TIPPU TIP

Hamed bin Mohammed al-Murjabi, also known as Tippu Tip, sits for his formal studio portrait in Zanzibar, *ca.* 1890s.

He was described by the Briton Herbert Ward as "a very remarkable individual in every way – of commanding presence, and a wonderful degree of natural ease and grace of manner and action. He stands nearly six feet in height, has brilliant, dark, intelligent eyes, and bears himself with an air of ultra-imperial dignity."
(Ward 1890: 491)

TIPPU TIP

Ivory, Slavery and Discovery
in the Scramble for Africa

Stuart Laing

Medina Publishing

Tippu Tip
Ivory, Slavery and Discovery in the Scramble for Africa

© Stuart Laing 2017

ISBN: 978-1-911487-05-0

Produced and published in 2017
by
Medina Publishing Ltd
310 Ewell Road
Surbiton
Surrey KT6 7AL
medinapublishing.com

Edited by William Facey
Designed by Kitty Carruthers
Maps by Martin Lubikowski

The moral right of the author has been asserted according to the
Copyright, Designs and Patents Act 1988

All rights are reserved. No part of this publication may be reproduced, stored or
introduced into a retrieval system, or transmitted, in any form, or by any means
(electronic, mechanical, photocopying, recording or otherwise) without prior
permission in writing of the publisher and copyright holder.

A catalogue record for this book is available from the British Library

Printed and bound by Interak Printing House, Poland

Contents

List of maps	vi
List of illustrations	vi
Foreword and Acknowledgements	xi
Introduction	1
1 A Young Arab in East Africa	11
2 Nile-seekers, Africa-crossers	37
3 Boy Trader	61
4 Business Start-up	81
5 The Far Side of the Lake	105
6 Between the Two Rivers	127
7 Down the Lualaba: Nile or Congo?	149
8 Tippu Tip and the Scramble	177
9 Fourth Journey: Back to the Centre	199
10 Fifth Journey: What a Relief!	219
11 The British and the Germans: Protection or Occupation?	247
12 Arabs versus the Congo Free State	261
13 Last Judgements	273

Appendices

1 Tippu Tip's Family Tree	288
2 British Residents, Agents and Consuls in Muscat and Zanzibar	290
3 Sultans of Muscat and Zanzibar	293
4 Timeline	294
Notes	301
Bibliography and Notes on Sources	309
Index	317

List of maps

East Africa in the 19th century	23
Explorers' routes	40–1
Tippu Tip's First and Second Journeys	83
Tippu Tip's Third Journey, 1870–82	115
Tippu Tip's Third Journey, final part	158
Africa: possessions and spheres of influence, 1885–86	196
Tippu Tip's Fourth Journey, August 1883 – December 1886	203
The Emin Pasha Relief Expedition	226–7
East Africa, 1886	252

List of illustrations

Tippu Tip. Studio photograph taken in Zanzibar; by kind permission of the Syndics of Cambridge University Library	Frontispiece
Zanzibar waterfront, 1874. Engraving from Stanley 1878	11
David Livingstone. Portrait engraving from Waller 1874	37
Bagamoyo. Engraved view from Cameron 1877	61
Maria Theresa thaler. By courtesy of Clara Semple	68
Central African weapons. Engraving from Stanley 1878	81
Chief Mirambo. Engraving from Becker 1887	105
Chief Kasongo. Engraving from Cameron 1877	127
Juma Merikani's hut. Engraving from Cameron 1877	129
Henry Morton Stanley in explorer's headgear. Engraving from Ward 1890	149
Stanley and Pocock tossing coins. Engraving from Stanley 1878	156
"Tippu Tip's grand canoes going down the Congo." Engraving from *The Illustrated London News*, 21 December 1889; by kind permission of the Syndics of Cambridge University Library	160–1

Sayyid Barghash bin Sa'id. Portrait engraving from a book of
letters of Dr Christie; by kind permission of the Syndics of
Cambridge University Library   170

Fort Leopold on Lake Tanganyika. Engraved view from Becker 1887   177

Le Stanley being carried in sections upriver. Engraving from
Stanley 1885   187

Taria Topan. Engraving from Stanley 1878   199

Emin Pasha. Portrait engraving from Stanley 1890   219

Carl Peters. Photograph by courtesy of the Bundesarchiv-Bildarchiv
(Federal Archives of Germany)   247

Tippu Tip's house at Stanley Falls. Line drawing from Ward 1890   261

Tippu Tip in old age. Photograph by courtesy of Zanzibar Archives   273

Between pages 176 and 177

1. Tippu Tip. Portrait photograph taken by 'GPA', published in Hoffmann 1938

2. Sayyid Sa'id bin Sultan. Painting; by courtesy of Bait al-Zubair Museum, Muscat

3. John Hanning Speke. Full-length portrait painted by James Watney Wilson; by courtesy of the Royal Geographical Society, London

4. Richard Burton. Photograph, from the portrait by Lord Leighton in the National Portrait Gallery, London; by courtesy of the Royal Geographical Society, London

5. Verney Lovett Cameron. Portrait photograph; by kind permission of the Syndics of Cambridge University Library

6. Livingstone in swamp near Lake Bangweolo. Engraving from Waller 1874

7. Ivory caravan. Photograph from the Fisher Collection; by kind permission of the Syndics of Cambridge University Library

8–11. Ivory objects. From the author's family collection

12. Henry Morton Stanley in Makata swamp. Engraving from Stanley 1872

13. Ujiji, Lake Tanganyika. Engraved view from Hore 1892
14. Henry Morton Stanley. London studio portrait; by courtesy of the Royal Geographical Society, London
15. Tusks in doorway of merchant's house, Zanzibar. Photograph from the J.A. Grant Collection; by kind permission of the Syndics of Cambridge University Library
16. The front door of Tippu Tip's house, Zanzibar. Photograph by the author
17. The plaque beside Tippu Tip's front door, Zanzibar. Photograph by the author
18. Detail of wood carving, Tippu Tip's front door, Zanzibar. Photograph by the author
19. Ivory warehouse, Zanzibar. Photograph from the Christie Collection; by kind permission of the Syndics of Cambridge University Library
20. Sayyid Barghash with his delegation visiting England, 1875. Photograph; by courtesy of Zanzibar Archives
21. John Kirk. Photograph reproduced from Foskett 1946
22. Dr James Christie. Photograph in a book of his letters; by kind permission of the Syndics of Cambridge University Library
23. Princess Salme bint Sa'id. Photograph; by courtesy of Zanzibar Archives
24. King Leopold II of the Belgians. Portrait engraving; from Stanley 1885
25. Hermann von Wissmann. Sketch portrait; from Brown 1892–95
26. Jérôme Becker. Portrait engraving; from Becker 1887
27. Tippu Tip's *majlis*, probably in Nyangwe. Engraving; from Ward 1890
28. Walter Deane escaping from Stanley Falls. Illustration; from Ward 1890
29. The steamboat *Le Stanley*. Engraving; from Ward 1890
30. Rooftop view of Zanzibar, early 20th century. Photograph, from the Royal Commonwealth Society Collection; by kind permission of the Syndics of Cambridge University Library

31. Zanzibar waterfront, early 20th century. Photograph, from the Royal Commonwealth Society Collection; by kind permission of the Syndics of Cambridge University Library

32. View from the roof of Bait al-Ajaib, 2012. Photograph by the author

Foreword and Acknowledgements

THE AIM OF THIS BOOK is to introduce the reader, through the life of Tippu Tip, to the extraordinary world of East Africa in the second half of the 19th century – the time of the 'Scramble for Africa' when European powers took over huge areas of the continent in a largely unplanned campaign of colonial and imperial expansion. Tippu Tip both spearheaded the Arab effort to open up Central Africa from the east, and watched from a ringside seat as Arab influence in the region was whittled away. In the latter process he played a significant role by co-operating with Western explorers, most notably with Henry Morton Stanley. His ability to face both ways found its most piquant expression when King Leopold II of Belgium engaged him as a governor in the eastern Congo. By following Tippu Tip's life, we can begin to understand how and why these momentous events unfolded – processes which have left strong traces in Africa still today.

I first came across Tippu Tip when researching for a dissertation on the abolition of slavery and the slave trade in East Africa and the Indian Ocean in the 19th century. He immediately seemed an intriguing character. Dismissed in some accounts as a 'notorious slave trader', there was obviously more to him than that. For one thing, the evidence suggests that he was primarily interested in ivory, not slaves. Not that this makes him an angel, since the quest for ivory had disastrous effects on elephant herds even in (and before) Tippu Tip's time, long before the terrible depredations we are seeing today. But he stands out from his Arab contemporaries. Partly this is because he engaged more closely with the world outside Africa. Mainly, however, it is because he left memoirs (the *Maisha*, which cannot quite be called an autobiography), through which the voice of a 19th-century Arab is clearly heard.

The book also fills a gap in the English-language bibliography of Africa of the Scramble. In François Renault, Tippu Tip has had his biographer in French, but in a form not easily accessible to the general reader. I hope that, through this book, more will come to enjoy a knowledge of this interesting episode in African (and European) history, with its cast of remarkable characters.

Acknowledgements

No author works alone. I have been helped by my wife, Sibella, and family members, all supportive of my apparent obsession with Tippu Tip. I am grateful to a number of Africanists who pointed me in the right direction in my research, and particularly to Felicitas Becker in Cambridge, who helped sort out discrepancies in the translations of Tippu Tip's memoirs. Clara Semple helped me with illustrations, and on information about the Maria Theresa dollar. Staff in the Cambridge University Library, especially in the Munby Rare Books Room, were invariably helpful in digging out source material. My editor, Will Facey, ironed out many wrinkles, and helped make the book more accessible. I thank them all.

Transliteration and presentation

References to Tippu Tip's memoirs (see the Bibliography and Notes on Sources) are given in the form *Maisha* § [paragraph number], using the paragraph numbers in the Smith/Whiteley edition.

I have wanted to make this book accessible to the general reader, and so have not used an academic style of transliterating all Arabic words and names, and have minimized diacritical markings, i.e. lines above letters or dots above/below them. In any case, the names of most of the characters in this book took on a Swahili form, in which the Arabic *'ayn* and the *hamza* disappear. Familiar Arabic names, of people and places, are spelt in a way used normally in English writing (e.g. Mohammed rather than the correct Muḥammad; Oman, not 'Umān), or in the form that they appear in Swahili writings. I have written the name of the Omani ruling family as Al Bu Sa'idi, although it is also found in the form al-Busa'idi and other variants. Where I have wanted to show the Arabic letter *'ayn,* it is shown as ', but omitted in names beginning with *'Abd* or *'Abdul* (which are normally shown in the form Abdul Rahman, Abdul Karim, etc, and not 'Abd al-Raḥmān, etc), and in other words with widely accepted familiar transliterations. For plurals of Arabic words or names, I have used a final s, and not the Arabic inflected plural, e.g. the Al Bu Sa'idis. I have normally used *bin* for 'son of', rather than *ibn* (which is equally correct) or *b.* (often used in scholarly writing).

Swahili nouns are prefixed to denote singular or plural, and (in some cases) place. For example, a Swahili person is a Mswahili; several are Waswahili. The prefix U denotes territory. In this book I have used Wa and U for peoples and territories, e.g. Wanyamwezi (Nyamwezi people), Unyanyembe (the land of Nyanyembe).

I have aimed at consistency of spelling of African, Swahili and Arabic names, but may not have achieved it; the sources are wildly inconsistent, to the extent that interpreting both people and places is often difficult or speculative, or both. Where an alternative spelling is often found in the literature, I have referred to it in brackets without further explanation, e.g. Sayf (or Sefu).

Most of the places named in the text are shown on the maps – but not all. Both Tippu Tip and the explorers often included names of villages which no longer exist; the earnest researcher can find these on the detailed (and very beautiful) maps in 19th-century editions of their travels. Names of Indian places are given with the spelling conventionally used before 1947, e.g. Bombay not Mumbai, Calcutta not Kolkata.

Stuart Laing
Corpus Christi College
Cambridge 2017

Introduction

TIPPU TIP WAS, as we shall see, an engaging and intriguing character in himself. His life and career were entwined with the themes mentioned in the sub-title: ivory, slavery, discovery, and the Scramble for Africa. He was principally an ivory trader but, like most wealthy Arabs of this period, bought, sold and owned slaves. In the course of his journeying through East and Central Africa, he met and at times collaborated with the famous European discoverers and explorers of Africa, including Livingstone, Stanley, Cameron and Wissmann. To these three themes we might add 'empire', since the latter part of the 19th century saw the expansion of European occupation of sub-Saharan Africa, and Tippu Tip even played his part in this process, at one time actually accepting a position in the employment of Leopold II, King of the Belgians, in the Congo.

Tippu Tip (one of several nicknames he earned in adulthood) was born probably in 1837, in Zanzibar, as Hamed bin Mohammed al-Murjabi. His father was a travelling trader, and from his youth he became involved in trading on the East African mainland. His life may be divided, for convenience, into five journeys, although some of these were so long that they might be more accurately thought of as absences from Zanzibar. To begin with he travelled to areas south and south-west of Lake Tanganyika, but then progressively moved north, setting up his base at Kasongo, on the Lualaba river (which, as we shall see, was later found to be the upper part of the River Congo). All these journeys, except the last, were primarily devoted to the collection of ivory and its transportation back to the coast in huge caravans of free and slave porters. He may have traded in other goods, but he does not record having done so. On the way to gathering his very valuable stocks of ivory, he asserted personal power and authority over numerous villages and tribes over a vast area in East and Central Africa, mostly through violent conquest. He has been described as a potentate or emperor, but the extent of his authority varied: in some places he practised rulership, in the sense of settling disputes and ensuring peace and stability, sometimes through a deputy, while in others his influence was felt only when he was personally present.

In his early journeys, Tippu Tip came into contact with various Europeans travelling in the region, notably Henry Morton Stanley. His Fifth Journey differed from the others because of its having been planned and implemented, in a contractual collaboration with Stanley, as the 'Emin Pasha Relief Expedition' of 1887–89. With Stanley, Tippu Tip travelled up the Congo River and based himself at Kisangani, an island on the Congo River right beside the Belgian station of Stanley Falls. By this stage, through Stanley's mediation, he had been in contact with King Leopold II, and been appointed by him as Governor of the eastern part of what by then was the Congo Free State, based at Stanley Falls. At first glance, this seems an improbable arrangement, from both of their points of view. But it suited the King; and it may have been Tippu Tip's high point. His influence and authority were then at their zenith, and he accumulated vast stocks of ivory. When he returned to Zanzibar in 1890, he found himself involved in court cases, mainly one brought by Stanley over interpretation of the contract made at the start of the Emin Pasha Expedition; and he had to watch from the sidelines as the Arabs in his former stomping grounds west of Lake Tanganyika were ousted by the Belgians, and his son Sayf (or Sefu) – whom he had left in command at Kisangani – was killed in battle. Although much had been lost, he retained wealth, including estates, in Zanzibar, and died there in June 1905, aged probably sixty-eight.

This book places Tippu Tip's life against the background of the strands of society and history mentioned above – ivory, slavery, discovery and empire. The characters include Arabs, Africans of the coast and the interior, and Europeans, all living in an environment where nature was often hostile, and (sadly) men and women were also often equally so. The narrative covers a period when vast tracts of territory in East and Central Africa became known to – and in part subjugated by – Europeans and Arabs who came as explorers, traders, occupiers, and missionaries.

Ivory

East Africa had been an area of interest to Arab traders from early times. But in the 19th century they came to realize the great profits that could be made from ivory. It was a product of little interest to the Africans of the interior, but valued both in India and increasingly in Western Europe and America. Some stocks of ivory were exported to India and worked there into items for re-export to European, American and even Chinese markets. As the Omani ruler Saʿid bin Sultan built up his control of Zanzibar and the coast in the first half of the 19th century, Arab traders developed the exploitation of ivory for export

Introduction

to those markets. Tippu Tip was foremost among such traders. The Arabs found that, as supplies of ivory became exhausted in the coastal areas, they could move farther west to find new supplies, and they established trading centres on the shores of Lake Tanganyika and on the trading routes between there and the coast. They then crossed Lake Tanganyika, travelled through the dense rainforest of what is now Eastern Congo, and made settlements on rivers such as the Lomami and the Lualaba. Their methods of acquiring the ivory became more violent as they moved farther west, inspiring fear and strong opposition from African tribespeople living in villages in the area. But they managed to export huge quantities, most of it still through the East African port of Bagamoyo and the market in Zanzibar, and some down the Congo river, as the Belgians developed river transport and communication in the latter decades of the century.

Slavery

The history of the East African slave trade is, not surprisingly, highly contentious. It is accepted that the trade was ancient: 4th-century CE sources mention trading of slaves in the Red Sea, there are records in the 9th century of a revolt among black slaves who were draining salt marshes in lower Mesopotamia (present-day Iraq), and Ibn Battuta, travelling in the 14th century, mentions slaves in Arab households in Mogadishu and Yemen. By the beginning of the 19th century African slaves were used mainly in domestic situations. We do not know how they were captured and brought to their eventual places of employment in the early period, but sources from the mid-19th century onwards describe how they were taken – often with extreme violence – from villages in the area near Lakes Victoria, Tanganyika and Nyasa, force-marched in chains to the coast, and shipped to markets in Zanzibar. Robert Alston and I have described the nature of this trade, the customs relating to slavery, and the attitudes taken by Islam to slaves and slavery, in more detail in our book about the relationship of Britain and Oman.[1]

Scholars now argue that the nature of the slave trade changed in the early and middle decades of the 19th century.[2] Until then, the wealthy would wish to own slaves as a sign of prestige and for their value in the household, including, of course, as concubines, permitted in Islamic teaching. Some were also used on public works projects such as the Mesopotamia salt marsh draining; and a number in agriculture, particularly date-palm cultivation. But as Sayyid Sa'id bin Sultan, arguably the greatest of the Al Bu Saʿidi rulers of Muscat and Zanzibar, consolidated his hold on the East African littoral, thus expanding the scope for Omani trade, the nature of commerce in the Indian Ocean changed. Sayyid Saʿid moved his court and his main place of residence from Muscat to Zanzibar in 1839, presumably seeing that his East African possessions were generating higher income than the homeland, and were also less prey to threats from his northern neighbours, the Wahhabis of central Arabia. Much of the Zanzibari wealth came from plantations, Arab investors having recently discovered that cloves – brought from what is now Indonesia via Réunion and Île de France (now Mauritius) – flourished in the soil and climate of Zanzibar and its sister island Pemba. These plantations needed imported labour, and so a different style of slave trading developed.

We shall see in more detail how this slave trade operated. Arab traders were largely responsible. They operated the local slave markets (chiefly the one in Zanzibar), and sailed the dhows that took the slaves to the northern markets in Arabia, Persia and beyond. While trading east of Lake Tanganyika, they mainly bought (and then sold) slaves who had been captured by one African chief at war with another. Much of this trade was not connected with the commerce in ivory: slaves were brought to the coastal markets purely for subsequent sale for work domestically or on plantations. It was this trade which so shocked David Livingstone, and then humanitarians such as those in the Anti-Slavery Society. But when the Arabs expanded their presence westwards, from the 1860s on, their methods became much more violent, as they burned villages and took hostages in order to acquire men and women for slavery, as well as ivory. This became well known in Europe, earning the African Arabs an appalling reputation for cruelty and violence.

Tippu Tip was inevitably closely associated with this trade. His attitude to ownership of slaves is described in the last chapter of this book: he claims, more or less, that it was the only way to acquire labour. This may have been true in the jungly area on the River Lualaba, but east of Lake Tanganyika (as we shall see in Chapter 1) the Unyamwezi people made a speciality of hiring themselves out as porters. The problem was that, in the latter decades of the 19th century, the trades of ivory and of slaves were inextricably intertwined. It was virtually impossible to get ivory to market from the Congo/Lualaba without using slaves. Although Henry Stanley tried to make the point, few purchasers of ivory luxury goods in Europe or North America seem to have been aware of the dreadful human cost of bringing the products to Oxford Street or Fifth Avenue. (The same may have been true, in the 1890s and early 1900s, of rubber from the Congo and those riding bicycles or driving cars on Mr Dunlop's pneumatic tyres.)

Tippu Tip cannot escape censure for his involvement with the purchase and use of slaves for transporting ivory. The record shows that in his early career he hired free labour for his journeys from Zanzibar and Bagamoyo, and on his Second Journey made a detour of several hundred miles to hire men in Tabora to carry home his stock of ivory. There is no reason to suppose that he did anything different later on, at least when travelling westwards, there being a thriving market for free men as porters in the coastal towns. However, for the huge caravans required in his later career to take ivory back from Kisangani or Nyangwe to Zanzibar, he makes no mention of hiring, and we must assume he would have used slaves. And, although there is no record of his selling slaves at the end of the journey, we must assume that he either disposed of them that way, or re-employed them on his spice estates.

There is one further indictment. Despite the agreements that he made with the Belgians in the period before the Arab–Belgian confrontation (Chapter 12), Tippu Tip failed to restrain his fellow-Arabs from patterns of horrific violence against African villages, the aim of which was the capture of both slaves and ivory. Taking the broad view, we can see that he would have preferred the Arabs to come to terms, in some way, with the Europeans – reluctantly, he could see which way this particular 'wind of change' was blowing through Africa. But it cannot be excluded that he connived at the way things were done because it suited him well: others could mount the raids (there is no evidence that he personally did so), and he could then take his tribute, or make his purchase, of ivory, and exploit the labour to carry it home.

In sum – and at the risk of seeming to split hairs – Tippu Tip was not primarily a slave trader. His main objective was not to engage in the slave trade for profit; he could make more money through ivory trading. But, like other wealthy Arabs of the time, he owned and used slaves; they were an essential element in the transportation of ivory from the interior to the coast, and for the management of his estates in Zanzibar. At several points in the narrative of his life, the presence of slaves is apparent and the issues of slavery and slave trading will come disturbingly to the surface.

Discovery

The second half of the 19th century was the period when Western European exploration of Africa reached its zenith. Explorers such as Burton, Speke, Livingstone and Stanley became famous from their extraordinary journeys, and as a result of their books and lecture tours. The public became fascinated by questions such as the long-unsolved mystery of the source of the Nile, and moved by the stories of the cruel traffic of slaves across and out of Africa. Tippu Tip met several of the well-known explorers – most of them by coincidence, as they criss-crossed the continent. These included Livingstone, who fell in with Tippu Tip south of Lake Tanganyika, and travelled under his protection for a few weeks in 1867; Verney Cameron, the first European to cross Africa from east to west, whom Tippu Tip guided from his headquarters on the River Lualaba south-west to Katanga, from where Cameron made his way to the coast at Benguela, in present-day Angola; Wissmann, the German explorer who crossed Africa in the other direction, and met Tippu Tip in 1883. Other explorers (Becker, Junker, Gleerup) also came his way, as did several missionaries who at this time were setting up their stations on and near Lake Tanganyika.

But it was with Stanley that Tippu Tip had the strongest working collaboration. With English-speaking audiences Stanley is best known for his having 'found Livingstone', in 1871; but a few years after that he organized and led a second expedition aimed at 'completing Livingstone's work' (of identifying the source of the Nile), which ended in his accomplishing an astonishingly arduous crossing of Africa on a journey which he only just survived, and which brought to Europe knowledge of the unexpected course of the Congo river. Tippu Tip travelled with Stanley for nearly two months, giving him some protection as his party travelled on foot and by boat down the River Lualaba; they parted before the river bent round to the north-west and then the west, causing Stanley to confirm his supposition that the Lualaba was not in fact the upper Nile, but the Congo.

Empire

Tippu Tip's life story was interwoven with the growth of European imperial conquest of Africa, the 'Scramble' as it became known. After his crossing of the continent and the journey on the great river, completed in August 1877, Stanley leaves our story for a few years. He

Introduction

was engaged by Leopold II, King of the Belgians, in the enterprise of developing the vast area of the Congo basin as a Belgian colony. Tippu Tip had by this stage established his base at Kasongo on the River Lualaba, some 200 km west of Lake Tanganyika. As the Arab traders had pushed westwards, their communications remained with the east coast, and their loyalties continued to be directed to Barghash, Sultan of Zanzibar and son of the great Sa'id bin Sultan. Barghash claimed a kind of sovereignty over the land – or at least over the Arabs living on the land – up to and beyond Lake Tanganyika. Later the ambitions of King Leopold, the claims of the Sultan of Zanzibar, and the imperial aims of the British and the Germans, clashed in a succession of struggles that ended with a *de facto* Belgian–British–German partition of central and eastern Africa, the departure of the Arabs, and the loss of the Sultan's power and prestige in all but Zanzibar and its neighbouring islands.

Tippu Tip was an active participant in this process. We shall see how Barghash, taking account of Tippu Tip's power and prestige, sought to enlist him in order to shore up his own position both east of Lake Tanganyika and in the upper Congo basin; and how King Leopold and Stanley, engaged in their own particular imperialist projects, persuaded Tippu Tip to come in with them – actually appointing him Governor in Stanley Falls, a station established by the Belgian administration high on the Congo River.

At this point, in 1887, Stanley and Tippu Tip collaborated on an expedition that was unusually risky, even for these two adventurers. The Emin Pasha Relief Expedition has been well narrated elsewhere, and in this book we shall consider it in the context of Tippu Tip's life and of the history of the Arabs in Central and East Africa. Stanley, having had good experience of Zanzibari recruits on his previous expeditions, contracted Tippu Tip to supply him with porters and fighters for a force that would ascend the River Congo to its most northerly point, and then branch out north-east in order to rescue Emin Pasha, a German appointed in 1878 by Khedive Ismail (ruler of Egypt under Ottoman tutelage) to govern Equatoria, Egypt's most southerly province. Emin Pasha needed rescuing, in the eyes of many in Europe, because he had been pushed south and isolated by the Mahdi's revolt in Sudan; popular opinion was enlivened to the danger of the revolt after the killing of Gordon in Khartoum in 1885. Tippu Tip accompanied Stanley on his ship from Zanzibar to the mouth of the Congo, and then up the river, but stayed in Stanley Falls or Kasongo while Stanley pushed through almost impenetrable forest to reach Emin Pasha at

Lake Albert. The expedition suffered dreadful losses, and afterwards recriminations flew – some directed at Stanley's poor leadership and organization, some at Tippu Tip for his alleged failure to make good on his contract. Arriving back in Zanzibar, using the eastern route past Lake Victoria and then south-east to Bagamoyo, and not the route via the Congo river by which they had come, Stanley sued Tippu Tip over the contract. Eventually the case was dropped, after Stanley had already returned to England, where he needed to defend his behaviour and his management of the expedition.

Tippu Tip lived on in Zanzibar as sovereignty slipped from the Al Bu Saʿidi sultans. In 1890, the British and Germans signed an agreement which divided control of Africa east of Lake Tanganyika into territories that later became, approximately, Kenya and Tanzania. The Sultan was left with Zanzibar and its islands, plus a coastal strip 10 km wide, up to Mombasa; and a British protectorate was declared over Zanzibar. Britain intervened in the succession crisis in 1896, in what is sometimes described as the 'shortest war in history' (about 45 minutes long); and more direct control was assumed by the British over much of the Zanzibari administration. By the time of Tippu Tip's death, in 1905, a British official was First Minister, and even took the position of Regent when Sayyid Ali bin Hamoud succeeded to the throne but was under age.

Sources

Generally the problem with historical writing about this area and period is the absence of the African, Arab or Swahili voice. In the case of Tippu Tip, however, we have his own memoirs, probably a unique document of its type. It arose because of a second law suit in which Tippu Tip was engaged, in 1894–95, with a fellow-Arab, Mohammed bin Khalfan, nicknamed Rumaliza. Because Rumaliza had been living in the German sphere of influence and was technically a German subject, his defence was assisted by the German Consul's Legal Counsellor, Heinrich Brode. Tippu Tip became acquainted with Brode during the court case, and was persuaded by him to write an account of his life, in Swahili though in Arabic script. Brode himself transcribed this into Roman script, and published it; later, in 1903, he wrote his own biography of Tippu Tip, which draws heavily on the memoirs but obviously also benefits from conversations Brode had with him.

The memoirs, entitled in the only English translation *Maisha ya*

Hamed bin Muhammed el Murjebi yaani Tippu Tip ('The Life of Hamad bin Mohammed al-Murjabi, known as Tippu Tip', referred to in this book as *Maisha*) is about 70 pages long, and contains many detailed and graphic accounts of episodes in Tippu Tip's action-packed life. Considering that it was written by a man in his late fifties, we assume without notes or a diary, recounting events stretching back forty years, it is a remarkable document. On occasions it is clear, from comparison with records made at the time by Europeans whom he met, that Tippu Tip's memory is defective, or that he wishes to portray his actions in a favourable light. French and English translations have been made, but they are not easy to acquire. Brode's biography has been republished in facsimile. Fine scholarly work has been done on Tippu Tip, but in French (Renault and Bontinck); and these are not easy to access, and not ideal for the English-speaking reader. Details are in the Bibliography.

Written communication between Zanzibar and the outposts on the mainland did exist, although it is difficult to tell with what frequency, since very few manuscripts survive. A few letters written by Tippu Tip while in Central Africa to diplomatic and consular agents in Zanzibar were translated by them and sent to their capitals, and so we can hear his voice, indirectly, by these means.

Otherwise we have to rely on the writings, of various kinds, of the Europeans travelling or living in the region. Fortunately, some of these are of high quality. The explorers, who needed to record data such as heights above sea level, location, temperature and atmospheric pressure, and who also wished to be able to write up their travels both for their sponsors and (to earn money from their books) for the public, went to great pains to keep diaries and journals. Famously, Livingstone used any scrap of paper, even old newsprint, to write his records. Stanley kept journals and then wrote with furious rapidity after each journey, to get his account into print while public interest, and his memory, were fresh. Other explorers acted likewise. The surviving participants in the Emin Pasha Relief Expedition almost all wrote and published their own version of events. All these men (no women) wrote letters home, some of which survive. The missionaries wrote reports for their British headquarters. The Agents and Consuls in Zanzibar – especially the British, but also the French, German and Belgian – reported carefully to their capitals. All these had their own motives for writing, and many of them could be tendentious, and were. But they should not be under-estimated: those who survived the rigours and difficulties of African life and travel were very robust, and took pains to understand the societies in which they lived. From their writings, and his own, we do in fact inherit a vivid picture of our unusual, actually unique, central character.

CHAPTER 1

A Young Arab in East Africa

TIPPU TIP ACQUIRED this nickname, and various others, only in adulthood. He was born Hamed bin Mohammed al-Murjabi, in Zanzibar, probably in 1837. Most writers and scholars refer to him as Hamed (or Hamad) bin Mohammed when writing about him in boyhood, and start to refer to him by his nickname only when describing his mature years; and this book will follow this convention. The date of his birth is uncertain. In his detailed commentary on Tippu Tip's, or Hamed's, memoirs, the *Maisha*, Bontinck argues convincingly for 1837.[1]

Hamed's father was Mohammed bin Juma al-Murjabi, an Arab originating from Muscat, who lived in Kazeh, modern Tabora, an African–Arab settlement some 700 km inland from Dar as-Salaam and Zanzibar, and 300 km from the shore of Lake Tanganyika. Brode, the German diplomat who during Tippu Tip's declining years persuaded him to write the *Maisha*, and then translated it, describes his family's connection with another well-known Omani clan, that of Nabhani.[2] Juma bin Rajab al-Murjabi, Hamed's grandfather, had married the sister of Mohammed bin Rajab al-Nabhani, another Arab trader; and

Brode recounts that Juma bin Rajab was himself an active trader, engaged in "daring raids" to Tabora and Lake Tanganyika. Brode does not give sources for many of his statements about Hamed and his family, and not all of what he writes is to be found in the *Maisha*. We have to assume that Brode made notes of conversations that he had with Hamed, and probably other traders, during the time that the *Maisha* was being written. His account therefore provides useful extra material to fill out the sometimes sketchy record in the *Maisha*.

Arabs in East and Central Africa

Already we see that Arab families were well established in East Africa, between the great lakes (Victoria, Tanganyika and Nyasa) and the coast, by the early 19th century. When we say 'Arabs', we really mean trading families and settlers from what is now Oman; only a few came from other parts of the Arabian Peninsula, such as Hadramawt, the ports and coastal plain of what is today southern Yemen. The tradition of sailing down the east coast of Africa was very ancient. Slaves were brought from this area to Arab lands from probably the 4th century CE, and certainly during the 9th: contemporary records refer to the rebellion of the slaves in Mesopotamia as the "revolt of the Zanj", or *black people*, a term thought to be the origin of the name of Zanzibar. This name, Zanzibar, is more properly applied to the archipelago of several islands, of which the largest is called Unguja, and the other main inhabited island is Pemba; in this book we shall follow common usage in referring to the largest island as Zanzibar.

The trading system was based on the convenient wind pattern: from approximately April to September the prevailing wind blows over the northern Indian Ocean from the south and west, and for the other half of the year from the north and east. This made it relatively easy to trade between India, the Gulf and the East African coast, using sailing ships and boats with the well-known settee rig of the *dhow* (a word not often used by Arabs, who have a number of more specific terms for their sailing vessels, depending on size and shape, etc). But whatever the variety of vessels used, the settee rig, basically a square sail modified into a fore-and-aft configuration for sailing closer to the wind, enabled efficient use of a following breeze in seas where prevailing winds remained steady in strength and direction, and complex manoeuvres such as tacking and wearing round before the wind were barely needed.

Indian Ocean trade was conducted by Omanis (and presumably others) from the early years of Islam, that is from the 7th century CE. This can be seen because traces of the Ibadi sect of Islam, which is predominant in Oman and only in small communities elsewhere, can be found in early mosques on the African coast. The trade extended to Sohar (on the north-east coast of Oman), then a significant port, and into the Gulf, where the Persians were trading actively, being consumers of products brought from Africa and India. Later, the Omani position on the African coast was eclipsed for about 150 years by the Portuguese occupation of both the coast of East Africa and Oman. Starting with the exploration voyages of Vasco da Gama in the closing years of the 15th century, and then the aggressive and invasive voyages of Almeida, Tristão da Cunha and Albuquerque a few years later, the Portuguese established themselves – generally by force – in a string of coastal towns, from Sofala (near present-day Beira, south of the mouth of the Zambezi river), to Zanzibar, Mombasa and Malindi farther north. In Oman, likewise, Portuguese rule was set in place; and to house their garrisons and governors, they built forts along the coast, several of which survive, with additions and alterations, to the present day. Two of the most famous, Mirani and Jalali, still watch over the enclosed harbour of old Muscat.

During this period the materials traded included foodstuffs, but also the export of gum-copal, ivory and slaves from Africa to India, with Indian cloth a significant import to Africa. Gum-copal was a resin from a forest tree, which was used in the making of varnish for carriages, and remained a staple in East African trade well into the 19th century. The explorer Henry Morton Stanley, arriving in Zanzibar in January 1871 at the start of his quest to find Livingstone, comments on the trade between Zanzibar and the Western markets of Europe and America: Zanzibari exports were "ivory, gum-copal, cloves, hides, cowries, sesamum, pepper and cocoa-nut oil ... and orchilla weed", while the Europeans and Americans brought "sheeting, brandy, gunpowder, muskets, beads, English cottons, brass-ware, china-ware and other notions".[3] By Stanley's time, some of the ivory was still exported to India, to be worked by craftsmen there into objects for the European market. Cowries were exported to West Africa, where they were used as currency. Orchilla weed is a lichen that was used to make a purple-blue dye. By then, also, Zanzibar and Pemba had developed their spice production, especially of cloves (see page 20). It is interesting to note Stanley's list containing alcohol and weaponry:

the trade in these products became of significance later, and was the focus of the Brussels Conference in 1889–90. We see also that American cloth ("sheeting"), and even English cottons, had taken over from Indian products. Indeed, lengths of cloth were a currency used by explorers and other travellers into the African interior, with tribes who preferred that to beads or copper wire, and – from the prevalence of the American imports – cotton cloth was known in Swahili as *merikani*.

Elephants and Ivory

In prehistoric and early historical times elephants lived wild in Asia and even Europe as well as in India and Africa. In this book we are concerned mainly with the African elephant, of which there are two species – the forest elephant and the slightly smaller savanna elephant. The Asian elephant is smaller still, easier to train, and has much smaller or no tusks. For centuries, the elephant population has been declining, due to loss of natural habitat (elephants have a huge appetite for grass, leaves etc, and may eat up to 150 kg a day), and hunting by humans for their meat and their tusks. They became extinct in China in about 200 CE, and the huge herds observed in East Africa as far north as Somalia and Sudan disappeared in the 17th and 18th centuries.

Even in the 19th century the continued decline was observable. Joseph Thomson, leader of a Royal Geographical Society expedition in 1879, comments on the changes since Burton was there in 1857, resulting in the Arabs having to obtain their ivory from much farther west (Thomson 1881: 134). In Tippu Tip's lifetime, elephants were rarely seen east of Lakes Victoria and Tanganyika. In the 20th century it has become possible to make calculated guesses of total numbers of surviving elephants, and from these we can see that the decline has become yet more severe, to the extent that they are classified as an endangered species. In just ten years, from 1979 to 1989, the number of African elephants in the wild is estimated to have fallen from about 1,300,000 to 600,000, despite efforts aimed at protecting them. This slaughter is mainly due to the demand for ivory, although the elephants' meat and hides are also used. A CITES ban on trade in ivory was introduced in 1990. In some places this has helped elephant herds to recover; but the ban has also raised the price of illegal ivory and thus increased the incentive to poach.

Ivory has been prized globally for centuries. (We are here talking of elephant ivory, although other types are found, for example from extinct mammoths, and from walrus tusks.) Its beauty, and its suitability for intricate carving, and then for polishing, is obvious. African ivory is generally considered better for such work: the tusks are larger than those of Indian elephants, and the material softer. It can be made softer still by dampening it. Craftsmen learned to minimize waste of this valuable material, devising techniques for cutting it very thin, so that it is almost translucent. Even the waste flakes could be used: by carefully roasting them in a closed furnace, the ivory goes deep black, and was used to make high quality and very dark ink ('Indian ink').

From the earliest times ivory has been used for carving figures and statues. The ancient Greeks made 'chryselephantine' statues, made of ivory with gold additions. Ivory was brought across the Sahara to the Arab rulers of Spain in late medieval times. In the 13th and 14th centuries, Europe saw a prolific period of ivory carving, mainly of religious themes, for example statues of Christian figures (notably the Virgin Mary, but also saints), and flat pieces showing scenes from the life of Christ. Secular subjects included scenes of courtly love. Later, in the 18th and 19th centuries, craftsmen produced high-quality forgeries of these earlier pieces.

By Tippu Tip's time, the trade in ivory was well established. There was steady and then rising demand from Europe, India and the Far East. Chinese craftsmen preferred the harder Indian ivory, while in India itself the demand was for African ivory. There was a long Indian tradition of working in ivory, which was greatly enhanced by the arrival of the British East India Company in the 17th and 18th centuries, with a growth in demand for European-style products, such as ivory inlay in fine furniture. The Indian custom of *suttee*, the immolation on her husband's funeral pyre of a widow who would still be wearing her jewellery, ensured continued demand for ivory bangles. Other Far Eastern markets included Japan, where ivory was (and still is) prized for making *hanko*s, personal seals used in place of a signature.

But the real growth in demand in the 19th century was in Europe and in North America, as machinery was invented for pieces that were either intricate (e.g. combs) or required precision difficult to obtain by hand. Billiard balls, for which ivory was thought the best material, are a notable example: they were made by special lathes that would shape from one block of ivory first one hemispherical side then the other, and – since after some years they would go out of shape – there was always demand for replacements. Before satisfactory synthetic substitutes were invented, piano keys were another huge 'consumer' of ivory: in 1900, it was estimated that 300,000 pianos were produced in America alone.

The Arab population of East Africa was reduced during the Portuguese occupation, as the occupiers took over much of the trade. But, despite some attempts to penetrate inland up the Zambezi river in search of gold and for missionary purposes, the Portuguese appear to have made few inroads into the interior, and to have made less profit from the region than they had hoped for. Wilkinson describes a "new world order" arriving in Indian Ocean trade during the late 16th and early 17th centuries, as the Ottoman empire extended its reach through the Red Sea and beyond, the Safavids grew in strength in Persia, and the Moghul Empire rose in India.[4] In the early 17th century the English also began expanding their presence in the Indian Ocean, after the grant of the Royal Charter to the East India Company in 1600; and the Dutch too were making their commercial mark, trading yet farther east. The result was a gradual weakening of the Portuguese position across the Indian Ocean. They were first removed from Hormuz, their base in the Gulf, by the Persians (with help from the English East India Company) in 1622, and then defeated and expelled from Muscat in 1650. This opened the way for the Omanis to press home their advantage, and seek to shift the Portuguese from bases and settlements in lands where Omanis felt they had a natural or historical presence. But the maritime campaign was not easy, even though the Omanis had developed improved ship-building techniques and could begin to match the heavily-armed Portuguese warships; and Omani fighting at sea (including along the Indian coast as well as the African) continued nearly until the end of the century, with some coastal towns alternating between Omani and Portuguese possession and repossession. Eventually the Omanis retook the important centres of Zanzibar and its neighbouring island Pemba, Pate (on the coast north of Malindi), and Mombasa, where the castle of Fort Jesus, built by the Portuguese in the 1590s, proved a hard nut to crack, but fell to the Omanis in 1698. Drawing on the writing of the German 19th-century historian Strandes, Coupland gives a graphic account of the 33-month siege in his *East Africa and Its Invaders,* published in 1938 but still a comprehensive history of this area.[5] The Omani reconquest went as far south as Cape Delgado (mid-way between Zanzibar and Mozambique town), which then became effectively the border between Arab and Portuguese territory, the coast of Mozambique and parts of the large island of Madagascar remaining in European hands. This effective partition remained valid until late in the 19th century: Captain Prior of the British Royal Navy reported in 1812 that Portuguese authority stopped at Cape Delgado, "neither fact nor courtesy ... giving them claim to a league farther; for the authority of the Arabs begins at the last-mentioned point".[6]

Since 1624, most of Oman (and by this, in the period up to the mid-19th century, we mean north and east Oman, not including Dhofar) had been under the leadership of Imams from the Ya'rubi dynasty. In the 1720s, a terrible civil war broke out between rival claimants to the imamate, who were supported respectively by the Ghafiri and Hinawi tribes. This spilled over to East Africa, where Zanzibar took the Hinawi side, and Mombasa the Ghafiri; and this disunity allowed the Portuguese briefly to re-occupy Fort Jesus, until Imam Sayf II emerged as ruler, and finally drove the Portuguese out of Mombasa to beyond Cape Delgado for good. The Ghafiri–Hinawi enmity, however, lived on.

By 1700, then, Omanis were relatively secure in a series of coastal towns from Pate and Lamu, north of Mombasa, to Cape Delgado. Many of these places were in fact on islands, presumably for defensive purposes, which made them dependent on imports for food supplies, and in part accounts for the importance of foodstuffs in regional trade. The Ya'rubi Imams were not able to consolidate their influence in these 'colonies', and a small number of Omani families strengthened their hegemony. The most notable example was that of the Mazru'i clan in Mombasa (often referred to in the literature in the Arabic plural or collective form, *Mazari'u* or *Mazari'a*), from whom a successive line of *liwali*s, Governors, was derived. An interesting feature of these families, as Wilkinson has shown, is that they came not only from Muscat and the coastal area of what is now the Sultanate of Oman, but from towns and regions of the interior, such as Nizwa, 'Ibri and Jabrin.[7] The Nabhani clan (or *Nabahina*), who at one time held the fort in Upper Nizwa, are of interest to our story, Tippu Tip's grandmother being from this family. At that time there was a clear distinction between those mountainous and desert regions of the interior, known as Oman, and the coastal plain of Muscat and the Batina; and while people travelled from one region to another, the influence of the Imam or – in later times – the Sultan in Muscat was often limited, particularly when Arabs from Najd in Central Arabia, under the leadership of the Al Saud (the Saudi ruling family), sought to impose their brand of Wahhabi Islam on the inhabitants of the Omani interior. And, in addition to the stream of traffic on land routes, Omanis travelled frequently by sea between Omani ports, such as Muscat, Qalhat or Sur, and East Africa.

The journey looks far on the map – about 4,400 km (2,750 miles) – but it can be done in three to four weeks of continuous sailing in a dhow: Alan Villiers records having sailed from Zanzibar to Muttrah (the port in the bay next to Muscat) in 23 days, in a Kuwaiti-built dhow.[8] Certainly the journey appears to have been commonplace for numbers of Omani sailors in the 18th and 19th centuries.

Thus Arab society in East Africa continued to be linked closely to the politics of Oman, and the collapse of the Ya'ruba dynasty and its replacement by the Al Bu Sa'idis had its ripple effect – and later a lot more than a ripple – on Mombasa and Zanzibar, and places in between. The story of this highly significant change in Omani affairs has been told in detail elsewhere, for example by the 19th-century Omani historian Ibn Ruzayq,[9] and most recently by Jones and Ridout.[10] For our narrative it is enough to say that out of a very turbulent period, which also involved intervention by a Persian military force, there emerged victorious Ahmad bin Sa'id, who was elected Imam probably in 1749 – the first Imam of the Al Bu Sa'idi dynasty (of whom the present Sultan of Oman is a direct descendant).[11] A table showing the Imams and Sultans of Muscat and Oman is at Appendix 3.

It took Ahmad bin Sa'id some years to assert his rule, and on his death in 1783 his sons contested the leadership. After further struggles, his son Sultan gained control of Muscat, which was by now becoming an important commercial and maritime centre, while another son, Sa'id, went into a kind of retirement as Imam, retaining thereby religious authority but virtually no secular power.

Sultan bin Ahmad came to power in 1792; and it was he and his son Sa'id bin Sultan, who ruled from about 1804 until 1856, who oversaw the strongest growth in Omani maritime power in the Indian Ocean in general and in East Africa in particular. This was also a period when European trading companies – mainly the Dutch, British and French – began serious expansion of their activities in the Indian Ocean. Historians have argued that their patterns of trade brought about a radical change in the ways of doing business in the region. Trading companies (rather than groups of individual traders) grew into enterprises which also sought to control resources and production of goods destined for particular (mainly European) markets, and were supported by national forces and the political systems which lay behind them.[12] Slave trading also changed in this period. Hitherto, slave traders had made money simply by carrying slaves from the African sources to markets to the north. Now slaves were used as a means of production, on plantations both on the African coast and on islands off-shore. For a time, and certainly during the life of Sayyid Sa'id bin Sultan (for 'Sayyid', see box below), the Omanis could live alongside this changed pattern, and even compete with it. But eventually, as we shall see as we follow Tippu Tip's career, European trading strength and political-military power eclipsed that of Oman.

Imams, Sayyids and Sultans

The term *Imām* (meaning 'the one in front') is generally used for the person who leads the faithful in prayer, and who often preaches the Friday sermon. In several Muslim societies, and particularly in the Ibāḍī sect (the branch of Islam followed by the majority of Muslims in Oman), the Imam has been the chosen leader in government and war, reflecting the people's wish to be led by someone who had spiritual and religious leadership qualities. Ibāḍī doctrine was that the Imam should be elected, and that there was no right of inheritance; and for much of Oman's history after the coming of Islam, the Imam was indeed elected, although it could and did happen that successive Imams could come from one family. Leaders in Oman took the title and responsibilities of Imam until and through the 17th and much of the 18th century. All the members of the Ya'ruba dynasty (1624–1728) used the title, as did two of the Al Bu Sa'idi who took power in the middle of the 18th century. After the civil wars of the late 18th century, Al Bu Sa'idi rulers did not think it appropriate to use the title, and called themselves 'Sayyid' (meaning 'Lord'), a title still used by close members of the Sultan's family today. Through the 19th century, British officials often transcribed this as Syud. Up to and including the early 1800s, British writers, including officials in Government correspondence, continued to use 'Imam' (or often 'Imaum') when referring to the ruler, and then 'Sultan' from about the middle of the 19th century: 'Sultan' was first used in an official document in the Anglo-Muscati Treaty of May 1839, and it has since become the customary title of the Ruler.

In the few decades before Hamed bin Mohammed's birth, then, the Omani presence and prosperity in East Africa were on the rise. It is curious that the Omani origin of the Arabs settled and trading there was not more emphasized: in the contemporary literature they are referred to as 'Arabs', occasionally as 'Moors', even though they were clearly proud of their ancestry. Tippu Tip himself usually mentions the *nisba*, family name, of those in his narrative of the same background as himself, not just the name and patronymic, and talks of his countrymen as 'Arabs'.[13] Perhaps this was because the adjective 'Omani' was not in such current use as it is today, and they would have assumed that hearers would know where their families originated. The descriptor 'Arab' linked them to Arabic, the language of the Qur'an, although most of their daily conversation was in Swahili, and they used Arabic only on religious or formal occasions, for example in talking with the Sultan.

The Omanis' strength in East Africa grew partly because of the stability brought about by the end of the civil war and the infighting within the ruling Al Bu Saʻidi house, and the firm leadership of Sayyid Saʻid bin Sultan. But the changing patterns of trade in the Indian Ocean also played their part, linked to the growth of plantation agriculture, particularly in spices. This was especially notable in Zanzibar and its neighbouring island of Pemba. In the early decades of the 19th century, Arab traders discovered that the two islands were well suited to the cultivation of several spices, but most of all cloves, which had been brought to the Mascarene Islands (see box opposite) from Indonesia. It is often thought that Sayyid Saʻid introduced cloves to Zanzibar; but Sheriff shows that the Omani responsible was Salih bin Haramil (or Huraymil) al-ʻIbri (that is, from ʻIbri, west of Nizwa).[14] Sayyid Saʻid appears to have confiscated Salih's estates in Zanzibar, because of an infringement of restrictions imposed by the British on the slave trade, and to have made great profits from cultivation of the land so acquired.

In the early part of his reign, Sayyid Saʻid was occupied with consolidating his Omani base against threats from the Saudis/Wahhabis, and (separately) the tribe of the Qawasim in what is now the United Arab Emirates. By the 1820s he was able to turn his attention to his East African possessions, and particularly to Zanzibar. Jones and Ridout argue that the choice of Zanzibar came about because Mombasa, a more natural base from which to manage an Omani and East African empire, had by this time become firmly lodged in the hands of the Mazruʻis, and that it was only after he had taken Pemba (on which Mombasa depended for food supplies) that Sayyid Saʻid was able to eject the Mazruʻis and regain Mombasa. This struggle may also have reflected a revival of the Ghafiri–Hinawi (Mombasa–Zanzibar) rivalry, mentioned above.

But the 'recovery' of Mombasa happened only in 1837, and meanwhile Sayyid Saʻid had needed to move forward with developing and exploiting his East African interests. He spent increasingly long periods in Zanzibar from about 1829, and moved there definitively in 1839, interspersed with visits to Oman. On his return from such a visit, in 1856, he died at sea, aged over seventy.

The Mascarenes

The Mascarenes are a group of islands east of Madagascar, named after the 16th-century Portuguese navigator Pedro de Mascarenhas. The Portuguese claimed the whole group during the 16th century, and used them as ports of call for reprovisioning on their eastern trade routes. The main two islands are now Mauritius (an independent republic) and Réunion (an overseas department of France). The Dutch occupied Mauritius in 1598, giving it that name after Maurice of Nassau, then chief magistrate of the Netherlands. The Dutch left in 1710, and the French took possession of the group of islands in 1715, naming the largest two Île de France and Bourbon. In 1793 the French Revolutionary leadership renamed Bourbon as Réunion. The British gained control over the islands during the Napoleonic wars in the early 19th century, but in 1815 returned Réunion to the French, keeping Île de France but giving it back its earlier Dutch name. On both islands the cultivation of sugar, as well as spices, was widespread in the 19th century, an agricultural system using extensive slave labour. Mauritius gained independence from the British in 1968; Réunion became an Overseas Department of France in 1946.

Arab expansion to the Great Lakes

The Omanis' trading took them inland from the ports and the coastal strip. Tippu Tip's father was based more at Kazeh (Tabora), the important inland town at the meeting-point of five main trading routes, than at Zanzibar. In his description of his journey from Zanzibar to Lake Tanganyika in 1856–59, Burton describes the welcome he received from the Arab merchants there, and reports on the history of their progress westwards. He arrived at Kazeh in November 1857, travelling with Speke, the explorer with whom he later fell out, in his quest to discover more about the water systems of the region, and specifically the source of the River Nile. They had marched 600 miles, and taken

134 days – less than 5 miles a day, on average! He calculated Kazeh at 3,480 feet (about 1,050 metres) above sea level, and 356 miles (570 km) from the coast as the crow flies.

Burton's writing is vivid, detailed and acutely observed, but he cannot suppress the pro-Arab prejudice he had absorbed after years of travelling in the Arab world – including, notably, his highly hazardous pilgrimage to Mecca and Madina. At Tabora, "nothing could be more encouraging than the reception experienced from the Omani Arabs … [and] the open-handed hospitality and the hearty goodwill of this truly noble race".[15] Burton says that the Arabs had colonized that area in about 1852, when they had been settled nearly ten years at a place "one long day's march" north. Most of the Arabs in Tabora were there on a visiting basis, making short stays for trading purposes. But we know that Tippu Tip's father based himself there for long periods, and some preferred to set up in agriculture, cultivating (with slave labour) quantities of food for sale to the large caravans passing through. By 1858, the Arabs had established a trading-post at Ujiji, on the shores of Lake Tanganyika, although Burton says that in his time they made only flying visits there, because of the unhealthiness of the lake shore and the dangers they faced from local inhabitants.

Certainly by the 1870s, and probably sooner, Ujiji had become a settlement; and once the Arabs had a base there, they were able to spread into neighbouring parts, both on the shores of the Lake and by crossing it in dug-out canoes which they hired or bought. They also spread themselves farther north: in September 1862 the explorers Speke and Grant, who had just seen the outflow of water on the north shore of Lake Victoria (and deduced that this river, called locally the Kivira, must be the Nile), were in Bunyoro – north-west of the Lake – and learnt that Arabs had been there forty years previously. In the area near Lake Tanganyika, Livingstone in September 1869 came across what was then described as the last (i.e. farthest west) Arab establishment 15 days' march west of the Lake. A few days earlier he had met an Arab trader who had reached Nyangwe (on the Lualaba river) and was returning to Ujiji with nine tons of ivory.

The incentive to move inland, up to and beyond Lake Tanganyika, arose from a general expansion of trading activity, but especially from the constant search to find new sources of ivory. In the early and middle part of the century, the easily accessible stocks in the coastal area became exhausted, and traders had to travel farther inland in order to satisfy demand. We can see how quick this process was: in 1858

A Young Arab in East Africa

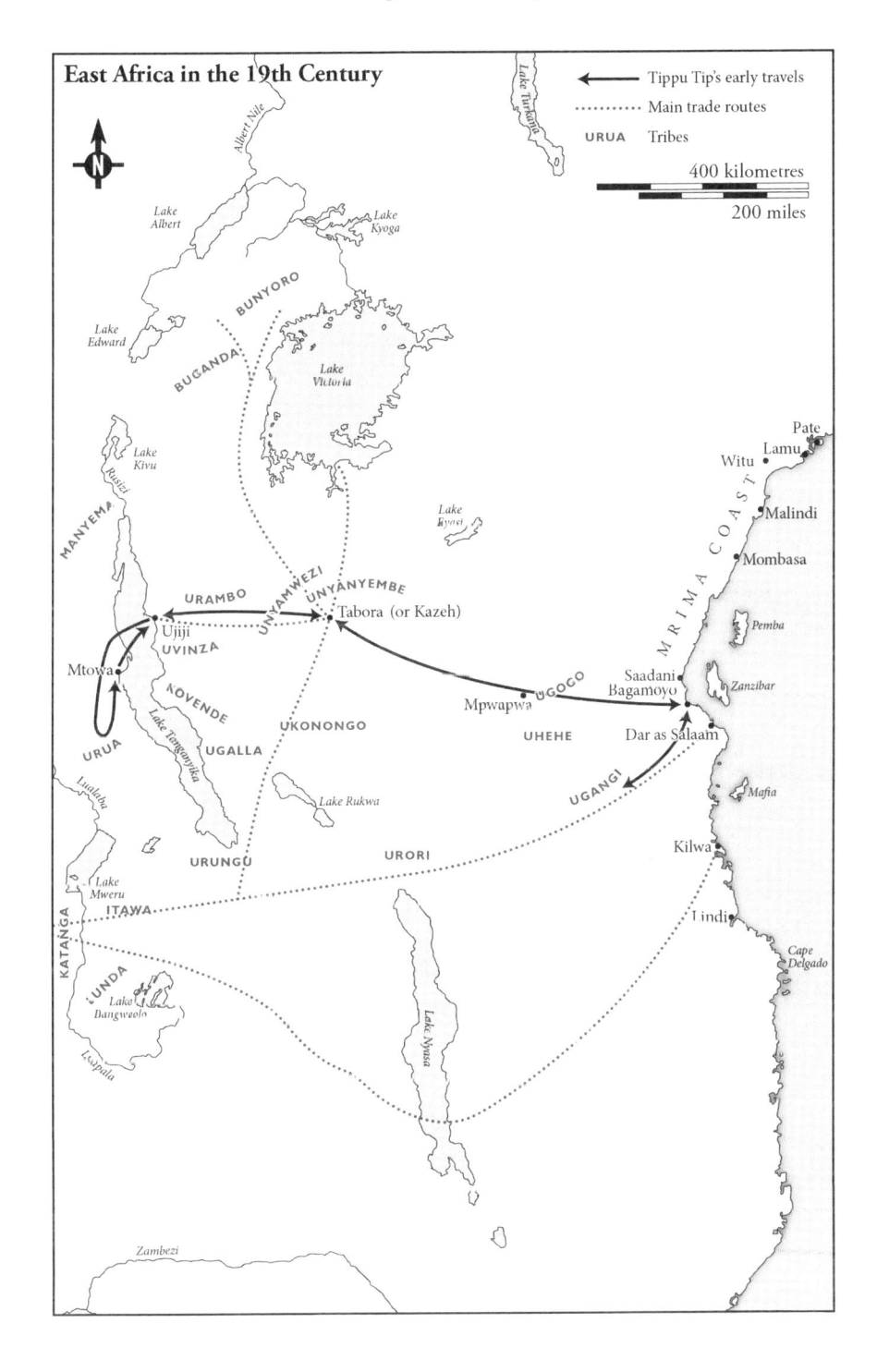

Burton commented that "the elephant roams in herds throughout the country", but in 1871 it was not until Stanley had reached south-west of Tabora that he observed for the first time "a small herd of wild elephants".

Only rarely did the Arabs catch and kill the elephants themselves. They mainly relied on being able to purchase the ivory from those living in the villages of the areas where they were trading. Often they would come across a store of tusks collected by a local chief. Sometimes they would buy, or take, tusks that were being casually used for some other purpose, such as a doorpost. And sometimes they would acquire tusks from freshly killed animals, buying from villagers for whom the elephant was as much a useful source of meat as a means of earning goods from Arab traders. With the passage of time, and as they moved into more western areas in the Congo basin where both the environment and the local population were hostile, their methods of acquiring the ivory became more violent, as we shall see later in the narrative.

For all that the Arab presence made itself felt in these areas, the Omanis were not (in our terms) numerous. At the start of the 19th century, there were about 300 Arabs in Zanzibar, and about 5,000 by the 1840s, when the population of the town would have been about 30,000. Arriving in 1857, Burton reports that those in the Unyanyembe area, where Tabora was situated, visited rather than colonized, and rarely exceeded 25 in number. Writing about the Arabs living in the Congo region about thirty years later, Wilkinson reckons that they were less than 150 in total, keeping under their control an area larger than France. In general, East Africa was sparsely inhabited anyway during the late 19th century, and also went through periods of severe depopulation as a result of war and/or disease. So a small number of Arabs, relatively wealthy and supplied with much more sophisticated weapons than the local inhabitants, could exert disproportionate influence, power and control.

Mainland tribes, towns and villages

Tippu Tip's travels took him through extensive areas of East and Central Africa. Between the coast and Lake Tanganyika, the main tribes whom he came across, and through whose land he travelled, were the Ugogo (south-east of Lake Victoria), and the Unyamwezi and Urambo (south and south-west of Lake Victoria respectively). The Unyamwezi had a reputation for encouraging trade, and also for making good porters on caravans; their young men were expected to go on caravan journeys as porters, to earn status as well as reward. Tippu Tip also had dealings with the Urori, north of Lake Nyasa, and the Urungu, west of the Urori at the southern end of Lake Tanganyika. West of that Lake were the Itawa, the Urua, the Manyema, and other tribes whom we shall come across in the narrative. They lived mostly in small villages, many of them with some defensive walls, and European explorers noted carefully the names of the villages and put them in the often beautiful maps that adorned the books they published on their return. Some of these villages were known by the name of the chief, and many of the names cannot be found on modern maps. Significant towns were not numerous. Tabora, where Tippu Tip's father was based, due south of Lake Victoria, was an important centre, as was Ujiji on the shores of Lake Tanganyika. Farther west, on the upper reaches of the Congo River, were Kasongo, Nyangwe and Kisangani, the latter being Tippu Tip's headquarters just near the Belgian station named Stanley Falls. Some of the towns have grown into important centres of population in the present-day Democratic Republic of the Congo.

Life and society in Zanzibar

How was the city into which Hamed bin Mohammed was born? In a famous passage in the first chapter of his *Last Journals*, David Livingstone records his unfavourable impression as he arrives in March 1866 at the start of the long expedition that lasted until his death in May 1873:

> The stench arising from a mile and half or two square miles of exposed sea beach, which is the general depositary of the filth of the town, is quite horrible. At night it is so gross or crass one might cut out a slice and manure a garden with it: it might be called Stinkibar rather than Zanzibar.[16]

Stanley, arriving there in January 1871, perhaps wishing to give the reader a more romantic start to his journey which was to have so dramatic a climax, lets purple prose take over:

> The island lay on our left, distant but a mile, coming out of its shroud of foggy folds bit by bit as the day advanced, until it finally

rose clearly into view, as fair in appearance as the fairest of the gems of creation.

He goes on to describe the masts of "several large ships" and "numerous dhows", the "dense mass of white, flat-topped houses", and the large houses of the Sultan and consular representatives on the seafront. A few pages later Stanley permits himself a less poetic style of description, when he takes a stroll through the city and observes "crooked, narrow lanes, white-washed houses, mortar-plastered streets", and then

> streets smelling very strong – in fact, exceedingly malodorous, with steaming yellow and black bodies, ... with a compound smell of hides, tar, filth, and vegetable refuse, in the negro quarter.[17]

Other contemporary writers also combine or juxtapose these two themes – the romantic arrival by sea, during which some claim actually to smell the cloves and other spices growing on the island's estates, and the dreadfully low standard of drainage and hygiene that contributed to the town's appalling stench of decomposition (including of human and animal bodies on the beach) and to water-borne diseases. There were indeed outbreaks of cholera, some with very serious effects. In late 1869 cholera was causing numerous casualties on the coast, and then came to Zanzibar, where these poor sanitary conditions made it almost impossible to control. James Christie, medical assistant to the Consul, records 12,000 deaths in Zanzibar in the three months between November 1870 and January 1871 – more than five percent of the population, if we are to believe Stanley's estimate of 200,000 on the island at that time. Other reports mention as many as 35,000 dying in the two-year period of the epidemic, 1869–70. (Estimates of the population of Zanzibar town, by European travellers or British officials, vary widely; taking averages of these estimates suggests that there were perhaps 12,000 in the 1830s, about 22,000 in the 1840s, 50–60,000 in the 1860s, and 80,000 in the 1880s.)

Zanzibar society: the Swahilis
This population was very mixed by the 19th century, as a result of the long tradition of maritime trading which we have already noted. The majority was, naturally, indigenous African. But, owing to centuries of contact with foreign traders – mainly Arabs, but also Persians and

Indians, and in later times Portuguese and other Europeans – the people of the coast and its off-shore islands became known as Swahili, from the Arabic word for 'coasts', *sawāhil*. Their language also became distinct, being one of the Bantu family, the group of languages spoken all over Central and East Africa, but with the adoption and absorption of a number of Arabic, Persian and other foreign words. Swahili became a common language of communication across Central and East Africa, including in areas where it was not a first language. The Swahili people were referred to as *wa(u)ngwana*, a word which by the late 19th century meant the free Muslim indigenous inhabitants of the coast.

The Swahilis adopted Islam from their Arab and Persian trading partners, mostly following the Shafi'i school, and not taking the Ibadi form, which remained distinctively a badge of Omani identity. This did not prevent them from retaining some animistic practices, for example belief in the evil eye (which is common in a number of devout Muslim societies) and in spirits. They observed Muslim fasts and worship ritual, though with varying degrees of strictness, and their schools gave the opportunity for the boys to study the Qur'an, and for some of them to become teachers, judges of *shari'a* law and *'ulamā* (Muslim scholars). True understanding of Arabic, however, was rare; even the *'ulamā* are reported as being able to read the Qur'an but not easily to write Arabic, which was used by the Sultan to communicate officially, and among the Omani Arabs themselves – although many of the latter were more comfortable in Swahili. One curious feature of the Swahilis' religious and social life was that they observed a solar calendar, not Islam's lunar one. They added 10–12 days to the Islamic year, with a respected old man choosing the New Year's Day by looking at the sun. This had the effect of bringing the seasons into line with certain months, which suited the Swahili way of life and the agricultural cycle of sowing and harvesting.

Swahili society was stratified, although it is not easy now to see how defined the class distinctions were. There does seem to have been a distinction between élite Swahili families, who were owners of property, and those of the artisanal class; the élite were styled 'Shirazis', as though claiming roots in the city of Shiraz in Persia, although this was more likely to represent a kind of status label than a real belief in this exotic family origin. These 'Shirazis' did inter-marry with Arabs, although in one direction only: an Omani man might take a Swahili wife, provided she were of similar or higher social status (this was the custom of *kafā'a,* equality or appropriateness), but an Omani woman would not be allowed to marry a Swahili man. We can see this in Tippu Tip's ancestry: he had dark skin and partly African features, and since his maternal grandmother's name is not given in accounts of his family, there must be a strong supposition that his grandfather Habib bin Bushir al-Wardi had taken a Swahili wife (or possibly concubine).

We should add that in Zanzibar there lived a number of indigenous Africans who were not from the coastal region. Some had come to the island, and to Pemba, as a result of the growing prosperity there in the 19th century. But the majority were slaves who had been brought there from the mainland to work in homes or on plantations, or descendants of slaves who had been freed. Islam encouraged the act of *tadbīr,* the owner freeing his slaves at his death by a provision in his will.

Zanzibar society: Indians
Like the Arabs, but not for so long, Indian traders had come to East Africa, bringing mainly woven cloth. A small number settled in Zanzibar, and at the start of the 19th century they also numbered a few hundred. Their numbers grew, and by the late 1850s they were a few thousand. Increasingly they turned to the financing of trade, at which they proved adept, and early in the century they had cornered the major share of banking and money-lending. As Arabs expanded their trading expeditions inland, this trade financing grew in importance: a trader would have to lay out considerable sums to buy the items (such as cloth, beads, wire, etc) that he planned to sell in the interior or barter in exchange for ivory, gum-copal and other exports, and would have to pay the wages and other costs of his *pagazi*, the porters. He would not know how long he would be away, or if he would be robbed en route, so the trade financier was taking a considerable risk, and possibly for a long period. Accordingly, to offset these risks, the Indian financiers set their rates high, and gave lower prices – for the goods brought back – than what they could actually receive in the market. Tippu Tip himself had a somewhat uneasy relationship with his Indian financier. In 1879, when he was in Kasongo, and had been away from Zanzibar for twelve years (having requested credit for two years!), he received a message from his financier, a Shiʻa Muslim named Taria Topan, requesting his return to Zanzibar to settle his account. Tippu Tip obeyed the summons, after a further year of settling his affairs. When he returned to Zanzibar he had with him such a phenomenal stock of ivory that we may assume

he could pay off his loans with ease, and conversations recorded in the *Maisha* suggest that the relationship was restored.

The majority of the Indian community in Zanzibar were non-Muslims, and were known as Banyans (from a Sanskrit word meaning 'merchant'), originating mainly from Kutch and Surat in north-west India, present-day Gujarat. A minority, settling from the 1830s on, were Muslims, including Khojas and Bhoras, or Bohoras (see box below). For caste reasons, the Hindus did not bring their families when they settled, and it is said there was not a Hindu woman on the island as late as 1857. Later this changed, and they became a self-sustaining community. Some of the Hindus were artisans – workers in wood, metal, or jewellery, or in small shops or businesses.

A small number of these Indian merchants specialized in a niche branch of finance: tax-farming. For an annual sum paid in advance to the Sultan, they had the right to collect taxes and customs dues payable to the state. The first record of this is the farming of the customs collection in 1804; and it was probably introduced because of the distance, and irregular communications, between the Sultan's seat in Muscat and his taxable possessions in East Africa. Later in the century it became big business, and the tax-farming contract covered the collection of duties not only in Zanzibar but in the ports in the Sultan's possessions on the mainland. The practice ended only in 1886, when Sultan Barghash created a government department in charge of customs.

Indian Muslims in East Africa

Historians of 19th-century East Africa refer often to the Indian Muslims as *Khojas* or *Bohoras*. The Khojas were originally a Hindu caste, who converted to Islam in the 15th century, and lived mainly in Bombay and Gujarat, from where numbers of them emigrated to East Africa. Most are Nizari Isma'ilis, and recognize the Aga Khan as their spiritual leader, their Imam. The name derives from a Persian word, meaning 'lord'. The Bohoras, whose name comes from a Gujarati word meaning 'trader', have a similar origin, having once been also a Hindu caste who converted to Islam, probably in the 11th century; and most of them are Musta'li Isma'ilis, who do not recognize the Aga Khan. Khojas and Bohoras are still found, both in the areas of origin (Mumbai and Gujarat), and in places of immigration such as Africa and Europe.

Foremost among these tax-farmers was Jairam Sewji, originating from Kutch, who held the contract from 1834 until 1853, at an annual rate initially of 110,000 Maria Theresa dollars (MT$), rising to MT$175,000 in 1848. (For an explanation of the role of the Maria Theresa dollar, see below, page 68) The business made Jairam Sewji very rich, partly from the profit on the actual tax-farming, but also from the special position it gave him in commercial circles in Zanzibar: he left MT$3million in cash when he died in 1866. Jairam Sewji left Zanzibar in 1853, but the customs farming contract stayed with his firm, by then led by his representative Ladha Damji. The contract cost was increased to MT$310,000 in 1865, and to MT$450,000 in 1876, when Taria Topan won the contract from the Jairam Sewji house. The sums were significant, but the Sultan had few other sources of income. Both Sultan Majid (ruled 1856–70) and Sultan Barghash (ruled 1870–88) went badly into debt to the Jairam Sewji company, from borrowing revenue in excess of the contract value. At his death in 1870, Sultan Majid was in debt to Ladha Damji to the tune of MT$423,000.

As described above, the Indian community included some Muslims too, who were also mainly engaged in trade and finance. The total Indian community in Zanzibar was estimated at about 1,000 in the late 1840s. Some of these Indians might have originated from British-administered India and claim to be British Indian subjects, and so under the protection of the British representative in Zanzibar. But the majority came from Kutch, and reckoned that, if they were anyone's subjects, they were subjects of the Rao of Kutch. This ruler had signed a Treaty of Alliance with the East India Company which had not placed Kutch under the British Crown. For most of Tippu Tip's life these British representatives in Zanzibar, listed in Appendix 2, held the dual posts of Agent (of the Indian Government, thus appointed by the Governor of Bombay) and Consul (of the British Government, appointed by the Foreign Office in London). Those claiming to be British subjects could therefore claim to have any legal cases heard by the (British) Consular Court, and not by the Zanzibari judicial system, which was for subjects of the Sultan.

There was in fact no rush by the Indian community in Zanzibar to try to claim British protection, because they knew that British subjects would be legally constrained to dispose of their slaves, and a number of Indians, especially those who had acquired plantations, relied on slaves for their prosperity. H.A. Churchill, Consul 1865–70, arranged to ask Kutchis on their arrival whether they wished to place themselves under British or Zanzibari jurisdiction; and, following the implementation of a regulation of 1867, only nine Kutchis had registered at the British Consulate by 1869. However, by the late 1860s the British Indian authorities in Bombay had come round to the view that, in order to oblige Kutchis in Zanzibar to disband their slaves, and not to trade in them, the Rao of Kutch should be induced to issue a proclamation effectively putting his subjects outside India under British jurisdiction; and this was done in April 1869. This left the British Consul in Zanzibar in a position to influence the commercial relationship between the Sultan and the leaders of the Indian community. For example, Churchill's successor John Kirk – who later became perhaps the most distinguished holder of this post – intervened in the placing of the tax faming contract, resulting in a loss to the Sultan of MT$410,000 over the five-year term, so Abdul Sheriff calculates.[18]

All these factors led to resentment building up against the Indian community, particularly among the Arabs. In 1864 Rigby, the British Consul, reported that "four-fifths of the entire commerce of Zanzibar passes through the hands of British subjects". In addition to their growing wealth from finance and banking, they began to acquire land, or the rights to land, from Arabs who had given land title as security but who had defaulted on debts, either because their trading had not been profitable enough to pay the sometimes high rates of interest, or because they had simply not returned to Zanzibar from their trading expeditions. Rigby also estimated that from three-quarters to four-fifths of the immovable property was owned by, or mortgaged to, Indians; but he may have been misled to exaggerate, since often the Indian financiers did not take full control of land on which they had foreclosed, instead allowing the original owners to continue to operate the plantations. The main reason for this was action taken by Rigby himself in pursuance of the British policy to reduce or remove the slave trade: in February 1860, he declared that Indians in Zanzibar falling under British jurisdiction might no longer own slaves. Some sought to avoid the ruling by denying that they were British subjects or by claiming that they were Arab. But many had to obey the instruction, because of their interest in retaining British protection. Spice plantations in particular could at that time not be operated except with slave labour – hence the Indians' preference for keeping them going without actually taking ownership.

Hamed bin Mohammed's birth and family

This was the mixed society into which Tippu Tip was born, probably in 1837. As we saw above, his father, Mohammed bin Juma al-Murjabi (also transliterated as Murjebi), was a trader based in Tabora, in the Unyanyembe district of the Nyamwezi tribe, where Arabs had settled since early in the century. Their presence seems to have met with the favour of the local chief, Fundi Kira, since he exempted their merchandise from taxation. And Mohammed al-Murjabi was singled out for special favour: he married Fundi Kira's daughter, Karunde, which would have put him in an advantageous position in Tabora society and trade.

A glance at the map (page 23) will show why Tabora was of commercial importance. From the east came the main overland routes from Bagamoyo and Saadani, the ports only 25 miles over the sea from Zanzibar. To the north went one route to Lake Victoria, and another round the west of Lake Victoria to Buganda. Due west from Tabora lay Ujiji, on the shores of Lake Tanganyika, from where dug-out canoes took people and traded goods to towns on the farther shore such as Mtowa. To the south-west was the route to the southern end of Lake Tanganyika, which led to Katanga, rich in copper mines. Katanga was also on a separate, more southerly, cross-continental series of routes that went from Luanda (now capital of Angola) to Lindi and Kilwa.

The Arabs living there had an uneven relationship with their compatriots in Zanzibar. At times they would claim to be loyal to the Sultan; and at times he appointed a *liwali* there – the equivalent term in Arabic, *wālī,* is usually translated 'Governor', but his main purpose was representational and to ensure that taxes could be collected. Generally, however, the Arabs of the interior behaved autonomously, and indeed Harthi clan members living there were in a kind of political exile, having been actively involved in the rebellion in 1859 which sought to put Barghash on the throne in place of Majid. (Barghash did in the end accede, in 1870.)

The Murjabi name is not a common one in Oman, but Hamed's great-grandfather had married into the prominent Nabhani clan, of the Riyami confederation, from central Oman. Mohammed al-Murjabi's second wife, Hamed's mother, was from the al-Wardi trading family, who originated in Bahla, but had been dispersed from there in the 16th century; some of their members had concentrated in Samad, in the Eastern (Sharqiya) region. Her given name is not recorded, and she is known to us only as the daughter of Habib bin Bushir al-Wardi. She had a husband other than, and before, Mohammed bin Juma: Hamed refers to "my brother Mohammed bin Masoud al-Wardi, older than I but of the same mother",[19] and Brode – who may have heard orally from Hamed more details than are written in the *Maisha* – records that she had been married to her relative Masoud al-Wardi but had been divorced by him.[20] He was probably the "Masud ibn Musallam el-Wardi, an old merchant of Tabora", whom Burton met in 1857.[21] Hamed's more distant ancestry must have contained African blood; several contemporary accounts mention his dark skin and African features. Brode asserts that his great-great-grandmother on his father's side, that is the wife of Juma bin Mohammed al-Nabhani, was African, but her name is not recorded. It is reasonable to assume, since many Arabs in East Africa took African wives, that other females in Hamed's recent ancestry were African. Herbert Ward, one of the British members of Stanley's Emin Pasha Relief Expedition (of which we shall hear more; see especially Chapter 10), was fascinated by Tippu Tip and writes much about him, not all of it accurate. Ward goes so far as to say that his mother was a "full-blooded negro slave woman of Mrima", the coastal area on the mainland opposite Zanzibar, but there is no other evidence for this, and the other sources all point towards the daughter of Habib al-Wardi as being his mother. Ward also says that Tippu Tip was born in Muscat.[22] This is just possible, since the Arabs of Zanzibar and the mainland travelled to and from Muscat and Oman more than we might expect, but again there is no evidence, and it is generally accepted that he was born and brought up on the island of Zanzibar.

We have little reliable information about Tippu Tip's childhood. The family farm or plantation was at Kwarara, near Stonetown, and there he appears to have had basic education from religious tutors, one of whom is described by Brode as "ignorant", and as having been dismissed so that young Hamed could learn from someone more competent.[23] He would have learnt enough reading and writing of Arabic to enable him to understand the Qur'an, to write letters, and – eventually – to compose the *Maisha*, which he did in Arabic script though in the Swahili language. Almost certainly he spoke Swahili at home as a boy and, later, with his business and other interlocutors. Arabic was his second language, which he used on formal occasions, such as when speaking with the Sultan. With imagination, we can picture a boyhood spent on a Zanzibari *shamba* (plantation), in comfort but without luxury.

The *Maisha* begins: "When I was twelve I started to go on local trips"[24] – the implication being that a young man in that society would naturally be initiated into the trading life. He made these trips with his half-brother Mohammed bin Masoud al-Wardi, his uncle (his mother's brother) Bushir bin Habib al-Wardi, and another uncle, Abdullah bin Habib al-Wardi. He mentions at this stage only gum-copal as the item traded on these trips. This curious resin, no longer in demand, but then used for varnish for carriages and also in the manufacture of other products including printing ink, was found buried in coastal areas on the mainland and on the western coast of Zanzibar. It was found as a fossil, having originally been exuded from the roots or the lower parts of a tree (*Hymenaea verrucosa* or *Trachylobium verrucosum*), just as amber is found on the shores of the Baltic. In an appendix to his book *The Lake Regions of Central Africa*, on trade to and from East Africa at this period, Richard Burton gives a lengthy and detailed explanation of gum-copal.[25] It was as important an export item from the coast as ivory was from the interior. A soft kind could be picked from the tree or was found in the loose soil, and a hard kind was dug out from pits between three and five feet deep – the hard kind being used for decorative purposes, like amber. Burton says that these pits were dug in locations up to 40 miles from the coast, and he is very dismissive of the miners:

> The exploitation of copal is careless and desultory ... the diggers are of the lowest classes, ... and although the labourers could ... easily collect from ten to twelve lbs [4–5 kg] per diem, they prefer sleeping through the hours of heat, and content themselves with as many ounces [i.e. 600–700 grams].

The export destinations appear to have been India and China, Hamburg, and Salem in North America.

Curiously, Tippu Tip says in the *Maisha* that he carried on this copal trade for a year, apparently leaving a gap between the ages of thirteen and eighteen. Bontinck suggests that he was doubtless married during this time. There is no evidence for it, nor any mention later of the ages of his sons which would enable us to place their birth in the early or mid-1850s. But an early marriage would have followed Arab and local custom, and seems probable. Later, when describing how he needed to get credit for a trading expedition, Hamed says that he had "no plantation nor a house in Zanzibar or anywhere else in the world; but I had a wife in Zanzibar, bint Salum bin Abdallah el-Barwanie, who had much property in Zanzibar and Muscat".[26] Again, like Hamed's own mother, her given name is not recorded, but it was a good match. The Barwani family were part of the Harthi clan (or al-Hirth), originally from the Sharqiya province of Oman, and were among the earliest Omani settlers in Zanzibar and thus well-established and wealthy. Hamed was proud of this part of his parentage: he used the Barwani family name when signing a contract which was preserved by John Gray.

With such education in religion and commerce, Hamed bin Mohammed lived as a young man, and began the trading journeys which – on a larger scale – would later form the pattern of his life. These would take place against the background of European exploration of Africa, to which we shall turn in the next chapter.

Chapter 2

Nile-seekers, Africa-crossers

We have already noticed that much of our information about East and Central Africa in the 19th century comes from European explorers. As Dane Kennedy has pointed out, their motivation was a mixture of inquisitiveness and acquisitiveness.[1] Organizations such as the Royal Geographical Society (founded in 1830) housed men (and women, but only from 1904) genuinely interested in the expansion of knowledge about parts of the world so far unknown to Europeans, and were eager for information on topography, geology, manners and customs, flora and fauna. At the same time, expeditions might be expected to reveal new markets for trading (items to buy, places to sell), as well as to open up possibilities for colonial or imperial expansion. Many of these explorers approached the new-found territories with an attitude that we should now consider patronizing – certainly with a feeling that European or American civilization was superior, and that by 'opening up' this territory they would be improving the standards of living of Africans as well as themselves. Some explorers were also driven by a missionary motive. David Livingstone, often described as 'saintly', believed that the scourge of slavery in Africa could be ended by a combination of the 'three Cs' – Christianity, Commerce (i.e. the substitution of legitimate trade for the slave trade), and Civilization. (See box on page 47 on Britain's role in ending the East African slave trade.)

Many of the Africans and Arabs whom the explorers met could not understand why they had come. Even the language of 'discovery' was strange: some asked, "What is there to discover? We know about this country; we have been here all the time!" Some were suspicious, believing that the incomers were there for hidden or criminal motives, for example to capture slaves or steal ivory, or to scout for later conquest. (The latter suspicion may well have been the reason for the attack on Burton and Speke in Somalia, described below.) It is nevertheless difficult to avoid using the language of 'discovery' and 'exploration', since that is how the explorers themselves thought of their activities.

Not surprisingly, explorers' motives were mixed. Stanley initially aimed to advance his journalistic career, and then sought further fame and immortality. A number of explorers had a strong sense of engaging in adventure; for men like Richard Burton, Samuel Baker and Joseph Thomson this was a significant motive. Beside them, or perhaps we should say following them, were the missionaries, with their own particular motivation. Nearly all the explorers, and several of the missionaries, had in mind the wish to record and to publicize their exploits, by books and lectures, if they survived and reached home.

The names of several of these, such as Burton, Livingstone and Stanley, are still renowned. Others may be less familiar. Their contribution to the development of European and American knowledge of the continent was hugely significant, and even now their writings form a valuable resource for the historian. They were assiduous in their note-taking and diary-writing. In part this stemmed from a deep curiosity about what they found, and often from a sense of wonder at landscapes, flora and fauna so utterly different from what they knew at home. Partly too they were duty-bound to keep careful and detailed records, because their expeditions had been financed by organizations such as the Royal Geographical Society or newspapers (in Stanley's case), or by wealthy individuals who expected reports on the results of these far-flung journeys. And partly the explorers knew that they could make an income (and in some cases a good deal of money) from books and lecture tours on their return. As a result, despite the awesome difficulties of writing and recording often quite technical data, and preserving what had been written, they returned with copious notes and diaries and sketchbooks. Livingstone died on his travels in Africa, but after Stanley had 'found' him in 1871, he asked Stanley to take back with him his journals completed up to that point. The problems he had encountered in making these records are vividly described by his editor:

> In the Manyema country he ran out of note-books, ink, and pencils, and had to resort to shifts which at first made it ... debateable ... whether the most diligent attempt at deciphering would succeed after all. ... Old newspapers, yellow with African damp, were sewn together, and his notes were written across the type with a substitute for ink made from the juice of a tree.[2]

Pertinacity of this and more striking kinds characterized these men, and the small number of women who travelled with them. They are important to our narrative, partly because their writings bring to life the picture of East Africa in the late 1800s, but also because several of them met Tippu Tip and took advice and help from him.

Richard Burton and John Speke

Among the earliest to come to this region was Richard Burton, one of those great Victorians who established a formidable reputation as explorer, adventurer and linguist. He is probably best known for having performed the Muslim *hajj* (pilgrimage) in disguise as an Afghan, in 1853. He enters our story because of his exploration of the area between the coast and Lake Tanganyika, with John Hanning Speke, a few years later.

Burton was born in 1821, and had an unconventional childhood: his parents separated (though later reunited), and his father brought up him and his siblings peripatetically in France and Italy. This may have sparked the young Burton's linguistic skills, a talent which he later developed in exhaustive learning of eastern languages. After a patchwork of schooling with an erratic succession of tutors, it was not surprising that his career at Trinity College, Oxford, was short-lived. His family then secured for him entry into the service of the East India Company's army. In India he spent immensely long hours mastering Arabic and various Indian languages, the soldiering duties being light. It was while on sick leave in England, recovering from cholera and an eye infection, that he conceived of the idea of the *hajj* adventure, which he later wrote up in his *Personal Narrative of a Pilgrimage to al-Madinah and Mecca,* a book containing careful and astute commentary on Muslim customs and practices. Like many outrageous incidents in Burton's life, it seemed an extraordinarily foolhardy exploit: discovery of his disguise would (or at least so he claimed) almost certainly have led to his death.

After completing the Arabian journey, Burton stayed for a while in Cairo, and then returned to India, where he wrote the *Personal Narrative.* There he found that a proposal had been made, a few years earlier, for an expedition to Somalia, to see if there were resources there of interest to the East India Company. He applied for and was granted the task; and while in Aden met the man who was to be his companion on two African adventures, and also his adversary when it came to claiming credit for their discoveries. This was John Hanning Speke, known as Jack, aged twenty-seven in 1854 and so six years Burton's junior. He was also an Indian Army officer and had gained experience in exploration – though of a different kind to Burton's: he had spent nearly five years exploring the Himalayas, and had crossed into Tibet. At first meeting in Aden he immediately impressed Burton with his energy and self-reliance. They made a contrasting couple: Speke was tall and thin, reserved and quietly confident, while Burton, though the same height, was dark with black hair, strong eyebrows and a long moustache, with a vigorous and often ferocious expression.

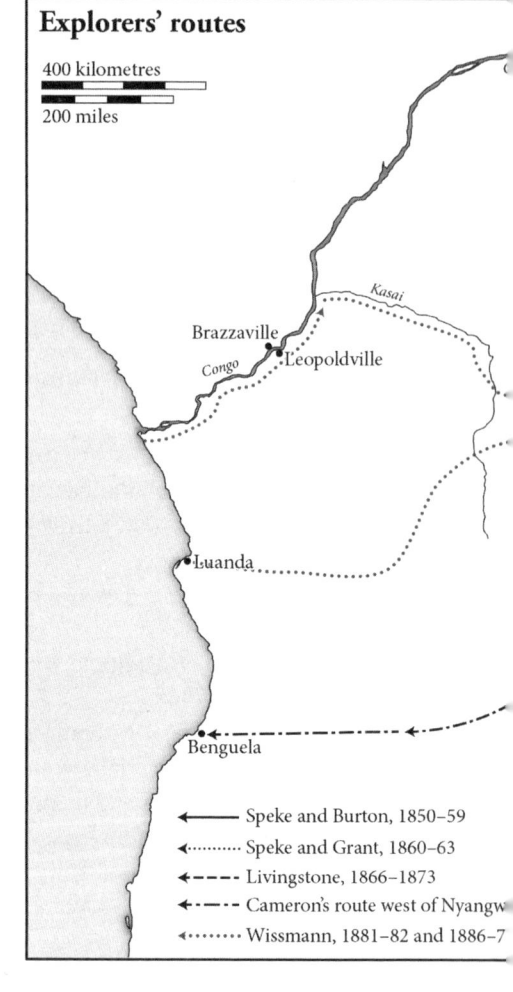

Burton and Speke's Somali expedition, recounted by Burton later in his *First Footsteps in East Africa,* was only a partial success, and

Explorers' routes

400 kilometres
200 miles

Kasai
Brazzaville
Congo · Leopoldville
·Luanda
·Benguela

⬅——— Speke and Burton, 1850–59
⬅········· Speke and Grant, 1860–63
⬅– – – – Livingstone, 1866–1873
⬅·–·–·· Cameron's route west of Nyangw
⬅········ Wissmann, 1881–82 and 1886–7

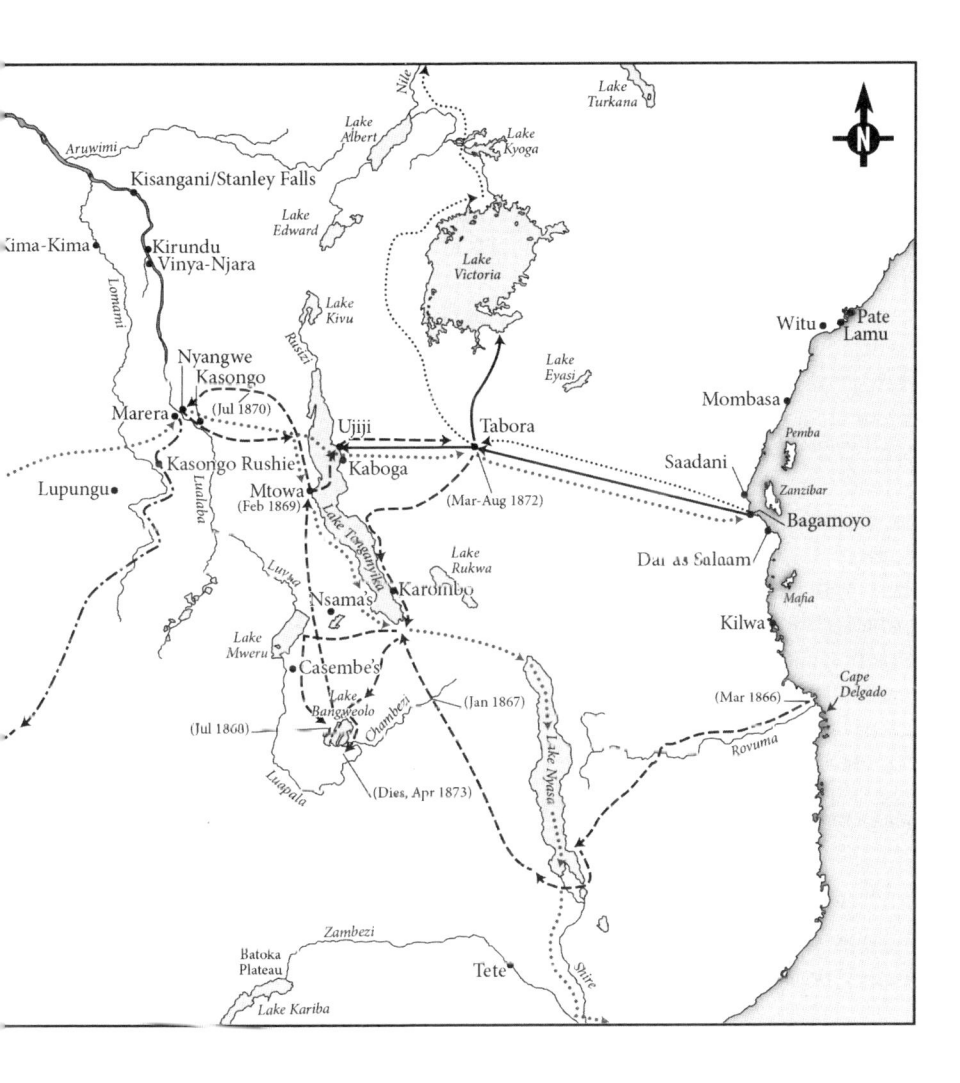

almost ended in total disaster for both men. Burton reached his first target, the ancient city of Harar (now Hārer) in south-eastern Ethiopia, although he sent Speke off on another journey while he did so. They then regrouped, with two other British officers, in Berbera on the Somali coast, waiting for new supplies and equipment to be delivered, and observing the great fair of Berbera. Here, in the middle of a night in late April 1855, they fell victim to a surprise attack of extreme ferocity, in which one of their companions was killed. Burton and Speke both suffered terrible injuries – Speke at one point being captured and very near death – but they made their escape from their camp to a small sailing boat in which they managed to reach Aden. Speke, against expectations, recovered in a few weeks from several spear wounds to his arms and his thigh, whereas it took Burton some months for a spear-wound to his face to heal. Their physical wounds were not the only casualty of this journey: they had differing memories of the frightful night attack, and Speke nursed a resentment of a command shouted at him by Burton during the height of the fighting, which he believed carried an implied accusation of cowardice.

While in Aden before setting out on the Somalia journey, Burton had spoken to Speke – and elicited a positive response – about an intention he had to travel into Central Africa from Zanzibar in the hope of finding the source of the River Nile. This was a bold ambition, which well accorded with Burton's nature. At that time, British geographers knew very little of the Nile above Khartoum. They were familiar with the writings of the ancient geographers and historians: the Greek Herodotus, who in the 5th century BCE had reached the First Cataract and had heard travellers' tales of a watershed from where the Nile flowed; and Ptolemy, who in the 2nd century CE had heard that the Nile started from snow-peaked hills named Mountains of the Moon, twenty-five days' march inland from somewhere near Mombasa in present-day Kenya.[3] They knew of the late 18th-century travels of a Scottish laird, James Bruce, who had reached the source of the Blue Nile, thereby accounting for the annual flood which then (before the building of the Aswan High Dam) gave Egypt its regular irrigation. And they knew of the extraordinary achievement of the wealthy and courageous Dutch woman Alexine Tinné, who had ascended the White Nile to the Sudd, the vast swampy area through which the Nile sluggishly oozes between Gondokoro and Fashoda. But no European had seen Lake Tanganyika or Lake Victoria, or knew the upper reaches of the Nile. The question held great fascination for the Victorians, and we can understand why. The reliability of the Nile's flood had lain at the root of the most ancient and longest-enduring civilization. Its length, even as it was known at that time, was beyond that of any other river then explored. And there was something awesome about this mass of water that flowed through arid desert to reach Cairo and the Delta. To identify its source was one of the great challenges of the age; and to travel there was akin to flying to the moon in the mid-20th century.

Speke therefore had every reason to be excited when Burton mentioned his project, and he claims to have himself conceived of a plan to "strike the Nile at its head, and then to sail down that river to Egypt".[4] The outcome was that, after they had recovered from their Somali injuries, and (in Speke's case) served in the Crimean War, they arrived in Zanzibar in December 1856 and, having made their purchases there and then sailed over to the mainland, they set out for the interior in June 1857. The details of the story of their expedition have been related elsewhere, notably by Tim Jeal.[5] We need to take note only that Burton's pursuit of his dream to solve the Nile mystery led him and Speke to travel through areas where Tippu Tip traded, and to meet Arabs and others who were his associates. They arrived in Kazeh (now Tabora),[6] a distance of some 600 miles from the coast, in just over four months. Burton's romantic description of the place, and his friendly reception by the Arab community there, has already been mentioned (page 22). He and Speke had already suffered hardship and illness, and some of the problems they encountered gave rise to differences of opinion which then kindled resentment between them. This has led writers to try to make judgements of right and wrong in the arguments that developed between Speke and Burton, which later led to downright hostility. The difficulty is that they were of radically different temperament and prejudice. For example, Burton, with his facility for languages, and for Arabic in particular, did not rate Speke – who spoke Hindustani but no Arabic – at all highly. Speke, on the other hand, was able to devise an ingenious system for calculating time and therefore longitude when their chronometers broke, and resented Burton's unwillingness to help him in the long and tedious calculations which he carried out when they reached camp each evening. Both suffered from serious illness on the journey, and it is fair to assume that they committed errors of judgement in their weakened conditions. In the extraordinarily tough conditions in which they journeyed, who would not?

Burton and Speke – the first Europeans to Lake Tanganyika

From Tabora they continued westwards to Lake Tanganyika, which had been well known to the Arabs for some thirty or forty years, or perhaps longer, but had not yet been seen by Western eyes. Burton had been very ill since leaving Tabora, and close to death. He was partly carried, partly assisted on his way, but in February reached the point on a hill from where he could see the lake – but, tragically, Speke could not, since he had been suffering from severe ophthalmia, which had left both his eyes inflamed and useless.

Once at Ujiji, on the lake shore, Speke began to recover, while Burton fell ill again. They nevertheless managed to discuss the question of water-flow – crucial to the issue of the Nile's source – which would engage explorers and geographers for years to come. Burton suspected that Lake Tanganyika might have an outflow at the northern end which connected with the Nile river system. Local people told them of such a river, the Rusizi; but they may have misunderstood whether their interlocutor was describing an inflow or an outflow. Settling this question would not conclusively prove where the Nile started, but it would provide strong circumstantial evidence. The balance of local opinion was in favour of the Rusizi flowing southwards into Lake Tanganyika, but if it turned out to be flowing north, it could well be part of the Nile headwaters. Speke made one journey across the lake in a dugout canoe. Then together he and Burton (still very ill, and barely able to walk unaided) were paddled northwards towards the mouth of the Rusizi, and came agonizingly close to it. But they turned back to Ujiji without having seen the river mouth with their own eyes. Burton's illness was certainly an inhibiting factor. Nevertheless it would probably have been possible for them to travel that little bit farther; and, ever since, there has been debate over why they failed to complete a quest so nearly achieved.

Speke – the first European to Victoria Nyanza

From Ujiji, Burton and Speke returned to Tabora, where they decided that Speke would venture north to see a large lake, locally called Nyanza, or Ukerewe (after an island in the lake), which he had thought could be a Nile source when he had first heard of its position some 200 miles north of Tabora. Burton would stay behind, to continue ethnographic research for the book he planned to publish on their return. This decision turned out to be one of the most important elements in the subsequent breakdown of their friendship. Speke set out with a small party in early July and, on 1 August, having walked 226 miles at nine miles a day, arrived on the shores of the Nyanza, which he later named Lake Victoria. And, although he was not able to set sail on it, or to go far along its shore, he was certain – from the accounts given him of its extent, and also from his measurement of its height above sea level – that "it would indeed be a marvel if this lake is not the fountain of the Nile".[7]

Speke, while deeply regretting that he could not explore the lake further, and in particular ascertain the flow of a river, the Kivira, reported to flow out of its northern side, returned to Tabora and reported to Burton what he had found. Burton appears to have disbelieved Speke's conclusion that he had found the Nile's source, or at least downplayed the importance of Speke's discovery. They could not extend their leave from the East India Company, to make another journey up the west side of the Nyanza, and so departed for the coast, which they reached in March 1859.

This summary of Speke's first, and Burton's only, journey to the Great Lakes region hardly does justice to their achievement. Though succumbing to unfamiliar infections and diseases they had walked (or in Burton's case been carried for some of the way) for hundreds of miles, had together been the first Europeans to reach and partly explore Lake Tanganyika, and – in Speke's case – reached Lake Victoria and correctly judged that its northern outflow was effectively an upper water of the Nile, a judgement that would be finally vindicated only after Speke's death. It was just highly unfortunate that their achievement was overshadowed by a quarrel that erupted into a very public enmity. The reasons for this, and the course of the dispute in British society, are well told elsewhere;[8] and even now it is difficult to relate that part of the history without taking sides between the two men.

Burton and Speke returned to Britain in May 1859, and discussion – often acrimonious – ensued over who should lead a successor expedition to explore the west and north sides of the Nyanza, and determine whether or not the Kivira was in fact a headwater of the Nile. The Royal Geographical Society decided in favour of Speke, who set out in April 1860 with another Indian Army officer, Captain James Grant. Their plan was to go to the Victoria Nyanza, as it was now called with the Queen's agreement, and follow the Nile to Cairo.

Speke and Grant on their Nile quest

After travelling out to Zanzibar, and crossing to the mainland, Speke and Grant left Bagamoyo on the familiar trail through Ugogo, and were not far from Tabora when they nearly became embroiled in the war between the Arab community there and the Unyamwezi chief Mnywa Sere. The chief told the explorer the history of his dispute with the Arabs of Tabora (see Chapter 3, pages 77–9), and Speke had some sympathy with him, especially when the chief offered to drop the imposition of the import tax which had been the cause of the quarrel.

Speke was known to have shared the widely held British belief that the evils of the slave trade could be ended if 'legitimate trade' could be encouraged and increased, and this may have been in his mind when he wrote: "I told Manua Sera I felt very much for him, and I would do my best if he would ever follow me to Kazé; but I knew that nothing could be done unless he returned to the free-trade principles of his father." Their paths then split. Mnywa Sere came near to meeting up with Speke again when the latter was in Kazeh/Tabora a few weeks later, but the chief – while uttering threats against the Arabs – could not be found again by Speke's messengers,

> for he was driven from 'pillar to post' by the different native chiefs, as, wherever he went, his army ate up their stores and brought nothing but calamities with them.[9]

Shortly after, the Arabs mounted an attack on Mnywa Sere, and suffered heavy losses, enabling the chief to start to plan to attack Tabora. Speke responded to an appeal from the Arabs by saying that he "had a duty to perform"; and, even though he was short of porters, set out northwards.

In all his account of the Arabs' confrontation with Mnywa Sere, Speke makes no mention of Hamed bin Mohammed. It is just possible that Hamed was amongst 'the Arabs' mentioned by Speke, since he would have been one young man there among many, and not – at this time – particularly wealthy or prominent. But it is more likely that he had already left for the coast. In the *Maisha* he records a "bitter war ... which lasted three months", and that "in the fourth month we removed the chief and made Mkasiwa chief in his place". The episode described by Speke, in January–March 1861, must have followed this, since Mnywa Sere was complaining that Mkasiwa had been installed as chief in his stead, and he was seeking reinstatement. This helps us place the date of Hamed's return to Zanzibar with his shipment of small ivory tusks at the end of his earliest journey to Tabora and Ujiji, probably in early 1861.

Speke and Grant continued their journey, and achieved remarkable success. They ascertained that the Kivira river flowed northwards out of the Victoria Nyanza, and were sure that its waters became the Nile. Just under two years later, in March 1864, the explorer Samuel Baker reached the lake north-west of the Victoria Nyanza, the Luta N'zige (later named Lake Albert), and found the river flowing into it (which

Britain and the East African slave trade

As noted in the Introduction above, the East African slave trade began much earlier, and ended some decades later, than the trans-Atlantic trade that took African slaves first to South America, and then (on a huge scale) to the Caribbean and North America. In East Africa, adults and children were seized near the Great Lakes of Victoria, Tanganyika and Nyasa, taken to the coast and then shipped to the market in Zanzibar. Many were retained for work on the plantations in Zanzibar and Pemba, but many were also taken – mainly for domestic service – to the Gulf and to Persia, or to Red Sea ports.

After Wilberforce pushed through the Act of 1807 which made slave trading illegal in British ships or through British ports, the British public demanded the Government exert pressure on foreign governments to act against the slave trade. In 1822, 1839 and 1845, the Ruler in Muscat conceded increasingly restrictive agreements with the British which forbade the carrying of slaves in his subjects' ships except in waters close to the coast, and then allowed inspections by ships of the Royal Navy. These measures reduced slave trafficking, but obviously could not stop it altogether. In 1873, the British Government decided on a more determined policy, and despatched a mission headed by Sir Bartle Frere, a former Governor of Bombay, to act tough with the Sultans of Zanzibar and Muscat (who were brothers, both sons of Sayyid Sa'id bin Sultan). Frere's instructions were to persuade Sayyid Barghash in Zanzibar to forbid all exports of slaves from his dominions, and Sayyid Turki in Muscat to forbid all imports into his, and both to allow extensive rights of stop and search to British vessels. Also, the slave market in Zanzibar was to be closed.

Frere failed with Sayyid Barghash; Arab plantation owners believed they would be ruined without being able to use slave labour. He had more success with Sayyid Turki, mainly through offering a financial incentive – Britain would pay the 'Zanzibar subsidy', the annual payment which the Zanzibar Sultan was supposed to pay his Muscat counterpart following the split of the sultanate on the death of Sayyid Sa'id in 1856. In the end, Barghash had to give way: a few months after Frere's visit, the British threatened him with a blockade, and John Kirk obliged him to sign the treaty.

Slavery continued in Zanzibar and on the mainland for some years after that, but declined, and it was more or less completely abolished soon after the British protectorate over Zanzibar was declared in November 1890.

he thought was the same as that which Speke had seen flowing out of the Victoria Nyanza) and one flowing northwards out of it, which he assumed was the Nile. In both conjectures he was right, although this was not definitively proved until thirteen years later. Baker was from a wealthy Devonshire family, and did not need sponsorship from the Royal Geographical Society or anyone else to pay for his exploring. All these explorers were remarkable in their different ways, and for many people what made Baker stand out was his having acquired his travelling companion, later his wife, in a slave market in Bulgaria. Not surprisingly, this colourful figure has attracted biographers as well as historians, and he wrote up his travels in a handsome pair of two-volume works.[10]

David Livingstone in East Africa

However, while these explorers naturally came into contact with Arabic-speaking people to the north of Lakes Victoria and Albert (the Victoria Nyanza and the Luta N'zige), the Arab sphere in East Africa, in which Hamed bin Mohammed was finding his feet, barely extended beyond Uganda. We return therefore to the region between the coast and Lake Tanganyika, and west of the lake, where David Livingstone would carry out his extensive last journeys.

Previously, in the late 1840s and early 1850s, Livingstone had journeyed widely in southern Africa, having originally gone out there as a medical missionary. His aim next in travelling beyond the border of the Cape province was the same, to win converts to Christianity, but as time went on other factors started to motivate him. He became interested in geographical discovery for its own sake. And, as noted above, he grew increasingly passionate about ending the slave trade and educating Africans to develop legitimate trade in its place. In pursuit of this goal, he aimed to "open up a path into the interior" for trade into Central Africa from the south. In a journey of two and a half years from late 1853 to mid-1856, he found a route from the territory of the Makololo people (in present-day Botswana) north and west to Luanda on the Angolan coast; and, having returned the way he came, he then continued east to the coast at Kilimane, near the mouth of the Zambezi river, which he had followed, or nearly followed, most of the way from the Victoria Falls. He was the first European to see these Falls, and the first also to complete a land crossing of Africa. (The Portuguese, who colonized the coasts of what is now Angola on the west and Mozambique on the east, had travelled far into the interior but not made the complete link.)

News of Livingstone's travels had been carried back to Britain, and when he returned in December 1856 he had achieved national hero status. He was able to make money from a best-selling book and from extensive lecture tours, including a famous address in the Senate House of Cambridge University in December 1857, when he inspired young men to the missionary vocation in Africa.

Livingstone's Zambezi expedition

Back in Africa in 1858, and appointed as British Consul in Kilimane, Livingstone organized an expedition, now with British Government financial support, aimed at proving possible the development of the Zambezi as a trade route to the central highlands. He had a vision of agricultural and commercial development (by the British) of the Batoka Plateau, which lies east and north-east of the Victoria Falls, and on the northern side of the Zambezi, and he also hoped that the Makololo tribe, who lived in an unhealthy swampy area to the west, could be persuaded to move there. The Makololo idea did not work out at all; the African tribespeople did not want to move, from fear of the Matabele who already lived there, and most of the missionaries sent to persuade them (and convert them to Christianity) died of fever. Overall the Zambezi expedition was not successful. It was a large-scale project, with a paddle steamer named *Ma-Robert,* and proper stores and supplies. Livingstone however was not a born leader of large teams. He preferred to travel with a small group of companions and porters, reckoning that it was a mistake to risk being seen as a threat by local chiefs and villagers. He had been successful as a lone traveller, but this had developed in him traits which led him to appear moody or aloof, though he did not lack a sense of humour. Jeal recounts, in the context of the awful hot and humid conditions on board the *Ma-Robert,* that Livingstone

> trapped two [cockroaches] in a bottle on one occasion to see how fast they reproduced, and discovered to his horror that from two of the female's egg cases, seventy-eight young ones appeared.[11]

Observing that a tame mongoose fed liberally off the cockroaches, but yet was losing weight, Livingstone noted in his journal that "this would be invaluable to fat young ladies". Jeal observes what a pity it was that he confined his humour to his journal.

The resulting unhappiness among the expedition members, the Zambezi's sandbanks which grounded the steamer, and its totally unnavigable sections of cataracts and rapids, caused Livingstone to give up the plan to establish the river as a channel of communication to Batoka, and to turn his attention instead to the Shire (or Shiré) river, which runs more or less due south from Lake Nyasa (now Lake Malawi) for about 250 miles, joining the Zambezi about 100 miles from its mouth. Lake Nyasa's existence had been reported by a Portuguese explorer in the early 17th century, and a Portuguese trader had told Livingstone he had been there a few years previously. It was also much talked about by local people, being nearly 400 miles long and 10-50 miles wide; but it had not yet been seen by any British person. Nevertheless, Livingstone was surprisingly unexcited when he reached the lake. He was depressed because he had observed the too-obvious signs of the spread of the slave trade in the area – hostility from local people who feared the approach of foreigners. This would clearly put at risk any idea of developing the Shire Highlands for agriculture or commerce. In addition, the Portuguese authorities, who still controlled the coastal area of what is now Mozambique, reasserted their grip on the Zambezi, partly to enable the export of slaves to the French Mascarenes, in the Indian Ocean, to continue. Personal tragedy also struck: Livingstone's wife came out to join the expedition, but died of fever, and several other expedition members, including Bishop Mackenzie (leader of the Universities Mission to Central Africa), succumbed to dysentery and malaria.

In June–November 1862, Livingstone made an attempt to reach Lake Nyasa from another direction, by ascending the Rovuma river, which reaches the sea about 800 miles (1300 km) north of the mouth of the Zambezi. It was a long shot, since the river is only about 300 miles (500 km) long, and Livingstone knew by now that Lake Nyasa was 1,200 feet (about 370 m) above sea level; so cataracts or waterfalls could be expected. His small expedition of selected men had to turn back before they discovered that the Rovuma has its source not in the Lake but in the hills above the Lake's eastern side.

Returning to the Shire river in December 1862, Livingstone made one last attempt to take a new small steamboat up to Lake Nyasa. On this journey, the Shire river (like the Zambezi) showed itself definitively as an unreliable communication channel: failure of the rains in 1862 caused drought and famine in the area, and Livingstone's expedition members, already disheartened by the difficulties of exploration, were dismayed by the sight of bodies floating downstream of those who had died of starvation and not been buried. When the expedition was about half-way to the Lake, Livingstone received a letter from Foreign Secretary Lord John Russell recalling them, the British Government having decided that no further funds should be allocated to the enterprise. When the message arrived in July 1863, Livingstone knew that there would not be enough water in the river for the boats to sail down until the end of the year. Remarkably, instead of waiting, he filled in the time by walking about 700 miles along the west side of Lake Nyasa and back to the boats, before going down the Shire and Zambezi, and from there to Zanzibar. Even then he did not take the easy way home: failing to sell the steamboat intended for Lake Nyasa, he decided to take it to Bombay – a 45-day voyage over open water with a very small crew. He arrived back in England in July 1864, having been away for six years.

When set against Livingstone's own stated ambitions, the Zambezi expedition was a failure; and so it was seen at the time. His hopes for establishing colonies either on the Bakota Plateau or in the neighbourhood of Lake Nyasa proved ill-founded, as were his plans for opening up this part of Africa for missionary endeavour. The reception he received on his return to the UK was very different from the hero's welcome that had greeted him in 1856: he had spent a significant sum of Government money, and some of his own, with the loss also of several lives but with no visible results. However, by the standards of 'normal' African exploration, the expedition had achieved a lot: Livingstone had determined the (limited) extent of the navigability of the Zambezi and Shire rivers, he had located and mapped Lake Nyasa, and his companions had recorded a large number of their scientific observations. As Jeal points out in his detailed description of the Zambezi expedition,[12] if Livingstone had confined his intentions to those of scientific and geographical exploration, without the exaggerated ambition of colony-building, his achievements would have been recognized.

As one of the contributors to the scientific reports, his party had included John Kirk, then a young botanist and the expedition's medical officer, on his first visit to Africa. Born in 1832, Kirk was of similar Scottish background to Livingstone, but he had a realistic appreciation of him, and his letters and diaries contain frank criticism of the Doctor's leadership techniques. He later became a distinguished Consul and Agent in Zanzibar, and he will reappear in the Tippu Tip story.

Livingstone and the source of the Nile

Livingstone next set foot in Africa in March 1866, but now with a modified agenda. He was still determined to do what he could to end the slave trade in East Africa, still believing that the combination of civilization, commerce and Christianity was key to achieving this. But he had also been bitten by the Nile bug, and when he writes, in his diaries, of the need to "finish my work", this usually refers to his determination to settle the question of the source of the Nile – still unresolved when he set out from England in 1865.

Livingstone's interest in the Nile stemmed from his having been invited to attend the confrontational debate being organized on the subject in Bath in September 1864. Speke was to explain why he believed that the Victoria Nyanza was the source, and Burton – still driven by angry jealousy of his former companion – was to set out his reasons for believing that those theories were far from proven. The debate never took place, owing to Speke's death in a gun accident the day before it was due. But the gathering of experts occasioned a meeting between Livingstone and Sir Roderick Murchison, President of the Royal Geographical Society, at which Livingstone became intrigued by the unsolved question, possibly believing that the Zambezi (which he knew and the other explorers did not) rose and flowed south from the same watershed as that from which the Nile rose and flowed north. Like Burton, he thought that Lake Tanganyika could be involved: it was such a huge body of water, and if a river flowed out from the northern end, it seemed likely to be the Nile, perhaps via the Luta N'zige (by then Lake Albert), of which only the northern part had been explored by Baker in 1864. The outcome, though some months later, of his conversation with Murchison was a commission by the Royal Geographical Society for Livingstone to solve the Nile mystery.

Exploration of the water systems of east central Africa was therefore high on Livingstone's list of priorities when he set out up the river Rovuma (again) in March 1866. He reached Lake Nyasa, went round its southern end, and then turned north-west, aiming to find Lake Bangweolo (of which he had heard, in today's northern Zambia) and the river which he hoped he would find flowing out of it northwards into Lake Tanganyika. In fact he passed to the east of Lake Bangweolo, and arrived at the southern end of Lake Tanganyika in April 1867. It was in this phase of his travelling that he began to have dealings with Arab traders, not surprisingly, since in the Lake Nyasa area he was on the slave-trading route leading to Kilwa, and when he reached Lake Tanganyika he encountered those on the route from Tabora to Katanga. Some have asked why, given his visceral hatred of slave trading, Livingstone would have anything to do with these people. The answer is that he needed help of various kinds, which could not always be supplied by local Africans – for example food, assistance in travelling (he suffered from a bout of severe rheumatic fever at this time), and protection from being attacked or caught in cross-fire among warring tribes.

Livingstone had hoped to explore the western shore of Lake Tanganyika, and to find a river flowing into it either from Lake Bangweolo or from Lake Mweru (Moero), another lake farther west of which he had recently heard. Fighting between Arabs and local tribes made this impossible, and only after a delay of three months, in September 1867, was he was able to start his journey to Lake Mweru. This he did in the company of Hamed bin Mohammed, by now known by his nickname of Tippu Tip. It was a slow journey – the 100 miles took over a month – because Tippu Tip was busy enquiring about new supplies of ivory. But he did at least help Livingstone in supplies of food, and in providing protection. Livingstone reached the Lake in November, and by discovery and enquiry worked out that a river (named Luapula) flowed out of Lake Bangweolo into Lake Mweru, and another river, a very significant one, named Lualaba, flowed out of Lake Mweru northwards. He thought it possible that the Lualaba might feed into the western side of Lake Tanganyika, or might carry on farther north and turn north-east into Lake Albert; and that therefore Lake Bangweolo could be the Nile source.

Tippu Tip offered to keep Livingstone in his party on the journey to Ujiji, which Livingstone was happy to do, since he could rely on the Arab for food, and needed to get to Ujiji where fresh supplies of barter goods and other supplies should have arrived. Tippu Tip wished first to go a short distance south, to Chief Casembe's village; but he then decided to continue westwards, to Katanga. ('Casembe', also spelt Kazembe or Cazembe, was a chiefly title held by a succession of chiefs in this territory.) Livingstone found another Arab prepared to go with him to Ujiji, but winter rains made impassable the whole area between Casembe's village and Lake Tanganyika, so instead he decided to head south to confirm the outflow from Lake Bangweolo to Lake Mweru. This was an appallingly difficult journey of about 200 miles through inundated territory, but Livingstone and his small party, with another Arab, Mohammed Bogharib, reached the Lake in July 1868. Now convinced that Lake Mweru was the Nile source, he set off back north again with Bogharib and other Arabs for Ujiji, where – after another serious illness which forced him to be carried in a litter – he arrived in February 1869.

Here Livingstone faced a fresh disaster. Nearly all the supplies he had ordered to be sent up from Bagamoyo had been stolen, and none of the mail and newspapers he had hoped for were there. Most of the supplies had in fact arrived, but up to two years previously; and it was not so surprising that most of it had been 'lost'. He sent a message to John Kirk, now appointed Consul and Agent in Zanzibar, requesting new supplies, and decided to go, still with Mohammed Bogharib, to Manyema, the area west of the northern end of Lake Tanganyika. Through this area, he had been told, the river Lualaba flowed; and thus he would be able to check its direction of flow – if north-east, then this would strengthen the likelihood that it was heading for Lake Albert.

In 1869 Livingstone and Bogharib crossed Lake Tanganyika and entered Manyema. But progress towards the River Lualaba was painfully slow. Partly this was because Arabs were expanding their presence and their trade in the area, often using violent methods which made the African villagers hostile towards any foreigner. But mainly it was because Livingstone's resistance to disease was very low, and he suffered dreadfully from pneumonia, dysentery, and horrible ulcers on his feet and legs. At times, and for six months in 1870 in Bambarré, he could not move for long periods. Finally he was able, in February 1871, to travel to the Lualaba, which he reached at Nyangwe at the end of March; this was the farthest west that he went on his 'last journeys'. There he spent time in fruitless negotiations for boats to cross the river, which might have been successful had it not been for an attack on the Nyangwe Africans by the Arabs there, at the market in July 1871. It is not easy to analyse the reasons for the attack, which Livingstone wrote up in graphic detail. It was presumably aimed at subduing the Africans into complete compliance with Arab demands for trading concessions and supply of ivory. Livingstone was so horrified by the incident, in which at least four hundred, and probably more, unarmed Africans died, that he could no longer bear the idea of depending on Arab support for his travels, and – still with great difficulty – he returned to Ujiji.

There he found that, again, his supplies – a fresh consignment sent from the coast by Kirk – had been stolen. This put him in a serious quandary: he would have to send for new supplies, but the process would take months, there was the added problem of continued fighting east of Ujiji, and in the meantime he would be forced to rely on Arab generosity. But, just one week after he reached Ujiji, he was saved, probably reluctantly (since he disliked journalists), by the arrival of Henry Morton Stanley.

Stanley, and how he 'found' Livingstone

Stanley's life story is one of the most remarkable, and for all his flaws he stands out among African explorers of the 19th century. From illegitimate birth in north Wales and an upbringing in poverty and deprivation, including a spell of several years in the workhouse, he took passage to America, rejected his given name of John Rowlands and adopted the name allegedly of his benefactor in New Orleans – although this, like many of his claims, is open to question. After fighting and being captured in the American Civil War, he became a journalist, and, demonstrating some competence as a writer, he was recruited by James Gordon Bennett, owner and editor of the *New York Herald*, to mount an expedition in Africa to find Livingstone, from whom nothing had been heard for two years. The details of his life have been excellently related elsewhere.[13] He is of interest to our narrative because he had closer dealings with Tippu Tip than did any of the other European explorers of Africa, not only on this journey but on later occasions and notably in the Upper Congo in the 1880s. He wrote extensively and vividly about his travels, but with an over-tinted palette which sometimes caused him problems with a sceptical British reading public, in books that sold well and made him famous: *How I Found Livingstone*; *Through the Dark Continent* (the account of the immensely long journey on which he established the source and the course of the River Congo); *The Congo and the Founding of its Free State, 1841–1904* (in which he recounts the years during which he worked for King Leopold II in the Congo); and *In Darkest Africa* (the story of his leadership of the Emin Pasha Relief Expedition). Tippu Tip features in all but *How I Found Livingstone*, and is a major player in the last one.

Stanley had been able to draw on the considerable resources of the

New York Herald to finance his expedition to find Livingstone, and he therefore arrived in Ujiji, on 10 November 1871, with equipment and stores that amazed the Doctor. The two men, radically different in temperament, seem to have established a friendly relationship – even allowing for the hyperbole common in Stanley's writing. They even did some exploring together, travelling by canoe to the north end of Lake Tanganyika where they found the mouth of the river Rusizi (also called Lusizé), and determined that the flow was into the lake, and not northwards towards Lake Albert. This was important for Livingstone's theories of water flows to the Nile, since (if one ignored Lake Victoria) it narrowed the field to the Lualaba and the Lomami, another north-flowing river roughly parallel to and west of the Lualaba, of which Livingstone had heard when in Nyangwe.

Both men showed a reluctance to part, but after five months Stanley returned directly to Bagamoyo, and then to London, to file his reports and to find fame. Livingstone waited in Unyanyembe for a few months, for the supplies that Stanley had promised to despatch from the coast. He set out in August 1872 (at about the same time as Stanley arrived in London), heading south-west to the southern end of Lake Tanganyika, from where he planned to travel west to Katanga and then farther, to discover the 'four fountains' mentioned by Herodotus. These fountains were said to be situated between two hills, and to flow both north and south. Livingstone desperately wanted to believe this story, especially when two Arab travellers in the area had given him evidence which partially supported it. He speculated that the Zambezi could derive from one of the south-flowing fountains, and the Lomami from one of the north-flowing, from where it made its way north to join the Lualaba and then (as he thought) north-east to Lake Albert and the Nile.

Livingstone's last journey

Livingstone did not make it to the fountains; and the story of his last months is told graphically in his *Last Journals* brought home by his faithful servants.[14] Making very slow progress because of his weakened condition, greater heat than usual, and then the onset of the rains, he reached Lake Bangweolo, and headed for the southern shore, to check that there were no rivers flowing in from that direction. Heavy rain, the difficulty of walking and wading through deep swamp, and his own weakness, led eventually to Livingstone's death in his camp south-east of Lake Bangweolo. Heroically his servants Chuma and Susi, having buried his heart near the camp, brought the remains of his body to Bagamoyo (a five-month journey of several hundred miles) so that it could be entombed later in Westminster Abbey.

Verney Lovett Cameron

Shortly before his death, another expedition for the relief of Livingstone was organized by the Royal Geographical Society. The leader, a Royal Navy officer named Capt. Verney Lovett Cameron, was instructed to meet up with Livingstone, convey to him mail and supplies, and to act under his guidance in furthering new geographical exploration. Cameron met up with Chuma and Susi in Unyanyembe as they were bearing home Livingstone's body, helped himself to some of the scientific instruments in their baggage, and decided "to push on towards Nyangwe to endeavour to follow up the doctor's explorations".[15] Though he was correct in surmising that the Lualaba was the headwater of the Congo, to what extent he shared Livingstone's obsession with the water systems of Central Africa is uncertain, since he clearly had an ambition to cross the continent, writing in what seem now rather patronizing terms.

> I became still more anxious to undertake some exploration in Africa on hearing that Arab merchants from Zanzibar had reached the West Coast; for I felt convinced that what had been accomplished by an Arab trader was equally possible to an English naval officer.[16]

Cameron did however succeed in his ambition, becoming the first European to cross Africa from east to west. He is of interest to our narrative since he met up with Tippu Tip in Nyangwe, and the advice he received from him, and his decision to travel with the Arab, affected his choice of route – south from Nyangwe and then south-west to Katanga and across to Benguela, instead of the descent of the Congo River that he had originally contemplated.

Wissmann and other Europeans

It was not only British explorers who made these great journeys in the course of which they encountered Tippu Tip and recorded their meetings with him. As European interest in East and Central Africa grew, others came on to the scene, notably Germans, Belgians and French. Some were explorers, some administrators – especially when King Leopold II began developing or exploiting the Congo – and some were missionaries. Two who give vivid descriptions of Tippu Tip were the German explorer Hermann von Wissmann and the Belgian administrator and explorer Jérôme Becker.

We shall hear more of Becker in the later narrative of the confrontation between the Belgians and the Arabs in the eastern Congo in the late 1880s and early 1890s. Wissmann was a German soldier who in 1881 took leave from the army to accompany Dr Paul Pogge, who had already explored in Central Africa, on a trans-continental journey. They started in Luanda, and travelled east and then northeast, crossing the Kasai and Lomami rivers, both major tributaries of the Congo, and arriving in Nyangwe on the Lualaba in April 1882. Here he met Tippu Tip, whom he describes as

> the powerful Arab, Hamed-bin-Mohammed, called Tibbu Tib, or, west of the Lualaba, Mutshi Pula and Tupa-Tupa. ... A man of about forty-five years old, completely black in his skin colouring, even though his father was a pure Arab. A little sturdy, he is lively in his movements, agile and polite, decisive in his gestures, like his son often has an attentive and watchful look, and seems to enjoy mockery.[17]

At Nyangwe, Pogge left Wissmann, turning back westwards in order to help establish one of the stations on the river Congo for the Belgian government of the Congo Free State. Wissmann continued east, reaching an outpost of the London Missionary Society on the west bank of Lake Tanganyika in July 1882, from where he crossed the lake to Ujiji, and then continued to the coast at Saadani.

Wissmann made a second journey across Africa in 1886–87, his purpose this time being to explore the Kasai river, and then make his way eastwards much as he had done four years previously. He travelled with a huge caravan; when he reached the Lomami river, and even though he had lost dozens of men through weakness and disease (because the region from the Kasai to Nyangwe was tragically depopulated, and food was hard to come by), he reports making the river crossing with 600 men! By the time he reached Nyangwe, in early 1887, Tippu Tip had returned to Zanzibar. But Wissmann met his son Sayf, whom he clearly did not like, describing his behaviour as "shocking", and his character as "hot-headed and insolent".[18] He comments in some detail on the methods used by "Tibbu Tib's hordes" to bring the Africans under their control, and extract slaves and ivory. Worried by the fighting that was breaking out between the Arabs and the forces of the Congo Free State on the Lualaba river, and by war in the Tabora area between Arabs and Africans, Wissmann took a long route to the east coast – to the south end of Lake Tanganyika and then south-east to the Shiré and Zambezi rivers. On this journey, in which Wissmann covered well over 3,000 miles in just under 22 months, Robert Brown comments – from the comfort of his armchair in London

that "Wissmann's journey may be said to have all but ended popular interest in these journeys across Africa", and "a trans-African journey had, indeed, by the year 1885 ceased to be a novelty".[19] Wissmann stayed in Africa, and later took posts in the German government of East Africa. We shall return to his accounts of Tippu Tip's control of Central Africa later in the narrative.

One other traveller deserves mention. Between Wissmann's two journeys, an Austrian explorer, Oskar Lenz, set out in 1885 to obtain news of Emin Pasha (see Chapter 10), and to discover more of the river systems between the upper Congo and upper Nile. In May 1886, he reached Kasongo on the Lualaba, and sought help from Tippu Tip: the Arab could not or would not give him the porters he requested, but made available canoes in which to travel downriver to Nyangwe, from where he could go on to Lake Tanganyika, and across it to Ujiji. Here Lenz reviewed his plan to find news of Emin Pasha, which would have required him to go due north through Uganda; but his party lacked the resources needed for this distance, and for self-defence, and he decided to take the Lake Nyasa and river Shiré route to the east coast.

As our narrative proceeds, we shall come across numbers of other Europeans who met Tippu Tip during their African journeys, and recorded their impressions. Notable among these are officials of the Belgian occupation of the Congo, of various nationalities, and the British team accompanying Stanley on the Emin Pasha Relief Expedition. One curiosity is the apparent absence of contact between Tippu Tip and the Christian missionaries who started coming to East and Central Africa, and to the Congo, from the late 1870s. References to them in his *Maisha* are very rare. He mentions a meeting with a British missionary during his last journey back to Zanzibar in 1891, and – a few weeks later – the care given to him by French missionaries when he fell badly ill with dysentery. But the missionary records themselves are oddly silent about him. It must be assumed that their paths did not cross. The missionaries were concerned with the objective of bringing what they saw as 'civilization' to Africa, through the introduction of religion, education and health (and the accompanying buildings of churches, schools and hospitals), whereas Tippu Tip was interested in expanding his wealth and influence through conquest and trade. He had no reason to think that the missionaries either posed a threat to him or could be of use as allies.

CHAPTER 3

Boy Trader

IN 1855, WHEN HAMED BIN MOHAMMED was eighteen, his father came to Zanzibar from Tabora, and took him on his first early travels inland, to a place he records as Ugangi, though this may have been wrongly transcribed. According to Brode, it was in the region north-east of Lake Nyasa (now Lake Malawi, see map on page 23), and they were trading in slaves and ivory, but Tippu Tip himself gives no details.[1]

Hamed does not describe in the *Maisha* what these journeys were like, except incidentally. European explorers give more explicit descriptions, and some went as far as to list, for the benefit of future travellers, the equipment that was necessary or useful. This seems curious to the modern reader, since only a handful of explorers and missionaries journeyed in those areas, and they were not exactly writing guidebooks. (Thomas Cook's handbooks to foreign countries started in the 1870s, but the 19th-century volumes never stretched south of the Sahara.) Perhaps they considered that their lengthy lists of essentials emphasized the complete non-availability of everything their compatriots took for granted. Even basic food was often difficult to acquire, due either to crop failure or to the hostility of local tribes. Given that we are looking at situations where survival depended on having the right supplies and equipment, and that everything had to be carried by *pagazi* (porters), the modern reader is sometimes surprised at what seemingly non-essential items the explorers carried. For example, Stanley had packed two silver goblets and a bottle of champagne to open with Livingstone if or when he found him. In the event, he was so emotionally overwhelmed when he met the Doctor at Ujiji that he forgot about the bottle, and had to produce it at the end of the day, when they had been sitting for some hours exchanging news, and having supper.[2] On another occasion, early in the Emin Pasha Relief Expedition, on the banks of the River Congo, Stanley handed Herbert Ward, an expedition member, "a cigar from the silver case given him by HRH the Prince of Wales on the night before his departure".[3] Stanley no doubt wanted to impress Ward with his royal connections. Even more extraordinary to the modern reader is the list of items which the Belgian explorer and colonial administrator Jérôme Becker provided for a year's travelling in Africa. This includes, after large quantities of tinned fruit and vegetables, tea, condensed milk, sugar and salt, and other provisions difficult to acquire locally, 50 bottles of "old Bordeaux [wine] (valuable tonic in humid weather), ... 25 half-bottles of champagne (prevents anaemia), 12 bottles of madeira (tonic and protects against fever), 12 bottles of cognac (in case of marches in marshy areas, night watches etc. Very healthy for neutralizing briny water)".[4]

Europeans, as we might expect, equipped themselves with medical supplies, some of which were crucial – notably quinine to counter the effects of malaria. Livingstone was particularly bitter about one of his *pagazi* who made off with his medicine chest, a loss which caused him protracted periods of illness and weakness that either slowed his progress or caused him to have to stop. Coupland reckons that this theft – in 1866 – hastened Livingstone's death, though in fact he lived over six years longer, until 1873.[5] Expeditions financed by bodies such as the Royal Geographical Society carried scientific instruments enabling the explorers to fix their positions and measure their height above sea level. The latter was essential for calculating likely water flow, and hence for identifying watersheds, all of which they needed in order to judge whether they were nearer to solving the burning question of the source of the Nile.

Caravans and *pagazi*

In the 18th century, trading was done using a relay system, so that each group of *pagazi* travelled a relatively short way.[6] In the 19th century the custom was adopted of employing *pagazi* for long trips lasting weeks or months. This may have been because certain tribes, and in particular the Wanyamwezi, developed a speciality in portering. One estimate, in the 1890s, reckoned that over 80,000 Wanyamwezi travelled between the coast and Tabora/Kazeh each year, that is about one-third of the male population of Nyamwezi. These were of course paid porters, who received cash (some of it in advance) as well as food during the journey. In *Through the Dark Continent*, Stanley complains at the inflation of the porters' wages – by 1874 they had risen from 2.5 dollars (Maria Theresa dollars – see below, page 68) to 5 dollars per month since his first journey to find Livingstone only four years previously.[7] Some caravan owners used slaves, particularly if they needed manpower to carry ivory from the interior to the coast, and in Zanzibar they could sell both slaves and ivory. Sometimes they would employ slaves belonging to someone else, and then they might pay a wage to the slave, or a fee to the owner, or both. They would also use Waungwana, freed slaves, of whom there was a reasonable supply in Zanzibar and in the coastal areas.

The Arab trading caravans travelled in long lines of dozens, sometimes hundreds, of *pagazi*. Stanley, setting out to find Livingstone 1871, had 153 *pagazi* and 23 soldiers; this was a medium-sized caravan. In his next and much longer journey, starting in 1874, his party numbered 228, including 26 women and children. Livingstone preferred a smaller party, but even he started out with about 60 (though this number was soon reduced as he fell out with groups of his company). At the end of the Emin Pasha Relief Expedition (see Chapter 10), Stanley was leading a line of nearly 2,000 people – porters, soldiers and some accompanying women and children. Tippu Tip does not describe the make-up of his company, but we may deduce from his narrative that he had a good number of armed men, and that when he had large loads to carry (for example when taking ivory back from Central Africa to the coast) he bought or conscripted slaves or forced labour to assist. Arthur Dodgshun, travelling with a London Missionary Society party, noted in a diary entry for 30 May 1878: "Both yesterday and today we met large caravans of Wanyamwezi carrying ivory to the coast. They are said to be Tipo-Tipo's men – 2,400 in number. Some of the tusks were very large."[8]

The routes were often only two feet wide, and sometimes less. They wound round and over the countryside, straight ways being made crooked by diversions to avoid swampy ground, or rocks, or fallen trees. Septimus Tristram Pruen, a medical missionary travelling in this area in the late 1880s, writes of them: "They are called 'roads', but the term 'paths' would more correctly convey their condition ... for they are only narrow tracks from 9 to 15 inches wide, bared of vegetation by the frequent tramping of naked feet, but as uneven as when originally made."[9]

At times the going was good and dry, at others the travellers would sink into water or mud even up to their shoulders; there is a graphic illustration of this in Livingstone's *Last Journals,* during his last rain-drenched weeks near Lake Mweru, west of the southern tip of Lake Tanganyika.[10] Even out of the rainy season caravans had to cross streams and rivers. Stanley describes how they had to stop to construct a small bridge over a river that was too deep to ford. His account of his preparations in Zanzibar and his early journeys are instructive, since (as he admits) he arrived in East Africa with extensive experience of European and Middle Eastern travel as a reporter, but no knowledge of what was required of an explorer in Africa; and so he looked at problems and requirements with an entirely fresh eye and uncluttered mind. Joseph Thomson, a young explorer who had to take over leadership of a Royal Geographical Society Expedition in 1878 when the leader died soon after the start, managed a more humorous take on African travel:

> If you want to get some idea of what an African road is like, I would like you to go out into some moorland place after rain, and march up and down in one of the drains for two or three hours. If there is a loch near at hand, vary your walk with a ramble into it, and now and then perambulate over some piece of dry ground. The effect will be highly realistic.[11]

The porters' loads were measured out to a norm of about 70 lbs, or just under 32 kg. Sometimes lighter loads per person were negotiated. On his first expedition, to find Livingstone, Stanley standardized on 60-lb loads in order to travel faster. Organizing his second expedition in 1874, Stanley distributed loads of different weights, depending on the strength of the carrier and the fragility of the load. Thus, cloth went in 60-lb bundles with the strongest men, beads in 50-lb packs with those who were "short and compact", and other stores at 40 lb per head for the younger *pagazi*. The precious loads of scientific instruments were allocated in 40-lb boxes to the older, more careful men, while the vitally important chronometers were in a light box of 25 lb.[12] If, as was common, the expedition had a boat intended for exploration on one of the lakes, this had to be constructed in sections, which were carried separately and then bolted together on arrival at the destination. Several of these sections were designed to be carried by two men, but even so caused difficulty on the march, especially on muddy paths in rainforests. The loads were carried on the porters' heads, or on their shoulders in cradles made of flexible sticks, or slung on poles between two porters' shoulders. Large ivory tusks had to be carried by two porters, since a good number of them weighed 80–85 lbs, and tusks of 140–150 lbs were not uncommon. Stanley relates how he collected all his goods and materials in a warehouse in Zanzibar, amounting to 11,000 lbs, or just less than 5,000 kg, and asked himself how he could carry 6 tons of goods across Africa.[13] (In fact 11,000 lbs is 5.5 tons, but Stanley was prone to exaggeration; it was still a great deal.)

Some travellers hoped to save on effort by using pack animals, either horses or donkeys, which could indeed carry heavier loads, or pull narrow carts with perhaps 200 lbs luggage. In 1877 a group from the London Missionary Society, drawing on the expertise of someone who had served in South Africa where bullock carts were in common use, attempted to train oxen to pull carts.[14] But these animals were all prey to the tsetse fly or other disease, and most did not survive more than a few weeks' travelling. In the late 1870s some British officials, having difficulty in recruiting reliable *pagazi*, brought four elephants from India to carry luggage for a Belgian expedition into the interior; two died quickly, and one survived for most of the expedition.[15] But the experiment was not repeated: overall, human *pagazi* were in the end more reliable. There are few records of Tippu Tip using pack animals. He received a donkey as a gift from Stanley when they parted on the River Lualaba in December 1876, and donkeys do seem to have been used occasionally, especially for carrying sick people.[16] Early in the Emin Pasha Relief Expedition (see Chapter 10), Stanley is described by an expedition member as riding "a fine henna-stained mule, whose silver-plated trappings shone in the bright morning sun".[17]

Pagazi, not surprisingly, created other problems. They often required part or full payment in advance, and their loyalty was not always unquestioned. They were aware that they were carrying loads which were of value, and – especially if they were travelling through country where they knew the local inhabitants – were often tempted to desert, taking their load (or other items of value, such as guns) with them. The expedition leader would make strenuous efforts to recover the missing person and goods, since maintaining discipline was thought to be vital, and sometimes vicious punishments were handed out to offenders. In addition to being prone to desertion, the porters' patience might run out. For example, at a crucial moment when Tippu Tip was travelling with Stanley on the Lualaba River, Stanley's *pagazi* said they wished to return to the East Coast with Tippu Tip, while Stanley wanted them to continue with him (see pages 160–1).

Human porters, incidentally, remained essential for transport even after railways started to be built in West and East Africa. As Simpson points out:

> The demand for men reached its climax in the Great War of 1914–18, when hundreds of thousands of porters were used on both sides during the protracted campaign between Allied and German troops, and in which very heavy casualties were incurred. It was not until the 1920s that mechanical transport and improved roads rendered large-scale porterage obsolete.[18]

Apart from *pagazi*, a caravan had soldiers, armed mainly for defence but also for shooting game. During this period, advances were being made in gun technology, and the Arabs attached importance to constant upgrading. Nearly all the guns used in Africa used gunpowder which was detonated by percussion caps; and the supply of both powder and caps is a constant theme in travellers' writing. During the Emin Pasha Relief Expedition it was this issue that played a major part in the fall-out between Tippu Tip and Stanley: Tippu Tip claimed that Stanley had failed in his undertaking to provide him with powder and caps, while Stanley actually sued Tippu Tip for breach of contract to supply armed porters (see Chapters 10 and 11).

In addition, caravans – particularly those of the European explorers – needed guides and translators. These men receive remarkably little mention in the diaries and records. Yet they must have been essential in any expedition or even trading travel, since the paths, especially through swamps, were difficult to trace, and communication with chiefs and villagers was necessary for obtaining food and permission to transit. And, as Hopkins points out, the guides and translators, or other leading men in the caravan, would have stepped forward to sort out problems on those frequent occasions when the caravan or expedition commander was laid low with disease or injury.[19]

Caravans were not only composed of adult males. Women and sometimes children would travel with traders' or explorers' caravans, and the women (probably carrying only their own personal effects, but sometimes helping to carry their husbands' loads) helped in the domestic work of setting up camp and cooking the meal at the end of the travelling day. In purely African trading caravans, some of the women were active partners in the commercial activity.

As may be imagined, with such large and disparate groups progress was slow. A typical day's march might be between 8 and 12 miles (13 and 18 km) depending on conditions, but could be as few as 4–5 miles. In the early phase of his journey to find Livingstone, Stanley reckoned that his caravan travelled at "a little more than four miles a-day", in 5–6 hours of marching.[20] The caravan started early, soon after sunrise, with the *kirangozi* (guide) leading, either carrying a flag himself or with a flag-bearer near him. Most caravans in the dominions of the Sultan of Zanzibar carried his blood-red flag, but Stanley made a point of having the American flag at the head of his caravan. The commander of the convoy would normally bring up the rear, although Stanley was often in the vanguard of his caravan, with another officer at the back, to round up stragglers. Distances were measured in days' marches, not in units of length or distance. During the march the porters would often sing, sometimes in response chanting between the *kirangozi* and the *pagazi,* as a help to maintain marching rhythm. At the end of the day's march, which would be not long after midday (the sun making the ground too hot for the bare feet of the *pagazi*), the afternoon would be spent pitching camp, gathering fuel for cooking, and obtaining food for the large company: although the loads on the porters' heads did include some supplies, it was more efficient to buy (or sometimes to steal) food from the villages near the camp.

Coinage and barter

Even this was not simple. In inland East Africa at this time, precious metals such as silver and gold were not valued, so the coins that were used for the trade on the coast, and across the Indian Ocean including in the Gulf, were of no use. These coins were of several kinds: merchants used Indian rupees, a French 5-franc piece (often called *franc d'or*), and the Spanish dollar. But the commonest, because most reliable (in

The Maria Theresa thaler

The Maria Theresa thaler or dollar was first minted in the middle of the 18th century, and named after the Empress Maria Theresa who ruled Austria, Hungary and Bohemia from the death of her father in 1740 until her own death in 1780. The word *thaler*, which is the origin of *dollar*, comes from *St Joachimsthal*, or the Valley of St Joachim, the site of an early silver mine in Bohemia. (For a fuller account of this remarkable coin, see Semple 2005.)

The coin became a standard for commerce in Europe, and then in the 19th century came to be recognized and widely used in the Arab world and in Indian Ocean trade. It weighed just over 28 grams, was known to have a reliably high silver content, and was difficult to forge or to clip – the edge is embossed, not simply milled, and contains the words *Justitia et Clementia* ("Justice and Mercy"), the motto of Maria Theresa's reign. The coins continued to bear Maria Theresa's image and the date of her death, 1780, for as long as they were minted. The explorer Sir Samuel Baker thought that "the effigy of the Empress with a very low dress and profusion of bust is ... the charm that suits the Arab taste".

The MT$ remained a common unit of currency throughout the Arab world, in North Africa and in the Sudan or Sahel (the region immediately south of the Sahara) long after it ceased to circulate in Europe. Both the MT$ and Indian rupee were Oman's currency from early in the 19th century until the Omani riyal was introduced in 1970. Mainly the system worked well, but after 1870 the cost and therefore the value of silver dropped. This was damaging to the Omani economy, whose cash receipts were in MT$.

So popular did the coin become that demand for it outstripped Austrian capacity to supply. In the 20th century several European countries minted their own, particularly after 1935 when the Italians gained a 25-year licence to produce it but refused to allow it to be issued to non-Italian banks. British-supervised mints produced the MT$ in London, Birmingham, and Bombay. In 1960 the Austrian Government asked foreign governments to cease production; the British were the last to do so, in 1962.

Visitors to the Arab world will be aware of the ubiquitous nature of this coin. For many years, and until late in the 20th century, thalers were melted down to be used for making jewellery, and often actually incorporated into head-dresses, belts, anklets and bracelets. The author saw one used as a weight (in order to value an anklet) in the souq in Nizwa in Oman in 2005.

terms of weight and purity of its silver) was the Maria Theresa dollar, referred to in this book as MT$. A short account of this remarkable coin is in the box opposite.

In the interior, instead of coinage a form of barter was employed. Travellers carried beads (of varying colours), copper and brass wire, and cloth. Some of the copper came from Katanga, some distance west from the southern end of Lake Tanganyika, and was used mainly for women's decoration. It was usually transported in the form of wire, this being easier than ingots to work into bangles, bracelets and so on. Beads, which were strung and used for bodily ornament, were of many different colours and types. The explorer Burton describes them in great detail, with an undertone of mockery for a people who could place such value on items of virtually no interest to the European: he claims there were 400 kinds – coral beads, pink, blue and white porcelain beads, beads "the size of a pigeon's egg", a bead that "resembles bits of broken pipe-stem", and many others; different tribes and villages valued certain kinds of beads. Burton reports that they were imported into East Africa by the ton, and that it was vital to lay in the right stock:

> Any neglect in choosing beads, besides causing daily inconvenience, might arrest an expedition on the very threshold of success. ... The utmost economy must be exercised in [spending] beads: apparently exhaustless, a large store goes but a little way: the minor purchases of a European would average 10 strings or necklaces per diem, and thus a man's load rarely outlasts the fifth week.[21]

Burton means here that a European traveller, purchasing food and a few other essentials, would need one load of beads for every five weeks on the road. The cloth was also of great variety. Burton similarly catalogues them – woollens, cottons and silks mixed with cotton, nearly all of it brightly coloured: "Their ... gaudy tastes lead them to despise sober and uniform colours." Some came from India, some from England, some from Europe which was then dyed in Surat (near Bombay), but much of it from America, giving rise to the generic term *merikani*, meaning cotton cloth. Tippu Tip had an Arab colleague named Juma Merikani, presumably because he traded chiefly in that cloth. The imported cloth was of different colours and quality, and – as with beads – different tribes had their own preferences for the 'currency' in which they wished to be paid.[22]

Not everyone travelled in caravans. In contemporary accounts there are references to letters and news being brought long distances much faster than caravans could travel. Although details of this system are not given, we must assume that messengers travelling either singly or in small groups carried letters between the inland centres and the coastal towns, on individual commissions.

A feature of travel, and a reason why Stanley and Burton were so exercised about the different kinds of cloth and beads that their caravans needed to carry, was the requirement to pay *hongo*, or transit money, to chiefs of villages and tribes through whose land they passed. Negotiations for *hongo* could be protracted and often caused European travellers much irritation, especially when they thought the chief too greedy. Even Tippu Tip had to face this problem; and the Arab conflicts with Mnywa Sere and Mirambo (see pages 77–8 and 116–20), in which Tippu Tip played a central role, arose more or less directly from Arab resentment at the high rates of these tolls.

Coast, plains and mountains

Hamed bin Mohammed's first recorded early journey, to Ugangi northeast of Lake Nyasa, in 1855 was mainly over the coastal plain (see map on page 23). This was how the terrain seemed to the missionary Pruen, travelling to Ujiji in 1890:

> As the traveller steams northward along the eastern coast from the southern limit of the dominions of Zanzibar [i.e. Cape Delgado], he notices the low-lying region that skirts the Indian Ocean; whilst lying behind, more or less dim in the perpetual African haze, he sees a range of hills, replaced in some parts by gently-rising ground. This marshy coast-line, malarious and deadly, which at Bagamoyo is about 10 miles wide, becomes narrowed at Saadani, opposite the town of Zanzibar, to four miles, and finally terminates north of this before reaching Pangani, from which point northwards the coast rises abruptly in coral limestone to a height of fifty feet or more. ...
>
> Behind the marsh to the south, and behind the shore to the north, the land rises by a gradual slope of 80 miles to a height of about 1,500 feet, from which ... stretches the first or coast plateau for 80 miles inland, in many parts broken up by spurs of the adjacent mountain-range, but in others extending for many days' march together in an unbroken level, with scenery not unlike that

of the fen-country at home. It is a continuous swamp through all the rainy season, a monotonous plain in the dry one, traversed by a few large streams, and consequently better covered with vegetation than most parts.[23]

Pruen goes on to describe how the first plateau gives way to a climb over "the great mountain-range which stretches in an almost unbroken chain from the Cape of Good Hope to Abyssinia", including Mount Kenya and Kilimanjaro, and then to a second plateau of 3,000–4,000 feet (910–1,220 metres) above sea level.

To describe the visual appearance of this countryside, Pruen resorts to likening it to an English landscape, at the same time giving points of comparison and demonstrating its strangeness through the exotic plants:

The traveller ... walks through continual woodland, not unlike the outskirts of Epping Forest in the late autumn, except for an occasional cactus-like euphorbia; a baobob, looking for all the world like a tree put in the wrong way up; or a still more occasional wild banana or fan-palm.

At other places, where there is more water, "typical tropical trees are thicker and more frequent, with an abundance of rank grass and undergrowth amongst them, giving the whole scene the appearance of our English country parks run wild". Pruen notes low scrub or dwarf thorn-trees, shadeless areas of "monotonous sameness", and villages at about 10 miles' distance from each other. These villages were protected by a double fence, and consisted of "low, circular huts of wickerwork and mud, with thatched roofs", seldom more than twenty huts in a village. There were farmed areas round the villages, where the inhabitants cultivated crops including millet, maize (referred to as "Indian corn"), sweet potatoes, beans, pumpkins and tobacco.

In fact, the countryside in the interior, viewed without Pruen's rose-tinted spectacles, is better described as having wide areas of low-rainfall scrubland or savannah, known in the Swahili language as *nyika*, wilderness. In these areas, in what is now northern Tanzania and southern Kenya, vast herds of wildebeeste and zebras graze, making their great migrations when the seasons change. During and immediately after the rainy season, between October and April, these regions drain badly and become flooded or swamped. Stanley describes days of splashing or wading through such places, in May 1871, with debilitating effect on himself and his caravan.[24]

Hamed's second early journey

From Ugangi, Hamed and his father returned to Zanzibar. Farrant's biography relates that they made a circuit of Zanzibar–Tabora–Ugangi–Zanzibar, but there is no supporting evidence for this in either *Maisha* or Brode's account.[25] Rather, it seems that Hamed's first visit to Tabora was after the Ugangi trip, when his father decided to take him to the interior (see map on page 23). On the way there, he fell ill with smallpox, but unlike many other sufferers from this disease he was not left with pockmarks on his face. Brode, who of course knew him personally, though in later life, unkindly comments that "his beauty would have suffered no loss even if [the disease had left visible traces], for ... Tippoo Tib can certainly not claim to be an Adonis"![26] Brode adds in this context – as others who met him also did – that Hamed's complexion was unusually dark for someone with unchallenged Arab paternity. As we saw in Chapter 1, while we know that his mother was also Arab, his grandmothers on both sides, and indeed other female ancestors, could well have been African, whether of chiefly family (like his father's first wife) or of slave origin. Jeal says (his source is Slade 1962: 88) that his grandmother was daughter of a Lomami chief.[27] For personal identity, and status in society, it was the father's clan and family that mattered, even at the highest levels: Sayyid Saʿid had several wives and a number of concubines, and his son Sayyid Barghash, who became Sultan of Zanzibar, was the child of a slave-concubine from Ethiopia. Tippu Tip himself had several children, but none of their mothers, so far as we know, was Arab.

Hamed was lucky enough, or constitutionally strong enough, to survive his smallpox. Those who caught this disease while on the march were often left behind, for fear that the infection would spread to other members of the caravan. Hamed arrived with his father at Tabora, or rather at his father's estate at Ituru, just nearby, in the district of Unyanyembe, right in the middle of the large tribal area of the Unyamwezi. They stayed there two months, and then journeyed on to Ujiji, on the shore of Lake Tanganyika, with some other Arabs. They were interested only in buying ivory, but found the prices too high. Renault speculates that this was because the people of Ujiji bought their ivory in Casembe (south-west of the southern end of Lake

Tanganyika), a region that was going through a period of instability due to disputes over the chiefly succession, and that this instability had reduced ivory collecting and trading.[28] Tippu Tip's party therefore decided to venture farther, and over the Lake, to the Urua area, which lies near the Lualaba river west of Lake Tanganyika. Before crossing the Lake, Tippu Tip had a confrontation with his father, who thought the young man too inexperienced to take charge of the tradeable goods and wanted to entrust them to a trading colleague. Tippu Tip resented this, and told his father (who in any case wished to return to Tabora) that either he took responsibility or he too would go back. His father consented, and Tippu Tip began his first expedition trading on his own account.[29]

There were no "proper boats", as Hamed says dismissively in the *Maisha*, only dug-out canoes in which to cross the Lake – a curious comment, since dug-outs were the norm in the interior; perhaps his point of comparison was the ocean-going dhow of Zanzibar. In Urua they arrived "at Mrongo Tambwe's place". It should be explained that in many contemporary accounts, including in maps, villages are identified by the name of the chief, and often took the chief's name for long periods. Chiefs also often took the names of their predecessors, making difficulties for historians who like to establish tidy chronologies with lists of kings or chiefs. In Urua, Tippu Tip took his first commercial gamble: he noticed that small tusks were much cheaper than large ones, and managed to buy a large quantity. He knew that the large ones would sell better when brought to market on the coast, and perhaps his more experienced companions took for themselves the better pieces, but Tippu Tip nevertheless reckoned that he had made the right choice. He wrote later that he was lucky: when he eventually brought his ivory to the market in Zanzibar, it was the small tusks that were fetching a good price.

Exporting ivory from East Africa

There was considerable difference between the more and the less valuable types of ivory. Large tusks, as Tippu Tip noted, were generally more costly, particularly the softer ivory, which was easier to work; in Europe this material was used for making billiard balls. Other types were used for piano keys, and the smaller tusks, though usually cheaper, could also command high prices in some markets, being used for ornaments sometimes mounted in silver. Later in the century, when the areas east of the Great Lakes came under British and German control, it was made illegal to kill young elephants, and so the smaller tusks became rarer and thus more highly priced.

Ivory had been exported from East Africa, notably to India and China, for several centuries. African ivory was in demand because it was softer than the ivory from Asian elephants, and widely used among Hindu women for bangles as bridal gifts and symbols of married status. These ornaments were destroyed at a woman's death, either when her body was cremated or when she died on her husband's funeral pyre, and so demand was continuously sustained. Abdul Sheriff describes how this demand was largely satisfied, up to the beginning of the 19th century, from the East African coast and Mozambique, but increases in export duty at Mozambique resulted in ivory traders turning to Zanzibar as a cheaper location for buying ivory from suppliers and shipping it on to its next destination – mostly Kutch, Surat (just north of Bombay) or Bombay itself.[30]

This trade saw remarkable expansion in the early decades of the 19th century. Indian producers sent their cotton goods to Africa, and their ships brought back ivory in increasing quantities. The trade patterns were affected by other industrial developments, as European (especially British) manufactured goods and cloth declined in price as a result of competition, heavy investment in plant, and economies of scale in production. The British also imposed tariffs and duties on Indian-produced cloth and cotton goods. At the same time, the vogue for ivory was growing in Europe, Britain and America. Until about 1820, most of the European demand for ivory had been for making cutlery handles, for which the harder ivory from West Africa was suitable. But from the second decade of the century, consumer demand rose rapidly for luxury items such as billiard balls, piano keys, combs and ornaments, for which the softer East African ivory was better, and this resulted in significant increases in the re-export of African ivory from Bombay to Western markets. Indeed, by 1850 the value of (African) ivory exported from Bombay to the United Kingdom in most years comfortably exceeded that of the ivory consumed on the Indian market, and in some years was almost double. From analysis of Indian and British customs records, Abdul Sheriff shows that British imports of ivory rose from an average of 10 tons a year in the first two decades, to 95 tons in the next two, to 280 tons in the 1840s, and more than 800 tons in 1875. This was all happening, of course, before the opening of the Suez Canal, so Bombay's position as a transit port for this trade was vulnerable to competition from ships trading directly between London and Zanzibar via the Cape of Good Hope. Curiously, attempts in the 1830s to set up such direct trading do not seem to have succeeded, partly from mismanagement but also because the investors probably over-estimated the profits to be made from it and ran up against existing vested interests.

American traders were also starting to arrive in Zanzibar from the 1820s, initially from the port of Salem (just north-east of Boston) in Massachusetts, and later (from the 1840s) from Boston, New York and Providence. Among other goods, they bought ivory for the comb-makers of Connecticut.

The sustained upward curve in demand led to a steady increase in the price, by weight, of ivory. Like most commodities in East Africa at this time, ivory was traded by the *frasila*, equivalent to about 35 lb (just under 16 kg). Its price per *frasila* in Zanzibar went from MT$22 in 1823 to MT$89 in 1873. The "good price" that Hamed achieved for his ivory after his first journey was MT$50–55 per *frasila*, less MT$9 tax. Many tusks weighed two *frasila* and thus constituted a full load for one porter; and the cost of transportation to the coast from the interior could account for 15–20 percent of its value at Bagamoyo. Traders of course profited from the high differential between the prices they paid in the interior and the sale price in Zanzibar. Capt. Loarer, a French naval captain who carefully recorded his impressions both in published books and in his reports back to base, reckoned in 1849 that profit rates could be about 25 percent, and Stanley, in 1871, calculated that 100 percent was possible (though he was prone to exaggeration).[31]

The Zanzibari state also got in on the act, through imposition of import duties, which were calculated not by percentage of value but by fixed amounts (in MT$) per *frasila*. These varied according to a complex system depending on the origin of the ivory: high rates of duty were charged on ivory coming from the Mrima coast (the area just opposite Zanzibar, stretching from Lamu in the north to Kilwa in the south), and lower rates per *frasila* shipped from farther afield – whether from ports beyond the Mrima, or from deeper in the interior. The Sultan's purpose in this was to keep Zanzibar commercially attractive for shipments not in its obvious hinterland, and to encourage Arabs to venture west of Lake Tanganyika and undercut their Unyamwezi rivals.[32]

The policy was successful. In the early 1860s, the value of ivory exports from Zanzibar averaged MT$586,000; at about MT$45 per *frasila,* this would have amounted to about 230 tons or 206,730kg.

This represented about one-third of Zanzibar's total exports. The process of expansion of trade was assisted by a positive shift (viewed from the African side) in the terms of trade of the principal traded commodities during the middle two quarters of the century: that is, the price of exported ivory was going up, while the prices of imported cotton and goods manufactured in America and Europe were going down, due to the pressures of competition in production. The outbreak of the American Civil War in 1861 had its effects on Zanzibar's trade in general and on ivory in particular, since that and gum-copal made up a large proportion of the commerce with America, and – being luxuries – were among the first products to experience a drop in demand. By this time, America was an important trading partner for Zanzibar, and the dip in American trade had noticeable effects, only partially mitigated by the ever-growing demand for ivory in Britain.

We shall see, as we follow Tippu Tip's life as an ivory trader, that supply of tusks was spread unevenly through the area. We have already observed that the movement of Arab traders westward from the coastal region was driven in large part by the need to find new sources of ivory. But exploring deeper into the interior did not automatically lead to finding new stores of the valuable commodity. For example, in his Third Journey Tippu Tip had to travel through wide areas of the region south, south-west and west of Lake Tanganyika before he could discover supplies of ivory sufficient to match his ambition. And in the late 1860s and early 1870s, when the Arabs were genuinely pushing their frontiers westwards, they had to create a market among people not used to dealing commercially with ivory, and sometimes had to hunt the elephants themselves. The need for a commercial and transportation infrastructure led the Arabs to create settlements in Manyema country some 200 miles (300 km) west of the northern end of Lake Tanganyika, notably at Nyangwe on the Lualaba River, and then at Kisangani (near the settlement, established later, of Stanley Falls). There ivory was cheap to buy. But the terrain of thick rainforest, the hostility of the local people (which may have been provoked by the Arabs' uncompromising and often violent ways of dealing with them), and the consequential difficulties of exporting the ivory and importing the goods needed for trading, all added to the costs.

From the 1880s onwards an alternative export route arose – down-river on the Congo, to its mouth at Banana Point on the Atlantic. As King Leopold II of the Belgians began his exploitation of the Congo, he made efforts to persuade the Arab ivory traders to use that method rather than the long overland route back to (and over) Lake Tanganyika and then via Ujiji and Tabora to Bagamoyo, and thence to Zanzibar. We shall see later that this became a key element in the tense and eventually confrontational relationship between the Arabs and the Belgians of the Congo Free State.

It is sometimes assumed that all the ivory was carried by slave labour, but, as mentioned above, this was not the case. The Nyamwezi *pagazi* described earlier were professional porters, and although it is not easy to gather evidence on the numbers or proportions of free and slave labour, comments in contemporary accounts suggest that a mix of labour was used to take the ivory from the interior to the markets where it was sold.

Hamed bin Mohammed returns from Urua

Hamed's trading party returned to Tabora via Mtowa, a village on the western shore of Lake Tanganyika, from where crossings were often made over the Lake. In Mtowa they heard the news of the death of the Nyamwezi Chief, Fundi Kira, who was Hamed's stepmother's father. His father Mohammed bin Juma played a significant part in the dispute over succession that followed, partly because of his being married to the late Chief's daughter, but also because the successful contender – Fundi Kira's nephew Mnywa Sere – could not get the better of his rival, Mkasiwa, without support from the Arabs of Tabora. To bring them on to his side he gave Mohammed bin Juma a supply of ivory ("many tusks", says Hamed in the *Maisha*) for distribution among the Arabs, and with his enlarged fighting force succeeded in expelling Mkasiwa. The latter took refuge with another Nyamwezi chief, Mirambo, who himself later became an important if contentious figure in the region.

Unfortunately, Mnywa Sere's relationship with the Arabs soon turned sour. He seems to have realized that he could increase his income by raising the *hongo*, or transit tax, levied on Arabs travelling through his lands. He may also have introduced a trade tax. As he told the explorer Speke, who was then passing through Unyamwezi on his great Nile discovery expedition:

> I established a property tax on all merchandise that entered my country. Fundi Kira had never done so, but I did not think that any reason why I should not, especially as the Arabs were the only people who lived in my country exempt from taxation.[33]

At this time, the Arab traffic had increased following another succession dispute – this one in Zanzibar. The great Sultan of Muscat and Zanzibar, Sayyid Saʻid bin Sultan, had died at sea in 1856, and two of his sons, Thuwaini and Majid, had assumed power in Muscat and Zanzibar respectively. Even this division of the mini-empire was disputed, since Zanzibar's revenue was much higher than Oman's. The argument was settled only by the intervention of the British, through an arbitration authorized by the Governor-General of India, Lord Canning. Canning's award, handed down in 1860, imposed on the Sultan of Zanzibar an obligation (not always observed) to pay his Omani counterpart an annual subsidy of MT$40,000. Meanwhile in Zanzibar, in 1859, Majid's brother Barghash had sought to dislodge him, but had been forced into exile in India after Atkins Hamerton, the Consul, had brought in British troops in support of Majid. A number of the Arabs who supported Barghash left Zanzibar to join the community in Tabora.

It was these Arabs, plus the regular traders, whom Mnywa Sere wished to tax. They and their Tabora compatriots would have liked to attack Mnywa Sere, but felt they could not, since Mohammed bin Juma, Hamed's father, who had access to a large number of fighting men, was still supporting him. However, Mnywa Sere managed to alienate this important ally by assassinating Chief Fundi Kira's widow and her brother. This widow was the mother of Karunde, Mohammed bin Juma's first wife. Infuriated at the murder of his mother-in-law, Mohammed bin Juma entered into discussions with leading Arabs, with the aim of deposing Mnywa Sere and bringing back the expelled Mkasiwa.

This was the situation when Hamed's trading party arrived in Tabora from Ujiji. Indeed, Mohammed bin Juma and his co-conspirators deliberately waited for the party to return, presumably to maximize their numbers for the forthcoming battle. Their campaign nearly came to a premature and disastrous end, because a large number of them gathered at the house of Salim bin Sayf al-Bahari, and their presence was revealed to Mnywa Sere by an Indian trader named Musa Mzuri, who had regular dealings with him. It was in fact unusual for Indians to venture in the interior, still less to live there; but Musa moved to Tabora early, even before the Arabs, according to Burton, and amassed a fortune. Burton, when he and Speke came to Tabora in November 1857, in fact had a letter of introduction to Musa, who however was away at the time of his arrival, although they met later. Brode remarks ironically that

> Musa ... had come to the country, in company with a compatriot who had since died, to promote civilization by the sale of brandy and other modern requirements. One of his principal customers was Mnywa Sere, who bartered the to him valueless ivory with the ingenious middleman for the marvels of European and Indian industry.[34]

Luckily for the Arabs, Musa's warning was ignored. They assembled their force, having brought Mkasiwa back, and fought a tough and ultimately successful campaign lasting three months. After the installation of Mkasiwa as Chief, Hamed stayed another two months before leaving for Zanzibar, to sell the ivory he had bought in Urua. This must have all have taken place at some time in 1860, since the deposed Mnywa Sere met up with the explorer Speke in January 1861, and sought his help in getting reinstated. As we have seen, Speke was sympathetic to him, and might have helped him; but their ways parted.

As mentioned above, Hamed's ivory sale in Zanzibar went well. He found that there was after all satisfactory demand for the smaller tusks, and he sold his father's consignment, and bought new supplies which he sent to Tabora. And then he took a momentous decision, which was to set up in business on his own account. He seems to have kept open the possibility of working in partnership with his half-brother, Mohammed bin Masoud al-Wardi, but at least at the start he was alone, borrowing goods on credit and setting out for the interior to make his fortune – which, in due course, he did.

CHAPTER 4

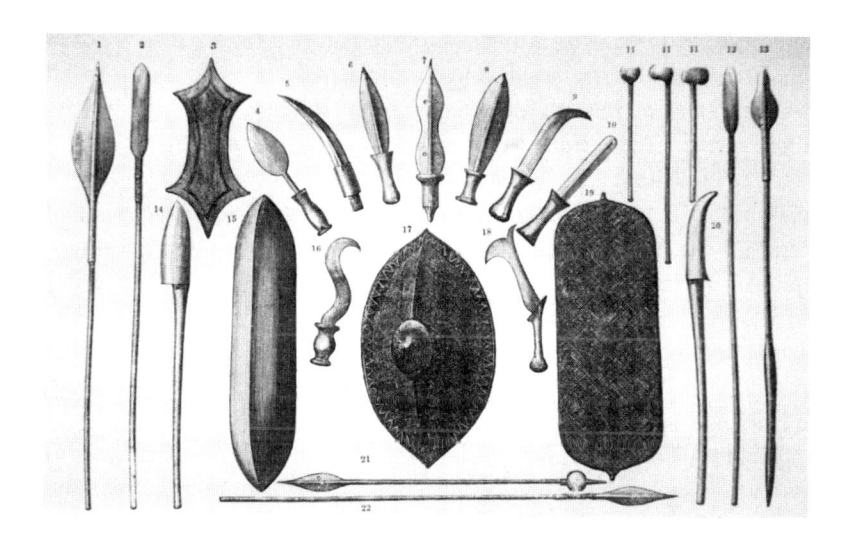

Business Start-up

UP TO NOW, HAMED BIN MOHAMMED had been trading on his father's account, but at this point he borrowed the funds necessary to finance a new expedition. According to Whiteley's translation of the *Maisha*, he had also been in partnership with his half-brother, Mohammed bin Masoud;[1] but this is misleading. In fact, while Hamed had been travelling with his father, Mohammed had gone south-west to the area between Lake Nyasa and the sea, which was well known as a major route for trading slaves captured west of Lake Nyasa. Livingstone had observed this both on his Zambezi expedition, and at the start of his last journey, when he travelled up the river Rovuma and round the southern end of Lake Nyasa to the river Chambezi. We assume that Mohammed too was engaged in slave trading – there was virtually no other purpose for an Arab trader to be in that area. Hamed reports that afterwards Mohammed went from there to 'Benadir', the name given to the coast of Somalia where there were several Arab outposts and trading ports, to which Mohammed was taking slaves he had collected farther south.

Hamed's first independent journey

In his teenage years, Hamed had probably engaged in small-scale trading trips, borrowing small sums to finance them. In 1860 or 1861, aged twenty-three or twenty-four, he determined on a larger venture. He borrowed trading goods to the value of MT$1,000, and started for the interior. Herbert Ward records that Hamed had "one hundred fighting men" and "four hundred natives loaded with merchandise, trading cloth and beads for ivory and slaves".[2] Ward, who was a member of Stanley's Emin Pasha Relief Expedition and met Hamed bin Mohammed during that time, wrote an account of the expedition on his return to England, and also another book describing his earlier experiences in the Congo. He took information about Hamed bin Mohammed from one of his associates, Selim bin Mohammed, and could plausibly have received direct reports from Hamed himself, enabling us to expand on the account in the *Maisha*.

On this, his First Journey as an independent trader, Hamed went to the region of Uhehe, south of Ugogo, and the town of Mpwapwa, on the usual trading route from Bagamoyo to Tabora (see map on page 23). He must have done some successful trading, since he decided not to go back to the coast to cash in on the ivory (and slaves, if we are to believe Ward), but to take a risk on further borrowing, and to continue farther inland, south-west to Urori. In the *Maisha* he does not mention the person – probably an Arab – from whom he borrowed these extra funds, nor does he remember accurately how much the loan was: "between 4,000 and 7,000 dollars", a curiously wide range given his normal precision in such matters.[3] He travelled on west. In Urori trade was bad, but he did well in Urungu, at the southern end of Lake Tanganyika. He "got a great quantity of ivory" (no mention of slaves), and returned to Zanzibar.

Hamed's second independent journey

Back in Zanzibar he joined up with his half-brother, Mohammed bin Masoud, whom he had not seen for twelve years. The two had enjoyed differing fortunes. "I had made tremendous profits," records Hamed in the *Maisha*.[4] Brode tells us that he had asked Hamed about the nature of his half-brother's trading, and that he replied "with a smirk" that it had indeed been slave-trading, but that he had not done well by it.[5] Hamed implied that commerce in ivory was more profitable than slave

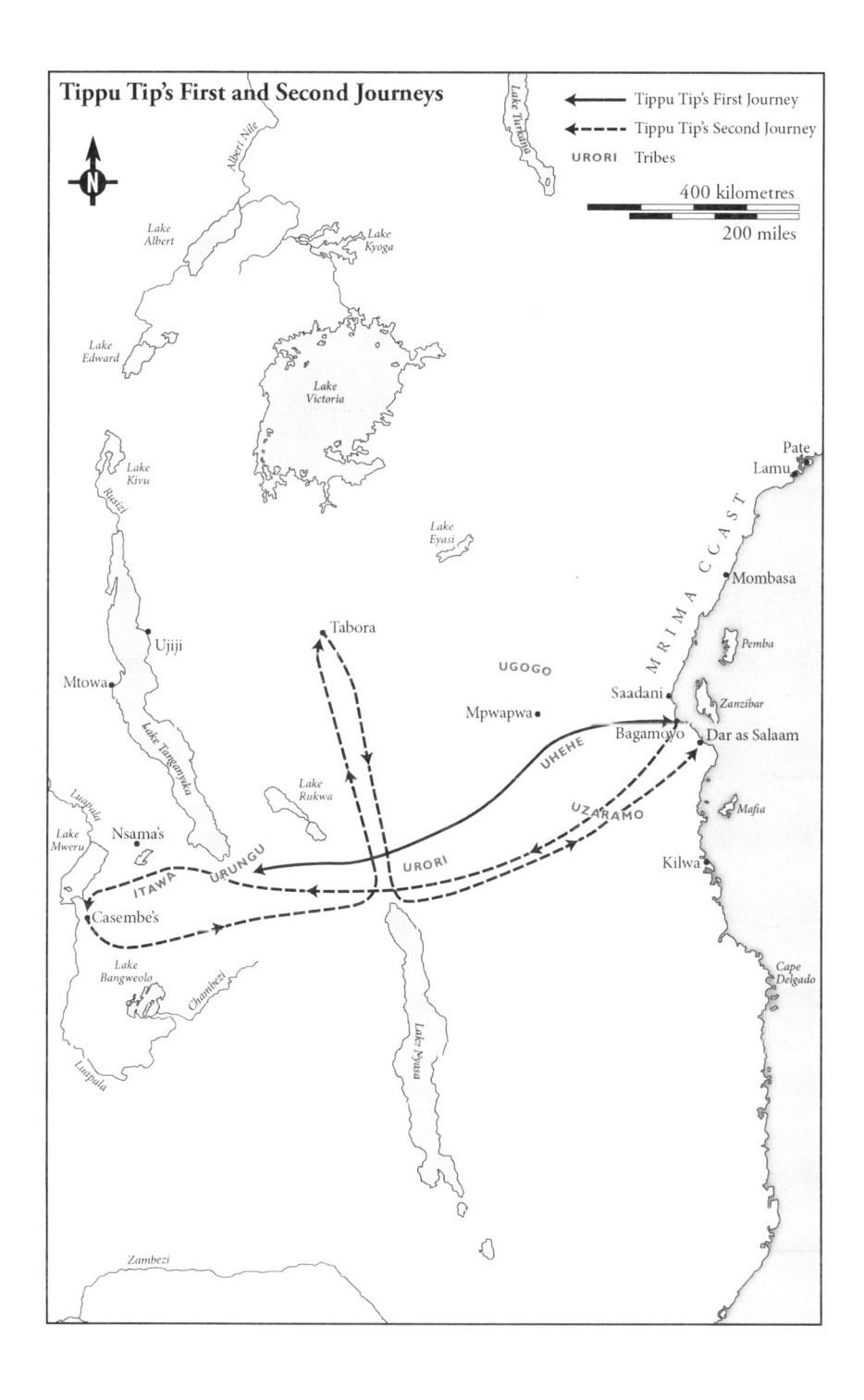

trading. In addition, Mohammed bin Masoud had been swindled by his partner, Mohammed bin Sa'id al-Harthi, who had squandered much of the profits. So when it came to planning a new trading journey, Mohammed bin Masoud was glad to be able to join forces with Hamed, although he could afford only MT$5,000 worth of goods for bartering, while Hamed splashed out with MT$30,000 – borrowed, he says, from at least twenty rich Indians and Banyans.

In planning the journey, Hamed and Mohammed had to reckon on a route to the south of that normally taken, because there was a famine (presumably due to failure of the rains) in the Mrima – the coastal area opposite Zanzibar. His caravan would rely on buying, through barter, food from the villages they passed through. As a result, he found it difficult to take the normal course of recruiting porters from Unyamwezi, as they preferred not to operate so far from their homeland. Instead he employed porters from the Zaramo tribe, from the region south of Dar as-Salaam, an area he knew from his earlier journey. Burton had come across this tribe in 1857, and comments on their physical strength and endurance, but adds that they were impetuous and quarrelsome – from which Hamed bin Mohammed was to suffer in due course. At first they refused to take on employment as porters, but were forced from hunger to do so. Hamed engaged seven hundred of them, paying some of them one-quarter, some one-third of the agreed fee in advance.

It is difficult to be sure of the date of this Second Journey. If Hamed was being accurate in his estimate of twelve years since he had last seen his half-brother, which was on his apprenticeship trip when he was himself aged twelve, then he would by now be twenty-four. Those who trust these figures and who place his birth in 1840 therefore reckon that this journey started in 1864. This could well be correct, since there is external evidence, from Livingstone, that Hamed's battle with Nsama (recounted later in this chapter) took place in May 1867. If however we accept 1837 as his birth year, then we must question his record of being aged twelve during his apprenticeship journey, and/or his estimate of twelve years since he had seen Mohammed. The most probable solution is to conclude that Hamed was indeed born in 1837, that he may not have been as young as twelve when he did his early journey, that it was more than twelve years since the two half-brothers had seen each other, and that this journey started in 1864 or 1865 when Hamed was twenty-seven or twenty-eight.

The large size of the party, the pre-payments made to the porters,

Business Start-up

and the fact that they travelled through Zaramo territory, soon caused problems. The first section of their journey took them along the slave-trading route connecting Kilwa with Dar as-Salaam. After walking for a week or two, they made a night stop billeted in different villages, a hundred men in one, sixty in another, and so on. But the next morning the porters refused to respond to the drums signalling the time to set off. They had received part of their pay, they had also been issued with food for the next few days, and they were in their home territory. Hamed was furious, collected his half-brother and a group of eighty armed men, and tied up two hundred of the older relatives of his porters. Under this pressure, the porters gave in and allowed themselves to be collected by Hamed as he went round the Zaramo villages. He somehow ended up with eight hundred, comfortably more than the number he had started with. And he yoked them together, either in the wooden neck-grip used for slaves or with iron chains and rods that he had had made for the purpose. As they progressed to the first trading location, Urori, Hamed made his half-brother walk at the head of the column while he brought up the rear, to catch any porters trying to escape.

This episode is an early indication of Hamed's force of character and determination. He was not one for half measures, and was not going to be thwarted by a group – even a large group – of recalcitrant porters. It also shows how people in this area (as elsewhere) could be used as hostages to put pressure on other members of the tribe, village or family. In this instance, no hostages are reported hurt; later we shall see how, in the hunt for ivory and slaves in Central Africa, the same tactics were used with grimmer effect. Hamed ends his account of this episode by recording his first nickname – Kingugwa, the 'Leopard' – "because the leopard attacks indiscriminately, here and there".[6] His half-brother, either at this point or later, was nicknamed Kumbakumba, the 'Gatherer of Wealth'. Hamed seems proud, looking back on his life as he dictates the *Maisha* in his old age, that early on he had established a reputation for firm, even violent, leadership.

A chief named Merere was ruling in Urori. Livingstone noted about two years later, in June 1867 (although it is not clear whether they met), that he had had "plenty of ivory when the Arabs came first, but now he has none".[7] Merere had previously been in dispute with the Arab traders, but at the point when Hamed, his half-brother and their caravan arrived, the region was at peace, and his stocks of ivory had clearly improved. More than that, conditions of trade were very favourable. Hamed records the exchange rates for barter: a *frasila* (35 lb, or 16 kg) of ivory could be bought for the same weight of beads, or a box of soap, or 15 lb (7 kg) of gunpowder. He also says that ivory could be bought "measure for measure" for spices, but he does not specify which spices. This exchange rate seems surprising to the modern reader, spices generally being valuable by weight, so perhaps Hamed was talking of some coastal foodstuff valued in the interior. A *frasila* of ivory could also be exchanged for 12 to 15 pieces of cloth, by which he would have meant the length of cloth needed for a single garment.[8] These equivalents would have been average prices, since the value of ivory varied depending not only on quality, and on whether the tusks were large or small (as we saw during Hamed's first trading journey), but also on the distance from the coast. Here at Urori there was porterage of 400 miles (600 km) to be paid for in order to bring the ivory to market. Stanley spells this out when describing how, until Arabs came to trade in ivory, local Africans barely valued it, using tusks as door-posts and supports to the eaves of their houses. He reports that in Zanzibar the price was MT$50–60 per *frasila*, in Unyanyembe "about $1–$10 per pound" (this higher figure cannot be right), but in Manyema – west of Lake Tanganyika – between half a cent and 14 cents per pound.[9]

Judging that he should take advantage of these trading conditions, Hamed decided to leave some of his men in Urori to carry on trade on his account, with MT$6,000-worth of beads and other barter goods.[10] They were left in charge of "a young man from Mbwamaji", a place on the coast. He does not record his name or his family, possibly because of the unfortunate sequel. His decision turned out to be a costly mistake. Towards the end of this journey, he came back to Urori, where he found that almost all these resources had been wasted. The young man had lost it all, except for 6 *frasila* of ivory and two slave girls bought for 20 *frasila* – and even they were not worth anything like what had been paid for them! Hamed was furious, and locked up the young man in prison for four days. He then released him, quoting a Swahili proverb: "The man who hurts himself doesn't cry." He clearly blamed himself for his poor judgement, and wanted to put the episode behind him. Unfortunately it was compounded by a similar error on the part of his half-brother, who had left MT$600 with another agent, who had also wasted all the goods and then died of smallpox. (Whiteley translates this amount as MT$6,000, but the Swahili text, which has the amount written in words, not figures, clearly shows 600.[11]) Such were the fortunes, and misfortunes, of trade.

Discipline restored, Hamed and his brother travelled on, south and west. He joined up with his uncles, Bushir and Abdullah, brothers of his mother, some other relatives, and some other young men, most of them armed. Together with the armed men in his existing caravan, Hamed now had 120 guns with him, an unusually large force. They travelled on to Ruemba, south of Lake Tanganyika, which is the region of the Bemba people, and where in fact he had been on his previous journey.[12] There they met up with "some of Mwamba's people" – Mwamba being actually a hereditary title of the chiefs of Ituna. They decided to go on to 'Mwamba's': both Whiteley's translation of the *Maisha* and most contemporary exploration writing uses this ellipsis the name of the chief, without specifying 'village', 'town' or 'district'. Livingstone was there in February 1867, though we cannot tell whether this was before or after Hamed's visit; and he describes the chief as

> a big, stout, public-house-looking person, with a slight outward cast in his left eye, but intelligent and hearty. ... He then showed me some fine large tusks, ... [and asked me,] "what do you wish to buy, if not slaves or ivory?" I replied that the only thing I had seen worth buying was a fine fat chief like him, as a specimen, and a woman feeding him, as he had, with beer.[13]

Hamed found no ivory at Mwamba's, and decided to go on to the Itawa (also written Itabwa, Itahua or Ituwa) district. He left Mohammed bin Masoud at Mwamba's village, with a number of 'guns' – armed men – about whom Hamed is interestingly precise. He left 15 with Mohammed at Mwamba's, and continued his journey with 105. Perhaps he wished the reader to know the strength of the forces he deployed in the battle to come.

Tippu Tip's small war with Nsama

Hamed's porters did their best to dissuade him from going on beyond Lake Tanganyika, to Nsama's (which Brode, and Farrant, presumably following him, mis-wrote as 'Samu'). 'Nsama' is in fact a title, and this one was the third chief to use it, his given name being Chipili Chipioka. In some histories he is therefore referred to as Nsama III Chipili Chipioka, in others Chipioka. 'Nsama' is however common usage, which we shall follow here.[14]

In advising Hamed, his porters admitted that Nsama had plenty of ivory, but described him as treacherous, and guilty of having killed several Arabs; and they advised Hamed to be more modest in his trading ambitions. The party also met an old Arab, who told them – as he had told Burton about eight years previously – how he and some other Arabs had gone to Nsama's some time previously, had been attacked, and had lost all their goods. He similarly told Hamed that he would do better to stay in the district where he was, and be content with less ivory but a more certain profit.[15]

But they pressed on, and crossed the river Lafu marking the border of Nsama's territory, to the south-west of Lake Tanganyika. It was densely populated: Hamed writes about "countless villages", and reports that they walked for six days, emerging from the bush into areas where there might be two or three hundred villages, several of them with headmen who were sons of Nsama. "In those six days we passed something like a thousand villages, and that of each chief was remarkably large."[16] Several tribes were paying tribute to Nsama. The Ngoni had recently raided the territory but had been repulsed. Nsama clearly headed a confederation of villages which was numerous, wealthy and strong.

Arriving at Nsama's own village, they found a well-defended settlement – a stockade with three lines of fortifications and a ditch filled with thorn trees. They were taken to see the chief, an old man of eighty or ninety. Livingstone met him a few months later, when he was settled in his new village, and records that he had "a good head and face and large abdomen, showing that he was addicted to *pombe* [beer]; his people have to carry him."[17] Nsama ordered his men to take him up and to lead the visitors to see his stock of ivory – a vast quantity in large houses.

At this point, what seems to have started as a genial meeting turned sour. When calling on the subsidiary headmen in the territory's villages, Hamed and his party had given modest gifts and been given two or three tusks in return. To Nsama himself, they had presented "a great quantity of goods", but when they suggested a reciprocal gift of ivory, he started cursing them. (With a chief, trade was not carried on by barter based on relative value of goods, but by approximate balancing of gifts freely presented.) Hamed and his party retreated to their camp.

The next morning, in response to a summons from Nsama, they returned to the village, expecting to collect the ivory they thought their due. Hamed was leading a party of twenty, with ten slaves. Without warning, they were attacked by a volley of arrows, and Hamed himself was injured by two of them, one in his leg. But their weapons were loaded, and they quickly opened fire. Hamed reports that the enemy fell and "died like birds", while others were trampled in the stampede to escape; a thousand died, against just two slaves killed and two injured from his own party. (Of course, he may have exaggerated the numbers of the enemy casualties and played down his own.) Nsama himself was carried out of the village, which was soon deserted except for the blind or maimed. Hamed comments on Nsama's cruelty as a chief; he was one of those who inflicted harsh penalties on offenders, including cutting out eyes or cutting off arms or noses. Such punishments were reported elsewhere by European travellers.

Livingstone, who was not far away at the time, and whose purpose of travelling to Lake Mweru was frustrated by the ensuing hostilities between the Arabs and the Africans over the whole territory, suspected the Arabs of having fired first:

> It was difficult to get to the bottom of the Nsama affair, but according to their [a group of "Arabs, mostly black Suahelis"] version that chief sent an invitation to them, and when they arrived called for his people, who came in crowds – as he said to view the strangers. I suspect that the Arabs became afraid of the crowds, and began to fire; several were killed on both sides, and Nsama fled, leaving his visitors in possession of the stockade village and all it contained. Others say that there was a dispute about an elephant, and that Nsama's people were the aggressors.[18]

Hamed collected all his people from the camp, and occupied the village. That evening they were surrounded by Nsama's forces, who stayed in their camps round the village, apparently confident of their numerical superiority, sitting by their fires and smoking pipes of tobacco or *bhang*, a cannabis mixture. Hamed was not sure what to do. He was severely enough wounded for his recovery to take several weeks; perhaps Nsama's men had been using poisoned arrows. He took advice from his uncle Bushir and organized small sorties of ten men at a time, who got close to the enemy under cover of darkness and shot at them – with considerable success, since in the morning they estimated some six hundred to have been killed. Later in the day, Nsama's forces attacked in strength, but were driven off by Hamed's men using the tactic of waiting until they were close before opening fire, with murderous effect – another 150 killed. A similar but larger attack two days later had a similar outcome: 250 dead. On both occasions the Arabs pursued the retreating Africans for some hours, presumably inflicting further damage.

Although there were no further attacks, Hamed was not sure that his party was yet safe, conscious as he was of the multitude of prosperous and powerful villages that he had seen on the way to Nsama's, and the distance he needed to travel to escape from this hostile territory. "We stayed in the village for a month, together with our fear," he records.[19] He decided on a reconnaissance expedition, to determine his enemy's intentions and strength. This was led by his uncle Bushir, since he himself had still not fully recovered.

Bushir took a considerable force, of more than five hundred men including twenty armed with guns. Hamed and those left behind spent a nervous day, but Bushir returned in the early evening with no casualties, and bringing numerous captives and a huge flock of about two thousand goats. It is not clear whether the captives, whom Hamed describes simply as "women and men, of small stature", were already slaves or were enslaved by him. But undoubtedly they would have been useful when it came to evacuating the village and its immense stock of ivory. Bushir's party also brought news of the slaughter of a caravan of sixty traders coming from Urungu into Nsama's territory by the same route as Hamed had used. They had been confronted and killed just as they had crossed the boundary river, it was assumed in vengeance for Hamed's initial battle with Nsama, which had taken place only shortly before. The caravan had consisted only of *waungwana*, or Wangwana, freed men living normally in the coastal area. (This term was also used to refer generally to non-slave porters hired near the coast, as opposed to Wanyamwezi, who were inland people.) It is surprising that it does not seem to have been led by any Arab, although those reporting the massacre reported that it had been owned by two Arabs of Tabora.

Hamed waited two days, and then decided that Nsama's forces were defeated and unlikely to cause them further trouble; and that it was safe to remove the ivory. They found that there were 1,950 *frasila* of it – 68,250 lbs, equivalent to 30,958 kg or over 34 tons. This would have required a caravan of nearly a thousand porters to carry it all. On top of that there were nearly 700 *frasila* of copper, from Katanga, the region some 300–400 km west-south-west of Itawa which was the main source of this valuable metal. Hamed loaded up much of this booty, plus his own supplies of beads and other barter goods, and took his party back to Urungu.

In Urungu they based themselves with a chief called Chungu, who bore resentment against Nsama from a dispute some years previously when he had been robbed of "three hundred tusks and several of [his] wives". Chungu welcomed Hamed, who sent off a party to investigate the killing of the caravan of *waungwana*. Kinsmen of the murdered men told Hamed that they knew of him only by the nickname given to him by local people in Urungu: Tippu Tip. In the *Maisha,* Hamed says that the old name, Kingugwa, given to him by the Zaramo, fell into disuse.[20] So, from now on, he will be referred to by the new nickname which stuck with him for the rest of his life. (See the boxes on pages 94 and 95 for Tippu Tip's various nicknames.)

Tippu Tip and Livingstone

It was at this point that Tippu Tip met David Livingstone, known as 'Bwana Daud' to the Arabs. Some of his men were on an expedition chasing down the remnants of Nsama's forces, came across Livingstone, and brought him into camp. He was reportedly without goods or food, and looking for guides to take him to Lake Mweru. Tippu Tip says that Livingstone and his party had narrowly escaped being killed, presumably by one of Nsama's sons, Kapoma, who was "killing all who came that way in revenge for what the Arabs had done to his father's people", and might have taken Livingstone and his small party for Arabs.[21] According to Livingstone's journal, they actually first met at a village east of Lake Mweru on 29 July 1867, and Tippu Tip gave him a goat, some white cotton, four large bushels of beads, and a bag of sorghum – and begged him to excuse his not being able to give more.[22]

Livingstone had in fact been knocked back by a particularly severe attack of fever a month or two before (April 1867). As recounted in the previous chapter, his interest in Lake Mweru arose from his belief (correct) that it was connected with Lake Bangweolo, and his conjecture (incorrect) that this would make Lake Bangweolo the most southerly of the headwaters of the Nile. But he was unable to go there because of the fighting between Nsama and 'the Arabs'. Tippu Tip relates that he helped Livingstone with guides to Lake Mweru, and then to Casembe's in the Runda area, and that Livingstone requested guides "to take him to other places, and wherever he wanted to go we sent him".[23] This is a telescoped version of what was actually an acquaintance spread over two months, as we know from Livingstone's diaries. Tippu Tip was not greatly concerned about the British explorer, being anxious to conclude the war with Nsama.

Nevertheless, whatever his other overriding interest, Tippu Tip lent considerable assistance to Livingstone who, having recovered from his fever, first came into contact with Tippu Tip's men in late May. He waited until August or September, by which time the fighting had died down, and then found that Tippu Tip, now able to resume his normal activity of searching for ivory to purchase, planned on heading west. Livingstone travelled with him, and reached Lake Mweru in early November. The journey was about 100 miles, but it took over a month because Tippu Tip stopped frequently for trading. Livingstone was glad to be at the lake, as it helped build up his picture of the water system that ran from the Chambezi river into Lake Bangweolo, on to Lake Mweru, and then into the Lualaba. He could not however afford the time to go south to Lake Bangweolo, since his supplies were now running very short. So he concluded that he should stay with Tippu Tip, which is why they went together to Casembe's, relying on Tippu Tip's assurance that they could then travel north, up the eastern side of Lake Tanganyika, to Ujiji. Livingstone had arranged for supplies to be sent there from Zanzibar, and thought he could re-form his party and then return to Bangweolo.

Tippu Tip mentions Livingstone's Ujiji stores in the *Maisha*, and also reports that Livingstone asked him to send some boxes from where they were, in or near Urungu, to Ujiji, by hand of some traders who had come from there to buy brass. Tippu Tip paid the transportation fee himself, and also gave the carrier some goods as a present. This is corroborated by Livingstone, whose diary for 10 September 1867 records that he sent a box containing papers, books and some clothes to Ujiji – although he says that the traders had come for ivory. It seems surprising that Livingstone should have sent personal effects off on such an uncertain journey, but his party was by now reduced, and he may have had insufficient hands and heads to carry all that he wanted. Tippu Tip – as was his custom – presents himself as the generous and hospitable dispenser of largesse; and we must remember that he was writing nearly thirty years later, after Livingstone had died and had become a legendary figure in Zanzibar as much as in Britain. But Livingstone was genuinely grateful, and in fact had much to be grateful for. He gave Tippu Tip a letter to take to John Kirk, then Consul in Zanzibar, in which he was at pains to point out how different were Tippu Tip and his companions from the Arabs he had met farther south, between Kilwa and Lake Nyasa:

> I met Hamidi Mahamad [Tippu Tip] in the Ulungu [Urungu] country and was very kindly treated by him and his brother headmen. ... Though they had suffered great losses in goods and men by a chief called Msama [i.e. Nsama], they generously gave me cloth, beads and provisions and tried to make peace with Msama that they might pass through the country in search of ivory and that I might go where I chose. I was three and a half months with them ... and believe they are totally different from the Kilwa traders on whose track we came up from the Rovuma to Nyassa and who fled from us invariably. ... I give this to Hamidi Mahamad in acknowledgement of his good services ... .[24]

"The Kilwa traders" clearly means slave traders, and Livingstone was implicitly but unambiguously drawing a contrast between those trading in slaves and those in the ivory business.

Meanwhile, and returning to the period of May–July 1867, Tippu Tip finished off the task of subduing Nsama's forces, which took two months. Peace was agreed, and Nsama paid Tippu Tip 50 tusks; and they traded a further 200 *frasila*. A little later Tippu Tip says that he visited Nsama to say farewells in a friendly atmosphere, before returning to the coast. Nsama refused to see Tippu Tip himself, although he received his relatives. Possibly this was because Nsama insisted that those who called on him should leave their weapons behind: Livingstone would have to comply with this condition when he met Nsama in September 1867, and was even frisked to make sure he was unarmed. Tippu Tip would never have agreed to the condition nor submitted to such an indignity.

Abdullah bin Suliman's narrative

The foregoing account of the Nsama episode is drawn almost entirely from Tippu Tip's own report in the *Maisha*, amplified a little by what was told to Livingstone. Interestingly, we do have another contemporary record, written by an anonymous British official in 1913, but based on reports, some from eyewitnesses, by Arabs and Africans. This is the *History of Abdullah ibn Suliman*, a text recorded in the Kawambwa District Notebook of the time (Kawambwa being a district

The nickname Tippu Tip

As we have seen, many of the Arabs in East Africa at this time were given nicknames. Perhaps Swahili speakers found them easier to deal with than the Arabic forms of their given names – even though these were themselves often simplified or adapted. Tippu Tip's son, for example, is always referred to as Sefu, an adaptation from Arabic Sayf, meaning 'sword', which is found more often in the form Sayf al-Islam, the 'Sword of Islam'. Or perhaps local Africans found that the nicknames helped them identify these 'foreigners' more easily. For the historian this is problematical, since the sources sometimes use the nickname, and sometimes the real name; and they often omit the family or tribal name, which is similar to referring to a British person as 'John son of James' without mentioning a surname.

Hamed explains his best-known nickname in a typical self-referential way. The Africans of this region had said: "This man's guns went 'tiptip', in a manner too terrible to listen to" (*Maisha* §30). There is no direct evidence about the weapons that Hamed and his party carried, although he several times points out that African forces such as Nsama's had little chance, with their bows and arrows and hand weapons, against the superior Arab firepower. This began to change in the 1870s and 1880s, when use of guns became more widespread. There was a brisk market in guns imported into Africa from Europe in the second half of the 19th century, particularly of second-hand weapons from European armies, as technology advanced and armies introduced new models. It is possible that Hamed determined to acquire more rapid-fire weapons than other Arabs, but unlikely, since much of his dispute with Stanley during the Emin Pasha Relief Expedition turned on the failure to supply powder and percussion caps. It is more probable that he had more and perhaps better-trained men, and that this enabled his forces to intimidate the Africans with greater firepower.

Others attribute the nickname to something in his eyes – either a nervous tic or a habit of fast blinking, especially when he was angry or excited, which was noticed by Europeans who met him. If this was a true reason for the name, Tippu Tip preferred to gloss over it, obviously preferring the military derivation!

Another explanation was given by Livingstone: his servant Susi stated that Hamed had stood over the massive booty gained after his defeat of Nsama, saying, "Now I am Tipo Tipo, the gatherer of wealth". But this corresponds with nothing in Arabic or Swahili. It might come from a local language, but on balance this derivation looks less probable.

I have not abbreviated it to 'Tippu', as some writers do, since the two words are not two names, but one. For a note on Hamed's other nicknames, see the next box.

> ### *Tippu Tip's other nicknames*
>
> As well as Kingugwa, 'the Leopard', the nickname given to him by the Zaramo on his first independent journey, Hamed bin Mohammed collected two others. Travelling in Ukosi, some way west of Lake Tanganyika, he found himself called Mkangwanzara, meaning 'He who fears nothing'. He adds, "Perhaps I would be afraid of famine, but certainly not war" (*Maisha* §157).
>
> Curiously, as though reflecting this in some way, Herbert Ward writes that "in the Kassongo and Nyangwe districts, he is commonly called by the natives Makangua Nzala (i.e. afraid of hunger), the only thing, they say, he is afraid of" (Ward 1890: 173).
>
> Finally, farther north in Manyema, as recorded by Jameson (one of the British officers on the Emin Pasha Relief Expedition), he was called Mutipula (also Mtipula, Mutshipule or Mtipoora), meaning 'Footprints', because when people came to a village that he had attacked, they looked at the footprints, or other evidence of his having been there, and said: "Tippu Tip has been here, it is a bad place, we will leave it" (Jameson 1890: 242).

of north-east Northern Rhodesia, now Zambia), and republished with commentary by Andrew Roberts in the 1960s.[25] It is not as direct a voice as the *Maisha*, in that it is not a transcription of oral evidence; but it is clearly written independently of the *Maisha* and our European sources, and so can be taken as a safe record of information obtained from Abdullah bin Suliman and other Arabs and Africans in the area at the time or soon after.

Abdullah bin Suliman's account differs from Tippu Tip's in several interesting ways. First, he suggests that the people at Mwamba's had an ulterior motive in warning Hamed of the dangers of going on to Itawa. They preferred the Arabs to stay there, because of the commercial advantage of having these coastal traders operating in and out of their territory. They went so far as to refuse to provide guides, forcing Tippu Tip to obtain guides from a village in the Walungu country (probably the same as Urungu, south-west of the southern tip of Lake Tanganyika, the letters L and R being often interchangeable in names in this region). A little farther on, Tippu Tip's party were met by a delegation from Nsama headed by the chief's son – and welcomed into the territory.

Tippu Tip

Once arrived in Nsama's headquarters village, they met a cooler reception; and – according to Abdullah – they made two or three return visits from their camp, but as affairs deteriorated they became victims of a process of harassment. Their women and slaves were molested when collecting wood or drawing water. Tippu Tip requested and was granted permission to build a camp within the village stockade. He suspected that Nsama was plotting mischief – with justification: with Tippu Tip's party inside the village, Nsama was more easily able to attack him, and a skirmish started round Tippu Tip's hut. One of his slaves managed to get away and bring reinforcements, and the Arabs succeeded in driving Nsama's men out of the village, and in repelling a number of counter-attacks over the next two weeks.

Abdullah's account goes on to describe fighting between Arabs and Africans for some time, as one side took revenge for killings by the other, while Tippu Tip loaded up the large tusks from the ivory store, retreated from Itawa southwards, and set up base in Walungu, i.e. Urungu. Nsama sued for a peace agreement, but did not stick to its terms, and fighting resumed. The Arabs now concluded that he did not want peace, and decided to use force in order to enable them to trade in Itawa. Tippu Tip, with other Arabs, with an African chief from Walungu, and also at this point accompanied by Livingstone, went in the direction of Nsama's territory. Nsama himself had built a new village near to his former one, now destroyed, and continued to defy the Arabs. According to Abdullah, Tippu Tip – though preferring to return to a peaceful trading relationship – was persuaded by the other Arabs to make war. He attacked and burned a village, and Nsama then sued for peace in a more serious way. In response to an ultimatum from Tippu Tip, he sent three sons as hostages and his daughter to be Tippu Tip's wife, and promised 100 tusks of ivory. He did not in fact pay all these tusks, but instead gave the Arabs freedom to buy ivory anywhere in his territory, and safe passage for Livingstone to Lake Mweru. As a result, the Arabs were able to collect 1,500 tusks, all weighing more than a *frasila*, and took slaves to carry the ivory to Dar as-Salaam on the coast. Abdullah adds that on their return to Zanzibar the Arab leaders were taken to task by the Sultan, Sayyid Majid, for attacking the people of Itawa, presumably because the Sultan thought he could gain more by taxation of peaceful trade than he would by having to keep large areas under forceful subjugation. In addition, other Arab traders had suffered from revenge attacks by Nsama's forces following Tippu Tip's small war with him, and destruction of African villages, and these traders may have complained to the Sultan. The Arabs explained the circumstances to Sayyid Majid, and were reportedly pardoned, though after that all caravans heading for the interior were told to avoid warfare with the Africans. Tippu Tip, not surprisingly, makes no mention of the contretemps with Sayyid Majid. His narrative consistently portrays him as having a cosy and confidential relationship with this Sultan and his successors.

The accounts of Tippu Tip and Abdullah bin Suliman of course give us the Arab point of view of this conflict. The same is true even for that of Livingstone, since – much as he liked the Africans – he heard the reports of the war with Nsama from Arab mouths. Looking back more dispassionately, we can perhaps see that there was a clear Arab interest in ensuring that they could travel and trade without hindrance, or excessive taxation or tolls, in this area south and west of Lake Tanganyika. Apart from their 'need' to purchase or acquire ivory there, now that there was little or none left east of the lake, it was a crucial transit area for the carriage of Katangan copper to Manyema (west of the northern end of the lake) and to Ujiji and places farther north and east. There were also valuable salt deposits east of Lake Mweru. There are hints in both accounts of the Arabs being too ready to exploit their armed strength, and some justification for the conclusion that all along they had been looking for an opportunity to quell any African resistance and ensure that they maintained long-term control over the area.

Livingstone's circuitous journey to Ujiji, 1867–69

Livingstone's plan to travel to Ujiji with Tippu Tip did not work out. He says that his new-found friend, having brought him to Casembe's, told him he was heading farther west to Katanga, so he set out northwards instead with another Arab, Mohammed bin Salih al-Nabhani, a relative of Tippu Tip's who had been living at Casembe's for over ten years, and whom Livingstone had met when he first arrived at Casembe's in November 1867. Remarkably, three months later, having made very slow progress northwards from Casembe's, he decided to turn back south and to battle through rain, swamp and mud to answer his questions about Lake Bangweolo, which he reached in July 1868, by now in the company of another Arab, Mohammed Bogharib. He fell ill again on his return, but Mohammed Bogharib had him carried and then transported by boat across Lake Tanganyika to Ujiji, where he eventually arrived in March 1869, and where Stanley found him on 10 November 1871 (see pages 55–6 above).[26]

It is not clear why Livingstone thought that travel to Katanga was being planned by Tippu Tip, who makes no mention of it in the *Maisha*. It may have come up in conversation between the two, Katanga being the main regional source of copper, another valuable commodity for the trader.[27] But, having forced Nsama to make peace, Tippu Tip now wanted to return to the coast, to cash in the enormous stock of ivory he held. He recruited porters in relays to carry the ivory from one district to the next, until they reached Urori, where Merere was still chief. There he could find no porters to take the cargo further, and he decided to go north to his father's home in Tabora, where he knew he could recruit porters from the porterage specialists, the Wanyamwezi.

End of Tippu Tip's Second Journey

Tippu Tip arrived in Tabora, but his father was absent, fighting Mkasiwa. What a turn-around! When he had been there on his boyhood travels, the Arabs had been engaged in the fighting surrounding the succession to the chief Fundi Kira, and had in fact installed Mkasiwa on the chiefly stool (Chapter 3, pages 77–9). Now some dispute had broken out, and they were enemies. The Arab party returned from the conflict, but without Tippu Tip's father, Mohammed bin Juma. Tippu Tip stayed two months assembling porters, and then began the return journey to Urori, in company with another trader, but still without having seen his father.[28]

He arrived without incident in Urori, where he discovered the loss of trade goods left there previously. But the large stock of ivory was intact. He left for the coast, and arrived in Dar as-Salaam in January 1869. This was fifteen months after leaving Nsama's territory; even allowing for the two-to-three months taken up by going to Tabora to recruit the porters, this was slow progress. We noted before the huge cargo of ivory he was transporting, requiring perhaps a thousand men to carry it. The account of this part of Tippu Tip's career given by Abdullah bin Suliman confirms the quantity – 1,500 tusks, all over a *frasila* in weight. Such a large caravan moves slowly.[29]

Tippu Tip found Dar as-Salaam bustling with activity. Sultan Majid was there; over the past few years he had begun building a palace for himself, and a major port at Dar as-Salaam, but the project failed to prosper. The palace was not completed, and the port project was dropped after his death not long afterwards, in 1870. But at the time of Tippu Tip's arrival many of the Sultan's court followers were with him. As well as consular representatives and other Europeans, crowds of business people and others were in the town, including the merchants from whom he had borrowed money, perhaps six years previously, to finance his journey. He comments on the "great joy" with which they greeted him, naturally delighted to see their loans repaid, with interest. Brode adds that Sayyid Majid entertained Tippu Tip and "loaded him with high honours".[30] Tippu Tip wanted to travel back to Zanzibar with the Sultan, but Majid told him to pay off his debts in Dar as-Salaam and then follow. The large caravan had arrived about a week before the end of Ramadan, so Tippu Tip celebrated the festival of 'Id al-Fitr there, and then he and a number of other Arabs sailed to Zanzibar in one of the Sultan's ships. 'Id al-Fitr fell on 16 January in 1869, so he would have crossed over during the last ten days of that month.

Tippu Tip plans his Third Journey

After six months (or perhaps within that time – the chronology is not certain), Sultan Majid summoned Tippu Tip, and – having checked that he was planning a new journey, and would therefore be needing loans for barter goods – tried to put pressure on him to do business with Ladha Damji, by now the principal agent in the firm of Jairam Sewji, who had the customs farming contract in Zanzibar. Brode interprets this approach as being one of encouragement to Tippu Tip to start on a new journey, on the grounds that increased Arab trading on the mainland added to his prestige – and also to his treasury, through the import taxes payable on goods (including slaves) brought into Zanzibar.[31] Tippu Tip did not want to give in to this demand, since he reckoned the Banyan traders had become too powerful. He preferred spreading his business among many merchants, but mentions two Arabs as his favourites, Nur Mohammed bin Herji and Rashid Warsi Adwani.[32] As we shall see, he needed no support from the Sultan to persuade Zanzibari merchants to advance him the loans and barter goods he needed. It may have been in this interview that Sayyid Majid reprimanded Tippu Tip for his violence against Nsama; as mentioned above, Tippu Tip avoids saying anything about it in the *Maisha*.

Late in 1869 or early in 1870, therefore, Tippu Tip started planning another trading journey. He had a convoluted time acquiring the barter goods that he needed. Initially he went to Nur Mohammed and Warsi Adwani, but they did not have enough for his requirements. They preferred him not to go the Banyans, presumably for the same reason as Tippu Tip himself had evinced after his interview with the Sultan, and they undertook to speak on his behalf to Taria Topan – presumably more acceptable because of his being a Shi'a Muslim. They were confident that Topan would provide the required goods and money. However, time passed, and nothing was actually forthcoming. Tippu Tip decided that after all he should accept the offer from the Banyans, who had been sending him persuasive messages aimed at getting him to sign up with them; and Ladha Damji (whom Tippu Tip describes as Set Ladda, *Set* being a Hindu honorific) agreed to advance him goods to the value of MT$50,000 – a very significant sum. As his men were collecting the first batch of goods, to the value of MT$6,000, they were spotted by Warsi Adwani, who immediately told Topan what was going on. Tippu Tip met Topan in the house of the American Consul, and there agreed that he would take his supplies from Topan and return those he had taken from Damji. The trouble was that Damji did not want to take back what he had advanced to Tippu Tip, who then had to arrange for the goods to go to his 'brother' (actually a relative, possibly a cousin), Juma bin Sayf bin Juma, for a separate journey up-country. Juma bin Sayf took an extra MT$4,000 worth of goods, making a total of MT$10,000, for which Tippu Tip acted as guarantor. This would have saved his reputation with Ladha Damji.

In the middle of the account of these negotiations, and just after he has reported Ladha Damji's willingness to lend him MT$50,000-worth of goods, Tippu Tip mentions that at this time he had neither plantation nor house nor any other property, but that he did have a wife.[33] The implication is that he was proud that Damji was prepared to advance him this large sum with no security – relying only on his confidence that Tippu Tip would return with enough to cover the debt and interest. It is also implied that, if he were to fail, none of his wife's money or property could be used as security or collateral; this is confirmed by Brode.[34] It is interesting to note this complete separation of assets between husband and wife.

This was the first caravan journey into the interior that Taria Topan had financed. Tippu Tip assembled what he reckoned was a "great quantity" of goods, which would have included supplies and equipment for the expedition as well as the barter goods of cloth, beads, copper wire, etc, packed them up into 200 loads, and sent them off to Tabora

– or in fact to his father's place at the nearby village of Ituru.

However, this large shipment did not include one essential commodity: gunpowder. Tippu Tip's arrangements for purchasing and despatching his supplies of gunpowder gave rise to a potentially humiliating and somewhat comic episode. He quotes the price of powder (MT$3.75 for 25 lb), and says he had nearly MT$5,000-worth of it. This would give a total amount of more than 33,000 lb (over 14 tons), or 15,000 kg, and it is difficult to believe that his figures are correct. Nevertheless, he admits himself that he bought "an enormous quantity"; perhaps the price was particularly advantageous, and he reckoned that he could sell it on at profit, either to Arabs or Africans in the interior. He took his purchase to a wide open area on the outskirts of the town, and then to a store in his own home in the town centre. From there he had it loaded into ships and taken to Bagamoyo on the mainland – where, incidentally, he had yet more.

One evening, at his house in Zanzibar a month later, he received a visit from two Arabs, one of whom was a kinsman of his wife's, a Barwani. No doubt this person's family ties had led to him being chosen for what turned out to be a delicate mission. They told him that he was required to go to see Sulaiman bin Ali, senior adviser to the Sultan. Sulaiman asked him if he had unloaded gunpowder near the Consulate, presumably meaning the British Consulate which was near the Barwani house where Tippu Tip lived with his wife. When Tippu Tip admitted he had, Sulaiman asked him, "Are you mad?", and went on to explain that transporting gunpowder in the town was forbidden, and that there were standard procedures for carrying and loading gunpowder into ships, using the Sultan's powder-depôt at Kizingo, about two miles out of Zanzibar to the south. (Presumably these procedures were designed not only to ensure safety in the town, but also to provide some extra income for the Sultan through a monopoly on storage and loading charges.) Tippu Tip claimed ignorance of all this – he had been travelling outside Zanzibar when these rules had been brought in. He was sent home, and told the next day that the penalty for his crime was either a month in prison or a fine to the value of the gunpowder – which he now claimed was worth only MT$4,000. Some bargaining went on, Tippu Tip saying that he would prefer to pay the fine than spend even ten days in gaol. But Sulaiman then told him that, in imposing the harsh penalty, Sayyid Majid had not realized that the guilty party was Tippu Tip, and reduced the penalty to two nights in jail. The prisoner clearly had a fine time of it: he was given

John Kirk

John Kirk has already appeared several times in this narrative, and remained significant in East African affairs for the major part of his working life. Born in 1830 (thus about seven years older than Tippu Tip) near Arbroath, he studied medicine, but also nurtured a passionate interest in botany. In 1855 he volunteered for service as a doctor in the Crimean War, but arrived too late to be of use, and instead profited from the journey by touring in Turkey and Greece, where he also collected a number of rare plant specimens. These were of great interest to Sir William Hooker, the director of the Botanical Gardens at Kew, with whom he remained friends – and conducted lengthy correspondence – for many years thereafter. Hooker recommended him as the botanist on Livingstone's journey up the Zambezi beginning in 1858. He was thus among the first Europeans to see Lake Nyasa. Weakened by dysentery, he left the expedition in May 1863 to return to the UK, six months before Livingstone finally had to abandon it. Kirk's diaries and letters reveal strong common sense and sound judgement, and also severe disillusionment with Livingstone's capacity as expedition leader.

Having gained a reputation as an explorer and geographer from the Zambezi expedition (and also having managed to avoid the controversy that followed it), he took an appointment as medical officer and deputy to the British Agent and Consul in Zanzibar. (A single individual, at that time G.E. Seward, was both Agent reporting to the Governor of Bombay, and Consul reporting to the Foreign Office.) He soon demonstrated that he had skills in addition to his medical expertise, and was appointed vice-consul in 1866, and in 1869 was acting Agent and Consul, replacing Henry Churchill, who had been invalided out of Zanzibar. He was promoted substantively to the post of Consul and Agent in 1873. He played a major part in the negotiations conducted by Sir Bartle Frere aimed at persuading the Sultan of Zanzibar to end the Indian Ocean slave trade – negotiations that were initially unsuccessful, but which Kirk brought to a conclusion in June 1873. He became a trusted adviser to Sultan Barghash and his successors, and left Zanzibar on retirement in 1887. He was knighted in 1881, and died aged 89 in 1922.

a good room, his servants were allowed to accompany him, and even women were allowed to stay there.

He was obviously luckier than some. The prison was a solid building behind the customs house, thought by some European travellers to have been constructed centuries previously by the Portuguese, but actually the work of Sayyid Sa'id earlier in the 19th century. Joseph Thomson, the leader of the Royal Geographical Society expedition in 1878, wrote, with characteristic irony:

> ... and as the Sultan does not believe in capital punishment, he simply puts the worst criminals into the deepest dungeons where they soon disappear from this earth.[35]

It turned out that it had been the British Consul, John Kirk (see box opposite), who had seen the unloading and loading of the gunpowder and reported it to the authorities, not knowing that Tippu Tip was the owner. Kirk apologized. According to the *Maisha* this was due to his being a friend of Livingstone, whose news had been brought to the coast by a servant travelling in Tippu Tip's caravan; and Tippu Tip (or, more likely, someone in a caravan just behind him) had also brought Kirk a letter from Livingstone. So he reckoned that Kirk was well-disposed towards him.

This letter, incidentally (dated 30 May 1869 and so nearly two years later than Livingstone's letter quoted from above), may have played a part in initiating Stanley's journey to find Livingstone. It was addressed to Robert Lambert Playfair, then Agent and Consul, who was absent; and Kirk communicated its contents to Bombay and from there to London. A summary appeared in *The Times* newspaper in October 1869, which presumably would have been seen by James Gordon Bennett, the proprietor and editor of the *New York Herald*. Two days later Stanley was summoned to Paris and (as he recounts) given the order – by Bennett, in bed in the Grand Hotel at 3.00 p.m.: "Find Livingstone!"[36]

Is there an element of snobbery, or name-dropping, in this part of the *Maisha*'s narrative? When he mentions Taria Topan, and John Kirk, in each case he adds 'Sir'; these two were indeed both knighted, but several years after the events he is describing. Is Tippu Tip reminding us that he was friendly with people in the top echelons of Western society? We may detect this surfacing later, when his acquired strength in the Congo brought him into indirect contact – they never met – with royalty, in the person of Leopold II, King of the Belgians.

So, with the goods sent on ahead to Tabora, and the gunpowder landed safely in Bagamoyo, Tippu Tip was ready for the next journey, his third, and one that would turn out to be his longest, keeping him out of Zanzibar for about twelve years.

CHAPTER 5

The Far Side of the Lake

Tippu Tip's style in the *Maisha* is not to tell the reader his intentions in advance. He simply narrates where he went and what happened there. Only very rarely does he give any dates (an exception is the day in Ramadan when he arrived in Dar as-Salaam, recorded in the previous chapter), although we can often work out some of the chronology from data elsewhere, for example the letters and diaries of Europeans who came across his path. In this case, the start of his Third Journey can be placed no more precisely than at some time in the first nine months of 1870, since it is known that Sayyid Majid returned from Dar as-Salaam to Zanzibar in late September, and Tippu Tip left Bagamoyo for Dar as-Salaam expressly to bid farewell to the Sultan. And we can also tell that he chose the more northern route towards Tabora, instead of the track direct to the southern end of Lake Tanganyika and Urori, where he had had difficulties on his previous journey.

His farewells were carefully choreographed. Having conducted the business in Bagamoyo necessary for efficient organization of the several caravans, and sending his half-brother Mohammed on to Kwere, not far inland from Bagamoyo, he went back to Zanzibar to say good-bye to his sponsor/lender Taria Topan – but then found that an important wedding was taking place, of the children of Warsi Adwani (one of the two Arabs whom earlier he had approached for finance for the expedition). He felt he had to stay for this event, and only then finally left for Bagamoyo and Kwere. This punctiliousness may have been because he knew in advance that he would be away for a long time; or perhaps his record, written twenty-five years later, reflected a wish to demonstrate that even in his younger days he had observed correct social behaviour.

Arriving at Kwere, he found that Mohammed and the caravans, having waited for a while, had gone on; he had after all been nearly three weeks in Zanzibar. They met up in Usagara, the region south of Mpwapwa, and continued on to Ugogo. There they ran into a serious problem: cholera.

Cholera and Tippu Tip's Third Journey

Cholera was more or less confined to areas round the Bay of Bengal until the early 19th century, when epidemics broke out – spreading along trade routes – as far as Turkey, East Africa and the Philippines. Further pandemics occurred in 1829, 1852 (which caused over 20,000 deaths even in the UK), 1863 and 1881; and twice in the 20th century. The outbreaks that affected Zanzibar and large parts of the mainland did not exactly correspond with the widespread pandemics listed, but were devastating in their effects. East Africa was hit hard in 1836, 1858, and now in 1869–70, and the disease was probably brought along the transport routes taking pilgrims to and from Mecca for the annual Hajj.

Cholera is an intestinal disease, spread when faeces containing the bacterium contaminate water that is then drunk by people. It can also be transmitted on food that has been irrigated, washed or cooked with contaminated water, or in fruit and vegetables that have been fertilized or irrigated with infected sewage. The bacterium causes the intestine to release huge quantities of fluid into the intestinal tract, causing intense diarrhoea and consequential extreme dehydration. Untreated (and no treatment was known in 19th-century Africa), the disease leads to death in more than half of those affected. Contemporary accounts suggest that the mortality rate in East Africa at this time was even higher. It is noticeably more serious than dysentery, although the method of transmission and many of the symptoms (including rapid dehydration) are similar.

The disease arrived at Pangani, the port almost opposite Zanzibar on the mainland, in October 1869, and in Zanzibar about the middle of November, spreading – it is thought – down the East African coast from an outbreak in Mecca. Contemporary accounts describe the terrible disaster. Kirk reported that the authorities were fatalistic as the disease approached; and he himself saw no way of avoiding the attack, although he thought that more could be done to remove the awful "accumulation of filth that spreads disease".[1] Once cholera struck the town, deaths came fast, with some victims surviving barely a few hours. Survivors found it impossible to arrange burials quickly enough, and bodies were left on the beaches for dogs to scavenge.

Another Scottish medical man was in Zanzibar at this time. James Christie, who had studied medicine in Glasgow, had arrived in late 1865 as the doctor to a Church of England mission, but built up a practice which included Sayyid Majid as one of his patients. He was interested in medical research, and after the epidemic died down he investigated the areas where the cholera had been most intense, and those where the inhabitants had been less affected; and he correctly analysed the causes of the spread of the disease, later publishing his *Cholera Epidemics in East Africa* in 1876.[2]

In their letters and reports, Kirk and Christie describe the town of Zanzibar as the disease was at its height. Casualties rose particularly during the month of Ramadan, which started in early December 1869, as resistance was weakened by the rigours of the fast. The streets became deserted except by burial parties. Christie, who himself worked tirelessly to provide relief where he could, was affected by the quiet that spread over the town; children's laughter was no longer heard, nor the sound of African music customarily played on the beaches in the evenings. People prayed to God for relief:

> When the plague was at its very height, raging in every quarter of the city like a devouring element, praying parties, and Koranic chanters were organized, and they perambulated the streets by night, invoking God to stay the pestilence, and spare the living. Sounds of prayer and solemn Amens issued from the mosques, and from private houses in the streets, and in the early morning the call of the Muezzin to prayers sounded over the city.[3]

In January 1870, the cholera abated, then resumed in March. Only in July could the damage be assessed – more than 12,000 deaths in the town, and more than 25,000 on the island of Zanzibar as a whole; and the casualty rate on the mainland, though not measured, would have been far higher. Slaves suffered particularly, because of the poor conditions in which they were transported and housed, often in extremely cramped conditions and always with crude or no sanitation.

Tippu Tip makes no mention of the disease on Zanzibar. Certain segments of society escaped its worst effects, for example the Hindu population and the Europeans, presumably because of their standards of cleanliness and access to uncontaminated drinking water. Perhaps the same applied to more wealthy Arab families, such as Tippu Tip's. He does however describe its effects on his caravan, progressing inland from Kwere in the early months of 1870. Villages refused them entry, and they found it increasingly difficult to barter for food. "We were in serious trouble, with men dying every day."[4] At one village in the Ugogo district, they were confronted by armed men barring their passage and insisting that they take a long route circumventing the villages, through the bush. Tippu Tip did not want to do this, since the detour would add twelve days to their journey, and they lacked sufficient supplies of food to survive the extra time. He threatened to use force in order to have his way and use the preferred route through the villages, and those opposing him eventually compromised, though insisting that he and his men camp outside by the river, and that they must move on after two days. Food and drink would be brought to them. Tippu Tip complied with these conditions, but still lost many men to the disease.

By the time they reached the last village in Ugogo, where more than seven more died, their numbers were so depleted that there were not enough survivors to carry the goods. They decided to bury some of their merchandise – beads, bangles, bullets, shot, bundles of chains, and even two cannon which Tippu Tip had brought. They carried on the next day, and during the four-hour rest they took after the first part of the march, six more men died.

Tippu Tip does not give absolute figures for his total numbers lost, although he does say later that he was lucky – compared with other caravans – in that he had lost no more than a quarter. The number of his *pagazi* could have been several hundred, depending on how much of the gunpowder he took up-country and how much he left in Bagamoyo or Dar as-Salaam. The losses must nevertheless have been significant, if he was forced into burying large amounts of his merchandise: "Only the goods were left [out] that could not be buried", he records.[5] He had other caravans, ahead, that had not been so badly affected, and this was also the case with other Arabs' caravans that had left the coastal area soon enough to escape the worst of the cholera outbreak. But some of those who had been travelling near Tippu Tip had also suffered badly. One had had to jettison all its goods.

Their caravan reached Tora, and then Rubuga, places in Unyamwezi, and the first in that district which caravans on this route from the coast would reach. In Tora they met up with the other caravans that had been travelling at the same time but on divergent routes. In Rubuga, Tippu Tip at last met his father, whom he had not seen for several years, since they had returned from Urua to the coast together after the fighting with Mnywa Sere, in about 1859. They went on to Tabora, and to the Murjabi home village of Ituru. Tippu Tip's father was in a period of relative prosperity: his African wife Karunde (not Tippu Tip's mother) had died, and he had married the niece of Mkasiwa, the current Nyamwezi chief. Mkasiwa had actually wanted him to marry his own daughter, but Mohammed bin Juma preferred Nyaso, a younger daughter of Mkasiwa's brother, Fundi Kira. This irritated Mkasiwa, not least because he had bad relations with his brother's family. Nyaso must have brought some dowry in the form of land, since all of Ituru now belonged to her and Mohammed bin Juma, who according to local custom would have inherited half of Karunde's property, the other half reverting to her father.

While Tippu Tip was in Ituru, an incident occurred which seems trivial on the face of it, yet which could have led to an outbreak of violence (Tippu Tip says 'war') in the community. An elephant wandered into or near the village, and was killed. Mohammed bin Juma planned to keep the tusks, which were unusually large, weighing 5¼ *frasila*, or 180 lb (82 kg) However, messages then arrived from both Chief Mkasiwa and the *Wali*, or Governor, Sa'id bin Salim al-Lamki, that the tusks should be handed over to them.

During this period, when the Sultan in Zanzibar considered that the Arabs on the mainland owed him allegiance, he appointed a *Wali* to be his representative in the territories where there was sufficient Arab concentration. The duties, and for that matter the powers, of the *Wali* were minimal. He would settle disputes between the Arabs, represent them in differences that arose with local Africans, and, if these became serious, organize and lead military campaigns. This *Wali* was in fact known to British explorers: Sa'id bin Salim, from the important Zanzibari family of Lamki originating in central

Oman, had been appointed by the then Sultan to be head of Burton and Speke's caravan in 1857–58, and had also accompanied Speke and Grant as far as Tabora in 1860. Livingstone had also had dealings with him, naming him as "Syde bin Salem" (he generally transcribed the Arabic name Saʿīd as 'Syde', probably reflecting the Swahili-speakers' pronunciation without the Arabic *ʿayn*), and curiously describing him as "a China-looking man".[6] Saʿid bin Salim does not seem to have been a strong governor, providing ineffectual leadership when the Tabora Arabs had to confront the powerful Mirambo (see below, pages 116–120), and a few years later, in 1878, he was ousted from his position as Governor by a rival faction grouped around another Tabora Arab, Abdullah bin Nasib (or Nasibu).

The tusk dispute arose because of a custom in a number of East African territories at this time, that the tusks of an elephant killed in or near a village should be divided: one to the person who killed the animal, and the other to the Chief. According to Livingstone, the Portuguese had introduced the custom, also giving half the meat of a killed elephant to local Africans. But the custom was not universally applied. An additional problem in the Tabora area was that there were two 'chiefs' – Mkasiwa and the *Wali*. Tippu Tip and his father were not going to surrender both tusks! In fact, they thought that they did not need to hand over either of them. Nyaso agreed. There may have been another point of principle at stake, as well as the interpretation of local custom: for Tippu Tip and his father to hand over the tusks would have been to acknowledge the superior authority of the Chief or the *Wali*, or both; it was akin to paying a tax. Mkasiwa and Saʿid bin Salim had decided to settle the dispute by force of arms when they were distracted by a greater common threat.

This was the prospect of an invasion by the Ngoni, a tribe who had been displaced by the Zulus from their territories farther south, and had been causing disturbance in areas near the southern end of Lake Tanganyika. One group of them had been ejected from Itawa by Nsama, and over a period of time had come north-east to Unyamwezi. They were known for their effective and disciplined military tactics, deploying broad shields and short stabbing spears. They had formed an alliance with Mshama (or Mushama), a nephew of Chief Mkasiwa, who took them towards Tabora, hoping to benefit from their support to oust his uncle. Tippu Tip claims that Mkasiwa and his tribesmen needed Arab help; but in fact the Ngoni approach also threatened the Arabs. The Arabs' relationship with Mkasiwa's family had its ups and downs, but at least they had consistently been allowed to trade, and they suspected that the Ngoni would not be so favourable to commercial activity. It was in their interests to support the resistance to the Ngoni.

Tabora was a collection of fourteen villages. Abdullah bin Nasib (who later had Sa'id bin Salim removed) was the Arab chief or owner of one of them, Kwihara, which lay first in the path of the invading force, and he went out to do battle with them. When he heard this, Tippu Tip sounded the drums, summoned support from Tabora itself, and followed after to the place where Abdullah had fought the enemy. They were met by bad news: the Arab force had been routed, and fifty of their slaves killed, as well as more than a hundred of the Ganda tribe, who were supposed to be escorting Abdullah's brother, Sheikh bin Nasib, to their chief. Sheikh bin Nasib had been entrusted with the task of carrying a gift for the Ganda chief from Sultan Majid, in exchange for a generous quantity of ivory he had sent. This was now not going to happen. The Ganda were all killed, and the Ngoni had made off with the Kwihara cattle.

Tippu Tip was all in favour of pursuing the raiders, but was given an unenthusiastic – even negative – response by his fellow Arabs, both immediately and on the next day, when they gave chase for a while. Others turned back, but Tippu Tip pressed on as far as the river Ngombe, at or beyond the border of Unyanyembe. In this energetic counter-raid he was accompanied by Sa'id bin Habib al-Afifi, another Arab trader and traveller who may have visited Luanda, now the capital of Angola, on the west coast of Africa (see box on following page).

At the river Ngombe, Tippu Tip and Sa'id bin Habib found that the Ngoni had crossed to the other side. They considered that further pursuit with reduced numbers would be pointless, and risky in territory beyond their borders, and so they returned to Ituru.

We should note in parenthesis that Tippu Tip's story[7] of the Ganda involvement does not tally with that of Livingstone, who records that the gift was to Sultan Barghash in 1872, not to Sultan Majid, who died in 1870. Nor does Livingstone record the massacre of the Ganda. So perhaps the record in the *Maisha* was a conflation of two or more episodes – easily done when writing twenty-five years after the event.

The Ngoni threat disposed of, Tippu Tip was anxious to be off to Itawa (or Itahua). But the Tabora Arabs, fearful of another attack and realizing that Tippu Tip was a useful ally in a crisis, asked him to stay to repel any second raid. He remained there for two months, but then sent

> ### *Sa'id bin Habib al-Afifi*
>
> Sa'id bin Habib's travels are first recorded in 1845, so we may deduce that he may have been born in the early 1820s, 15–20 years before Tippu Tip. He was active in trading in areas frequented by Tippu Tip, and gave an account of his travels to Rigby, the Consul in Zanzibar, in 1860. According to this account, he was one of a group of Arabs who travelled west from Casembe's to Katanga in the late 1840s. At this time the Portuguese had stations extending eastwards from their bases at Luanda and Benguela, and the Arab party met up in Katanga with trading agents of the Governor of Bié, the most easterly of these provinces. Persuaded to go back with them to the coast, the Arabs reached Benguela in April 1852. Their return across the continent took them to the upper Zambezi (where Sa'id bin Habib met Livingstone in 1853), and then down the River Rovuma to Mozambique island, where they arrived in September 1854. Despite his claim to Rigby that he had crossed Africa twice, and visited Luanda three times, there is some doubt as to whether Sa'id bin Habib actually participated in the whole of this journey. His path crossed Livingstone's again on Lake Mweru in 1867, and then he moved his operations northwards and traded on the Lomami down to Stanley Falls. There he became an enemy of Tippu Tip, being one of those Arabs whose violent methods of acquiring ivory and slaves Tippu Tip was trying to moderate. He died in 1889, on the road back to Zanzibar. (Wilkinson 2015: 91–98; Bontinck 1974: 215.)

on his half-brother Mohammed bin Masoud and another close relative, Juma bin Sayf, with most of the goods, and made arrangements for his own departure. The goods that he had buried in Ugogo were delivered to him, mostly intact, though some of the beads had been lost or stolen. After a further argument with the Tabora Arabs who still wanted them to stay longer, he set off. In the *Maisha* he mentions the names of several prominent Arabs who stayed behind, plus a number of young men from the Mrima coast and fifteen of his own men – presumably to demonstrate that he was not entirely indifferent to Tabora's need for defence against a possible renewed attack.

Heading south-west from Tabora, he took a route towards the south end of Lake Tanganyika which had only recently been opened up by Arab traders. He first passed through an area called Ukonongo, where a brother or near-relative of the deposed Tabora Chief, Mnywa Sere, had usurped the chieftainship and installed himself under the name Simba (Lion). The caravan then arrived in a region named Ugalla, where the chief was named Taka, but the actual power was exercised by Taka's brother Riuva (or Riova, or Liova). Here occurred another of those incidents where extreme violence was provoked by an apparently trivial cause, although we have only Tippu Tip's account of it, and there may have been different underlying reasons for the fighting.

Arriving in Riuva's territory, Tippu Tip's party decided to stock up on basic foodstuffs, in exchange for generous quantities of cloth and cattle. Prices were much lower than in Simba's territory in Ukonongo. These basics included a large supply of millet, a food grain which was and is used in Africa for grinding into flour for bread and porridge, and also for brewing beer. Tippu Tip's men were each given enough for a week, and they went into the surrounding villages to have it ground. One of them claimed he had been attacked without provocation by villagers, and all his millet spilt; and he was determined to fight the men responsible. Tippu Tip tried to restrain him, promising to replace the lost millet. He did not want to cause trouble (he said), and Riuva was known to be treacherous and cunning. But the man, a slave of one of the Arabs, seemed bent on revenge. He took out his gun, and a fracas broke out which ended in Riuva being shot. Immediately the villagers disappeared; Tippu Tip thought they were drunk on millet beer. His narrative of what ensued is confusing. He won control of Riuva's village and captured some women and some ivory, but about sixty of his own men had deserted and returned to Tabora, making it impossible for him to continue on his journey. He waited in the village, and fought off a counter-attack led by Riuva's brother, the actual chief Taka. Tippu Tip's weaponry must have made it an unequal fight, since he records seventy enemy killed, against only four of his own men.

A few days later a group of about fifty arrived from Tabora, consisting of twenty Baluchis and thirty slaves. There is a long tradition of immigration to Oman from Baluchistan, the mountainous area of what is now south-west Pakistan; many Baluchis were recruited into Omani military forces, as well as more peaceable occupations. So these men may have been in the service of Sultan Barghash, or some kind of militia serving the *Wali*. They brought messages from principal Arabs in Tabora, and also from Tippu Tip's father, to the effect that they had heard about the fighting and that the chief Taka had taken refuge with the Arabs and wanted peace. After another interval of a few days, a much larger contingent appeared – five hundred men, led by prominent Arabs from Tabora, including his father, deputed by the *Wali* to bring about a peaceful solution. Their persuasiveness, backed up by overwhelming strength in numbers, led to a settlement. Mutually acceptable compensation was paid: Tippu Tip returned the prisoners he had taken (mostly women), and received 15 *frasila* of ivory in exchange. Then he was able to travel on.

Tippu Tip gave a different account of these events to Herbert Ward, one of the British members of the Emin Pasha Relief Expedition, several years later when they were on the Congo. Then he said that he had complained to Riuva about mistreatment of his women while collecting wood or drawing water, and that when the African chief had refused to take any notice of him, Tippu Tip had lost his temper and started a hand-to-hand fight. One of his men had then shot Riuva and killed him. Abdullah bin Suliman also refers to this incident, as a 'war' between Tippu Tip and 'the chief Lyowa'; but he does not know the cause of it.[8]

It seems improbable that such a violent incident, involving the death of a chief, could have been caused by spilling one man's share of millet, even though it did happen that tempers could rise and fighting erupt very quickly. It is more likely that Tippu Tip wished to assert his position in Ugalla, and in the neighbouring Ukonongo, where Simba was chief. On this interpretation, Tippu Tip may not have been actively seeking violence, since what he needed was influence and the ability to take his caravans through and to barter for provisions; but when violence came, he was confident of coming out on top. The arrival of the significant force from Tabora headed by his father, with Abdullah bin Nasib (who later became *Wali*) and his brother Sheikh bin Nasib carrying a message from the *Wali*, suggests that the influential Arabs of the interior wanted to avoid provoking unnecessary conflict with African leaders, either from their own policy or in order to comply with Sultan Majid's wishes. We saw this when Sultan Majid reprimanded Tippu Tip after his confrontation with Nsama (see previous chapter, page 96). The Tabora delegation may also have wanted to ensure that they and their Arab kinsmen were not caught up in a cycle of revenge fighting. They certainly seem to have travelled with the intention of giving Tippu Tip some plain speaking, since when they arrived they refused to come into the village, or to accept customary hospitality, until they had a commitment that their demands would be met.

The compromise agreed suggests a partial climb-down by Tippu Tip. From the Ugalla episode he emerged with a paltry 15 *frasila* of ivory, though he may have felt he had the long-term advantage of having secured a compliant piece of territory on an important trade route.

The Far Side of the Lake

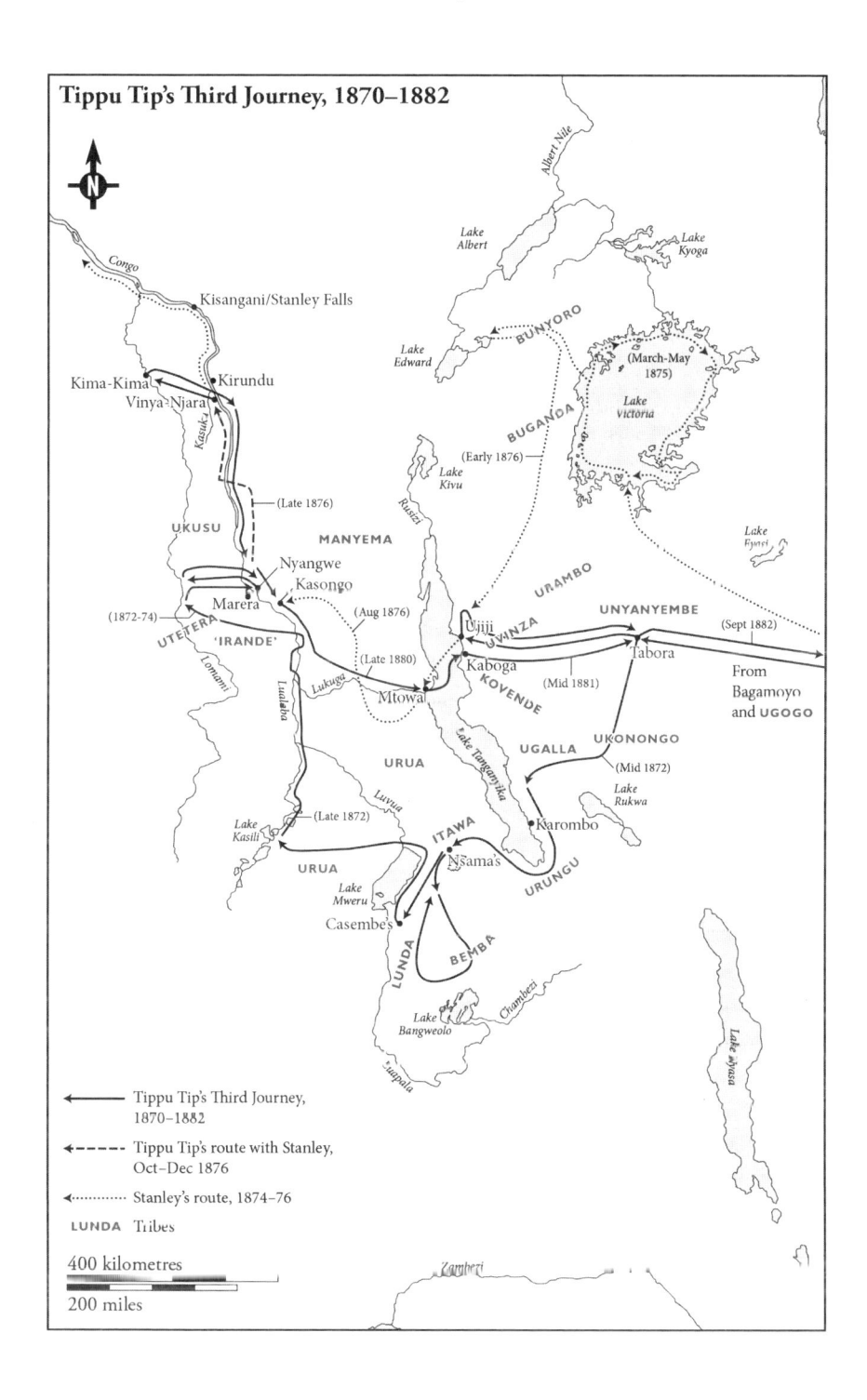

Chief Mirambo

It is during this incident that the great Chief Mirambo makes his first appearance in Tippu Tip's narrative. When he was telling the slave not to make a fuss about the spilt millet, he had said to him, "Don't make a dispute of it! ... [The Chief here] is treacherous, and even Mirambo came here and couldn't do anything."[9]

Mirambo was a Nyamwezi Chief of what even he admitted was an insignificant territory of half a dozen villages and 4,000 people, small by comparison with the Nyamwezi Chiefdom of Unyanyembe (which included Tabora). But by bravery and skill he extended his influence well beyond his homeland, eventually forcing the Arabs to confront him and start a war which lasted nearly five years, from 1871 until 1875. It is worth giving some attention to him: although he left no lasting legacy, his presence and influence was a powerful one in the region east of Lake Tanganyika for some twenty-five years between about 1860 and his death in 1884, and his career is illustrative of the times in which Tippu Tip flourished.

Mirambo's date of birth is uncertain, probably between 1830 and 1840, and he was thus of the same generation as Tippu Tip. We know little about his early years. In his excellent biography of Mirambo, Norman Bennett speculates that, like other Nyamwezi young men, he would have travelled in trading caravans and also acquired skills in fighting and warfare.[10] He appears to have won the position of chief by force or subterfuge, since he was a chief's son and the office would normally have passed not from father to son, but to a nephew in the female line, according to the custom of matrilineal succession. Soon after becoming Chief of Uyowa, he absorbed the neighbouring territory of Ulyankulu, and the combined chiefdom became known as Urambo, the country of Mirambo. It was a well-organized entity, with sufficient manpower and agricultural surplus to enable Mirambo to engage in almost perpetual warfare or raiding. His forces, made up of warriors who remained unmarried until they were allowed to 'retire' with rewards of land and slaves, overcame villages over a wide area to the north and west of Unyanyembe, almost as far as Lake Tanganyika.

Mirambo's warlike conduct led him into natural conflict with the powers in Unyanyembe, where – following the conflict over the succession to Fundi Kira (pages 77–8) – the Arab and African leadership had established a form of stable collaboration. Mutual and complementary interests were served, based on the Arabs' wish to trade safely through the area to Ujiji (to gain access to the profitable regions of Manyema west of Lake Tanganyika), and the Nyamwezi aim of selling provisions and the services of their young men as *pagazi*. Mirambo's aggression, plus his demands for increased *hongo* (transit dues), put this symbiosis in peril. Fighting broke out in 1871. An early episode, in June 1871, involved the explorer Stanley, then in an early stage of his search for Livingstone; he had made good progress from the coast to Unyanyembe, and was then persuaded by the Arab–African coalition there to join forces in a battle against Mirambo, who was portrayed by them as a lawless leader of bandits. It did not turn out well for the combined force: after an initial success, the Arabs and Stanley's men were ambushed by Mirambo's better-disciplined followers, and Stanley was lucky to escape alive from the chaotic retreat back to Tabora. He dubbed Mirambo 'the African Bonaparte' (sometimes amended to 'the Napoleon of Central Africa'), and after the failed mini-campaign he took a long détour to the south to avoid having to go through his territory.

Campaigns continued, with sometimes one, then the other, side gaining temporary advantage. When Stanley returned to the coast through Tabora some eight months after his first visit, he thought Mirambo was on his last legs; and in July 1873, when V.L. Cameron came on his expedition to find Livingstone, and (after finding that the Doctor had already died) carried on to cross Africa, he described him as a harassed fugitive in the bush. But Cameron also observed that the Arabs had divided loyalties, some following the leadership of the Nasib brothers, while others preferred to take orders from Amir bin Sultan al-Harthi, who had been sent with some troops by Sultan Barghash of Zanzibar in a vain and half-hearted attempt to bring the anti-Mirambo campaign to a close. Barghash was pressured into this intervention because the war was curtailing trade from the interior to Zanzibar, particularly in ivory, on which in normal times he was able to levy a valuable import tax.

Eventually Mirambo decided to seek a settlement. The reasons for his coming to terms are not clear, especially as in 1874–75 he remained a formidable enemy of the Arabs. Reports reaching British officials in Zanzibar suggested that he was very short of ammunition, Barghash having imposed an embargo on gunpowder earlier in the conflict. Mirambo may simply have come to the conclusion that he could not actually defeat the Arabs and force them out of the region, and that a war without end was not in his interests. Indeed, it may not have been sustainable, since his 'business model' was to motivate his warriors by dividing up among them the booty captured from defeating other villages and tribes. This booty included slaves (who had value as agricultural workers) and cattle. But after some years of guerrilla fighting against Arab enemies, he may have calculated that this kind of interference no longer generated sufficient booty.

Accordingly, he sent a gift of a large quantity of ivory to Sultan Barghash with a friendly message saying that he would allow Arab traders to transit the areas under his control. Barghash sent back gifts of equal value, and the *Wali* in Unyanyembe, Saʿid bin Salim, concluded peace shortly afterwards. Both sides had suffered from the four-year war, and although the Arabs remained hostile to Mirambo, they held back from engaging in further armed action.

In the late 1870s, Mirambo had contact with the now-emerging European missionary societies. There had been a missionary presence in Zanzibar since the 1860s. Now, partly as a result of the publicity given to the region by the death of Livingstone in 1873, and the remarkable recovery of his body to Zanzibar by his faithful servants (and from there to Westminster Abbey), increased donations made possible a rapid growth of the establishment of missionary stations. Mirambo had good relations with several of these missionaries, and also with other Europeans. These included a Swiss adventurer, Philippe Broyon, who assisted Mirambo in trading ivory (conveniently for the latter, since he would obviously not have wanted to use Arab intermediaries to sell his tusks). Another was Ernest Cambier, one of the first to arrive in East Africa from the International African Association, the body set up by King Leopold II to initiate his ventures in Africa, which eventually led to the Belgian colonization of the Congo. Cambier went on to build the Association's first station, at Karema on the eastern shore of Lake Tanganyika.

Mirambo's relationships with the Europeans, including John Kirk (now Agent and Consul in Zanzibar, and a close adviser of Sultan Barghash), were put at risk when two British employees of the International African Association were killed in cross-fire between Mirambo's forces and those of a village he was attacking. For a while Kirk, the Sultan and the Unyanyembe Arabs were not sure whether this action signified a renewed attempt by Mirambo to seize control of all the routes from the coast to Lake Tanganyika, and it looked as though another war with him might start. But the spat died down, although Mirambo continued to find supplies of gunpowder difficult to acquire as a result of a tightened blockade imposed by Barghash. He continued to facilitate travel by the missionaries, and on occasion tried to use them as intermediaries with Kirk and Barghash, claiming that his was a rule of peace, enabling safe passage for traders through his territory to Lakes Victoria and Tanganyika.

It was only late in his life that Mirambo met Tippu Tip. Their paths did not cross until 1882, since Mirambo confined his activities to his sphere of domination between Unyanyembe and Lakes Victoria and Tanganyika, while Tippu Tip was at first travelling on the journeys described earlier, and then for a long time in Manyema, west of Lake Tanganyika. They did in fact have a family connection — somewhat remote, but perhaps enough to give Mirambo grounds for hope that Tippu Tip might persuade Sayyid Barghash to get the Tabora Arabs to soften their hostility towards him. The reader may recall that Tippu Tip's father, Mohammed bin Juma, had been active in installing Mnywa Sere as Chief in Unyanyembe; it was widely believed that Tippu Tip's grandfather, Juma bin Rajab, had played a similar role for Mirambo's grandfather as Chief in Uyowa.

Whether or not there was a family-based relationship, the two had a mutual interest in becoming friends. While Mirambo could benefit from having an Arab friend in court in Zanzibar, at the end of his Third Journey Tippu Tip needed an easy transit for his prodigiously large caravan of ivory porters on its way back from Manyema, through to Tabora and the coast. This was especially so since he had run into some violence in Uvinza, west of Unyamwezi, and obviously wanted to avoid having to confront an alliance between Mirambo and his neighbour. He sent his son Sayf to negotiate the agreement, and successfully reached Zanzibar without further incident. (Details of this episode, with its added complications created by the Tabora Arabs, are recounted below, in Chapter 7, pages 164-5.) Tippu Tip met Mirambo in person a year later (in late 1883 or early 1884) when he returned to Manyema on his Fourth Journey. Arabs in Tabora sought to dissuade him from going to Urambo, and even sent messengers to Mirambo claiming that Tippu Tip was coming with hostile intent. These spoiling tactics failed, however, and Tippu Tip was received with "great honour", and "a great friendship was established".[11] They exchanged valuable presents, Mirambo promised to send generous gifts of ivory to Sayyid Barghash and notable Arabs in Zanzibar, and Tippu Tip stayed a week before travelling on to Ujiji.

Mirambo continued his pattern of constant campaigning in 1882 and 1883, but with increasing difficulty because he faced a serious rival in the form of his uncle, Kapela, chief of a territory near Urambo. He was forced into more fighting with the Ngoni, and began to suffer from an illness in his throat, possibly cancer. He died while campaigning in December 1884, probably from the throat illness.

After Mirambo's death, Urambo strength soon declined. Kapela came near to uniting his chiefdom with that of his deceased nephew, but he too did not survive long. Urambo reverted to its previous independent component territories. Mirambo was – and is – remembered as a brave, brilliant and charismatic military leader rather than as an administrator or empire-builder. He stood out from other chiefs in his willingness to engage with Europeans (mainly missionaries), apparently interested in learning from them about the wider world, possibly in the hope of making Urambo a centre for development in East Africa. There was, however, no sign that he was interested in the faith that they wanted to propagate, or in the education that they hoped to bring.

Tippu Tip in Itawa

Our narrative left Tippu Tip in 1870 as he was departing from Riuva's territory south-west of Tabora, on his way to the southern tip of Lake Tanganyika. He passed through Ukonongo (reinforcing the suggestion that his aim in the confrontation with Riuva and Taka was to ensure easy passage through this region), and came to the district of a chief called Karombwe. This might be the same as the 'Kafumfwe' recorded by Livingstone in October 1872: on his last journey from Unyamyembe to Lake Bangweolo (where he died), Livingstone was following a route similar to Tippu Tip's in 1870–71.

In Karombwe's district Tippu Tip met up with his half-brother Mohammed, who had found abundant supplies of food there, thus enabling both caravans to stock up. This was just as well, since they were now a very large party (Tippu Tip claims 4,000 men), and the next part of their journey was difficult – steep inclines, and no food to buy. They were following a track close to Lake Tanganyika, and as they rounded the southern tip of the lake, at Urungu, the lack of supplies caused them some hardship.

They did succeed in reaching Itawa, probably in July–September 1872 (the date can be deduced from comments in Livingstone's journals). But in their eagerness to satisfy their hunger many of the caravan tried to short-cut the method of preparing and cooking cassava, the local crop. In the *Maisha*, Tippu Tip kindly explains how cassava, a tuberous root crop (also known as manioc, yucca or tapioca) which is a staple in many tropical and sub-tropical regions, has to be soaked for several days until it ferments, then dried and then cooked before it is safe to eat.[12] Failure to give cassava this treatment allows residues of cyanide to poison the person or animal eating it. Tippu Tip was not aware that it was cyanide that made his men ill, but describes graphically how seven hundred of them were overcome with violent vomiting and diarrhoea, and forty of them died. His kinsman Juma bin Sayf bin Juma appeared on the scene, and luckily had the antidote – a broth made from goat's meat with peppers and ginger. The sick men lived on this for three days, and then those who had survived the initial illness recovered enough to continue. We shall see later how a similar failure to deal with manioc's toxicity caused terrible problems in Stanley's Rear Column on the Emin Pasha Relief Expedition.

They were now in the region of Chief Nsama, whom Tippu Tip had subdued on his Second Journey (see Chapter 4, pages 88–90). Nsama agreed to see all his kinsmen, but not Tippu Tip himself; the previous defeat still rankled. As the days passed, however (and the party stayed there nearly a month), Nsama seems to have relented, and even to have made available to Tippu Tip a decent quantity of ivory, though nothing like as much as Juma bin Sayf managed to acquire – 300 *frasila*. But the difference seems to have been that Tippu Tip did not have to pay for his; and he had the impression that Nsama wanted him to go away. Whatever was in his mind, his behaviour towards Tippu Tip was not far off that of a vassal towards a feudal superior, and his 'gift' of ivory equivalent to tribute.

The caravan members themselves went out hunting, and killed large numbers of elephant and buffalo. Tippu Tip decided to go visiting tribal chiefs in Ruemba (or Bemba), the area south of Itawa, towards Lake Bangweolo. He describes them as his friends, but his transactions with them look like a kind of one-sided trading. In each case, he reports the chief as giving him a quantity of ivory, and himself as having responded with unspecified quantities of goods plus an advance of goods to the value of specified numbers of tusks or 'loads' of ivory. (A 'load' is not explained, but might be 2 *frasila*, since each porter was expected to carry 70 lbs weight.) In other words, Tippu Tip did the rounds of a number of chiefs, making it clear that he expected that when he next came, each chief would have to pay him certain quantities of ivory in exchange for the advanced goods.

At this point in his narrative, for no apparent reason, Tippu Tip relates how he had bought four slaves at a cheap price from another Arab, and he gives their names. Brode's biography suggests that these slaves were of special value to Tippu Tip because of their ability in woodcraft and hunting, and he reckons that they paid for their purchase price several times over, through the ivory and meat they brought in.[13]

On returning to Nsama's village, Tippu Tip found that his men's hunting expeditions had been remarkably successful: they had amassed a huge quantity of ivory – at one point he says 400 *frasila*, although two paragraphs later it has become only 100. Whichever was right, and both would have been approximations, it was significant. He also held a large quantity of goods, and made arrangements with his brother to stay at Nsama's village to separate the cloth from the beads, on the grounds that beads were in demand in Urua, west of Itawa, where he wanted to go next, whereas the cloth would sell well in Itawa and Ruemba.

Conquest of Casembe and on into Urua

Tippu Tip made careful preparations for the next part of his journey, probably in about November 1872. He took 800 porters, 150 guns, and all his own beads and those of his brother. With him came Sa'id bin Ali bin Mansur, with goods that included cloth as well as beads. The rainy season had started when they set off, and progress was slow. Urua extends to the west of Lake Mweru, and Tippu Tip seems to have intended to go round the southern end of the lake. A particular hurdle was the River Karangosi, the border between Nsama's territory and that of Runda (or Lunda), where the hereditary chiefs took the name Casembe (or Kazembe). At the time of Tippu Tip's visit the chief was the eighth of the line, named Mwonga (also referred to as Kazembe VIII Mwonga). Some of Tippu Tip's men crossed the river, swollen by the rains, and four of them were killed, seemingly by Casembe's men wanting to pick a fight or to challenge the travelling party. There was no reason for them to attack the Arab party; Casembe was on bad terms with Nsama, whom the Arabs had subjugated, and Tippu Tip was surprised that they should have laid down this challenge to him. The two powerful men of the region were Nsama and Casembe; and before deciding to fight, Tippu Tip warned his brother (still in Itawa) that a battle was imminent, and brought in reinforcements from him.

The Casembe chiefs had indeed been powerful and important in the region. Their Lunda territory covered the strategic gap between Lakes Mweru and Bangweolo, astride the trade route from Katanga (rich from its copper deposits) and the east coast; from Lunda the routes split – the northerly one to the southern tip of Lake Tanganyika and on to Tabora, and the southerly one to Lake Nyasa and on to Cape Delgado and Kilwa on the coast. Their territory had been known to the Portuguese, who had traded with them from the Mozambique coast, up the River Zambezi and past Lake Nyasa, for perhaps two hundred years. Livingstone met the then Casembe chief in November 1867, and was impressed and appalled at the same time:

> The present Casembe has a heavy uninteresting countenance, ... and his eyes have an outward squint. He smiled but once during the day, and that was pleasant enough, though the cropped ears and lopped hands, with human skulls at the gate, made me indisposed to look on anything with favour. ... Casembe's smile was elicited by the dwarf making some uncouth antics before him. His executioner also came forward to look: he had a broad Lunda sword on his arm, and a curious scissor-like instrument at his neck for cropping ears. On saying to him that his was nasty work, he smiled, and so did many who were not sure of their ears a moment ...[14]

But by the time Tippu Tip arrived in this region in late 1872, a new Casembe was in place, and his power in decline.

The battle with Casembe's forces lasted a month, at the end of which Casembe was killed and the Arab forces seized what Tippu Tip describes as "an enormous quantity of booty – a great number of guns, much ivory, and innumerable prisoners".[15] He does not say, but we have to assume that the prisoners would have been either kept or sold as slaves. Again, Livingstone's journals help us put a date on this fighting, by an entry in early December 1872 mentioning reports of the death of Casembe.

On to the Lualaba

It is not completely clear how Tippu Tip travelled from Casembe's territory in Lunda, due south of Lake Mweru, to Chief Mpweto's territory on the lake's northern tip. He followed the lake shore round, either on east or west, and reached the River Lualaba, which in the *Maisha* he correctly names the Congo – but using knowledge (writing in the 1890s) which he did not have in 1872. Livingstone, even when he died in 1873, believed that the Lualaba flowed north and then northeast to join, or to form, the Nile. For Tippu Tip, the eastern branch of the Lualaba (called the Luvua on modern maps, and named "Webb's R. Lualaba" by Livingstone) formed an obstacle to be overcome: even in dry times of year, but particularly during the rains, the Lualaba was a significant river as it flowed out of Lake Mweru, and his party crossed it in dug-out canoes in order to enter Urua. This reference to the difficulty in crossing suggests that he had travelled up the east side of Lake Mweru, and crossed the Lualaba for the first time from east to west.

Tippu Tip had been in Urua before, on his second early journey (Chapter 3, pages 72–3), and no doubt reckoned that there was much to be gained from acquiring ivory. But on this occasion he was disappointed. First, there was not much ivory to be found. The villages were poor and small, and some of the villagers lived in caves. They were vulnerable to attack from their stronger neighbours in Katanga to the south-west, and indeed soon afterwards the Katangan Chief Msiri (or Mushili) did bring them into subjection, having forced them to come to terms by smoking them out of their caves from behind their defensive stockade. Secondly, when Tippu Tip and his party did find ivory to trade, the terms and conditions were barely acceptable: negotiations were painfully slow – it might take ten to fifteen days to conclude a transaction for a single tusk – and the chief, Kajumbe Chakuma, who was powerful with many followers, insisted that traders should stay until all their barter goods had been exchanged. On top of that, he charged a tax of 25 percent, payable directly to him as chief, on each piece of ivory traded. They found this doubly frustrating because they knew that areas nearby had ivory in plenty, but the people were for some reason afraid to bring it in to them. Kajumbe was one of a number of chiefs who had carved out an area of influence from the region, extending from Manyema in the north and to Lake Tanganyika in the east, that had previously been subject to a great paramount chief, Ilunga Kabare.

During this enforced stay with Kajumbe Chakuma, Tippu Tip received messengers from Chief Msiri in Katanga. They delivered a gift of twelve tusks, and a message giving him the distinct impression that Msiri was afraid that, having effectively brought Nsama and Casembe under subjection, Tippu Tip would do the same to him. His reply amounted to: "Too right! I shall attack Msiri unless he buys me off with a further twenty tusks." He was assuming the status, once more, of chieftain receiving tribute from a subject ruler. The messengers departed, and Tippu Tip was left with the problem of how to escape from Kajumbe. He had now been a year without moving. Having sought permission to leave, and been refused, he was forced to fight; Kajumbe, defeated, sued for peace, which he was given – at a price of nine tusks.

Tippu Tip travelled onwards and westwards, doing some small-scale trading in ivory on the way, making for the territory of Chief Mrongo Tambwe, who was in conflict with his brother Mrongo Kasanga over the inheritance of the chieftainship. Whichever brother was in the ascendancy (and it seems to have been now one, now the other) occupied the villages on the shore of Lake Kasili (or Kasile, now Lake Lukenga), while the other took refuge in the nearby forest. The victor – until himself ousted by the other – profited from the revenue from the extensive trade done on the lake shore, at that time a significant market for all sorts of goods – general goods such as beads and bracelets, slaves, goats, etc, but principally fish from the lake (much of which was exported, either smoked or dried), and *viramba*, a cloth woven from palm fibre, and sold in fringed pieces about 80 cm square in such quantities that it was almost equivalent to a currency.

The lake itself is described in the *Maisha* as half or one-third the size of Lake Tanganyika; it is actually much smaller than that, although it is one of a series of lakes lying in a north–south line about 250 km west of Lake Mweru. In attributing this size to Lake Kasili, it is possible that Tippu Tip was confusing it with the huge 'lake' (more accurately an expansion of the river) below the confluence of the two branches of the Lualaba. The western branch flows through Lake Kisali and its companions, while the eastern branch – called the Luvua on some old and most modern maps – drains from Lake Mweru. Today this large 'lake' has disappeared, or become marshland surrounding the river. In the 19th century, it was called the Kamolondo or Landji, and travellers related how the clear waters of the eastern branch and the muddy water of the western channel hardly mix until some distance after leaving the lake.

Tippu Tip stayed on the shores of Lake Kasili for nine months. The lake was at this time prolific in fish production. The local people also killed elephants by scaring them into the lake, or into the marshy surrounds, where they became stuck and therefore easy prey. The villages were large, and clearly prosperous. But Tippu Tip complains that he managed to buy only 100 *frasila* of ivory there, compared with the 150 he acquired at Kajumbe's. We must assume that the disadvantage of a sluggish ivory market was offset by the comfortable life supported by cheap food – "small fish fetched one or two glass beads, while the largest fetched only seven or ten".[16] The Chief made sure that dug-out canoes full of fish were supplied to them each day, and they also shot duck flying over the lake – "one barrel would bring down thirty or more" (!).

Shortly before they left Lake Kasili, Tippu Tip's friend, Saʿid bin Ali bin Mansur al-Hinawi, was persuaded by new messengers from Chief Msiri to go to Katanga to trade. The messengers brought a gift of twenty-five tusks, promising that there was more where it came from. The venture was risky, and at one point he was robbed of most of what he had, and had to start afresh. But Tippu Tip wanted Saʿid bin Ali to go, partly because he had refused to leave behind his loads of cloth at various points when they had run short of porters, and the cloth had not been in demand at the villages where they had traded. Now it seemed that Msiri did want cloth in exchange for ivory. So Saʿid bin Ali was the man to take up Msiri's invitation. His departure left Tippu Tip in sole charge of the caravan, his brothers Mohammed bin Masoud and Juma bin Sayf having stayed behind in Itawa.

Tippu Tip had now, in 1873, been away from Zanzibar for more than two years. He had exhausted the areas rich in ivory east of Lake Tanganyika and in the regions close to the lake and to its south and south-east, and needed to push farther westwards to explore new possibilities for trade. Making enquiries about the best places for commerce, he was advised to go to 'Irande'. It is not certain where this would have been, but from references in the writings of the explorer Wissmann it seems likely that this was the region north-west of Lake Kasili, between the rivers Lualaba and Lomami. One Arab had penetrated this far – Juma bin Salim al-Bakri, who was nicknamed 'Merikani', presumably because he traded particularly in American cotton. Tippu Tip would have an up-and-down relationship with this man as he entered into a new phase his career, and set out into a region that was to offer him vast new opportunities in exploration and commerce.

Chapter 6

KING KASONGO.

Between the Two Rivers

TEN DAYS AFTER Sa'id bin Ali had left for Katanga, probably sometime in 1872, Tippu Tip and his party set off from Lake Kasili, crossing the western branch of the Lualaba, and heading northwest. Hearing – apparently for the first time – about Juma Merikani, Tippu Tip decided to visit him, and crossed back to the eastern side of the river.[1] Juma Merikani had been in the area west and south-west of Lake Tanganyika for some years, probably since the early drive into Urua by Omani Arabs in the late 1850s. He was one of the leaders of the Arab penetration into Central Africa, and had at one point been prospecting the gold and copper mines of Katanga. This was the period, as Wilkinson relates, when increased demand for ivory, and reduced supply because of scarcity east of Lake Tanganyika, had led Arab traders to look for new sources in the catchments of the Rivers Lualaba and Lomami (or Lomani, or Rumami).[2] The Lomami is a significant tributary of the Congo, running more or less south–north and parallel with the Lualaba for about 1,000 km, and joining the Congo just over 100 km west of Kisangani, the settlement which later became one of

Tippu Tip's headquarters near Stanley Falls. Juma Merikani met several of the European explorers – Burton and Speke in Ujiji, previous to this in 1858, and later Cameron in 1874–75. Stanley thought he had been living more or less permanently in Urua since 1867. Wissmann, who met him in Nyangwe in 1882 and again in 1887, describes him as "a medium-height, corpulent man with a shiny grey beard, of mixed-race colour and with pop-eyes, giving the impression of a good-natured *bon vivant*".[3]

Juma Merikani told Tippu Tip that he could do decent trade by staying where he was, and relying on the Warua to bring ivory in to him; he himself preferred not to take the risk of venturing into even less known territory. Tippu Tip told him he had made up his mind not to stay. Perhaps he thought there was not enough ivory in Urua to provide profit for both of them, or perhaps he simply had a stronger sense of adventure. Nevertheless, he trusted him enough to leave 300 *frasila* of ivory with him, and pressed on.[4]

It is difficult to be certain of the geography of this part of Tippu Tip's travels. He came to a chief whom he calls Kirua, but this may have been a family or even tribal name. At any rate, from Lake Kasili he reached the great 'lake', or widening of the River Lualaba, known as Kamolondo, where it is known that Juma Merikani had a base. After his meeting with Juma, he continued northwards, and met chiefs whom Cameron came across about two years later, in October 1874. Reference to Cameron's narrative enables us to place Tippu Tip's route very near the River Lomami. Indeed, Cameron relied on one or more of Tippu Tip's men to guide him for ten days through this part of his journey. One of these chiefs was Chief Rumba, a subordinate of the chief at Kasongo, who was described by Cameron as "a dirty, drunken old man without much sense";[5] and another was Chief Sangwa, about whose territory Cameron was more complimentary:

> [It is] a fairly populated country, with large villages of well-built and clean huts disposed in long streets with bark-cloth trees planted on each side. All the streets ran east and west, but the reason for this I was unable to discover. The people seemed friendly, and the chiefs usually brought small presents of corn or dried ants – which are eaten here as a relish on account of the scarcity of animal food.[6]

Cameron goes on to describe the ingenious method used to trap the ants, clearly an important source of protein:

A light framework of cane or twigs is built over a large ant-hill and covered with leaves cleverly fastened together. ... A very small entrance is left open at the bottom, and under this is dug a round hole a foot in diameter and two feet deep. When the winged ants come out of the hill ready to migrate they all make for this entrance and hustle each other into the hole, where they lose their wings and are unable to get out. In the morning they are collected by the natives who smoke them over slow fires to preserve them.[7]

Tippu Tip's description in the *Maisha* accords with Cameron's. He found country which was rich but undeveloped. The villages were very large, seemingly built to a regular design, with houses round a large courtyard where the craftsmen plied their trade, which was mostly in the palm-tree fibre *viramba* textiles such as the caravan had seen at Lake Kasili. But the villagers had no guns, only bows and arrows, and very little ivory, and few traces of elephants were to be seen. The Arabs told the villagers that their guns were pestles for grinding corn, and were apparently believed. They allowed this delusion to continue, with the result that they suffered from hostility and robbery: "We couldn't do much to defend ourselves," says the *Maisha*, "because they behaved as though we were not carrying weapons, but had only pestles in our hands."[8]

Juma Merikani's hut in Urua, as depicted in Verney Lovett Cameron's *Across Africa* (1877).

Tippu Tip takes power in Utetera

The caravan also suffered from lack of communication. They had left Lake Kasili with guides provided by Mrongo Tambwe, but these guides seemingly left them, since Tippu Tip records with relief that the caravan met someone who spoke Kirua, the language of Urua, and with whom they could converse. This man told them that they needed to cross the River Lomami, and he named areas and chiefs from whom they would be able to purchase plenty of ivory. He went on to say that they should go on to meet Chief Kasongo Rushie, Chief Mwana Mapunga and Chief Mwinyi Nsara, but especially the first and last of these, who were friends. Chief Kasongo was (the informant went on) an old man, and his people, the Watetera, "very numerous and somewhat stupid". They faced several enemies, and tended to lose their battles against them because of their timidity.[9] ('Kasongo' is probably an honorific, but is used in the *Maisha* to refer to this chief, in place of the full 'Kasongo Rushie', or Lushi.)

The message about plentiful ivory was just what Tippu Tip wished to hear; and he followed the advice and travelled yet farther westwards. This proved an excellent source of good and cheap ivory: two or three *frasila*s could be bought for two bangles, a cowry and a piece of cloth. A great quantity was brought in to them, but supply became exhausted after twelve days. So they continued their journey, telling those whom they met that they were still aiming to see Chief Kasongo Rushie in Utetera (or Utetela) mentioned by their recent informant. As they got closer, they began to be embroiled in the tribal warfare from which the Utetera people suffered. They had to pay a high rate of *hongo* to secure passage through one territory (Mkahuja), and then had to deal with a people (Kirembwe) who wanted Tippu Tip's support in fighting the Watetera. They offered to divide up the booty – the ivory for him and the women for themselves.

Tippu Tip wanted none of it, insisting that meeting Chief Kasongo in Utetera was his objective. He seems to have been trapped by the Kirembwe, but was rescued by the arrival of messengers from Chief Kasongo, asking for him by name and promising him quantities of ivory.

At this point Tippu Tip demonstrated his quick wits, combined with a somewhat wicked sense of humour. He told Kasongo's messengers that two generations previously a Chief of Urua, Rungu Kabare or Kumambe, had crossed to Utetera, where he had taken captive two women "of the royal house". Tippu Tip's grandfather, Habib bin

Bushir, he claimed, had bought one of them, who had given birth to his mother. She had later told him, Tippu Tip, about the powerful chief in Utetera, and he accordingly claimed kinship with Chief Kasongo. This, said Tippu Tip, was why he was determined to meet Kasongo, his long-lost cousin or uncle.[10]

This story was almost certainly fabricated, but cleverly aimed at putting Tippu Tip in a position where he might even claim power in Utetera. Farrant suggests that he had planned the deception in advance, and that he had been given the corroborative details – the names of the two captured girls, for example – by a slave concubine of his own who came from Utetera; but there is no evidence for this.[11] Indeed, in the *Maisha* he recounts how he heard the names of the slave-girls from the informant who had told him about the Watetera having many enemies and being rather stupid. The idea may have occurred to him when he heard the informant's story, since he specifically says that he noted it down carefully, as though he had in mind to use it somehow; and he had also observed the informant say that Chief Kasongo Rushie was an old man, and therefore perhaps looking to name his heir.[12]

Tippu Tip gave a different version to Herbert Ward, the member of the Emin Pasha Relief Expedition in whom he confided years later. In Ward's account, the two girls are "sisters of the aged king, [and consequently] persons of importance ... his ruse succeeded in imposing on the people, the old king even abdicating in favour of Tippo Tib, who he declared was the heir, as his sister's grandson."[13]

Whatever they thought of his story – and it was so constructed as to be very hard to contradict or disprove – Kasongo's messengers agreed to take him to their chief. But before they could go, fighting broke out. The people of Mkahuja and Kirembwe had banded together with the aim of blocking Tippu Tip's passage to Chief Kasongo in Utetera. The Arabs were in the middle of trading some ivory when they realized that fighting could not be avoided – they had heard the war-drums all the previous night, and knew that they were surrounded by large villages and by a force of several hundred men. But the Arabs, with their Wanyamwezi men, had the advantage of guns over spears and arrows, and soon secured an overwhelming victory, with several hundred Mkahuja and Kirembwe killed. This enabled them to capture more than a thousand women and countless goats. In talking to survivors the next day, they reckoned that the Africans had been unaware of the lethal power of the guns, thinking them to be a form of thunder, and that those killed could somehow be revived.

It turned out that Tippu Tip's numerous prisoners included some Watetera, and he was advised to separate them out from the Mkahuja and Kirembwe enemies. This was going to help him on two counts: he would graciously release the Mkahuja, and so bring a peaceful end to the fighting, and he could present the rescued Watetera to Chief Kasongo Rushie as a gift at an appropriate moment. But he needed assistance in distinguishing the ones from the others; and help was at hand in the shape of a chief whom he had met previously. This man, named Pange Bondo, had been headman of a village where the custom was to replace the headman periodically. He had refused to step down, been ousted, and had then sought Tippu Tip's help to be reinstated. Tippu Tip had turned down that request, but this time thought the man could be of use. He installed him as chief, in a ceremony that involved adorning him with a necklace of ten very small live chickens, which Tippu Tip obviously thought ludicrous, commenting that they would be dead in a few days. But he and Pange Bondo worked out a scheme whereby all the prisoners would be passed in front of Tippu Tip, standing by holding a book to add credence to his reputation as a diviner, while Pange Bondo looked up or down depending on whether the prisoner in question was or was not Watetera. The deception worked well, and Tippu Tip's reputation was enhanced.

The caravan travelled on into Utetera, where Tippu Tip was introduced to a member of the Chief's clan, named Ribwe, to whom again he told his story of being the grandson of a woman of the "royal house", whom his grandfather had taken to the coast, and that his grandmother had encouraged him to return to his familial area. Ribwe was amazed at his determination to fight his way over such a distance to come home, as it were, and prepared to take the Arab caravan on to Chief Kasongo Rushie, another four days' journey. As they travelled, Tippu Tip noted that the villages were large and prosperous. Arriving at the Chief's village, they pitched camp beside an "extremely fine" river. This could have been the Lomami: we know, from Cameron's account, that Tippu Tip later made his headquarters close to the Lomami, and that he (Cameron) had travelled from there to Kasongo Rushie's, also named as Ibari, in two days – say twenty miles.

Now Tippu Tip had the pay-off from his ancestry tale, which had obviously gone before him. Kasongo Rushie straightaway ordered his men to recognize him as chief, to invest him with all authority, and to bring him any ivory that they had. An enormous quantity was brought in – 200 tusks weighing 374½ *frasila* (which must also have meant that they were large tusks, if averaging nearly 2 *frasila*, or 70 lb, apiece). In return, Tippu Tip gave Kasongo Rushie those captives that he accepted as "his people". This reinforced Tippu Tip's prestige and authority, and he now described himself as Paramount Chief.

There are unanswered questions about Kasongo Rushie. Tippu Tip presents him as having various eccentricities, for example that he had not seen tusks for a long time, and that he did not eat elephant meat; and also that he did not look at the sun around sunrise or sunset. All this was because he thought it improper to lay eyes on his fellow-chiefs, that is the elephant or the sun. Apparently this inhibition did not apply to the sun at midday. He also hints that Kasongo Rushie was old, and for this reason prepared to surrender his power. But this does not tally with the description given by Cameron, who met him a year or two later, in September and again in December 1874. He recounts how Kasongo Rushie "performed a jigging dance with his two daughters" for the visitors when they first met – thereby confirming the eccentricity but suggesting some youthfulness, or certainly not a man in decline. Cameron's sketch of Kasongo Rushie also depicts a man in his late forties or early fifties.[14] So why should he have handed the chieftainship to Tippu Tip? Why did Tippu Tip seek it (through the ancestral story ruse) and accept it? His main interests were normally in maximizing profit from trading in ivory, not in establishing territorial power. On Kasongo's side, there may have been the possibility of a succession dispute which he hoped to avoid by transferring power to a powerful, well-armed and charismatic outsider. For Tippu Tip, perhaps the combination of a steady supply of ivory, with a comfortable life for his followers, all of which could be ensured by his assuming the position of chief, proved irresistible. We have no clear evidence.

The arrangement worked to their mutual advantage. Tippu Tip stayed in Utetera for nearly three years, from the middle of 1872 until late in 1874. He came across cannibalism for the first time, and was obviously both angered and disgusted. This was when his uncle Bushir bin Habib went on a journey, probably coming from the north-east (where other Arabs were already established) and then heading west, to a chief named Kitete. Here he and sixty of his men were killed and eaten. Bushir bin Habib was the uncle with whom Tippu Tip had done his very first trading journeys, from the age of twelve. He set out to attack his uncle's murderers, and was soon followed by Kasongo Rushie with a very large force, of about 40,000. Again citing the chief's age, Tippu Tip told him to stay at home because he could not keep up, but Kasongo Rushie insisted on coming along. More joined their army, and they attacked several districts where they tried to make the local people give up eating human meat, but in vain. The reply they received was, "OK, but you give up eating goat!" Tippu Tip's disgust is shown by his comment that they could not camp near their villages because of the smell. Eventually they made the people their subjects, collected a good batch of ivory, and returned home.

During their absence, the old enmity with the Kirembwe and Mkahuja had flared up again. These tribespeople had attacked villages on the borders of Utetera. So Tippu Tip and Kasongo Rushie (who still would not stay behind, but at least brought along a sizeable force) went again to battle, and subdued a substantial area. "Our domain was very large," claims the *Maisha*, and their booty included goats and pigs, and some ivory, in return for which they gave 'guarantees', presumably of peace and security.[15]

It is possible that, during this period in Utetera, Tippu Tip established some form of administration, or at least a system of security of a basic sort. That is, in exchange for tributes or taxation in the form of livestock for his followers and ivory for himself, he imposed a rudimentary centralized order, with support from the considerable forces available to Kasongo Rushie. This would account for his bestowal of 'guarantees' after the subjugation of the Kirembwe and Mkahuja peoples. He also reports this as the system used about a year later in the town and area confusingly called Kasongo – a town some way east of Utetera and near, though not right beside, the Lualaba, on its east bank south of Nyangwe – as we shall see below. Whether we can go so far as to describe it, as Renault does, as a 'system of government' is less certain.[16] Brode records that Tippu Tip exercised justice, exacted heavy penalties from all who committed offences, and appointed subordinate rulers who had to pay him heavy tributes; but there is almost nothing of this in the *Maisha* or in any other contemporary source.[17] His authority ensured a relatively high level of security, particularly on the main travel and trading routes, which brought about social as well as commercial benefits: "Even women travelled [safely]".[18] But the system, if system it was, contained fragility: where someone remained in charge with direct responsibility to Tippu Tip (for example the man he left in Utetera, when he left for Nyangwe and Kasongo), then order could be maintained and tribute collected. In that case, much of the tribute was in the bark-weave *viramba*, of which a large quantity was brought in after just two to three months, and some sold for ivory. But when Tippu Tip and his men moved on, the old fragmentation of inter-village rivalry would have returned.

Tippu Tip encounters other Arabs in the region

Tippu Tip now judged that the time was right to leave. He had come to realize that he was in fact not far from places where Arabs had penetrated, using a route quite different from his own. He had come from the large Arab centre in Tabora round the south end of Lake Tanganyika, and then north and west past Lake Mweru to the River Lomami; other Arabs had travelled directly west from Tabora to Ujiji on Lake Tanganyika, across the Lake to Mtowa, and then farther west (and only a little north) to Nyangwe on the River Lualaba. The two groups were soon to meet. Tippu Tip came to realize the proximity of his compatriots through contact with a chief in Marera (or Malela), named Rusuna (or Lusuna). Marera was two days' journey (i.e. about 20 miles) from the left (west) bank of the Lualaba, almost on the same latitude as Nyangwe on the east bank. Chief Rusuna, when Tippu Tip's men first came to his village, commented that he wanted friendship with their leader, and rather charmingly asked them, "What does he want, women or ivory?" On being told that it was ivory being sought, he gave them ten tusks, a prudent way of finding favour. Soon afterwards he met Tippu Tip and got into conversation with him, particularly over the repair and maintenance of guns. Rusuna told him that he could find people like himself, with guns (and therefore the means to repair Tippu Tip's damaged stock), east of where they were and on the other side of the river 'Ugarrowa' – a local corruption of 'Lualawa', as the people of Nyangwe called the River Lualaba.

Tippu Tip decided to go there, to meet his fellow Arabs and have his guns repaired. The journey was not straightforward, since his men fell to looting in Rusuna's territory, and peace and good order had to be restored. Tippu Tip actually entrusted his guns to Rusuna, and returned to his headquarters near the Lomami. Rusuna and his men, probably a little short of half-way between the Lomami and the Lualaba, ran into further danger, since an Arab force travelling west from their base in Nyangwe feared they were being attacked and opened fire. After some parleying they realized that Rusuna was in fact allied to their kinsman, Tippu Tip was summoned for the four-day journey from his base, and "there was great rejoicing". Tippu Tip's party were delighted to catch up with the news from Zanzibar. They had been entirely out of contact for about three years, and had not even heard of major events such as the succession of Sayyid Barghash as Sultan on the death of Sayyid Majid in 1870, and the disastrous cyclone that had struck the island in April 1872 and done terrible damage to houses, ships, dhows and plantations.

Tippu Tip names the principal Arabs then in the area: Mwinyi Dugumbi and Tagamoyo (both of mixed parentage; and more about both of these anon), Sa'id bin Habib al-Afifi, Abed ('Ubayd) bin Salim al-Khaduri, and Sa'id bin Mohammed al-Mazru'i. Tagamoyo encouraged Tippu Tip to travel on to Nyangwe, and also to Kasongo (the other settlement on the Lualaba, upstream from Nyangwe), where he could meet more Arabs "like ourselves". After seven days' walking they reached the river, and crossed it. Tippu Tip seems to have been impressed with Nyangwe – "an extremely large village, one part of which was for Arabs and another for those from the Mrima coast".[19] He comments warmly on the availability there of rice: "Not for more than three years had we seen rice."

Nyangwe, on the right (east) bank of the Lualaba, in the area known as Manyema, had become a significant Arab settlement since about 1860. As they went farther inland from Tabora, the Arabs had established themselves at Ujiji, on the east shore of Lake Tanganyika, but balked at attempting to penetrate what looked at first like dense forest on the opposite shore. In fact the local population engaged not only in subsistence agriculture, but in trade over relatively long distances, involving copper from Katanga, salt from south-west of Nyangwe, bark-weave products, iron tools, and foodstuffs including fish from the abundant rivers. Some of these products have been mentioned as being of importance in the places that Tippu Tip was passing through. But ivory was considered of little or no value. Elephants were useful for their meat (the heart was especially appreciated), for their skin (for leather items), for their fat, and for the hairs on their tails, used for adornment. It was only when the Arab traders penetrated the continent, seeking ivory for the European, American and Indian markets, that the balance of trade was disturbed. To begin with, when their numbers were small, they secured a certain level of collaboration with local chiefs. But as they grew in strength, saw the advantage they had in weaponry, and required forced labour to carry the ivory back to the coast, the use of violence became more common. This in turn gave rise to resistance and to deep suspicion of the stranger, whether

> ### *Ivory exports and ivory products*
>
> Analysing the western movement of the Arabs in the 19th century, in their search for more ivory, Ceulemans ironically remarks that it is "a product which by its nature is renewed very slowly": *l'ivoire, qui par sa nature est une marchandise se renouvelant très lentement* (Ceulemans 1958: 324). Yet the amounts exported, at first nearly all through Zanzibar, then later via the Congo, and also other African ports, notably Mombasa, were prodigious. From customs figures we can calculate the value, and hence the weight, of ivory exported from Zanzibar – an average of 228 tons a year in the early 1860s (Sheriff 1987: 124). With the continued efforts of Tippu Tip and his colleagues it would have increased in the 1870s and 1880s. After Leopold and Stanley had opened up the Congo route, exports from the Congo went from just under 6 tons in 1888 to 324 tons in 1900 (Gann and Duignan 1979: 118).
>
> Where did it go, and what was it all used for? In the earlier box on Elephants and Ivory (Chapter 1, pages 14–15), we noted the steady demand in China and Japan (for both raw ivory and carved items) and the 19th-century growth in ivory purchases in Europe and North America. Apart from the mass markets for piano keys and billiard balls, ivory artifacts were very varied, as a visit to the Victoria and Albert Museum will show. Many of them were carved in India from African ivory exported from Zanzibar (there were virtually no ivory carvers in Zanzibar itself), and then re-exported elsewhere. Many were small, but they were very numerous. There were statuettes and other ornaments (such as carved concentric balls), boxes, paper knives (important for uncut books), hairbrushes and combs, fans, chess sets, and so on. A fashion grew up in the 18th century for the production of portrait miniatures – small head-and-shoulders portraits on thin slivers of ivory, just a few centimetres across, beautifully painted in exquisite detail. The fashion spread from Europe to India, where many of the best examples were made, including of Indian rulers and others. Another large-scale use was for knife handles, by the cutlery manufacturers of Sheffield. (See Barbier 2009; Pedersen 2015).

Arab or European. Despite not having guns until later in the century, the Africans could pose a significant threat through their superior knowledge of the environment and their ability to conceal themselves before choosing the moment to attack, and through their own weapons of spears, and bows and (often poisoned) arrows. The literature of the European explorers is full of stories of the dangers presented by these formidable enemies; and we have already seen, in the case of Tippu Tip's uncle Bushir bin Habib, how the Arabs themselves could suffer serious losses as a result of this confrontation.

Of the Arabs he met on this occasion, Tippu Tip mentions first "their leader", Mwinyi Dugumbi, who was probably of mixed parentage and came from Winde, on the Mrima Coast. His Arab name is not recorded, although he met several European explorers, including notably Livingstone when he was in Nyangwe in March–July 1871. For weeks Livingstone negotiated with him in the hope of persuading him to acquire canoes to cross the Lualaba or to travel downstream, his aim being to demonstrate that the Lualaba was in fact the upper reach of the Nile. Later, on the stage of his journey that killed him, and still fostering this false belief about the Lualaba, he sought the Nile's source which he thought was in or near Katanga, far to the south, but west of Lake Bangweolo. Livingstone ended up being tragically disappointed by Dugumbi. On 15 July 1871, Dugumbi's men started a fight in the market-place in Nyangwe, which soon turned into a massacre as a small number of gunmen fired into the throng of buyers and sellers. Many sought refuge in the river, but were carried downstream and drowned. On the other side of the river, an associate of Dugumbi's, Tagamoyo, had embarked on a campaign of murder and arson that carried on into the next day. Livingstone was horrified by the incident. His journal entry for 15 July spreads to four printed pages, and on 16 July he wrote separate entries in the morning, at 12 noon, 2.00, 3.00 and 4.00 p.m. Two days later, he writes:

> The murderous assault on the market people felt to me like Gehenna, without the fire and brimstone; but the heat was oppressive, and the firearms pouring iron bullets on the fugitives was not an inept representative of burning in the bottomless pit .... The terrible scenes of man's inhumanity to man brought on severe headache ... I was laid up all yesterday afternoon, with the depression the bloodshed made – it filled me with unspeakable horror.[20]

After this no further collaboration with Dugumbi was possible for Livingstone, and he left soon after for Ujiji where, a few weeks later, he was 'found' by Stanley.

It is not easy to establish the motives for the massacre at Nyangwe. It was clear that Dugumbi had initiated it; indeed he did not deny his responsibility. Wilkinson attributes it to a turf war, or a demonstration of power by the Arabs, relative newcomers to the region.[21] Renault thought it was due to the 'violence breeds violence' atmosphere brought about by African reaction to the Arabs' use of force to acquire slaves and ivory, and to the Arab wish to assert their superiority and authority.[22] In his vivid description of the massacre and analysis of it, Coupland, the great historian of 19th-century East Africa, attributes it to a dispute between Dugumbi and an ex-slave named Manilla, who had provoked Dugumbi by trading on his own account, burning villages, and binding village headmen on both sides of the River Lualaba in ties of 'friendship', presumably under duress.[23] Dugumbi wished to punish those headmen who had linked themselves with Manilla, whatever pressure they had been under; and the people massacred in the market were thought to come from those villages. It was considered particularly horrifying because of the convention of immunity from harm covering those attending the market, even when there were inter-tribal hostilities, and the custom forbidding the carrying of arms there. Livingstone estimated that between 330 and 400 were killed.

Dugumbi's associate Tagamoyo is also mentioned by Tippu Tip as being one of the principal Arabs in Nyangwe, in the capacity of "commander of the forces". He was also known as Mwinyi Mtagamoyo bin Sultan, or more often in the literature as (Mwinyi) Mohara, and we must assume was of mixed blood, like Dugumbi. It was he who led a major expedition from Nyangwe north and west in 1869 or 1870, in an Arab attempt to find new sources of ivory and slaves. They were ambushed early in the expedition, and found out that those who were killed were also subsequently eaten, but they went on to cross the Lualaba and enter Ukusu. Hearing of land farther west occupied by pygmies, where ivory was so cheap that a tusk could reportedly be bought for one cowrie, they continued over the Lomami. They did indeed collect a huge number of tusks, about four hundred, but the pygmy chief refused to let them leave, and in fighting their way out they lost almost everything they had. Only thirty of the large force escaped back to Nyangwe. Later, however, Tagamoyo did establish himself as the major power in an area between the Lualaba and the Lomami, operating from a base named Riba-Riba on the Lualaba. But Tippu Tip came later to despise him. Two years later, when Stanley asked him, just before their travel together on the Lualaba, what he thought of Tagamoyo, Tippu Tip turned up his nose and said, "He is brave, no doubt, but he is a man whose heart is as big as the end of my little finger. He has no feeling, he kills a native as though he were a serpent."[24]

In the same passage Stanley describes Dugumbi as having the "rollicking look of a prosperous and coarse-minded old man ... [dealing] in humour of the coarsest kind – a vain, frivolous old fellow, ignorant of everything but the art of collecting ivory". Cameron met Dugumbi on arrival in Nyangwe in August 1874, and reports that "he had collected round him over three hundred slave women, and the ill effects of this arrangement and his indulgence in *bhang* [cannabis] and *pombé* [beer] were plainly noticeable in his rapid decline in idiotcy [*sic*]".[25] Brode uses plainer language, describing Dugumbi as "ruined by drink and sexual excess".

Dealings with V.L. Cameron

It was here in Nyangwe, in August 1874, that Tippu Tip met Verney Lovett Cameron, recently arrived from Tabora and Ujiji. To explain his presence there we need to go back to 1871, and reconnect with the story of Livingstone. Late in 1871, there was growing concern in England that Livingstone might be in need of support, and perhaps even rescue. Reports from Kirk in Zanzibar, and his superior as Consul, Churchill, were reaching the Royal Geographical Society (RGS) that the Mirambo war in Unyamwezi might cut Livingstone off from the coast, or prevent supplies from reaching him. The RGS decided to raise a public collection for an expedition to go to relieve him, and contributed from its own funds for the purpose. All this happened in a few weeks, and the expedition set sail in early February 1872, arrived in Zanzibar in March, and in Bagamoyo in April. However, the day after their arrival, messengers came from Tabora, sent on ahead by Stanley, who – having 'found' Livingstone in November 1871 – had bidden him farewell in Unyanyembe in March 1872 and was about to arrive on the coast. So the RGS expedition was aborted. Moving forward now to later in 1872, the RGS organized two further expeditions aimed at making contact with Livingstone. They knew from Stanley's reports that his obsession now was to identify the source of the Nile; but some in London thought (correctly) that in exploring the Lualaba and its headwaters, Livingstone might have been near the source of the Congo, not the Nile, and that he might therefore emerge from Africa on the west coast – as Stanley was to do in 1877. So, to bring relief to Livingstone, the RGS organized one expedition to go up the

Congo, and one to take the customary route to Lake Tanganyika, and if necessary beyond, via Bagamoyo and Tabora.

V.L. Cameron, leader of this second expedition, was an officer of the British Royal Navy, who had spent some years on ships tasked with suppressing the East African slave trade. His experience of the region (or at least its ports) made him a good choice for the command of the RGS expedition. He was briefed to place his expeditionary group at Livingstone's disposal, the RGS envisaging that Livingstone might want some personnel to explore to the north of Lake Tanganyika while he investigated to the south. They started from Bagamoyo in late March 1873. In the event, their main purpose was soon undermined. Cameron and his three British companions (one of them, Robert Moffat, a nephew of Livingstone's) were stricken by a particularly vicious strain of malaria, which killed Moffat. They struggled to reach Unyanyembe, where they were then held up for several weeks, trying to regain strength. While there, in October 1873, to Cameron's complete surprise, Livingstone's faithful African companions, Susi and Chuma, were brought in to see him, with the news that the great explorer had died near Lake Bangweolo five months previously, and that they were carrying his body to the coast.

Three weeks later, Cameron had recovered enough to be able to continue travelling. His objective was Ujiji, since Susi had told him that Livingstone had asked him to ensure that a box of papers he had left there should be sent back to England. Susi obviously could not do this himself – he still had to go on to the coast with Livingstone's carefully wrapped body. Cameron set out, now the only British member of the caravan, the two others having decided to go back to the coast with Livingstone's body. But his journey was interrupted by news of the death of a second of these Britons, who had shot himself while almost out of his mind from dysentery and blindness caused by acute malaria. He turned back, to meet up with the sole other survivor, and then resumed his journey. He reached Ujiji in February 1874, his journey lengthened by having to avoid areas affected by the ongoing war with Mirambo, and recovered Livingstone's box, which he sent back to England. He did however retain some of his instruments, which he considered would be useful for the travel he was about to undertake.

Based at Ujiji for a short time, Cameron explored Lake Tanganyika and succeeded in identifying its only outflow, the river Lukuga, which however – as Stanley discovered a few years later – does not flow all the time; its mouth on the Lake silts up, and only when the water level rises high enough does it act like an overflow pipe and allow water to flow down to the Lualaba.

As we have seen (Chapter 2), Cameron intended either to fulfil Livingstone's aims to solve the mystery of the Central African water systems, or to achieve a crossing of the continent; or perhaps a combination of the two. Writing about his journey afterwards, Cameron claimed to have proved the Lualaba to be the Congo and not (as Livingstone believed) the Nile, and also to have opened up the area south and south-west of Nyangwe to commercial exploitation.[26]

From Ujiji, therefore, he crossed Lake Tanganyika, and went on westwards to Nyangwe, a place which impressed him as it had done Tippu Tip:

> Nyangwe has been well chosen by the Zanzibari traders as a permanent settlement on the Lualaba. It takes the form of two villages, each set on an eminence above the river, divided by a small valley watered by little marshy streams and affording admirable rice grounds.[27]

Like Tippu Tip, he distinguishes between the part occupied by the people from the coast, among whom he too includes Mwinyi Dugumbi, and the Swahili and Arab part, where he stayed.

As soon as he arrived, in August 1874, Cameron started enquiries for canoes on which to "float down the river to the sea". But he faced the same obstructiveness as Livingstone had three years before and as Stanley would two years later. In his own account, he adds that in order to obtain the necessary canoes he would have had to countenance the buying and selling of slaves (presumably as crew members), which he was not prepared to do. Tippu Tip arrived (with Tagamoyo) as Cameron was deliberating how to proceed. One of his men told Cameron of a large lake, Sankoru, to the west and a little north, which was fed by the Lualaba after the Lomami had joined it. This caused Cameron to believe that the Lualaba turned west much sooner – i.e. farther south – than actually it does; and, because this man also mentioned that there were traders there with big boats, Cameron's curiosity was aroused. Lake Sankoru does not exist, although Cameron still thought it did when he published his *Across Africa* in 1877, and marked it on the beautiful and detailed map tucked into the end-paper: his informants must have confused it with the Congo itself, which below the confluence with the

Lomami becomes very wide and slow-moving, and could be thought of as a lake.

Cameron was impressed with Tippu Tip, although there is a touch of the sardonic in his description:

> He was a good-looking man and the greatest dandy I had seen amongst the traders. And, notwithstanding his being perfectly black, he was a thorough Arab, for curiously enough the admixture of negro blood had not rendered him less of an Arab in his ideas and manners.[28]

The 'dandy' characterization accords with that of others who commented on his perfectly white *thawb* in circumstances hardly conducive to cleanliness of either person or dress.

Cameron reports that Tippu Tip promised him that, if they were to go together to his headquarters on the Lomami, Cameron could get guides there to take him across the river and on to the lake. Tippu Tip says that Cameron's aim was to get to the west coast preferably by going down the Congo in canoes, but if not, over land. The problem with this account is that, in 1874, Tippu Tip did not know (and nor did Cameron) that the Lualaba was the Congo – we can tell this by the way he behaved with Stanley two years later; so in the *Maisha*, written in the 1890s, he is using knowledge acquired subsequently.

Whatever their expectations, Tippu Tip and Cameron set out for the Lomami headquarters together, in August 1874. Tippu Tip had to cancel a planned visit to the village of Kasongo, a short way up the Lualaba, to do this, to the surprise of his fellow Arabs, who could not understand why he should put himself out for a European. Probably it was because he had more ivory in store on the Lomami, which he needed to bring back to Nyangwe or Kasongo: his meeting up with his kinsmen made him realize that he could bring his ivory to market far more easily via the Ujiji–Tabora route than by the way he had come, round the south of Lake Tanganyika.

From Cameron's account, we can tell that he and Tippu Tip arrived at the latter's camp, near the village of Kasongo Rushie, in September 1874. Kasongo undertook to help Cameron towards achieving his ambition of reaching Lake Sankoru, whose existence seemed to be confirmed by travellers' tales of men in trousers there, and boats with masts. But when they started negotiations for safe passage with the chief on the far (i.e. west) bank of the Lomami, the headman said he had never let through people carrying guns, and was not going to start now. Cameron did not wish to fight his way through, writing piously: "True to my principle that one drop of blood unjustly or unnecessarily spilt would tarnish the greatest geographical triumph, I made my way further south."[29] His book *Across Africa*, in which he writes a similar sentiment,[30] was published in 1877, and he may have been having a sly dig at Stanley, whose fame in England was indeed tarnished by his having been too quick to take African life on what were considered flimsy pretexts of self-defence. Articles criticizing Stanley for this were appearing in England in mid-1877. Realizing that he could not cross the Lomami and travel due west, Cameron accepted Tippu Tip's advice to loop round by the south and south-west.

Tippu Tip mentioned his encounter with Cameron when talking to James Jameson, another member of the Emin Pasha Relief Expedition, in 1888, saying that Cameron had wanted to travel down the Congo but received no support (presumably in the form of supplying canoes) from the Arabs in Nyangwe, and that Cameron had pestered him, Tippu Tip, to take him back to Utetera. His account of this episode in the *Maisha* concentrates only on the guides he supplied, from Urua, who left Cameron some ten days later when the latter met up with some 'Portuguese traders' from the west; by this he probably meant either mixed-race Portuguese-Africans, or people who had come under Portuguese influence from their occupation of points on the west coast, in what is now Angola. Tippu Tip adds that Cameron reached the coast at or near Luanda.[31] This was almost correct. Cameron's loop south-west from Kasongo Rushie's led him to a relatively well-trodden trading route from Katanga to Benguela, on which in November 1875 he completed his remarkable crossing of Africa, the first recorded by a European from east to west. In *Across Africa* he left a full and entertaining account of his journey, with a large number of delightful illustrations based on his own sketches.

Tippu Tip takes control of Kasongo

Tippu Tip stayed in his camp near Kasongo Rushie's for three months, waiting for news in case Cameron should need further help. But, except for the return of his guides, no news came. So he collected his ivory, left a small force under the command of a Mrima coast man to assume authority in his place, and returned once more to Nyangwe. Again, as when he himself had taken the chieftainship, he claimed that Kasongo

Rushie willingly abdicated power during his sojourn in his country.[32]

At Nyangwe, his fellow-Arabs asked him to stay. He was obviously in a position of wealth and strength, and could help protect them against local enmity stirred up by their own actions. He may also have had a reputation for more balanced relations with the Africans: on his recent journey to Kasongo Rushie's, his party had included people from Nyangwe who were shot at, with arrows, by some Africans who recognized them as old enemies. Tippu Tip's appearance had helped calm the situation, and he then sat everyone down and forced the Nyangwe people to pay blood-money for those whom they had previously killed. Just after this incident he also got his lieutenants to discipline some porters who had taken advantage of the stoppage to loot a nearby village.

However, he would not stay. He was determined to see his relative (or possibly half-brother, according to Bontinck[33]) Mohammed bin Sa'id, known as Bwana Nzige, a nickname meaning 'locust', no doubt because of the destruction wreaked by his raids. He was in Kasongo, a town near, though not right beside, the east bank of the Lualaba some 50 km south-east of Nyangwe. Bwana Nzige had been one of the early Arab settlers there, in the late 1860s, and had introduced the cultivation of rice. Livingstone had passed through it in July 1871, on his despondent journey back to Ujiji after the massacre at Nyangwe, calling it 'Kasongo's' after the chief in the area, Kasongo Luhusu. The Arabs also called it 'Kwa Kasongo' (Great Kasongo), but later simply 'Kasongo'. Cameron, transiting in July 1874, remarks that it was a settlement of some size, and that there were fifteen tons of ivory stored there, waiting to be sent to the coast when the roads were clear; this was while the Mirambo war was still going on. The Arab who owned the ivory

> employed 600 Wanyamwezi, all armed with guns. These fellows get little or no pay, but are allowed to loot the country all round in search of subsistence and slaves. Some of the slaves they keep for themselves, giving their employers a sufficient number in return for the powder supplied to enable them to oppress the natives.[34]

A curiously balanced economic system!

On his way to Kasongo, village chiefs asked Tippu Tip to stay and become their chief as he had done with Kasongo Rushie. There was famine in the area, and perhaps they hoped that firm control would bring peace and a return to prosperity. But he was not to be deflected from his aim to reach Kasongo, where he found that law and order had broken down, and that even two hundred of his own slaves had been stolen. He held a council with the leading Arabs there, assumed leadership, and decided that they would have to assert their authority over the local people by force. They fought a campaign of three months, at the end of which the Arabs had reasserted control – which meant establishing a monopoly on ivory and requiring labourers to be supplied for 'necessary work'. The reciprocal benefit was that food became plentiful, to the extent that people from Nyangwe came to buy the surplus, in exchange for ivory, and nicknamed the place 'Bengal', because of the quantity of rice.[35] But it is interesting that in describing the peace brought about by Arab control, Tippu Tip does not mention – either here or on other occasions – other institutions that are often associated with imperial or colonial systems elsewhere, such as courts, taxation or maintenance of utilities. The main objective was simply to settle a place and an area which was already a hub for trading routes west of Lake Tanganyika, and which Tippu Tip could perhaps discern – with his recent experience of Utetera – would grow in importance.

Tippu Tip stayed in Kasongo for eighteen months, consolidating his position and using the time to check on other parts of his commercial empire. To the west, the man he had left in Utetera reported good results: "The people of those parts feared him more than they feared me" (!), and brought in ivory, men, goats, and the bark-weave *viramba*, which was currency then in Kasongo. To the south, he learned that his half-brother Mohammed bin Masoud, who it will be recalled had separated from the caravan in Itawa, had managed to take back to Tabora a large amount of ivory – about 700 *frasila* – some belonging to each of them. To the east he set up a messenger system to Tabora, and made contact with his father there, who was delighted to meet up with his son Mohammed after a long absence. This must all have been after the end of the Mirambo wars in 1875, for the travel in Unyamwezi by messengers and porters to be possible.

His father and brother wrote back urging him to join them, and also reporting that they had despatched some ivory to Taria Topan, the merchant in Zanzibar who had advanced Tippu Tip money to finance the trading journey. After five years of little or no news, the merchant would have been glad to see some return on his capital. But Tippu Tip did not want to go back, not to Tabora, still less to Zanzibar, being still busy trading in the region to the north, down-river from Nyangwe.

At about this time, he was reunited with his friend Saʿid bin Ali al-Hinawi, who had separated from the main caravan at Lake Kasili in order to trade in Katanga (end of Chapter 5), and in the meantime had met up with Mohammed bin Masoud in Tabora. He and Tippu Tip stayed a further four months in Kasongo, when they heard that "some Portuguese had come to attack Utetera", and Tippu Tip decided to go and sort out the problem. From Portuguese sources we can place this incident in about July 1875.

As when he had mentioned 'the Portuguese' previously, this group of traders would have contained both mixed-race men and Africans coming from the south-west, where Portuguese influence remained strong and some stations and settlements continued to be occupied. The traders did commerce mainly in muskets and powder. Tippu Tip wished to maintain the Arab monopoly in the area, and his forces drove out the interlopers. But the expedition was tinged with sadness: he heard news that Saʿid bin Ali had been taken ill, and then that he had died in Kasongo before Tippu Tip could reach him. He was much affected by this loss.

But there was still trading to be done, and he stayed another nine months while his men carried on bringing in ivory. And then there arrived another European, whose collaboration with Tippu Tip materially affected the lives of both men, and also the history of exploration of Central Africa, and of the politics of the region. This was John Rowlands, by now known, and universally celebrated, as Henry Morton Stanley.

Chapter 7

Down the Lualaba: Nile or Congo?

In Chapter 2, we left Stanley as he parted from Livingstone in Unyanyembe and headed for the coast, London and fame. But, when he arrived back in Britain in August 1872, it was not plain sailing. He was mocked for his reported "Dr Livingstone, I presume" greeting; he ran into hostility from the Royal Geographical Society; and he was worried that the truth of his humble (and illegitimate) origins in Wales might emerge and destroy the image of the courageous American that he had constructed over the years. Even his book, *How I Found Livingstone*, produced at great speed and published in November 1872, met mixed reviews – partly because of the stories of his rough treatment of Africans.

The same month, he sailed for the United States to carry out a lucrative lecture tour, and to return to his employment with the *New York Herald*, whose proprietor James Gordon Bennett had commissioned him for the Livingstone expedition. Late in 1873, Bennett sent him to cover a story of a British military campaign in West Africa. It was on his journey back from this, in February 1874, that Stanley learnt of Livingstone's death. He had been coming to realize that his calling was African exploration, a feeling that was now intensified by the belief that he could finish his hero's work and settle finally the unresolved questions about the White Nile and Congo basins. After attending Livingstone's funeral and burial in Westminster Abbey, at which he was one of the pall-bearers, Stanley got together the finance for a new expedition with those aims. The *Daily Telegraph* of London and Bennett's *New York Herald* were co-sponsors.

Stanley arrived in Zanzibar, with the companions he had chosen for the journey, in September 1874. There he gathered supplies for the expedition, which was to be an enormous undertaking. He planned to travel north-west first, to Lake Victoria, and then south-west to Lake Tanganyika, circumnavigating them both to ascertain finally whether either or both had outflowing rivers that might be sources of the Nile or the Congo. By this time some geographers were beginning to suspect that the Lualaba either was the Congo or flowed into it, so Stanley did not know whether – if he followed the Lualaba to the sea – he would emerge in the Mediterranean or the south Atlantic. In the end, the journey would turn out to be 7,000 miles long, a huge distance when we remind ourselves that most of it was done walking, some in canoes, and only a small proportion on animals, since horses and donkeys soon fell prey to the tsetse fly.

The story of Stanley's expedition has been excellently told elsewhere, and what follows is intended to put it into the context of Tippu Tip's collaboration with him. His own account, in *Through the Dark Continent*, is graphically written, although he is prone to exaggeration and even fiction; and it is prudent to read it alongside a modern critical biography.[1] Coupland comments with puzzlement about Stanley's style, so completely different from that of other explorers,

> with its strong colours and racy language, its forced dramatization, [exemplifying] the best sensational journalism of the day .... Was he saying in effect: "I was a workhouse brat ... I am tough and proud of it. Would you expect anything else?"[2]

The party set out from Zanzibar in November 1874, heading for Lake Victoria (also referred to as the Victoria Nyanza) by a direct route, not via Tabora. It was an extremely hard journey; the caravan had to overcome difficulties caused by rains and then drought, and then dangers from attacks by hostile tribespeople armed with poisoned arrows. When he reached the lake, Stanley had lost about sixty of his party of 230. In March–May 1875, he carried out the planned circumnavigation, in a 24-foot (7-metre) boat which they had carried in pieces and assembled on the lake shore. She was named *Lady Alice* after his fiancée, an American heiress called Alice Pike. Eleven crewmen and a guide came with him in the boat, the remainder of the party staying in a camp on the southern shore of the lake.

In terms of discovery, the circumnavigation was successful. Stanley confirmed that the lake was a single expanse of water, not several, and that the one outflow at the north-western corner, discovered by Speke, was likely to be an upper water of the Nile. However, two incidents that occurred on the lake – or rather, the way in which Stanley reported these incidents, one of which ended in his party killing thirty-three Africans – caused revulsion in the British public. As a result, his moral authority was undermined, and his extraordinary achievements on his trans-African journey did not win the recognition that they deserved.

From the north-west corner of Lake Victoria, Stanley went west and north hoping to reach Lake Albert, but in January 1876 was turned back by hostile Bunyoro forces, and so had to surrender his aim of establishing whether or how that lake fitted in to the Nile system. It was later established that the outflow from Lake Victoria which he had seen does indeed supply Lake Albert, at its north-eastern part, and that the White Nile flows out from its north-west corner, not in fact very far away.

Forced to turn south, Stanley headed for Ujiji, spending some time en route in exploring the River Kagera, which flows into the west side of Lake Victoria. He measured it at 84 feet deep at its deepest and 150 yards wide at its mouth, and reckoned that it might be "the real parent of the Victoria Nile".[3] In this he has been shown, though not until early in this century, to be probably right – some uncertainty remaining because of the large number of rivers that feed the lake.

Shortly before reaching Ujiji, Stanley met the famous Mirambo – not without some nervousness, since the warrior chief headed an army of 15,000 men, and had a reputation for having taken tens of thousands of lives. He knew of Mirambo's ferocity and skill in battle first-hand, having narrowly escaped from him in 1871, when he had become involved in one of the early battles in the five-year war between Mirambo and the Tabora Arabs (page 117). The meeting passed off peaceably: not just that, but they went through a ceremony that made them blood brothers.

Stanley arrived in Ujiji in May 1876, having (as he reckoned) travelled 3,500 miles on land and water since leaving Bagamoyo. He spent the next two months mapping Lake Tanganyika. This was important to him since, if the River Lukuga flowed out of the lake (as Cameron had found, but Stanley did not know), and if it joined the Lualaba, and if the Lualaba turned north-east into or past Lake Albert, then Lake Tanganyika would be a more southerly source of the Nile than Lake Victoria. On returning to Ujiji, he was delighted to hear the news that Cameron – whom now he considered a rival in the field of Nile-source discovery – had turned south to Katanga and had not been able to follow the Lualaba downstream. He was becoming personally more and more convinced that by sailing down that river he would end up in the Atlantic. Recovering from a bout of malaria, he set off in August for Manyema, but with some anxiety, since he had lost more men to disease and desertion, and his remaining total of 132 included only just enough trained in the use of his Snider-Enfield breech-loading rifles.

When he and Livingstone had spent several weeks together at Ujiji and on the lake in 1871, Stanley had acquired information about Manyema from the older explorer. He agreed with Livingstone about the natural beauty of the region, but set against this the physical problems presented by sharp grasses and thorns, and the wild exuberant growth of many of the trees and plants. In addition, the villagers sometimes showed their savage side: Livingstone had told him how one of his younger followers had been killed and eaten by cannibals, and on several occasions local chiefs tried to buy support from the passing explorers in their battles or civil wars with neighbouring villages. At the same time, he was moved to pity them to a certain extent, since the ravages of fighting of various kinds – including notably that caused by Arab raids on villages for slaves and ivory – had within a decade significantly depopulated the region.

In October 1876, Stanley reached the Lualaba, at a point 30–40 miles upstream from Nyangwe. It was clearly an emotional moment for him, and not just because of the distance they had had to travel, and the difficulties they had had to overcome, to reach this point. Stanley had hoped to name the river after the explorer he so much admired, and it sometimes appears thus in his writings, as here, though of course the name did not stick:

> Suddenly from the crest of a low ridge saw the confluence of the Luama [the river they had been following from near Lake Tanganyika] with the majestic Lualaba. The former appeared to have a breadth of 400 yards at the mouth; the latter was about 1,400 yards wide, a broad river of a pale grey colour, winding slowly from south by east. We hailed its appearance with shouts of joy …. I likened it even here to the Mississippi, as it appears before the impetuous full-volumed Missouri pours its rusty brown water into it. A secret rapture filled my soul as I gazed upon the majestic stream. The great mystery … was waiting to be solved. For two hundred and twenty miles I had followed one of the sources of the Livingstone to the confluence, and now before me the superb river itself! My task was to follow it to the Ocean.[4]

Tippu Tip helps Stanley down the Lualaba

Marching fast, they reached Mana (or Mwana) Mamba, south-east of Nyangwe, two days later. This was the village of Kasongo Luhusu, which later (known simply as Kasongo) became Tippu Tip's headquarters. They were greeted there by a delegation of Arabs, on whom Tippu Tip made the deepest impression – or so Stanley records in his book. This may have been because, writing after the event, he wanted the reader to have a clear characterization of someone who would be so closely involved with the expedition for the next few months. *Through the Dark Continent* was however published in 1879, well before Stanley had any inkling of the years that he would spend on the Congo, or the close collaboration – later to turn to enmity – which they would have during the Emin Pasha Relief Expedition. He writes:

> He was a tall, black-bearded man, of negroid complexion, in the prime of life, straight, and quick in his movements, a picture of energy and strength. He had a fine intelligent face, with a nervous twitching of the eyes, and gleaming white and perfectly formed teeth. … He reclined vis-à-vis, while a buzz of admiration of his style was perceptible from the onlookers. After regarding him for a few minutes, I came to the conclusion that this Arab was a remarkable man – the most remarkable man I had met among the Arabs, WaSwahili, and half-castes in Africa. He was neat in his person, his clothes were of a spotless white, his fez-cap brand-new, his waist was encircled by a rich dowlé, his dagger was splendid

with silver filigree, and his *tout ensemble* was that of an Arab gentleman in very comfortable circumstances.[5]

Stanley and Tippu Tip discussed the problems of travelling on the Lualaba, or west of it, where one or two Arab expeditions had penetrated. Stanley was naturally interested in knowing why Livingstone and then Cameron had not managed to move an inch downstream from Nyangwe. As he summed it up, after his talk with Tippu Tip and the others present, the reasons had been a lack of canoes, hostility of Africans, reluctance of the Arabs to permit him (Cameron) to proceed "from an officious regard for his safety", and his party's unwillingness to face the reported dangers. (Actually Stanley says "cowardice".) He immediately realized the difficulties he would have in overcoming all these problems, which were just as valid in his own current circumstances as they had been for Livingstone and Cameron.

Stanley went on to discuss the possibility of Tippu Tip accompanying him onwards from Nyangwe, either over the Lualaba and westwards (as Cameron had hoped to do) or down the river, to see if it would turn north-east, to become the Nile, or north-west, to become the Congo or at any rate to flow into the Atlantic. Stanley estimated that a commitment of sixty days would be enough for his purposes. It was during this discussion that Tippu Tip asked one of his men to tell the story of Tagamoyo's expedition that had gone north, then as far west as the pygmies beyond the Lomami (see page 139). It was a graphic and detailed account, taking six pages in Stanley's book, and including such wonders as plantains as long as the pygmy people were tall; but the reports of cannibalism and fiercely hostile tribes cannot have encouraged Stanley. Nevertheless, he continued the parley, and finally reached an agreement – to which Tippu Tip said he was agreeing against the advice of his comrades, because he did not want to disappoint Stanley.

From Stanley's account in *Through the Dark Continent* the reader assumes that, at the time of the discussions and the conclusion of the agreement in Kasongo, he was already fixed in his decision to travel down the river. But Bontinck has shown, through close reading of Stanley's diaries and 'Despatches', that originally he planned to head west, and that while in Nyangwe he changed his plan and decided to follow the river.[6] These details are omitted in *Through the Dark Continent*, presumably because Stanley wanted to portray himself in that book as single-minded of purpose, and prescient of the discovery of the actual course of the Lualaba/Congo.

Stanley spells out the details of the agreement: that Tippu Tip should go with him for sixty marches, each march lasting four hours, that there should be one halt for every two marches, and that the journey should not last more than three months in all. Stanley also committed himself to accompanying Tippu Tip back to Nyangwe after sixty marches, unless they met traders from the "western sea", in which case Stanley would go on with one-third of his force and allow two-thirds to go back with Tippu Tip. This was because Tippu Tip feared that if he returned with only half the number they had started with, he would be vulnerable to attack on the return journey. Finally, there was a payment clause and a break clause: Stanley would pay Tippu Tip MT$5,000 and victualling for 140 men, and, if he decided at any time that the journey could not be continued, he would still pay the MT$5,000.

Tippu Tip had driven Stanley a hard bargain. MT$5,000 was a very large sum of money, about £1,000 in the middle of the 19th century. (The value of silver, and with it the Maria Theresa dollar, dropped sharply towards the end of the century.) It would have been just under one-tenth of the total sum raised for the whole expedition. We may deduce from this that Tippu Tip was genuinely not over-enthusiastic for this assignment, well outside his normal way of doing business. There may have been some advantage in his having an expenses-paid journey to an area north and/or west of Nyangwe which so far he had not visited personally (although other Arabs had been there), and whose possibilities for trading he would certainly have been interested in discovering. But for Stanley it was the only way that he could hope to make progress towards his objective of going where Cameron had not or of solving the Nile mystery and "completing Livingstone's work". Tippu Tip's presence in the capacity, as it were, of joint leader of this sector of the expedition would ensure safe passage through those areas where his power and influence were known and respected, and would double the defensive capability of the party in places where they would come under attack. This increased security was also an encouragement to those free men (Wangwana) in Stanley's party who might have been tempted to desert when learning of the dangers ahead.

Tippu Tip's account of his first meeting with Stanley is briefly given, in two paragraphs of the *Maisha*.[7] In the first, he describes his amazement at Stanley's rifle, which may have been the Snider-Enfield mentioned above, capable of firing ten rounds a minute. He reports that, a couple of days later, Stanley asked him if he would go with him to 'Munza', that is, the country of the chief Munza, about thirty days' march north, and offered him MT$7,000 for the trip; but he gives none of the other details of the contract. (For the difference between the MT$5,000 recorded by Stanley and the MT$7,000 mentioned by Tippu Tip, see below.) Tippu Tip replied that, if he were to accept, it would not be for the sake of the MT$7,000; he had plenty of wealth, witness the ivory stocks he had – but it would be because he wished to oblige Stanley. He asked to sleep on it, and the next day agreed – to the shock of his Arab friends, who thought he was mad. He does not say either why they wanted to dissuade him, or why he went ahead.

Stanley had also used the time overnight, but to consult Frank Pocock, the sole survivor of the three companions who had started from Zanzibar. He offered Pocock the choice between going north to the unknown, or turning south to Katanga, where some exploration had been done and Livingstone had hoped to find the source of the Lualaba, or Lomami, and thus possibly the Nile. (No mention, we

"HEADS FOR THE NORTH AND THE LUALABA; TAILS FOR THE SOUTH AND KATANGA."

Stanley and Pocock toss coins to decide whether to go north or south, as depicted in H.M Stanley's *Through the Dark Continent* (1878).

note, in Stanley's dramatizing of the story, of possible travel to the west of the Lomami.) They tossed coins and drew straws to help them decide; Stanley even includes a lively picture of them doing so. Despite the coins and the straws advising them to turn south, Stanley's determination to go down the river won through, Pocock agreed to support his decision, and the next day the contract was signed with Tippu Tip.

So from Kasongo they set out, on 23 October 1876, on an exciting sector of a dangerous and historic journey. Stanley's party now numbered 146; Tippu Tip had 140 armed with rifles, 60 Wanyamwezi with spears, and 300 others (*pagazi*, women, etc). There was also with him a group of 300 led by one Bwana Shokka, meaning 'Master of the Axe', described by Stanley as a

> confidential man of Tippu Tip's staff, of great strength, tall and gaunt of person ... a man of great tact, and worth a fortune to his master, as he is exceedingly cool, speaks slowly, and by some rare gift conciliates the savages (when not actually attacked on the road), and makes them friends.[8]

At Nyangwe a few days later, Stanley changed the contract. He now decided, finally, to follow the river and answer once and for all the water-system question: was this the upper water of the Congo or the Nile? This added MT$2,000 to the deal – hence Tippu Tip's record of MT$7,000 as against Stanley's original MT$5,000.

Heading north from Nyangwe, the combined expedition initially made good progress, over pleasant meadows and grassland. But then they entered the dark forest of Mitamba, where the going was slow and conditions horrific – damp and dark, with biting insects and hazardous snakes. Most depressing, they could see no end to it. Even the *Maisha*, usually matter of fact in tone, betrays their mood: "the forest where one cannot see the sun .... We were in difficulties because of the mud ... One day's journey took three days."[9] Tippu Tip, under pressure from his exhausted men, asked for a reduction in the number of marches, which Stanley agreed to, provided the fee was cut in proportion, to MT$2,600.

Eventually the expedition branched west, and came to the Lualaba, where they bolted together the launch *Lady Alice*. They commandeered some canoes in order to carry the majority across to the west bank (where the forest was less dense), and to provide extra

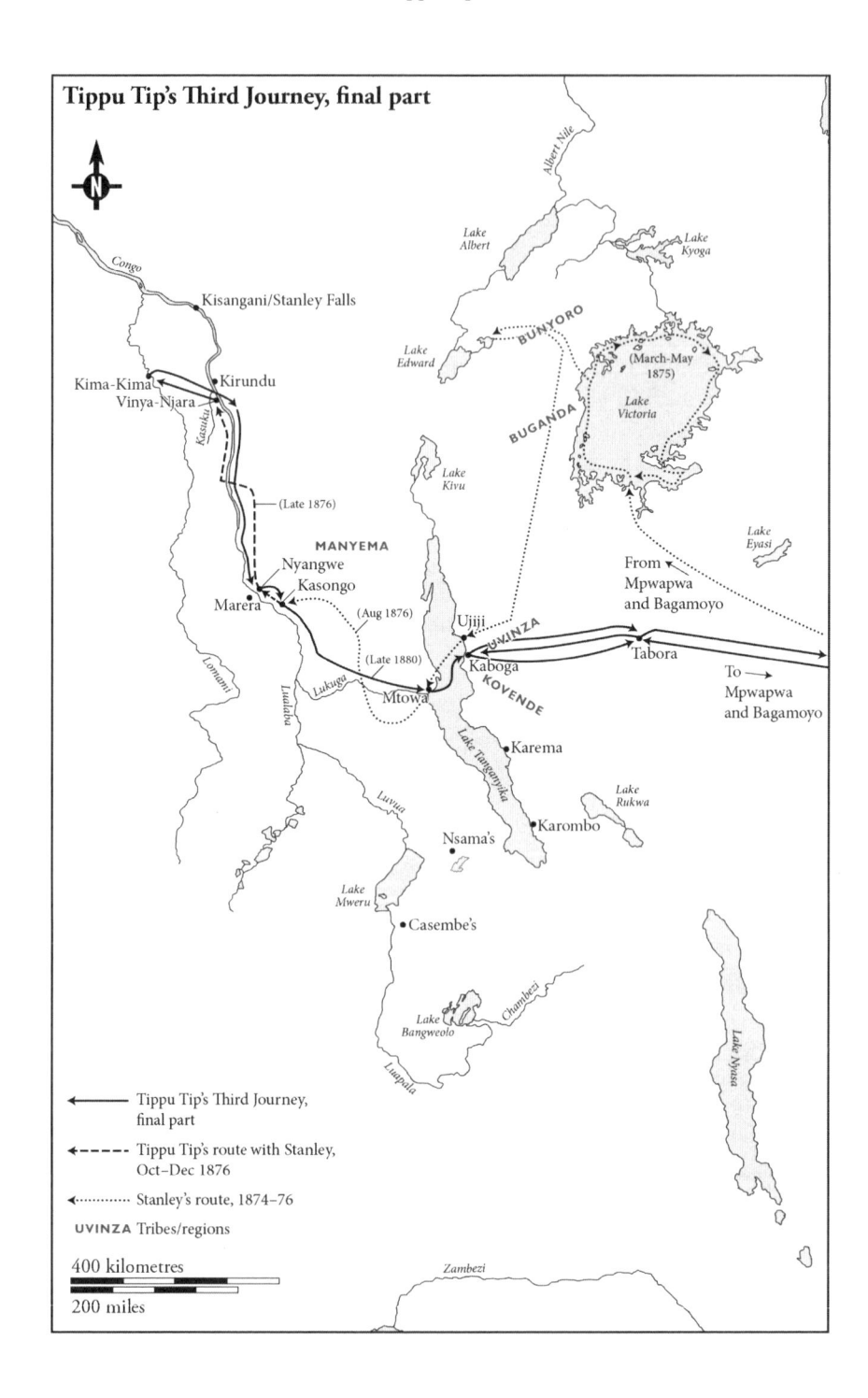

Tippu Tip's Third Journey, final part

river transport for a small number to sail along with the launch. They all then proceeded steadily downriver. Stanley says that Tippu Tip, Frank Pocock and most of the party travelled by land, with himself in the launch; Tippu Tip says that he too was in the launch at least for some of the time. Stanley's narrative mainly treats of the people they came across, the skirmishes with Africans, and the difficulties they found in obtaining food, and occasionally branches out to comment on the natural history, as though he only periodically recalls the likely interest of the members of the Royal Geographical Society and their friends. Tippu Tip's account portrays the local Africans entirely as enemies, describing how actually they seldom saw the villagers, because they would evacuate their homes when the expedition came into sight, leaving him free to organize raids for goats and additional boats. This suggests that the African villagers believed they had something to fear from the strangers, because Arab traders had been in the area before, to take either ivory or slaves. At this period, few Arabs had come this far north and west from Nyangwe, but apparently enough for their reputation to go before them. Another result of this hostility was that rapids on the river, when they came across them, became a double hazard: not only did the expedition risk losing canoes and lives to the occasional fierceness of the current, but, if they drew in to the bank or decided to carry the launch and the canoes on shore past the rapids, they risked attack from the villagers on land. Sometimes the expedition would come under attack from warriors in canoes, but mostly their guns were powerful and accurate enough to see them off. Tippu Tip also comments on the effective system of *mingungu*, war-drums, which conveyed news of the expedition's approach from one village to the next. These were not normal drums: they had no skin, but were wooden, in shape like a flat bell. The drummers used a system of coded 'language' to pass news up and down the river with great speed. Stanley's *Through the Dark Continent* is littered with occasions when he heard what to him became the sinister sound of the drums, since he knew that his boats would be 'welcomed' with spears and arrows as he turned the next corner or came to the next village, news of his progress preceding him. This was made all the more frightening by the frequent reminders – in the form of skulls on display outside the villages – that many of these people were cannibals.[10]

On 18 December 1876, the expedition arrived at a village named Vinya-Njara about four miles upstream of the confluence of the River Kasuku, which joins the Lualaba from the west rather more than half-way between Nyangwe and Kisangani/Stanley Falls. Here they rested for twelve days. And here Stanley decided that he could, or should, let Tippu Tip consider his contract fulfilled and go back to Nyangwe. Curiously, Tippu Tip records that Stanley asked him to make a special effort to steal a dug-out large enough to carry his donkey: it is extraordinary that a donkey could have survived this long on the expedition, or that Stanley had picked one up in a village, and also very odd that he wanted to take it downriver on a boat.[11]

Much more importantly, a big issue then arose over persuading enough of Stanley's men to continue with him. We can understand their hesitation. Behind them lay a difficult but feasible journey to the relative comforts of Nyangwe and Kasongo. In front lay uncertainty and great danger, since there was no reason to believe that the tribes farther downriver would be any less hostile than those they had already encountered, and the river itself had been shown to be treacherous, with whirlpools and rapids in place of the lazy grey calm of the stream at Kasongo. Illness also affected the expedition: not just malaria (though that was bad enough), but also dysentery and smallpox, which struck three of Tippu Tip's favourite concubines.

Stanley's men claimed that their contract, originally for two years, had now expired and, given the circumstances (and the risks), they intended to go back with Tippu Tip to Nyangwe. How exactly Stanley and Tippu Tip managed to combine persuasion and bribery to get them to stay with the expedition is not clear, since the accounts in the *Maisha*

and in Stanley's diaries do not tally. It is likely that Stanley threatened to report Tippu Tip's behaviour to Sultan Barghash if he simply allowed the men to come back to Nyangwe with him, and that Tippu Tip threatened the men with violence if they came, on the grounds that this would create a risk that his property would later be seized by the Sultan. And the men were offered extra rewards, in money and goods. In his published book, Stanley says nothing of all this: he "reproduces" the stirring speech he delivered, which was greeted by "a loud shout of applause", and attributes the change of mind on the part of his men to this fine oratory. He even quotes an extract from Tennyson's *Ulysses*, which he claims a friend pointed out bore close similarities to the sentiments he had presented in the jungle.[12]

It was Christmas Day 1876. They celebrated by holding games, including canoe races, running races, and – "the great event" – a 300-yard race between Tippu Tip and Frank Pocock, in which "the sinews of the muscular Arab carried him to the front at the finish by 15 yards". The prize was a "richly chased silver goblet and cup", a present Stanley had been given before leaving England; we wonder why it had been in his baggage for these thousands of miles! Somehow they persuaded ten young women also to compete for a prize on the same race-course (the village high street), which Stanley relates "convulsed

"Tippu Tip's grand canoes going down the Congo": a typical scene of traditional traffic on the great river, as depicted in *The Illustrated London News* of 21 December 1889.

the hundred assembled to witness the unusual scene". To return the hospitality, Tippu Tip gave the whole company a feast the next day, with rice, roast sheep, and palm-wine. Stanley is at pains to play up the good spirits of all on the expedition – both those going on downriver, and those going back.[13]

By dint of stealing more canoes, Stanley was able to make his entire party water-borne, and he set off with 143 people (including 24 women and children) in *Lady Alice* and 22 canoes. He claims to have paid Tippu Tip a bank draft for MT$2,600, and various goods including a donkey, brass wire, cloth, beads, cowries and ammunition. But the amounts Stanley actually paid, and the promises he made, are open to question, and became later a source of enmity between the two men which was to end in the courts in Zanzibar.

At this point in the *Maisha*, in which he has gone into unusual detail in recounting what the mutinous men had said to him, and his replies, Tippu Tip makes no mention of receiving any money or gifts. He quotes Stanley:

> "I don't know how to pay you back, to recompense you for your kindness, nor how much to give you. But when I get back to Europe I shall receive esteem and much wealth. I'll bring you back a watch worth 1,000 dollars, mounted with diamonds, and as for money I'll bring you a countless sum …"[14]

Years later he told Brode that he had received a draft for money, but had not been told the amount; and that, when he presented it to the Indian merchant and banker Taria Topan on his return to Zanzibar, he had been astonished that it was for between MT$2,000 and MT$3,000, not the MT$7,000 he had expected. He admitted to receiving the donkey; in fact he told Brode there were two, since Stanley had four but could transport only two in the river boats. He did not consider the cloth a gift: this was payment for the food for the men, which was part of the contract.[15]

He did consider that Stanley owed him moral, if not financial, debt, as he explained to the Belgian Jérôme Becker in Tabora in 1882:

> In this critical situation, I came to his aid. Not only did I accompany him, personally, with my soldiers, for long days of marching through almost impenetrable forests, but I also brought him … to

1. Tippu Tip: portrait photograph taken by 'GPA' in Zanzibar, perhaps in the 1870s.

2. Sayyid Sa'id bin Sultan, Ruler of Muscat 1807–1856, and of Zanzibar 1839–56.

3. John Hanning Speke, pictured with his navigating instruments in front of the Ripon Falls, where the Nile flows out of Lake Victoria.

4. *Below, left* Richard Burton, first European to see Lake Tanganyika.

5. *Below* Verney Lovett Cameron, the first European explorer to travel from East to West across Africa.

6. Livingstone in a swamp near Lake Bangweolo, shortly before his death in 1873.

7. Ivory caravan resting, late 19th century.

8. *Left* Ivory carving, East Africa, early 20th century.

9. *Above* Ivory paper knife, India/China, early 20th century.

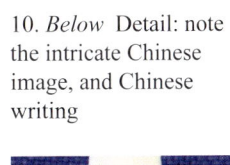

10. *Below* Detail: note the intricate Chinese image, and Chinese writing

11. *Left* Lamp made from ivory tusk, East Africa, early 20th century.

12. Stanley and his caravan struggling through the Makata swamp, on his way to 'find Livingstone'.

13. Ujiji, an early Arab settlement on the shore of Lake Tanganyika.

14. Stanley in a posed London studio portrait, with African 'scenery' background.

15. Ivory tusks displayed in front of a merchant's house in Zanzibar. Note the Christmas greeting above the doorway!

16. The front door of Tippu Tip's house in Zanzibar.

17. The plaque beside Tippu Tip's front door.

18. Detail of wood-carving above Tippu Tip's front door.

19. Ivory collected at a warehouse in Zanzibar, with European, Swahili and Arab figures.

20. Sayyid Barghash with his delegation visiting England, 1875.

21. *Left* John Kirk, doctor then British Agent and Consul in Zanzibar from 1866 until 1886; died 1922.

22. *Below left* Dr James Christie, doctor in Zanzibar and researcher into cholera.

23 *Below* Princess Salme bint Saʿid, later Emily Ruete.

24. *Left* Leopold II, King of the Belgians from 1865 until his death in 1909, owner and ruler of the Congo Free State from about 1878 until 1908.

25. *Above* Herman von Wissmann, German explorer and later administrator in German East Africa.

26. *Right* Jérôme Becker, Belgian explorer and later official in the Congo Free State.

27. Tippu Tip's majlis, or council, probably in Nyangwe.

28. Walter Deane being rescued after escaping from (and setting fire to) the Stanley Falls Station. He failed to save his colleague, Lieutenant Dubois.

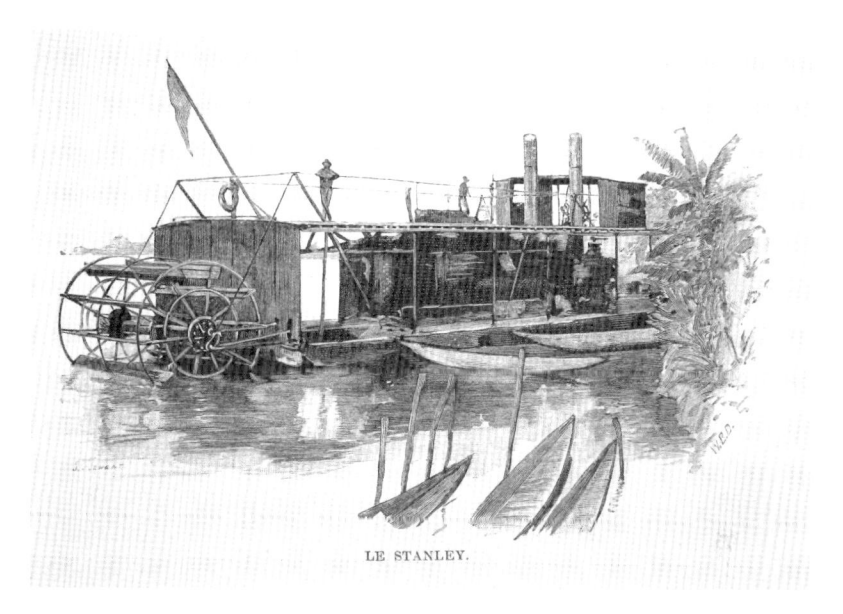

29. The steamboat *Le Stanley*, one of several of this type used by Congo Free State personnel on the upper Congo.

30. Roof-top view of Zanzibar, early 20th century. Bait al-Ajaib, Sultan Barghash's palace, is on the right, and the waterfront visible on the left.

31. Zanzibar waterfront, early 20th century.

32. View from the roof of Bait al-Ajaib, 2012.

the point on the Lualaba ... where he could embark, while on the bank I threatened to kill those of his men who were making as if to desert him.[16]

Three years later, in mid- or late-1879, in Kasongo, Tippu Tip received a letter from Stanley, enclosed with one from Sayyid Barghash. After completing his descent of the River Congo, Stanley had negotiated passage back to Zanzibar for his surviving *pagazi* and companions, and travelled with them, arriving in Zanzibar in November 1877. His letter to Tippu Tip would have reached him in Kasongo in mid-1880. Even though writing or dictating nearly twenty years later, Tippu Tip's fury is apparent, as he repeats himself and writes with heavy sarcasm of Stanley's 'kindness':

> Of the 7,000 dollars of mine (which he'd promised), he offered in his kindness 3,000, for the services I'd rendered him. He also sent a photograph of himself, that was what he sent me. I thought to myself, "When he gets to Europe he'll get this wealth, or send it, or at any rate my money". Yet when he arrived, not even greetings did he send. Of the money he gave me only 3,000 of the 7,000. And the photograph, that was all he gave me.[17]

Brode, recounting the incident, lapses into unrestrained mockery at Stanley's insensitivity: "If there is anything for which the Arab or Swahili has by nature no appreciation, it is photographs ...." The 'gift' still rankled when in 1891 in Zanzibar Tippu Tip was answering questions about the Emin Pasha expedition:

> "All the great kindnesses that I showed him [Stanley] were not enough for him – by way of thanks he wants to drown me now as well. I had a specimen in the promises that he made me: 'When I get to Europe I do not know what I shall not give you, for I shall obtain boundless wealth and great influence.' And he sent me his photograph! And when we met again he presented me at Cape Town with a dog. ... It was a wretched little dog."[18]

There is of course an element of over-reaction in this. While it is true that, without Tippu Tip's help and support, Stanley might well have experienced at Nyangwe the failure of Livingstone or the diversion of Cameron, Tippu Tip may well be allowing his memory and judgement to be clouded by his resentment at the fame and fortune which Stanley achieved as a result of his support and assistance. And was his memory accurate? Stanley is specific in *Through the Dark Continent*, based on diaries that he kept at the time, that the MT$7,000 contract was amended to MT$2,600 when Tippu Tip cut his number of days' marches by more than half; and, as we have noted, he records in detail the gifts he gave him when they separated at Vinya-Njara. Why was Tippu Tip so angry? After all, he was quite proud of his collection of photographs: in 1895, he showed the German explorer Oskar Lenz his "collection of photographs of world-famous European travellers, all with signatures, who had all requested and received his help" and he did the same when Richard Meinertzhagen visited him a few years later.[19] Farrant suggests that the MT$3,000 mentioned here had been directly paid into his account with Taria Topan in Zanzibar, and was in addition to the draft for MT$2,600 which Stanley had given him in Vinya-Njara; but evidence for this is lacking. Perhaps his account was coloured not only by resentment, but also by his financial losses caused by his dispute with Stanley over the Emin Pasha Expedition. which ended in a costly lawsuit between them. At the same time, in a culture where friendship and collaboration is sealed by gifts, Stanley's apparent failure to deal generously with Tippu Tip seems egregious.

Tippu Tip undertook to wait at Vinya-Njara in case Stanley found the journey impossible and was forced to turn back. In the event, Stanley overcame the very considerable obstacles, human and natural, presented to him by and on the river. A determining moment came not much more than a month after he separated from Tippu Tip, in early February 1877 when, soon after getting past the long series of cataracts later known as Stanley Falls, he observed the river definitively turning west and first heard it referred to as the 'Congo'. Surviving many attacks from hostile tribes, and other dangerous parts of the river (in one of which Frank Pocock, his last surviving British companion, was drowned), Stanley eventually arrived at the mouth of the Congo in August 1877. He had completed probably the longest and most significant African journey ever accomplished.

Tippu Tip pioneers to the northern Lomami

Back at Vinya-Njara, Tippu Tip gathered his forces and set out, not back to Nyangwe, but west and a little north to Kima-Kima on the

River Lomami. He had with him 4 *frasila* of copper that he had bought for one *frasila* of beads in Kasongo, and on the Lomami, having turned some of the copper into arm bangles, he was able to buy 200 *frasila* of ivory with it. Even allowing for the distance that the beads and the copper had been brought (from the coast and from Katanga respectively), this represented an immense profit. Brode calculates that Tippu Tip had earned MT$10,000 from an investment of MT$3! – but he takes no account of transportation costs, which were not negligible. The people in that area had no appreciation of the value of ivory. They did hunt elephants, but for their meat, and they used the tusks for simple things like fencing, or for making flutes or pestles and mortars. To illustrate the easy way in which he could buy tusks cheaply, Tippu Tip found a couple of old hoes, fitted new handles to them, and bought a tusk with each one.

He spent a month there, and then returned to Nyangwe, but had a difficult time on the journey, fighting every day. It is interesting that he had not become involved in any violence with the people in Kima-Kima, so we must assume that slave raiders had not yet come their way. The Wagenia tribespeople, who had caused them trouble on the way out, fought them using arrows tipped with a particularly virulent poison, right up to a few days' journey from Nyangwe. After just one night there, he went upriver to Kasongo, travelling in a boat overnight, and then walked for over two hours from the river to the town. He records "great rejoicing at my arrival", we may assume from friends who had advised him against the escapade with Stanley. In addition, not only had Tippu Tip brought a great deal of ivory from his journey, but his own agents in Utetera and other traders had also accumulated significant quantities.[20]

Three quiet years in Kasongo and news from Zanizibar

There followed another relatively stable period in Tippu Tip's life. He stayed based in Kasongo for about three years, continuing his trading. This would have been from mid-1877 until mid-1880. Although the *Maisha* does not mention it, we know that the travelling routes to the coast were open, so that he and others could send back some of the ivory they had collected, and receive more supplies of barter goods of cloth and beads. In May 1878, the missionary Arthur Dodgshun saw a huge caravan of about 2,400 *pagazi* carrying Tippu Tip's ivory to the coast (see pages 63–4).

Although Kasongo was his base, he did not stay put there continuously, but moved about the region, checking on his agents in different places. His kinsman Mohammed bin Saʻid (Bwana Nzige) asked if he could go and represent Tippu Tip in Marera, where Chief Rusuna lived. Tippu Tip agreed, and gave him letters of authority to use with the local people, as well as instructions to bring in more ivory. Bwana Nzige was happy with his assignment, finding both Marera and Ibari (Chief Kasongo Rushie's village) peaceful, "because the people of this area were an amiable lot, so were their women, and the country was fertile".[21]

Probably in mid-1880, messengers arrived from Zanzibar with presents and letters for Tippu Tip. Sultan Barghash sent him a repeater rifle, somewhat to Tippu Tip's surprise, since they did not know each other personally, and the merchant and banker Taria Topan sent him a shotgun and "clothes for wearing" – presumably to distinguish them from cloth for trading. Both of them also sent letters. Barghash urged him to return to Zanzibar, on the grounds that his loan from Taria Topan was for two years, and he had now been away for twelve. Barghash was exaggerating: Tippu Tip had left Zanzibar in early 1870, and the letter would have been written in 1879. Nevertheless, the debt was long overdue. It is not recorded what was in Taria Topan's own letter. Both of them would have known of Tippu Tip's wealth and status from the arrival of caravans such as that seen by Dodgshun.

Tippu Tip returns to Tabora

Tippu Tip was not too concerned about the appeal to return to Zanzibar. He stayed in Kasongo another year before beginning to plan the journey back to the coast. This was a large-scale logistical operation. The top priority was the need to arrange the carriage of what he described first as "a large quantity of ivory", and then – two sentences later – as "immense". Then he had also to make sure that his interests in the area were protected during his absence. He left agents in Marera and Ibari, where Bwana Nzige had been, and in Kasongo.[22]

To ensure proper supervision of the caravan, Tippu Tip went ahead on a four-hour march with one group of *pagazi*, organized a place for overnight storage of the ivory, sent the men back to collect more, while he slept, and then supervised the arrival of the remaining tusks. Day after day he repeated the process. But because the caravan made only the distance of one four-hour march per day, and no doubt also because of the sheer numbers of *pagazi* needed to carry the "immense quantity", the whole process was very slow. The journey from Kasongo to Mtowa, on the west bank of Lake Tanganyika, which normally took a smaller caravan one month, took them six.

At Mtowa, Tippu Tip met two Europeans, a missionary and a doctor. These may have been Mr Griffiths and Mr Hutley of the London Missionary Society, as Whiteley suggests in a footnote to the *Maisha*, but it is more likely to have been Griffiths and a Dr Palmer, who arrived at the missionary station at Mtowa (which they named 'Plymouth Rock') in October 1880, and left in June 1881. This therefore enables us to date Tippu Tip's arrival at Mtowa within these seven months. He claims to have been accorded great respect by them, and decided to stay on there for a while. Being concerned about safety on the road, he sent Bwana Nzige on ahead to reconnoitre the route, asking him to check for news of Mirambo. The war with Mirambo was in fact by now clearly finished, but his influence and capacity for raiding was widespread over the area between and to the north of Ujiji and Tabora, and Tippu Tip needed to minimize his risks. The account in the *Maisha* hints (though not clearly) that he was still considering taking the caravan by the much longer, but safer, route round the south end of Lake Tanganyika. Bwana Nzige reported back that the route to Tabora was dangerous, but that boats would come to ferry the party across the lake. Tippu Tip decided that he would leave the bulk of the ivory at Mtowa, on the west side of the lake, in the care of Bwana Nzige, take to Tabora a small force and just the small tusks, and return for the rest with new supplies of gunpowder and provisions.[23]

He crossed the lake, arriving at a harbour named Kaboga south of Ujiji, and decided to leave the ivory there and make a quick trip to see his kinsmen in Ujiji – which he did by boat, sailing all night. Renault places this in February 1881.[24] The head of the Arab community there was a Swahili, Mwinyi Khayri bin Mwinyi Mkuu al-Ghassani, whom he wanted to meet. This trader had impressed Stanley with his fortune estimated at MT$18,000, made up of items that included 120 slaves, 80 guns, 80 *frasila* of ivory, nine canoes, plus land, cattle, goats, beads, brass and iron wire, and so forth. But Tippu Tip also met here, for only the second time, Mohammed bin Khalfan al-Barwani, better known by his nickname Rumaliza (or Rumaliza, or Lumanisha), who also enjoyed a prominent position among the Arabs and Swahili in Ujiji, and was in a sense a rival of Mwinyi Khayri. Tippu Tip later developed a successful partnership with him, but the two finally fell out during his retirement in Zanzibar. Rumaliza was about ten years younger than Tippu Tip, and came from a prominent Omani family which had been established in the region since about 1840. The British missionary Hore describes him as "polite and hospitable ... an educated and liberal-minded man, free from many of the prejudices of the half-castes and others who have not seen the world".[25] Tippu Tip had business contacts and friends in common with him, and had actually borrowed from him, for his trading expeditions, before taking loans from Taria Topan.

Tippu Tip was still worried about which road to take to Tabora – the shorter but more dangerous route through Uvinza, or the loop round to the south through Kovende. He brought up all his men, and the ivory, from Kaboga, and set out from Ujiji. He also took into his caravan an Arab named Salim bin Abdallah al-Marhubi, who was operating as a kind of executor for Sa'id bin Ali, Tippu Tip's friend who had died in Kasongo (page 147 above). Salim was collecting ivory belonging to Sa'id bin Ali, which was needed in order pay off those who had given him advances for trading. Some of Sa'id's ivory was stored in Mtowa, and Tippu Tip had it transported to Ujiji. He and Salim sent the ivory of both of them on ahead to a village called Ruanda (no connection with the kingdom, now a country, of that name, to the north), about six hours' march away. But here trouble struck: two of Salim's men had been killed in a skirmish, for no apparent reason, he claimed. He said that their Unyamwezi *pagazi* had been "collecting wood", a phrase that Wilkinson interprets as "pillaging the local villagers' fields"![26] Whatever it was, this event had led to further fighting on a larger scale, in which Salim himself had been attacked and lost clothes and personal effects. The Arabs and their men had suffered no further casualties, but they had killed twenty-six or twenty-seven of their enemies (presumably Wavinza, but the account in the *Maisha* is confused at this point), and burnt fifteen villages.[27]

Despite this local hostility, Tippu Tip decided that this was the better route to use for bringing the rest of his ivory that was still in Mtowa to Tabora and then to the coast. The Arabs had at any rate had the better of the fighting, and presumably were confident that they could suppress further opposition. He established a base in Ruanda, and stayed there for six months (approximately until mid-1881) while all the ivory was brought over the lake, and on from Ujiji to Tabora.

While he was in Ruanda, a friend (Sa'id bin Habib al-Afifi) brought Tippu Tip's son Sayf (or Sefu, or Sef) up from the coast. The boy had been in school in Zanzibar, but father and son had not seen each other for eleven years at least. Tippu Tip records, "We were very glad to see them". He does not mention Sayf's age, but the Belgian official Jérôme Becker met both of them in Tabora a few months later, and describes Sayf as being about twenty, and as dark as his father, being the son of an African wife.[28] He married a daughter of Bwana Nzige. The party contained other Arabs, and also a number of *pagazi*, of which Tippu Tip was also glad, since his numbers were depleted.

For reasons that are not clear, he now decided to send half his ivory back to Ujiji, in the care of Bwana Nzige, where it was to be stored in Rumaliza's house. The other half he took himself, but brought it to Tabora with some difficulty: the Chief of Uvinza first demanded an exorbitant toll, which Tippu Tip paid, and secondly stole 150 slaves from the caravan. Tippu Tip was inclined to take his revenge by fighting, but was dissuaded by his Arab companion, Sa'id bin Sultan al-Ghaythi, who pointed out that, with their large quantity of ivory, they had a lot to lose, and their men were young and inexperienced. By comparing Wissmann's account of his meeting with Tippu Tip in September 1882, we can tell that this tough journey was made in about February 1882.[29]

A further family reunion took place when he reached Tabora. His father was there, in their village of Ituru, as were his mother (making a rare appearance in the *Maisha*) and his half-brother Mohammed Masoud al-Wardi, as well as other family members. "There were celebrations for a fortnight; cattle were slaughtered and food was prepared. This was a time of great rejoicing."[30]

Presumably anticipating a return to Zanzibar before long, Tippu Tip decided to mend fences with Sayyid Barghash and Taria Topan, his Sultan and his creditor, by sending them messages. He took the opportunity to request fresh provision of gunpowder from Barghash, which he records as being "extremely scarce" at the time; this was because Barghash had kept the monopoly of gunpowder for himself, and had in any case restricted supply into the interior to put pressure on Mirambo, who was still causing problems for the Arabs, despite the settlement made in 1875. Indeed, in October 1881 Mirambo subdued the village of a chief who had been his ally, putting him now in control of a significant area that included the route going south-west from Tabora to the southern end of Lake Tanganyika, and also the route from Tabora to Ujiji.

Barghash responded positively to Tippu Tip's request, passing

Sayyid Barghash bin Sa'id, Sultan of Zanzibar

Sayyid Barghash was born within a few years of Tippu Tip (accounts vary between 1834 and 1837), the son of the great Sayyid Sa'id bin Sultan and one of his Ethiopian slave-concubines. He was travelling with his father when Sa'id died at sea in 1856, on his return from a visit to Muscat, and tried then to seize power. But he was unsuccessful and, after a few years of disputes between Sa'id's sons, the Sultanate was split under British arbitration, Thuwayni and Mājid becoming Sultans in Muscat and Zanzibar respectively. Barghash tried again to displace Mājid, but the British intervened, fearing a breakdown of law and order, and Barghash was exiled to Bombay in 1859.

After giving a pledge of loyalty to Mājid, he was allowed to return to Zanzibar in 1861, and lived there peaceably until he succeeded to the throne on Mājid's death in 1870. Sultan for eighteen years, his was not an easy reign. He was under constant pressure from the British to end the slave trade – indeed even while Mājid was on his death-bed, Barghash had been approached by Churchill, the British Agent, and been coerced into giving an undertaking to reduce and then eliminate the traffic in slaves from the mainland. Under pressure from his advisers, he reneged on it soon after his accession.

In April 1872, Zanzibar was struck by a cyclone of extraordinary violence: perhaps one-third of the clove plantations, and all the ships and dhows in the harbour, were destroyed. This disaster was uppermost in his mind when in 1873 he rejected the attempt by Sir Bartle Frere to 'negotiate' an end to the slave trade once and for all – Barghash thought the broken economy could not tolerate this further disruption. He had to give way a few months later, but only under threat of a British naval blockade. He conceded the treaty to the Consul John Kirk, who became his confidant and trusted adviser in the following fifteen years.

He was rewarded for his compliance by being invited to England in 1875. He and his delegation were warmly received, including by Queen Victoria in Windsor, and they visited Birmingham, Liverpool, Manchester and Brighton. They then spent ten days in Paris, and returned to Zanzibar via Egypt.

Through the 1880s, as explained in the main narrative, Barghash watched as his power on the mainland was eroded as the European powers encroached during the 'Scramble for Africa'. The French–German–British Delimitation Commission in 1886 awarded him sovereignty over just the islands of Zanzibar and Pemba and a ten-mile-deep strip along the coast from Cape Delgado to just north of Mombasa. He did not live to see the conclusion of the Anglo-German Agreement of 1890 and the declaration of the British protectorate over Zanzibar.

Barghash inherited a sultanate encumbered by debt, but managed Zanzibar into a state of fair prosperity. He oversaw a number of public works, and built as his palace the magnificent Bayt al-Ajā'ib ('House of Wonders'), still a central tourist attraction on the Zanzibar waterfront. But his personal life cannot have been happy. He suffered from elephantiasis, a horrible affliction of the lymphatic system which causes huge swelling in the lower limbs. Stanley commented on it when he met Barghash in 1871. With his unerring eye for the grotesque, Burton remarked that the disease affected up to 20 percent of the population, and that in afflicted male patients "the scrotum will often reach the knees". (Burton (1872 i: 185) It is not known if Barghash suffered as severely as that – possibly not, since he did have children. But his sons were considered too young at his death to take over the Sultanate, and when he died in 1888, in his early fifties, he was succeeded by his brother, Khalifa.

2,000 lb (907 kg) of powder to Taria Topan for onward transmission, and not demanding payment. Tippu Tip was now able to arm his men with enough guns and ammunition.

Tippu Tip spurns a Belgian overture

During this period in Tabora, Tippu Tip first encountered a new element – which variously presented itself as a threat and an opportunity – in his business affairs: this was the more active involvement of European powers in the region. He was of course accustomed to the presence of the British in Zanzibar, and the steady level of trade conducted by foreign traders such as the Americans and French; and he had met some of the European missionaries who had begun establishing stations in his area. But in the 1870s and 1880s the European political and economic interest intensified, in what became known as the Scramble for Africa. In particular, in the central belt of the Congo basin and Lake Tanganyika, Belgium – or rather, King Leopold II of the Belgians – started the process of invasion and colonization which would deeply (and adversely) affect the lives of hundreds of thousands of Africans, and lead to confrontation with Arab interests in Central Africa and to the foundation of the Belgian Congo.

We shall look at these developments in more detail in the next chapter. In Tabora in 1881–82, Tippu Tip encountered Belgians for the first time. As part of the move to explore and 'develop' the upper Congo, the Association Internationale Africaine set up by King Leopold had decided to send a mission to establish a 'scientific post' on the eastern shore of Lake Tanganyika, while another expedition sought to link up with it from the west.

A four-man Belgian party arrived in Zanzibar in December 1877. After overcoming the usual difficulties of disease, deserting *pagazi*, and extortionate *hongo*, the one surviving member, a Lt Ernest Cambier, reached Tabora in late 1878, and in August 1879 he set up his post at Karema on the lake, about 150 miles south of Ujiji. Further Belgian expeditions to Karema, via Tabora, followed, until in 1884 a party arrived in Zanzibar but was ordered home; Leopold had decided that his efforts should be concentrated on imperialism from the west coast and no longer from the east.

The first Belgians of whom we need to take note, because of their activities east of Lake Tanganyika, were Lt Jérôme Becker and Capt. Émile Storms. Becker arrived in Tabora in mid-1882, on his second visit to the region; he had first come in 1881, on his way to bring relief to Lt Cambier in Karema. His book graphically describes his journeys, and includes magnificent appendices explaining how to organize an expedition, listing supplies required for a caravan of 200 *pagazi* and 100 armed men. His recommended provisions for a year included 50 bottles of old Bordeaux wine, 25 half-bottles of champagne, 12 of madeira and 12 of cognac – plus of course medical supplies and scientific instruments.[31] The juxtaposition of luxuries in the provisions and the extreme hardship undergone while travelling is intriguing to the modern reader.

Becker had a house in Tabora, from where he went to call on Tippu Tip in September 1881. He records a conversation in which Tippu Tip revealed that he was curious about the Belgian intervention on the Congo, and how Leopold managed to finance it.[32] It was in Becker's Tabora house that his colleague Storms met Tippu Tip in August 1882, pursuing a particular Belgian agenda. (Becker was absent in Fort Karema, after the death there of the commander Ramaeckers.) By now, the success of Stanley's journey down the Lualaba/Congo was well known, and Leopold was working for the development of the Congo as a trading route, in the hope that the ivory wealth of Manyema and surrounding areas could be brought to market that way instead of on the heads of *pagazi* walking hundreds of miles via Ujiji and Tabora. Storms asked Tippu Tip if he would go back to Manyema, help the Belgians build a station on the upper Congo or Lualaba, and pursue that option of exporting downriver, offering him an equal share of the profits of the operation, plus arms and ammunition which would be useful to him in maintaining his regional power and his trading operations.

Tippu Tip demurred. In the *Maisha* he explains his reluctance in terms of his loyalty to Sayyid Barghash, adding that both he and the territory of Manyema were under the authority of the Sultan. Storms responded (he claims) that he need have no such qualms, since he – Tippu Tip – had full autonomous authority in Manyema.[33] Perhaps an innate conservatism influenced Tippu Tip: the routes from the coast to Lake Tanganyika and beyond, though prone to interruption by warlords like Mirambo and obstructive tribes such as the Wavinza, were well known and mostly reliable, whereas the risks of disaster from the poisoned arrows of the villagers on the Congo were high. He was inclined to leave the Belgian offer on one side.

With Wissmann to the coast

Before finally collecting together the various stocks of ivory needing transportation to the coast (his own, Bwana Nzige's, Salim bin Abdullah's, and perhaps others), Tippu Tip decided to subdue the Wavinza, whose trouble-making could block the way of caravans between Tabora and Ujiji. It turned out to be more difficult than he had expected. He needed to go via a chief named Mgombera, and the route there was through country where water was scarce and access to wells limited, and where Mirambo was still active and hostile to the Arabs of Tabora. However, Mirambo sent a message saying he had no quarrel with Tippu Tip, whose forces were then free to attack the Wavinza. Subduing them took time, and cost lives: their villages were protected by extremely effective stockades, and Tippu Tip's small army had to advance under a kind of siege-engine improvised from inverted dugout canoes to defend themselves from gunfire, and then build siege-towers to shoot over the stockade walls. Eventually the campaign was successful, and the chief replaced by one more compliant. It was a relatively long and expensive campaign for the sake of one village, but it secured free passage along a crucial part of the route to Ujiji, and in addition allowed access by traders to the salt deposits in a nearby river valley. This far from the sea, salt – a vital preservative for meat – was a valuable commodity.[34]

Herbert Ward, the British member of the Emin Pasha Relief Expedition who collected a number of stories from Tippu Tip and his companion Salim bin Mohammed, recorded that this small war in Uvinza was actually the result of a struggle between two brothers for the chieftainship. Tippu Tip (says Ward) became involved when one of the brothers, Katarambura, bribed him with a hoard of ivory greater than what he could have gained by raiding the villages, and the incumbent chief, Kasanura, under attack from his rebellious sibling, who was now allied with Tippu Tip, took refuge with Mirambo and sought his help. This appeal fell on deaf ears, since – as we have seen – Mirambo did not want to find himself opposed to Tippu Tip. Ward goes on to claim that Mirambo did however agree to mediate, bringing about a solution under which Kasanura was allowed back into his territory, but his brother Katarambura was installed as Chief. Kasanura tried to buy his way back to the chieftainship by offering Tippu Tip presents of ivory and his sisters – gifts which Tippu Tip apparently accepted, but without involving himself further in the fraternal dispute. In any case, he probably preferred to have as Chief the compliant Katarambura, who owed him a debt of gratitude.[35]

Tippu Tip now had easy passage to Ujiji, in order to make up the caravan and begin the journey back to Tabora and on to the coast. He did not in fact have as much ivory to take as he had expected, since Bwana Nzige had already arranged for a quantity to be carried to the coast. Mohammed bin Khalfan, Rumaliza, asked if he could join the caravan, since he had collected only 40 *frasila* of ivory and was short of provisions and barter goods. A few years later, in 1883, when Tippu Tip was preparing his next journey into the interior, he advanced money to Rumaliza, who was still unable to get credit in Zanzibar. This left Rumaliza morally as well as financially in debt to Tippu Tip.

Arriving at Tabora, he went to see his step-mother, Nyaso, the daughter of Chief Fundi Kira. While in Ujiji a short time before, he had heard that his father had died, and in the *Maisha* he recalls a request by his father to look after Nyaso "with both eyes". Mohammed bin Juma had reminded his son of the internal rivalries in the family of Mkasiwa, the former rival to Fundi Kira for the chieftainship; presumably these rivalries could put Fundi Kira's daughter in peril. Tippu Tip undertook to protect her.[36]

One more Mirambo episode occurred before the caravan could depart. Mirambo sent an invitation for either Tippu Tip or his son Sayf to visit him. Tippu Tip decided to send Sayf, with other Arabs who were going on to Ujiji and Manyema. Sayf, able to give Mirambo presents from the store of goods being transported to the west, was well received by Mirambo. A group of Tabora Arabs, angry at Tippu Tip's having reached a settlement – and indeed established close and friendly relations – with someone with whom they had been fighting for so long, plotted to trick Mirambo into killing Sayf and his accompanying party. Mirambo was not taken in, and in fact sent Sayf back loaded with gifts and with declarations of friendship for his father.

Just as Tippu Tip was about to leave for the coast, the German explorer Hermann von Wissmann arrived in Tabora. He was making the first of his two crossings of Africa, having started from Luanda and travelled due east until he struck up north and north-east to the River Kasai and then the Lomami. From there he had joined the relatively well-trodden route via Nyangwe, Kasongo, Mtowa and Ujiji, and he arrived in Tabora in September 1882. He was in fact with Mirambo when Sayf called on him, and suggests that Tippu Tip was really the suppliant in the establishment of friendly relations, for the familiar reason of wanting to ensure free passage of caravans through that part of Unyanyembe.[37] The interest was probably mutual, since Mirambo would not have wanted continued harassment from the Arabs, and particularly from one as well-armed and ruthless as Tippu Tip. In addition, he also had stores of ivory which he needed to bring to market on the coast along routes frequented by the Arab traders, and ultimately in territory under the control of the Sultan of Zanzibar.

In Tabora, Wissmann stayed at the Roman Catholic Mission House, and noted that they paid less attention to efforts at conversion than their Protestant colleagues, and more to education in European civilization, for example agriculture and improved cattle-breeding. He gives a pen-picture of Tippu Tip that tallies with those of others, although he is not correct in his father's lineage:

> about forty-five years old, with completely black skin-colour, although his father was a pure Arab. A bit sturdy, but very lively in his movements, agile, polite, decisive in his gestures, but like his son has something watchful about him, and seems to enjoy joking and mockery.[38]

Wissmann was also short of provisions and barter goods, but Tippu Tip agreed to take him on to the caravan at his own expense, with a rather uncertain promise to repay on reaching the coast. No doubt glad of the added protection he received by being part of the caravan, Wissmann travelled with the Arabs through Ugogo to Mpwapwa, where they ran into difficulties caused by an outbreak of smallpox in the caravan, and extortionate demands for *hongo*. Getting away, their ways parted; Wissmann took more supplies from Tippu Tip, and headed for Saadani on the coast, where he arrived on 15 November 1882. He made subsequent journeys in the Congo, in the employment of King Leopold, and in the late 1880s became involved in the German takeover of territory in East Africa, where he was appointed Governor in 1895.

After parting from Wissmann, Tippu Tip went to Bagamoyo, a short distance south. He left his ivory and other goods with Taria Topan's agent there, and took passage to Zanzibar, arriving on the 9th day of Muharram 1300, as he records it, equivalent to 20 November 1882.[39]

CHAPTER 8

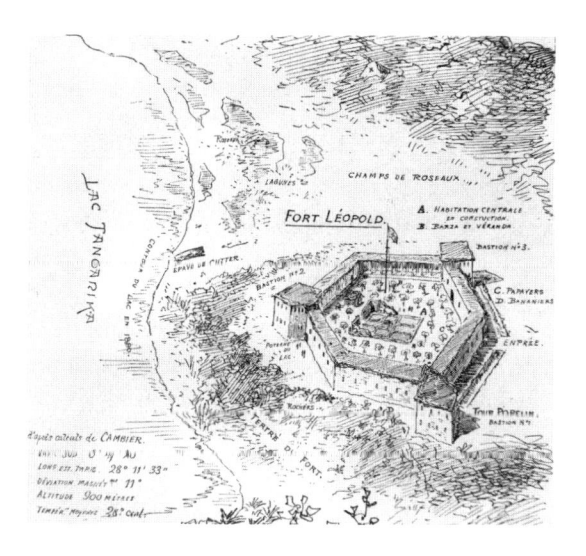

Tippu Tip and the Scramble

WHEN TIPPU TIP ARRIVED back in Zanzibar in late 1882, he found that a great deal had changed in external politics, in ways that would deeply affect the Arab community in East Africa, himself included. For a variety of reasons, and with a variety of motives, European governments were intensifying their involvement. British and German interest weighed heavy in the territory of the Sultan of Zanzibar and his areas of influence on the mainland. But it was Leopold II, King of the Belgians, whose ambitions and achievements — for good or ill — most directly concerned Tippu Tip.

Tippu Tip rejects the governorship of Tabora

Tippu Tip knew that change was in the air from his meeting with the Belgian Émile Storms in Tabora earlier in the year. It may have been the first time he had heard of the relatively new European kingdom of Belgium, which had become independent, after a rebellion against the Dutch, only in 1830, a few years before his birth. Now, in November

1882, the very evening of the day he arrived back in Zanzibar, Tippu Tip went immediately to see his banker and creditor, Taria Topan. (There are internal inconsistencies in the chronology of these meetings, but this seems the most likely reconstruction.) Here he learned that Sultan Barghash wanted to appoint him Governor (*wali*) of Tabora, in place of Abdullah bin Nasibu, whom he had recalled – a proposal that Tippu Tip greeted with derision: why should he want to be a *wali* when he was 'great chief' of Manyema?[1] There were two points of comparison, or contrast. First, the position of *wali* of a place like Tabora meant little more than being the Sultan's representative, with some obligations (such as collecting taxes, and providing armed men to protect the Arab community) and with virtually no compensatory advantages. Second, Tabora and its surrounding district of Unyanyembe was under the influence of the Sultan of Zanzibar, but not in any sense under his rule or control. So Tippu Tip's position there would be modest in terms of status or power, when compared with the power and prestige he enjoyed in Manyema. And this was to say nothing of the possibilities for further expansion of trade which he could reasonably expect in the barely explored areas north and west of Nyangwe.

That same evening, after seeing Taria Topan, he was visited by an Arab named Mohammed bin Masoud al-Mugheri, who does not appear elsewhere in his narrative, with the same message about the offer of the governorate.

Next morning he went again to Taria Topan. It is at this point in the *Maisha* that he records his meeting in Tabora with Émile Storms the previous August, perhaps because he expected soon to receive the formal offer from Barghash, and he was mentally comparing existence as *wali* in Tabora with the profits he could make in Manyema, either by continuing to trade to and from the east coast, or in some form of collaboration with the Belgians on the Congo.[2]

It was now time to see Sultan Barghash, whom he was meeting for the first time. Tippu Tip brought him up to date about events on the mainland, filling out information he had given him in letters sent on ahead about a month previously from Mpwapwa. Then he told him about the proposition put to him by Storms. He had of course clearly turned it down; but the fact of his telling Barghash (whom he knew would be violently opposed to Arabs trading westwards rather than through Zanzibar), rather than keeping it to himself, makes it certain that he was genuinely not interested, and indeed was willing to see efforts made to prevent such trade developing. He may also have had in mind the considerable quantity of his ivory still in Tabora, which he mentioned to Barghash; he would presumably wish to export that eastwards, and therefore to keep open the trade route between Ujiji, Tabora and the coast. Barghash replied that he had been planning to appoint Tippu Tip *wali* in Tabora, but in the light of what he had heard, he judged it more important for him to return quickly to Manyema and protect Arab/Zanzibari interests there. At the same time, Barghash issued an order prohibiting the Belgian Ernest Cambier, then in Zanzibar, from recruiting a large number of slaves to act as porters – presumably either to frustrate the Belgians in any attempt to expand their influence on the mainland, or to allow Tippu Tip a free hand in recruiting the men he would need for his return to Manyema, or both. Cambier managed to enlist the support of Col. S.B. Miles, who had formerly been Agent in Muscat but was then Acting British Consul during two years' leave taken by John Kirk (August 1881–August 1883), and somehow managed to recruit *waungwana* (Wangwana) free men of the coastal region, instead.

Before following Tippu Tip through the preparations for what would be his Fourth Journey, we should step back in time to see how it was that the Belgians Becker, Storms, Cambier and others, came to be involved from coast to coast across Central Africa in the early 1880s.

King Leopold turns his gaze on the Congo

Unlike the processes of imperial or colonial acquisitions by other European powers, the Belgian takeover in the Congo was driven, initially, by one man: King Leopold II. He came to the throne in 1865, aged thirty, and already by then had ideas of expanding the new and small country's horizons through somehow acquiring a colony. It is not clear why this developed into such an obsession. Writers have drawn attention to the unhappy marriages that Leopold endured – his own, and that of his parents – but this hardly seems a satisfactory explanation. He seems from an early age to have been interested in geography and exploration, and to have looked beyond Belgian shores for ways of enriching the new nation as other Europeans had done through trade and then empire.[3]

Leopold II's parents were Leopold I and Louise-Marie, daughter of King Louis-Philippe of France. Leopold I was the youngest son of the Duke of Saxe-Coburg-Saalfeld (a very small duchy in what is now Bavaria), and his first wife was Princess Charlotte of Wales, the only child of the then Prince Regent, who later became King George IV. Charlotte died in 1817, and had no children. Leopold then married the daughter of the French king probably to strengthen connections to a major European power, in a move similar to his activity in arranging the marriage of (Queen) Victoria, his niece, to his nephew Prince Albert of Saxe-Coburg-Gotha (as the name of the duchy had now become). Whatever the effects on his family life, he had good reason to walk carefully to protect the interests – indeed the survival – of the new kingdom: Belgium, declared an independent nation in 1830, remained under attack from the Dutch until 1839, when eventually King William I of the Netherlands recognized its independence. In addition, the revolutions of 1848 brought an air of uncertainty to sovereigns on European thrones.

The relationship between the Leopolds, father and son, was formal and distant; but the young Leopold was at least given a good education and helped to prepare for his future role as king. However, when he was eighteen, his father, eager to make another dynastic match, this time with the Austro-Hungarian imperial family, arranged for him to be betrothed to the Archduchess Marie-Henriette Habsburg. It was a disaster from the start. The two were ill-matched, and irritated each other. While Marie-Henriette pursued her hobby of equestrianism, Leopold travelled widely, including to the Balkans, Egypt and Spain. Everywhere he saw opportunities for developing Belgian trade, and enabling his countrymen to make the most of the industrial and financial strength that had been built up during an economic reform programme of the 1850s. To a certain extent, he was right: Belgian factories and the Belgian banking system were well placed to grow and prosper, and there was some sense in looking to markets outside Europe where growth rates were likely to be rapid.

Unfortunately (as it turned out), Leopold could not resist going a step further than commerce. He was attracted by what he believed were the enormous profits to be earned from actual acquisition of lands abroad. He maintained the connections with Britain originally created in his father's marriage to Charlotte, and continued to visit: the gains made by the British from India and other territories of the British Empire would have been obvious to him. In 1862, when he was twenty-seven, a look back into history in the Spanish archives in Seville opened his eyes by to the wealth that had flowed from Spain's possessions. Even before that, the idea had taken firm root: "Belgium must have a colony".[4] In 1864, pursuing the obsession, he visited south and south-east Asia, and was able to conclude that size did not matter: the Dutch, from a country about the same size as Belgium, had developed their colonies in the Dutch East Indies, now Indonesia, and made profits from plantations that had financed infrastructure investment back in the homeland. Leopold appears to have taken particular interest in a book about colonization in Java, written by a British author, which described features that Leopold was to draw on later in the Congo, for example personal investment by the king, and the use of forced labour.[5]

He faced two problems in particular in pushing this agenda. One was that there was no obvious place to go in which land on this scale could be bought, or even acquired on long lease. Leopold looked all over – in South America, Fiji, the East Indies. He asked the King of Spain if he could buy the Philippines, but without success. It was only later that his eye would fall on Africa. The other problem was that there was little appetite in Belgium itself for a colonial adventure. His father had attempted investment in Guatemala, with unhappy results. His officials, including Belgian ambassadors in places he visited, found his continued foreign travels annoying and unproductive. Most of all, the business people – on behalf of whose profits Leopold thought he was acting – saw no advantage in the high risks of imperial acquisition. Interestingly, the British in this period thought similarly: when Livingstone was exploring the Zambezi, he suggested that the best solution to the problems of slavery and poverty would be to found a colony on the river, but found little support at home. The British were prepared to make efforts and spend resources on maintaining the existing empire, but – at least in the second half of the 19th century – saw little point in gratuitously expanding it. The Belgian people's reservations about the King's project for growing colonies was to be an important feature in the development of the Congo, right up to the point where the Belgian state took it over from Leopold in 1908.

Leopold was not particularly troubled by the lack of Belgian popular enthusiasm for his colonial project, not least because he did not need the tax-payer's money to finance it. He was wealthy on his own account, having inherited a comfortable fortune from his parents, which he had increased by successful speculation in Suez Canal shares. (The Canal opened in 1869.) He also reckoned that with this he could leverage loans from Belgium's solid banking sector.

In the mid-1870s, he turned his attention to Africa. He was a regular reader of *The Times* newspaper, which he had delivered (or tossed out of a train) daily to his palace at Laeken outside Brussels, and he would have been well aware of the news reports about the search by Livingstone and his predecessors for the source of the Nile, and Livingstone's much-publicized death in 1873, just as he was aware of the coverage given to these matters in the proceedings of the Royal Geographical Society (RGS). In particular, he noticed the reports of Lt V.L. Cameron's arrival in Benguela in late 1875 after his crossing of Africa, and made an offer (which in the event was not taken up) to the RGS to pay the very significant sum of Belgian francs (BFr) 100,000, equivalent to £4,000, to cover Cameron's expenses. Cameron's reports had glowingly played up the wealth of the African interior, ready for exploitation by an "enterprising capitalist".

Leopold's subsequent exploitation of the Congo was so deliberate, and the suffering of the indigenous population so acute, that historians have tended to attribute to him malign intentions from an early stage in his career. At this point, for example, when in the mid-1870s he began the process which was to lead to the foundation of the Congo Free State and its cruel administration, it is tempting to assume that his actions were driven from the start by a sinister and ignoble plan to gain huge personal wealth by deception of his European colleagues and violence towards his future African subjects. However, there is no real evidence for this. It is true (according to Adam Hochschild) that his father compared his young son to a fox, with a subtle and sly approach to handling people and problems. But this does not prove malign intent towards the Congo from an early age. It is also recounted that he displayed a different persona on public occasions, in Parliament for example, from that which he used with his officials. Thus, on the issue of the wished-for colony, he said little or nothing in public while not concealing his ambitions from his staff. But in this Leopold was not so different from many public figures. He was practising a prudence which was perhaps well-advised in the light of the still fragile state of monarchies in Europe – Belgium itself being only a few decades old. It is more likely that he set out to establish the colony with the dual aim of aggrandisement for Belgium and a good return on investment for himself, and that the problems (and the blind eye that he turned to them) came later.

It is also said that Leopold deliberately cloaked, with a pretence of caring for the abject plight of Africans downtrodden by slavery, his allegedly well-formed plans for self-aggrandisement and colonial conquest. This is of course possible; but again the interpretation projects back onto the early 1870s attitudes, policies and activities that evolved only in the 1880s and 1890s. It is more realistic (and possibly more interesting, because the analysis is more subtle) to consider the events as they unfolded, and the characters as they made their progress across our European and African stage. Leopold was not alone in mixing his motives as he went along. Others too, as we shall see, could play the philanthropist and colonialist at one and the same time.

In 1876, Leopold took the initiative that propelled him from theory to activism in his involvement in Africa. He convened a conference of explorers and geographers with the aim of opening up the continent, by establishing routes into the interior and bases for scientific study, bringing peace in place of war, and imposing justice, the rule of law, and of course an end to the slave trade, which Europeans knew was going on despite their own legislation against it. He avoided specific mention of his interest in linking any outcomes of the conference with the creation of a Belgian presence on the ground in Africa, but made clear the role that Belgium, a small but central and neutral country, could play in advancing this civilizing mission in Africa.

The Brussels conference was impeccably organized, with every detail attended to by Leopold himself, and on a grand scale. But it was not large by modern standards: the twenty-four foreign guests were carefully chosen to include notable explorers and to represent government, business and other institutions concerned with exploration, commerce, and missionary and anti-slavery activity. The outcome was a decision to form the *Association Internationale Africaine*, referred to widely in the literature as the AIA. There were to be national committees of this body, and also an international committee chaired by Leopold. The conference, and the formation of the AIA, was applauded as a great humanitarian action. In the event, the national committees barely met, and the international committee continued to re-elect Leopold chairman. The result was to afford him an ideal platform from which to take forward the still unformed plan for a Belgian colony.

Leopold draws Stanley into his web

In 1877, Stanley appeared at the mouth of the Congo after his extraordinary journey "through the dark continent", as he called his second exploration book. Almost immediately Leopold set about courting the great explorer. Shortly before the 1876 Brussels conference he had met Cameron in London, and the latter's enthusiastic description of the wealth of the Congo basin, combined with the discovery of a river route to the heart of Africa, awakened in Leopold the realization that here lay the region, hitherto unclaimed by any European power, where his dream of a Belgian colony could be brought to fruition. It is clear that by now he wanted to use exploration as a cover for, or preliminary to, colonial bases, and he sought contact with Stanley to persuade him to join – or indeed to lead – the venture.

Stanley was flattered by the attention, particularly as Leopold sent as his envoys an American ex-diplomat, Henry Shelton Sanford, and a Belgian aristocrat, Baron Jules Greindl. Sanford had a chequered business history, and styled himself General (on the grounds that he had given some cannon to a regiment during the Civil War), but lived in Belgium and was useful to Leopold. He and Greindl met Stanley in Marseille and Paris. These initial approaches failed to win Stanley over, but Leopold kept up the pressure, through his Embassy and through arranging for Sanford to visit London to see him again. Stanley's reception in London was not quite what he had hoped, or expected, after his astonishing and gruelling trans-African journey. He came under public criticism for the violence he had used against Africans during his epic adventure, both on the Congo but most particularly in the incident on Lake Victoria referred to earlier (page 151). Then, under considerable provocation but not actually forced to shoot in self-defence, he had ordered his men to open fire in an engagement that resulted in 33 or 43 (accounts differed) Africans being killed. In vain he cited other killings – some on a large scale – by Europeans in colonial or imperial situations. Somehow comparisons with military engagements were thought irrelevant or inapposite, and it was hard to dispel revulsion at a well-armed exploration party taking the lives of 'natives' armed only with spears or bows and arrows.[6]

Stanley faced other problems in his reception in England. Despite the ambiguity about his origins (and he continued to present himself as an American, from a wish to conceal his inauspicious start in life), he persisted in hoping that the British would take advantage of what he considered were tremendous opportunities in developing the Congo. He envisaged these opportunities as being balanced, that is as bringing advantages to the Africans living on and near the river as well as to the investors or colonial developers. He wanted to see roads and railways built alongside the impassable stretches of the Congo, making the great waterway a continuous route from the Atlantic to the heart of the continent, open to international free trade. At the same time, he remained strongly influenced by his conversations with Livingstone in 1871–72, and firmly believed that a European presence could end slavery and human trafficking, either by repression or by introducing (or expanding) regular commerce. And he would much rather that that presence should be a British one. So it was disappointing for him that, although he attended numerous receptions and met with plenty of the great and the good, he was not received formally by the Foreign Secretary, and his hopes that he might be sent back to Africa at the head of a mission to develop trade remained unfulfilled. The truth is that, as we saw earlier in the context of Livingstone's similar hopes for a colony on the Zambezi, there was little appetite either in British society or in the British Government for additional imperial adventures at this time. Nor was this surprising: Disraeli's government had various foreign crises on their hands – Russian threats to Turkey, a financial crisis in Egypt (now of strategic importance, after the opening of the Suez Canal), problems in South Africa. The public also knew, because Stanley could not resist writing up stories of the danger he had experienced from disease and tribal hostility, that any European travelling in Central Africa did so at great personal risk. With Stanley looking a little like damaged goods despite his extraordinary achievements as an explorer, his advocacy for investment or a colony in the Congo was not going to win a friendly hearing.

So Stanley reverted to his fall-back position: he had in fact kept his options open, and told Sanford and Greindl that in a few months' time he might reconsider. Now he decided to take up the Belgian invitation and, in the summer of 1878, he had his first meeting with Leopold, confirming that this was the King's best chance of achieving his ambitions for the Congo basin. In October he signed an agreement to serve Leopold for five years, and in December he signed another, for three years' service, with the *Comité d'Études du Haut Congo*, a body that Leopold had established independent of the AIA, with the aim of creating stations for scientific, philanthropic and commercial purposes on the Congo. Several British subscribers, clearly motivated by these ostensibly philanthropic aims, put money into the *Comité*. Among them was the Scottish industrialist William Mackinnon, who had made a fortune from founding the shipping line that became the British India Steam Navigation Company. Mackinnon was to maintain his interest in Africa, and would later be involved with financing the Emin Pasha Relief Expedition.

Is it possible to be certain of Leopold's actual plans and aims at this stage? All his actions are consistent with his overt and long-standing purpose of creating a colony for Belgium. He clearly considered that the Congo basin was an ideal location – the explorers had determined the geography and declared that there were riches to be made from trade, and no other European government had an interest in the interior. (There were Portuguese possessions at the mouth of the Congo, and some British 'factories' or trading stations, but nothing farther up the river.) But, if at this stage he had the intention of enforcing a royal monopoly, or of building a personal fiefdom, or of ruthless extraction of natural resources, this was certainly not apparent to his staff, and obviously not to the international subscribers.

One of these subscribers, a Dutch company, went bankrupt in early 1879, an event prompting further corporate changes in Leopold's structure for Congo development. With the agreement of the other subscribers (who had little option), he dissolved the short-lived *Comité d'Études*, and substituted for it the *Association Internationale du Congo* (AIC), in which he was the major shareholder and in fact the overall controller. The closeness of the name to that of the *Association Internationale Africaine* (AIA), which had emerged from the Brussels conference, and the risk of confusion, was almost certainly deliberate: Leopold wanted to allow people to think that the AIC (which was incorporated with him in overall control) was either the same as, or the natural successor to, the AIA (which had a genuinely international origin). As he travelled out to start his new job, in February 1879, Stanley commented in his diary on Leopold's apparent ambition to turn the Congo basin into a Belgian dependency – seemingly concerned that his own hopes of opening up the continent to free trade and improved lives for Africans were already diverging from those of his employer.

Stanley's operations on the Congo, 1879–84

Stanley's achievements on the Congo, over a period of five years, were considerable.[7] He established a series of stations on the river right up to Wagenia Falls (then called Stanley Falls), near Kisangani, where Arab traders were by then well established, and not in fact very far from where he and Tippu Tip had separated at the end of 1876 (see pages 159–60). He fulfilled his contract with Leopold, working with steadiness and determination to build the road that by-passed the huge and dangerous cataracts below Malebo Pool, a huge widening of the River Congo which was then named Stanley Pool. On the south bank of this Stanley established an important station that became Leopoldville and has since developed into Kinshasa, capital of the Democratic Republic of the Congo. Much of his labour force were East Africans, including Wanyamwezi, brought by ship round the Cape from Zanzibar: he was accustomed to working with them, and they were generally loyal to him – even though at times he was tough with them, using punishments that in modern terms would be considered brutal, and even then had already been abolished in the US army and virtually eliminated in the British army and navy. It was at this stage that he earned his Swahili nickname: *Bula Matari*, Rock Smasher. Some have attributed this to his habit of driving his men so hard that he could break rocks, let alone men. But he drove himself hard too, and his own claim that it was because he personally taught them how to use a sledgehammer, and because he used explosives for his road-building, rings true. At any rate, he was proud of the nickname, and often referred to it in later life. The words are on his tombstone in Pirbright, Surrey.

The demands placed on the men, together with the fatigue brought on by the climate, took its toll on Africans and Europeans alike. Malaria was common; there were no prophylactics, but by this time Europeans could often survive it by heavy doses of quinine. Other

The steamboat *Le Stanley* being carried in sections upriver, as depicted in H.M. Stanley's *The Congo and the Founding of its Free State*, 1841–1904 (1885).

forms of fever could prove fatal. Stanley himself was near death twice from 'fever', and the second time – after nearly three years in the Congo – he decided to take a recuperation break in Europe. He had in fact done remarkably well: by then he had established a station at Vivi, at the bottom of the cataracts descending from Stanley Pool, and built a track enabling him to lay down a Belgian (or AIC) presence at the Pool itself. And he had achieved all this with virtually no violent confrontation with local Africans. His team had brought up a paddle steamer, in pieces, and assembled it on the Pool, enabling him to go upstream on the Upper Congo in April 1882.

Arriving in Brussels in September 1882, Stanley may have been pondering the wisdom of a return to Africa, but interviews with Leopold in October made it clear that the King wanted him to complete his contract and finish building the roads and setting up the stations on the river. To facilitate this, Leopold raised the annual budget from £12,000 to £60,000, and authorized the recruitment of more officers (several of whom were British, Stanley preferring them to the comfort-loving Belgians), and of many more labourers. For the Brussels end of the operation, he relied on Col. Maximilien Strauch, who had been Secretary General of the AIA since its early days, and also titular president of the *Comité d'Études du Haut Congo*. Strauch was a kind of Permanent Secretary of the administration of the Congo, and so the normal point of contact for Stanley and others in posts of command on the Congo.

Back in Africa after only a two-month break, Stanley continued his progress in station-building up the river, now also under instructions to conclude 'treaties' with local chiefs. This was partly to ensure loyalty to the (Belgian) AIC, which was facing competition from the activities of the explorer Pierre de Brazza, who aimed at claiming territory for France on the northern and north-western side of the River Congo in what is now Gabon and land to the south and west of it, near the River Congo. De Brazza, of Italian origin but exploring with French financial backing and on behalf of the French government, believed (with some justification) that he could find an easier way to Stanley Pool, and thus to the Upper Congo, by travelling up the river Ogowe and then a relatively short way south-west to the Pool. He made good progress, and established a French connection with local chiefs, and in particular Chief Makoko. But Leopold had another purpose in mind: the signature of treaties was normally an act of sovereign states, and he actually wished to assert the right of the AIC to sign agreements granting a trading monopoly in the area, and the use, even the ownership, of land for the stations. It is of course doubtful that the chiefs knew what they were signing away. By these means, Stanley ensured that the AIC flag, a gold star (for hope) on a blue background (dark, for Africa), was flying over 450 villages.

The negotiations with the village chiefs were often complex. One of them, Ngaliema, was central to success in controlling large areas on the south side of Stanley Pool, while de Brazza, assisted by a highly competent sergeant named Malamine, was securing a range of alliances on the north side. Ngaliema had earned a fortune from ivory trading, and remembered Stanley from his journey down the Congo in 1877. But, despite being lavished with gifts, he was not to be won over easily. In the midst of all this Stanley, though not famous for his sense of humour, yet contrived to pull a trick that still brings a smile to the lips. Knowing that Ngaliema was on his way to see him at his station beside Stanley Pool, bringing an armed band intended to drive out the white man, Stanley briefed his own men to stay hidden but to spring out if they heard the sound of a gong. He then sat in a chair, reading Shakespeare, with just two attendants. Ngaliema arrived, sword unsheathed, only to be greeted with friendly smiles by Stanley – and then noticed the gong beside his chair. He asked if it could be rung, but Stanley refused, saying that it was a fetish and only trouble would come of ringing it. Ngaliema insisted, Stanley hit the gong, all his men jumped out, and Ngaliema's men, scared witless by this display of magic, took flight.

It could be said that it was here, on the Congo, as Leopold and the French, Stanley and de Brazza, struggled to gain tactical advantage with the chiefs either side of the river, that the physical Scramble for Africa really began – that sense of competition between European powers motivating them to seize territory not because they saw immediate profit or security advantage, but from a belief that it was important to keep out the opposition, just in case a treasure-store lay behind the dark wall of impenetrable rainforest.

Stanley dutifully continued his progress upriver, and by mid-1883 had established a station at Equatorville (now Mbandaka), just over 400 miles from Stanley Pool, and in December 1883 established one at Stanley Falls itself. Late in that year he had his first encounters with Arab traders, who had taken further their expansion north and west from Nyangwe and Manyema. Stanley had heard them tell stories of their first attempts in this direction when he had been with Tippu Tip and others on the River Lualaba a few years before. These Arabs may have been emboldened by Stanley's own success in going down the river past and beyond Stanley Falls, or it may just have been the result of their desire to extend their trading areas. It is not clear whether at this stage they were selling their ivory and slaves down the Congo, or whether they were still exporting to their traditional markets on the east coast. One of his Belgian officers, Branconnier, had infuriated Stanley by purchasing ivory with such a quantity of the goods stored at Leopoldville (on the Pool), that they had been left without enough to buy food and had to beg from the Baptist missionaries there; he may have been buying ivory collected from elephants in that part of the Congo, or product brought down river from (for example) Manyema. Leopold had already, by this stage, started demanding that ivory be collected and sent back to Belgium.

Whichever it was, ivory was sadly not the merchandise that these Arabs were mainly interested in. Stanley reached the confluence of the River Aruwimi, some 800 miles from the Pool and only 200 from

---

Slavery in the Ottoman Empire

In this book, the slave trading routes with which we have been concerned have mostly been those in East Africa and the Indian Ocean. Africans were captured in the area of the Great Lakes, in what is now Tanzania, Kenya, Malawi and the eastern part of the Democratic Republic of the Congo, taken to markets on the coast or in Zanzibar, and then either retained in Zanzibar or Pemba or traded (in dhows) to the Gulf or Persia. Some were taken to the Red Sea, for example to Jiddah (Jedda) and Mecca, and a few to India.

But there was high demand for slaves in the heartlands of the Ottoman Empire too, and much of this was satisfied by supply over land routes. Slaves captured in the Sahel (the semi-arid area south of the Sahara, referred to as 'Sudan' in much 19th-century writing), and even as far south as the Ituri (in north-east Congo), were taken east and north through modern Sudan and Egypt, some to be sold in Cairo, and some shipped across the Red Sea to the Hijaz, where the large number of Muslims converging for the pilgrimages to the holy places of Mecca and Madina provided a lively market. From there slaves would be taken to the great cities of the Ottoman Empire such as Damascus and Baghdad, and of course Istanbul itself. Contemporary reports suggest that in Upper (southern) Egypt, on the land route parallel with the Nile, there were places where boys were castrated in order to provide eunuchs for the Egyptian and Ottoman markets. On a trade route

Stanley Falls, in late 1882, and found that slave traders had come downriver from the north-east, and taken women and children as slaves. These traders may have been Arabs from Nyangwe, but it is equally likely that they were from Sudan, using a route similar to that which Stanley was to take a few years later on the Emin Pasha Relief Expedition. Then in November, back on the Congo, Stanley came across burnt villages from which men as well as women and children had recently been taken in large numbers. Closer investigation brought him into contact with Abed bin Salim, one of the founders of the Arab settlement at Nyangwe, whom he had met previously. (Abed bin Salim's correct name was 'Ubayd bin Sālim al-Khadūrī, but he is always referred to as *Abed bin Salim* by writers in English, *Obed-ben-Salem* in Ceulemans; Livingstone and Cameron had also met him.) There was clear evidence of the capture of many hundreds of slaves and of appalling cruelty in their treatment, and of the murder of many others. The Arabs had also been collecting ivory, presumably by robbery.

---

of incredible hardship, slaves were taken from around Lake Chad either due north to Benghazi or north-west across the Sahara to Tunis, where there were slave markets from which they were distributed along the North African littoral, and also to Turkey and the Levant.

These were the main trading routes for Central and East African slaves. As is well known, the Ottoman élite also had a great appetite for Circassian slaves, brought to Istanbul from the Caucasus, present-day Abkhazia and Georgia. And there were also slaves taken from Ethiopia into the Levant and Arabia; Sayyid Barghash's mother was one of Sayyid Sa'id's Ethiopian concubines, prized for their beauty and fair skin.

The British and other European states, who had close diplomatic relations with the 'Sublime Porte' (as the Ottoman imperial court was called), made efforts through the 19th century to persuade the Ottoman authorities to end slavery and the slave trade in the Empire. For a long time such appeals fell on deaf ears: the institution (particularly concubinage, and domestic and agricultural slavery) was too deeply entrenched, and not considered morally reprehensible. What was thought evil was to treat your slaves unkindly. Eventually the Sultan gave way – in fact before the Sultans of Zanzibar and Muscat – and *ferman*s were issued to the Governors of Egypt, Tripoli and Baghdad to forbid trade in black slaves. Implementation was however erratic, and slave trading in Egypt and on the Red Sea continued well into the 1870s, and declined only in the 1880s and 1890s.

This episode brought Stanley up against a paradox that would bedevil the AIC occupation of the Congo up until the final dénouement in the Belgian–Arab battle at Stanley Falls in 1893. If the humanitarian objects of the AIC were genuine, in creating a modern communications infrastructure for trade and civilizing influences they risked undermining their own avowed purpose by providing a pathway for the expansion of the violent trade in slaves and ivory from East Africa (where it was bad enough) to the Atlantic. And if, as is more likely, the AIC's objects were merely a smokescreen for colonial exploitation aimed at enriching the King and the Belgian people, they still faced the actual reality of the extension of the slave trade into 'their' territory. Yet there was so far no sovereign state, and so no legal base for using force to end the inhuman traffic. Until this point, Stanley had appeared suspicious of Leopold's ambition to create a fiefdom; still less would he have countenanced the foundation of a state. The explorer's interest was in establishing stations on the river for the purposes of expanding trade – but free trade, enabling British and other shipping concerns to benefit from, and bring benefit to, Africans prepared to do business. He even invited a delegation of Arabs to bring a small quantity of ivory to one of the stations on the lower Congo to demonstrate that this trading route was feasible. But the contact with the Arabs under Abed bin Salim made him come round to the idea that only a recognized entity such as a state could exercise the power to confront the slave trading and its accompanying violence that was inexorably moving west across Central Africa.

Stanley left the Congo in June 1884. In five years and a few months he had effectively laid the foundation for what would turn out to be a personal estate of King Leopold for about twenty years, until the Belgian Government, under intense international pressure, removed it from his control. The atrocities that accompanied the exploitation of this immense territory, mainly for the purpose of extracting rubber, came later. Stanley's methods may have been tough, and he expected hard work from his subordinates, but his name is not associated with the extreme cruelty that was practised later. His achievement was to have established a Belgian presence from the coast nearly to Lake Tanganyika, marking out European control over hundreds of miles of this formidable river – to which he, with Tippu Tip, would soon return just a few years later.

Leopold and the Congo Free State

Meanwhile in Europe, King Leopold also – but for reasons different from Stanley's – wished to convert his *Association* into a state.[8] He realized the importance of Stanley's achievements, and saw that his chances of profiting from trade on the river would be much enhanced if he could monopolize the commerce. His personal investment in getting this far had been significant, and it was becoming necessary to see a return. He looked first to the USA for official recognition of statehood, using as his agent the American former diplomat Henry Sanford who, as we saw above (page 184) had acted for Leopold in recruiting Stanley in 1878, and was still living in Belgium. Sanford had for some time, from a distance, been cultivating President Chester A. Arthur, and conducted a clever and sophisticated propaganda campaign to convince the Republican President, leaders of the US business community and members of Congress, of the humanitarian nature of Leopold's enterprise and the commercial opportunities available in the Congo. In April 1884, the US Senate recognized the AIC flag as "the flag of a friendly government", and two weeks later the Secretary of State announced that the USA recognized Leopold's claims to the Congo. Intriguingly, and no doubt as a result of Sanford's deliberate spreading of confusion, as Hochschild has pointed out, Secretary Frelinghuysen used both 'International Association of the Congo' (i.e. the AIC) and 'International African Association' (the AIA) in his declaration, as though they were the same body.[9] Leopold had only a few steps to take before the transition from international scientific collaboration to personal ownership was complete.

With American recognition in the bag, Leopold turned his attention to the Europeans, whom he could expect to look at African affairs more critically, given their existing political, commercial and territorial interests in various parts of the continent. The French posed a pressing problem, having made claims to land to the north and north-west of the River Congo through de Brazza. Leopold came up with a brilliant plan for defusing this threat: he offered France a first option, or right of first refusal, on possession of his Congo territories should the AIC at any time in the future decide to relinquish them – on condition, of course, that France recognized his current claims. This seemed a good deal to the French, who judged it quite likely that the necessary investment – particularly for the railway required to bypass the rapids on the lower Congo – would be beyond Leopold's means. They were also concerned that Stanley might succeed in bringing round British public and government opinion into favouring a British protectorate in the Congo basin.

Leopold now needed German acquiescence. At first Chancellor Bismarck was suspicious, and was apparently able to see through Leopold's attempts at sleight of hand (for example, when Leopold tried to avoid delineating the borders of his territorial claims, explaining that they would be defined later). However, in time, and after the involvement of a German financier who was willing to advance Leopold's cause, Bismarck seems to have concluded that it was better for Germany that the vast tract of the Congo basin should go to Belgium, a minor player in European power politics, than to serious rivals such as Britain or France. He probably also reckoned – wrongly, as it turned out – that under Belgian rule the Congo territory would be more open to German traders than if it were controlled by one of the other traditional imperial powers. As a final inducement to Bismarck to come round to Leopold's scheme, it happened that Stanley was staying as a guest of Leopold in Ostend when, in the summer of 1884, Bismarck's questions about the AIC borders arrived with Leopold himself; and Stanley was able to draw them on a map, to Bismarck's satisfaction.

As this process unfolded, Leopold was able to exploit another ambiguity in terminology, this time arising from the 'agreements' signed by the AIC (or Stanley on the AIC's behalf) with local chiefs. He had presented the AIC as presiding over a federation of 'independent states', but gradually slipped into describing it as a single 'independent state'. This allowed him to manoeuvre the creation of the *État Indépendent du Congo*, known in English as the Congo Free State (occasionally the Independent State of the Congo), but generally referred to in the historical literature as the EIC, which emerged from the next big international conference on Africa, the Berlin Conference of November 1884 – February 1885.

It was in 1884 that the Scramble for Africa reached its political climax – although action on the ground in Africa would continue for some time after that. In February, the British and Portuguese had reached an agreement admitting Portuguese claims on territory at the mouth of the Congo. This had originated in Portuguese claims there going back to the establishment of 'factories' (trading posts) following early sailing expeditions round Africa's coast, and more immediately because the British considered this the best way of keeping the French out of the region, as de Brazza's claims seemed to threaten free trade in the Congo basin. The Anglo-Portuguese treaty was never ratified, foundering in Parliament, and also as a result of protest from the French. In Britain there was opposition from business interests, including particularly from Mackinnon (now Sir William). It may seem strange in retrospect, but Mackinnon and others believed that free trade on the Congo stood a better chance under Leopold's rule than if Portugal controlled the territories round the river mouth.

Other claims on the West African coast now began to catch the attention of British politicians, especially when actions by Bismarck made it clear that Germany was changing policy and beginning active involvement in Africa. Consistently up until 1883, Bismarck had insisted that Germany had no wish to start colonies; the Chancellor was kept busy enough in ensuring Germany's position in Europe, and in any case feared that colonial adventures would incur expenditure. Circumstances changed in late 1883 and early 1884. Bismarck began to fear that the British and French would seize all the West African coast, to the exclusion of German commercial interests. In May 1884, he caused German flags to be hoisted in Cameroon, and in August agreed to give protection to a German businessman wanting to take possession of Angra Pequena, a trading post on the aptly named Skeleton Coast in south-west Africa, now Namibia. This caused confusion between Lord Granville in the Foreign Office and Lord Derby of the Colonial Office. Granville, busy trying to resolve problems arising from the Egyptian financial crisis, wished to avoid further entanglement in Africa, while Derby was under pressure to protect the interests of the Cape Government, who for their own reasons wanted to assert claims over south-west Africa and to push back against perceived German advances. The outcome was British occupation of Bechuanaland and the port of St Lucia on the east coast.[10] And this marked the first use of the term 'Scramble' in official writing, when Derby observed that there was "something absurd in the sudden Scramble for colonies ...", and that there was "a difference between wanting new acquisitions and keeping what we have; and both Natal and the Cape Colony would be endangered ... if any foreign power chose to claim possession of the coast between the two."[11]

During this period, Britain's informal influence over large parts of the West African coast was forced to give way to a system of formal claim

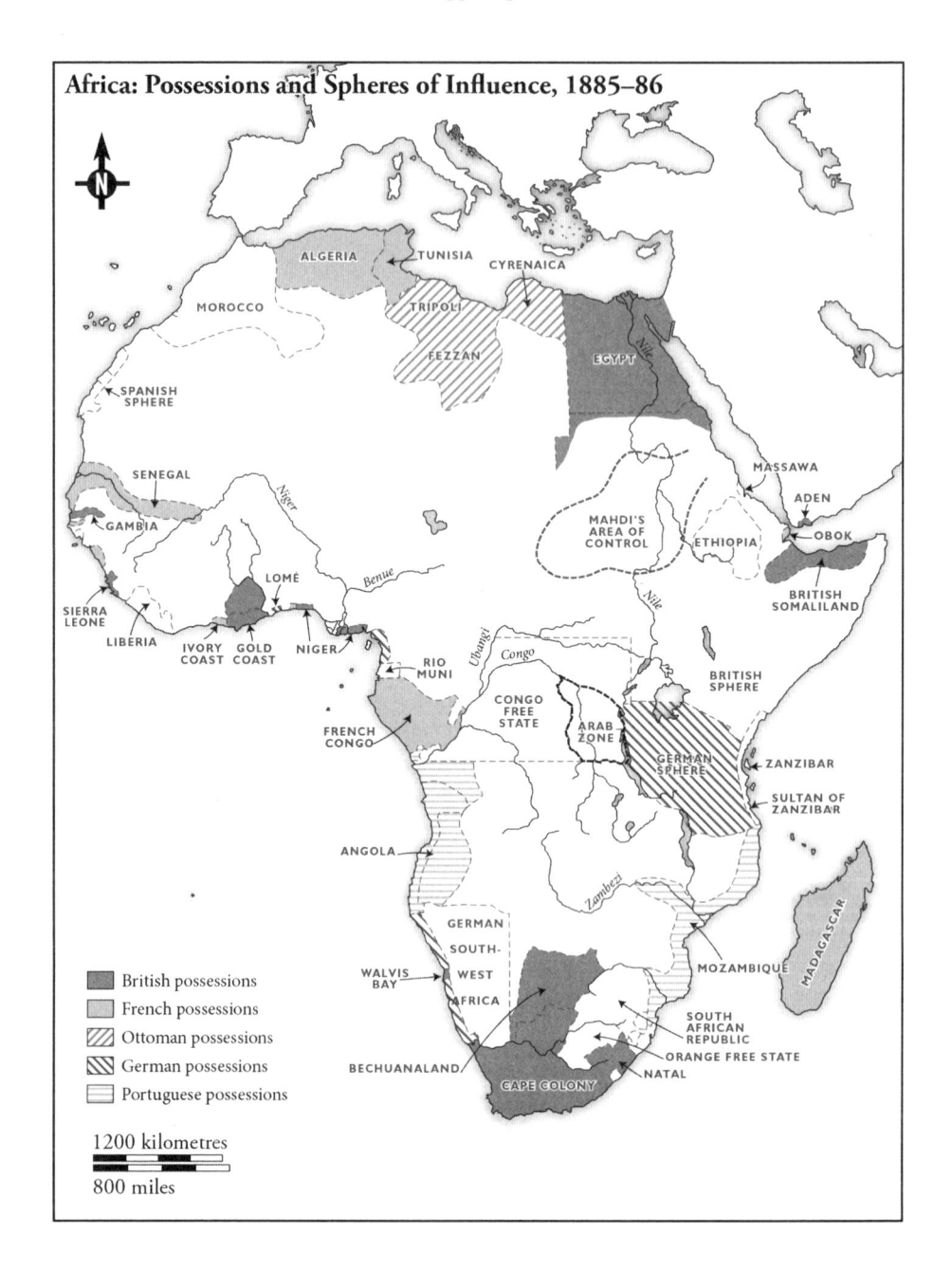

Africa: Possessions and Spheres of Influence, 1885–86

- British possessions
- French possessions
- Ottoman possessions
- German possessions
- Portuguese possessions

1200 kilometres
800 miles

and direct territorial domination and control. The Berlin Conference of November 1884 arose from a joint French–German proposal aimed at getting international agreement on free trade on the Congo and Niger rivers, and on the process for defining future territorial claims. The British did not object, hoping that the conference would help them to maintain their pre-eminent position on the Niger and to ensure trading rights on the Congo. In addition, the Foreign Office aimed to bring in international safeguards against the slave trade. In the course of the conference, other issues were introduced, such as the need to restrict the import into Africa of arms and munitions, and liquor. In both of these sectors, trade was well established and increasing, and seen in some European circles as bringing evil to African society, while of course in others it was considered a valuable source of profit.

The Berlin Conference was attended by the European powers already engaged in colonial activity in Africa, and by other governments interested on the margins, or in trade (Russia, Austria, the Scandinavians, Holland, Belgium and the USA). There were of course no African representatives. Bismarck opened proceedings with high-flown language, referring to a "[shared] desire to associate the natives of Africa with civilization, by opening up the interior to commerce, by furnishing the natives with the means of instruction, ... and by paving the way to the suppression of slavery."[12] The outcome was more prosaic. A Berlin Act was concluded in February 1885, providing for freedom of trade in the Congo basin, protection of Christian missionaries in Africa, a condemnation of slavery and the slave trade, and rather ambiguous attempts to restrict the liquor trade. Nothing was done to contain the growing export of arms to Africa. Although it was not directly discussed, Leopold was able to emerge from the Conference with general recognition of his 'federation' on the Congo river as the Congo Free State, or État Indépendent du Congo (EIC); and, as a state, the EIC adhered to the Act immediately after signature.

Back in 1882, where we left Tippu Tip in negotiation with Sultan Barghash about Zanzibar's influence in the African interior and the Sultan's ability to control trade from there to the coast, this kind of infrastructure on the Congo was less than half built. But even by then the arrival of the Belgians signalled a significant change in African and Arab relationships with European and American Incomers. Up till the 1870s, Tippu Tip and others had met such visitors, but always as birds of passage: the explorers came and went, their trading limited to their need to barter for survival. Even the diplomats and agents, although long-term fixtures in the sense that they consisted of a chain of successor appointments, were on the edge of society. Imperialists – and missionaries – were of different character, in that they were there to stay, and penetrated far into the interior. Indeed, by 1880 the Church Missionary Society had two stations on the mainland, the London Missionary Society had two on Lake Tanganyika, and the Société des missionaires d'Alger had three on and north of Lake Tanganyika. The missionaries had mixed success in converting Africans to Christianity, and were seen in many areas as a threat to ancient customs and traditional religion – as was also sometimes the case with Muslims attempting to make converts. Consequently, missionary effort was often diverted away from direct religious activity into health and education. As for the imperial or colonial presence, Tippu Tip was soon to experience first-hand how Europeans were to transform Central Africa.

CHAPTER 9

TARYA TOPAN.

Tippu Tip's Fourth Journey: Back to the Centre

AFTER HIS INTERVIEW with Sayyid Barghash, and having agreed to return to Manyema to protect the Sultan's (and his own) interests from his established position of strength there, Tippu Tip was requested (by the Sultan) to return to the merchant Taria Topan. Messengers soon arrived at his door bringing lavish gifts – cash, clothes, valuable oils (essence of roses and aloes), a *khanjar* and a sword, a diamond ring and a gold watch – presumably from Barghash, as an expression of his confidence in him, and also as a way of sealing his loyalty. Abdullah bin Nasibu, who had been *wali* of Tabora until a short time before, happening to pass by, expressed astonishment at this stash and asked if Tippu Tip had been appointed *wali* to succeed him. Tippu Tip again made it clear that he scorned such an offer: why should he be *wali* when he had 'domination' over an area larger than Unyamwezi and Tabora combined?[1]

The situation was in fact more complicated than that: it was in both Tippu Tip's and Barghash's interests that he should go back to Manyema because, from there, Tippu Tip could not only exploit further trading opportunities, but also keep his options open in case the export route down the Congo turned out to be more promising. (His use of the term 'domination' was probably an exaggeration: while he was widely respected and feared over large areas of the interior between Lake Tanganyika and the River Lualaba, and indeed beyond, his influence fell short of the kind of command and control that we normally associate with a state or government.) For Barghash, Tippu Tip's presence in the interior could provide a watching brief over Belgian ambitions, while at the same time keeping open the trading routes to Tabora and Ujiji. At this time he was becoming more anxious about such security questions, as can be seen by his decision in 1880 to follow John Kirk's advice and recruit a former British naval officer, Lloyd Mathews, to establish a fortified post on the road to Tabora. (See box on page 249.) This was planned to be the first of several. But, although Mathews was retained in the Sultan's service and later became an important figure in Zanzibar,[2] no further posts were set up.

It was at this time, November 1882, that Barghash sought to prevent the Belgians from recruiting porters or fighting men in Zanzibar, as mentioned above (page 179). It is likely, as suggested by Renault and as we shall see below, that Barghash saw more opportunity for developing the Sultanate in the African interior, where the Arabs were well established, than on the coast, where Europeans might want to expand their commerce, and that he feared this could be frustrated by Leopold's and Stanley's occupation of the Congo basin.[3] Direct evidence for this is lacking, although it is suggested by Barghash's efforts to persuade Tippu Tip to leave quickly for Manyema. Whatever the case, he had to back down over the recruitment ban not long after. Tippu Tip says that this was following the intervention of S.B. Miles, the British Consul,[4] but it is more likely that it resulted from Barghash's receipt of a telegram of protest from King Leopold, and Cambier was able to take about 200 with him to the Congo. It is interesting that Barghash gave way so easily. Perhaps he was by now beginning to feel the mounting pressures of European influence: he had been forced to sign an anti-slavery treaty in 1873 under threat of blockade by the British, and in 1875 he had visited Paris and London and seen for himself the technological and political power of those advanced economies.

Despite Barghash's urgings, Tippu Tip chose not to leave for Manyema straightaway. This may not have been from a sense of independence, or refusal to be ordered about by Barghash, since he used the time – about ten months, from January to October 1883 – in organizing deployment of barter goods in Bagamoyo and the dispatch of caravans into the interior, for example one led by Rumaliza (Mohammed bin Khalfan) and his own son Sayf. Delay was also due to difficulty in recruiting porters (or so he claimed to Barghash), and his needing to wait until his consignment of ivory arrived from Tabora, brought by his half-brother Mohammed bin Masoud. During this time he seems to have built up friendship with the staff of the British Consulate and Agency: S.B. Miles (Kirk's stand-in) and his deputy Frederick Holmwood gave him presents of "fine guns", and when Kirk returned from his long leave in August 1883, Tippu Tip renewed a friendship which he said went back some years.[5] Kirk, with his interest in maintaining the Sultan's influence in the area on and near the coast, suggested that Tippu Tip should be used to restore peace in Ugogo; Barghash had asked a Swahili leader to undertake this, but the Swahili had gone independent and begun charging *hongo* on his own account. Nevertheless, Barghash told Tippu Tip that he preferred him to leave for Manyema.[6]

Tippu Tip returns to Central Africa

Perhaps hinting at the confrontation with him that was to occur later, Tippu Tip records at this point a general reluctance by others to advance money to Rumaliza. As we have seen, this was an essential feature of Arab trading – but "neither in the town of Zanzibar nor in any town of the Mrima coast did anyone trust [Rumaliza] with 1,000 dollars".[7] Even Ali bin Isa, Rumaliza's kinsman, said that he could not give any goods to him – "he has no head for business". Tippu Tip advanced him goods of his own, and brought him in his caravan to Tabora, where they arrived in October or November 1883, at the start of Tippu Tip's Fourth Journey.[8]

In Tabora, he met with his agents from Manyema, who brought mixed news. There was ivory ready to be brought out, in addition to the 250 *frasila* which they had brought with them, but the men left behind were causing trouble, and would not carry out orders from Tippu Tip's cousin, Bwana Nzige. Urgent action was needed. Tippu Tip went on ahead with a lightly laden party, having first borrowed 200 men from Mirambo, there being a shortage of porters in Tabora. Rumaliza was to take the ivory to the coast, and then come back and deliver the caravan's large load of barter goods from Tabora to

Manyema. Seemingly he could be trusted with leading caravans, but not with business!

Tippu Tip made a small diversion on his route to Ujiji in order to meet Mirambo. Presumably he was curious to encounter the famous warrior, and perhaps wished to thank him for kindly making porters available; and, as explained above (Chapter 5, page 119), the two had complementary interests in some kind of alliance. They exchanged presents, and Mirambo undertook to send gifts of ivory also to Barghash, Taria Topan and two Arabs in Zanzibar, no doubt to protect his trading concerns.

Tippu Tip continued on to Ujiji, and then without delay into Manyema. He was clearly in a hurry, recording with unusual precision his dates of arrival in Kasongo and Nyangwe, and how many days (only a few) he spent in each.[9] His immediate intention was to suppress the malcontents, but he may also have had – as we shall see – other motives connected with his relationship with Sultan Barghash. In the area of Marera ("my domain"), between the Lualaba and Lomami rivers, he collected an army, no doubt using also the force he had brought with him, and, during a campaign of three months, restored order. As Renault points out, a three-month campaign must signify determined resistance from the African villages he wished to subdue, given that he had a large force with him, armed with powerful weapons, and the area was relatively limited.[10] To be sure that his authority was maintained, he also appointed in Kasongo Rushie a new chief of known loyalty to himself, in place of one who had died. Named Ngongo Lutete, he was of slave origin, and either this or his reputation occasioned a protest from local leaders. Tippu Tip put this down firmly, declaring that anyone who objected to him would be whipped into obedience.

He needed to continue campaigning, however, as a result of a letter he received from Juma bin Salim Merikani, the trading colleague with whom he had travelled in this area in 1872 (see Chapter 6). Juma had apparently been taken prisoner or hostage and had many of his goods stolen by Kasongo Karombo, Chief of Urua. Tippu Tip had an interest in rescuing him, partly from loyalty to a fellow-Arab, but also because he had left some ivory with him previously. He set out, but somewhat indirectly, having heard that there was copper to be bought at Ukosi. This place has been identified with Lukosi or Lukasi – but that is about 1,000 km south, in fact south-west of Lake Mweru; and Tippu Tip says in the *Maisha* that he crossed the Lomami (i.e. travelled west), went on to a Chief Lupungu (or Rupungu) and then pressed on for a month

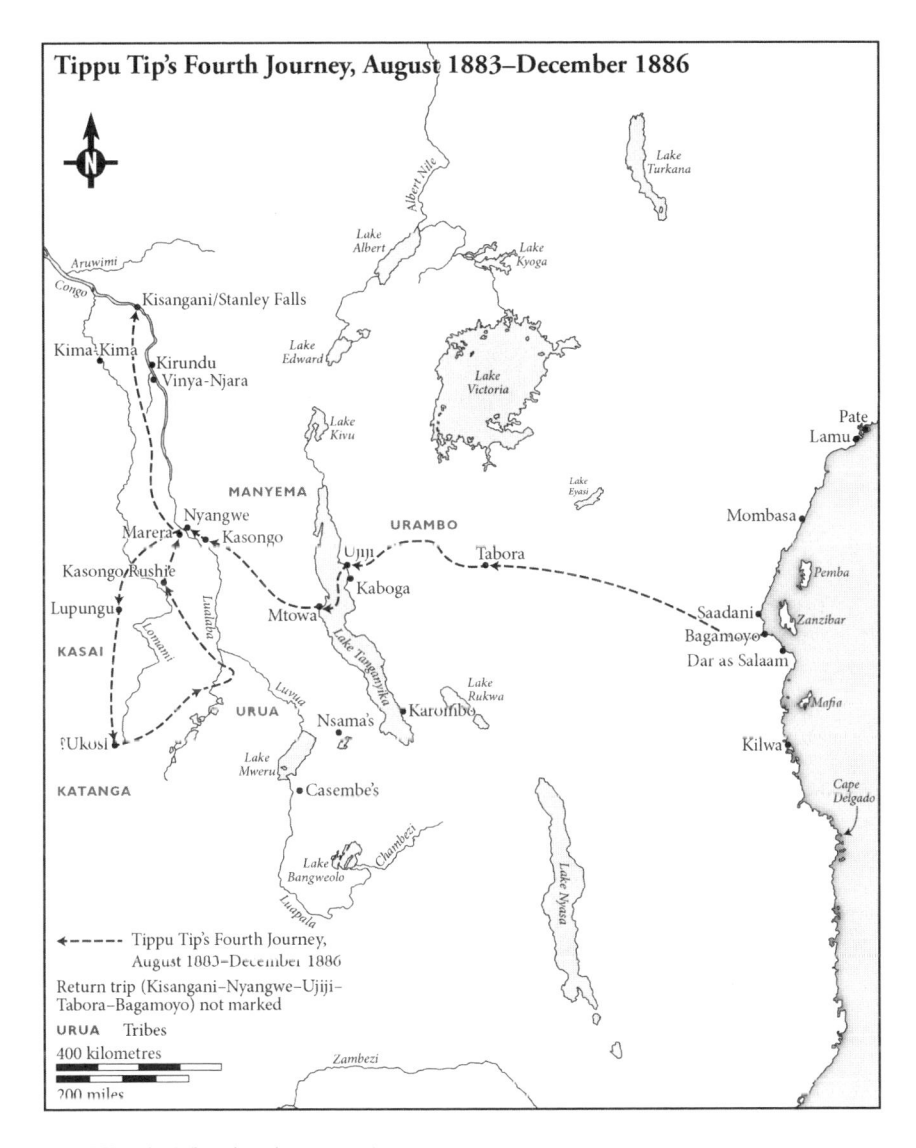

Tippu Tip's Fourth Journey, August 1883–December 1886

(Map showing Tippu Tip's Fourth Journey, August 1883–December 1886. Return trip (Kisangani–Nyangwe–Ujiji–Tabora–Bagamoyo) not marked. URUA Tribes. 400 kilometres / 200 miles.)

to Ukosi. After buying 700 *frasila* of copper (more than 4.5 tons) very cheaply, he then turned north to find Juma Merikani after only eleven days' travelling (which might have been 150 miles). So it is likely that Ukosi was some way west of Lake Mweru, possibly even in the Kasai region, or on the borders of Katanga, where the copper mines were. Tippu Tip comments on this journey that, although he found plenty of food in the villages he passed through, people fled on his arrival. Almost certainly this was because by this time, in the early 1880s,

Arabs looking for ivory and slaves west of the Lualaba had earned a reputation for violent attacks on villages. Their method was often to capture women and children as hostages, and return them only if the menfolk could redeem them with supplies of ivory – and sometimes not even then.

A strange scene met him when he found Juma Merikani: "In this village there were about 3,000 men or more, all drunk, except for one Muslim, by name Musa, ... who was sober." Juma Merikani had been at the same party: "He managed to drag himself to greet me and immediately collapsed in a drunken stupor." The trader's taste for liquor was confirmed by the German traveller Wissmann, who records that Juma distilled his own spirits for medicinal purposes, to relieve the pain of gout![11] Next morning, Tippu Tip sorted out matters with the chief, insisting that Juma Merikani have his goods returned to him, and be allowed freedom to travel when he wished.[12]

Why did Tippu Tip spend this extra time in sorting out the problems of a drunkard? Apart from the fact that Juma Merikani had some of his ivory, and of his being an old colleague, Tippu Tip was set on a mission to assert his own and Arab authority in Manyema and surrounding areas, so that he and others would be able to trade freely, and that the routes to the east coast remained uninterrupted. In what follows we shall see how the development of the Congo as a trading route really did present a direct threat to the Arabs of Zanzibar, just as Tippu Tip and Sultan Barghash had feared.

For this period, it is difficult to be sure of Tippu Tip's route since he does not name the village where he met up with Juma Merikani. He reports on the state of the villages subject to the Paramount Chief of Urua, the area between Lake Mweru and Lake Kasili. Here the Chief had enforced the loyalty of troops in his huge army, reckoned by Tippu Tip at 7,000 or more, by cutting off some of their noses, ears or arms. The explorer V.L. Cameron also records such mutilations. Neither he nor Tippu Tip explain how a man's fighting capacity can be improved by amputation of an arm! Cameron considers that the chiefs did this simply to demonstrate their power over their subjects. Somehow this Chief had gained control of large areas between the upper reaches of the Lualaba and Lomami rivers, and even west of the Lomami. But the mini-empire collapsed when Chief Rungu Kabare died and his children took over.[13]

The scale of operations had by now significantly increased. Instead of the armed caravans of a few hundred that featured in Tippu Tip's early journeys, he was now dealing in large numbers of men and guns. He revisited Ngongo Lutete, the chief he had installed in Kasongo Rushie, and gave him 10,000 guns; and then set out, with 3,000 armed and 6,000 unarmed men, for Stanley Falls.

Travelling with Stanley in October–December 1876, Tippu Tip had gone as far as Vinya Njara on the River Lualaba, more than half-way from Nyangwe to the series of cataracts which then were given Stanley's name. Shortly downriver from Stanley Falls the river turns west, and it was not far from there that Stanley first heard the river referred to as the 'Congo', so achieving absolute certainty that Livingstone was wrong and the Lualaba had no connection with the Nile river system. In the late 1870s, Arabs other than Tippu Tip extended their operations north from Nyangwe, and by 1879 they are recorded as being well established in Stanley Falls, presumably using it as a base for expeditions farther north in search of ivory. Meanwhile, as we saw in the previous chapter, from 1879 onwards Stanley and the Belgians had been developing communications up the River Congo, and in December 1883 Stanley established a station there. This was not only to be an important base for the Belgians in the Upper Congo: it would also be the place of confrontation between them and the Arabs moving westwards and downriver from their previous bases of Ujiji and Nyangwe.

Tippu Tip at Stanley Falls, 1884–85

Tippu Tip arrived at Stanley Falls in December 1884. The base established by Stanley was on an island in the river, Kisanga (hence the name Kisangani), opposite the Arab village of Singitini. Tippu Tip based himself at the latter both on this journey and during the Emin Pasha Relief Expedition in the late 1880s.

It now really does become apparent that Tippu Tip's journey – in fact more of an expedition – had a motive distinct from his previous trading travels. Sultan Barghash, in loading him with presents but also with superior weapons, and in urging him to make haste to Manyema, had indeed reckoned that a strengthened Arab presence on the Lualaba, under Tippu Tip's leadership, would define the limits of the Belgian sphere of influence, and would ensure that Arab trading continued along the Ujiji–Tabora–Bagamoyo route rather than succumb to the enticements of the Congo river line of communication. Barghash, and the Arabs of Zanzibar, were increasingly aware of the competition they were facing in Manyema. There were even rumours that Stanley had gone farther upriver than Stanley Falls/Kisangani, and had hoisted the AIC flag at Nyangwe. This accounts for the large number of men Tippu Tip had with him, and the stream of letters he records he received from Barghash – to which he replied that he would need yet more men and munitions.[14]

The Belgians were acutely aware that action needed to be taken to confine Arab influence and operations. They wanted to halt what they saw as Arab expansion down the Congo, and reckoned that the way to do this was to occupy and control territory alongside the river, and/or to conclude alliances with chiefs of villages on the route. Partly this was so that the AIC, later the EIC, could monopolize trade and charge import and export duties, and partly it was to prevent the spread of the slave trade beyond Manyema. Competition with the Arabs, even confrontation with them, was inherent in these policies.

Lt A.M. Wester, a Swedish national appointed as commander of the Stanley Falls station in July 1884, reported that relations with the Arabs were then good. Nevertheless, no doubt reckoning that good fences make good neighbours, he concluded a written agreement in November 1884 with a certain Mwinyi Amani, who signed on behalf of Tippu Tip. Some historians have described him as a 'lieutenant' of Tippu Tip, but he was almost certainly his son, by a non-Arab concubine. He signed the agreement "Aman bin Malu and Hamed bin Mohammed bin Juma al-Murjabi", unusually giving the name of his mother, Malu, as well as the fullest possible catalogue of his father's names (father and grandfather, and *nisba*, family name). But his other appearances in narratives of the period are incidental. By this agreement, the Arabs would go no farther downriver than the seventh cataract of Stanley Falls, "nor on any territory of the *Comité d'Études du haut-Congo,* either for fighting, or for trade, or for taking slaves, goats or chickens".[15] A translation of the agreement made by the Belgian official Camille Coquilhat either then or very soon afterwards (he published his book in 1888) adds the important word "ivory" between "slaves" and "goats".[16]

The ink was scarcely dry on this agreement when Tippu Tip himself arrived, and he promptly disavowed it, declaring that he had been sent by the Sultan to stop Arabs trading with the Europeans. The Wester–Amani agreement did not in fact specifically permit trade, although it did prohibit Arab movement below the seventh cataract for purposes of trade, among other things. Tippu Tip's objections are more likely to

Fourth Journey: Back to the Centre

have been directed against the asymmetric nature of the agreement – it purported to stop the Arabs going downstream but with no parallel prohibition of the Europeans encroaching (and trading) upstream.

Tippu Tip promptly set about defying the agreement. He organized a number of caravans to trade outwards from Stanley Falls, including down the river to the confluences with the Lomami and Aruwimi. One of these came badly to grief; they were taken by surprise by a force of local people at a large village, according to one account having been tempted to over-indulge in palm wine given them by the Africans, and lost 1,500 men. But the others brought back huge quantities of ivory; Tippu Tip reports 2,000 *frasila*.[17]

Some British missionaries encountered Tippu Tip on this occasion. George Grenfell, who had come with his companions up the River Congo, spent Christmas 1884 at Stanley Falls and noted that Tippu Tip had brick-built houses constructed, and large areas of land cleared for cultivation, to supply the numerous personnel both resident and expected to pass through. Grenfell also reported that Tippu Tip

> had sent 700 men down river trading (rather 'raiding', for we counted 20 burnt villages and thousands of fugitive canoes). He ... talks of making his way down to the Atlantic – says that the Sultan of Zanzibar claims all the Congo, right down to the sea.[18]

Coquilhat, recording the conversation between Tippu Tip and another Belgian EIC officer, Alphonse Vangèle, in January 1885 (see next paragraph) also mentions this exaggerated claim by Barghash. It seems out of character, especially as not long afterwards the Sultan recognized the EIC and its territorial claims. It is more likely that Tippu Tip was asserting the right of the Sultan's subjects to trade wherever they wished, including down to the Atlantic.[19]

Just over a month later, at the end of January 1885, Vangèle arrived at Stanley Falls with instructions from EIC superiors to re-open discussions with Tippu Tip. Similarly to Storms's proposal in 1882 (see Chapter 7 pages 172–3), but more specifically this time, the aim was to persuade him to visit Europe, set himself up as independent of the Sultan of Zanzibar, and to handle all his trading activities via the Congo. Tippu Tip's instructions from Sayyid Barghash were to assert the Sultan's authority all the way down the Congo – at least, that is what he said; but, as mentioned above, he must have known that in practice he could not have done more than ensure trading rights down to Stanley Falls, and perhaps as far as the confluence with the River Aruwimi. We have a detailed account of the conversation between Tippu Tip and Vangèle, based on a debrief given by Vangèle to Coquilhat three weeks later.[20] They engaged in frank speaking, at the end of which Tippu Tip gave some ground, ("very conciliatory" in Ceulemans's interpretation) promising to withdraw his men from the Lomami and Aruwimi, and requesting the Belgians to persuade the locals not to run away at the Arabs' approach, so that they could do trade with them. (Unfortunately, as we have seen, this was a vain hope, since too many Arabs – not necessarily those under Tippu Tip's command – were using barbaric violence towards African villages in their pursuit of ivory and slaves.) Following these discussions, Arab raiding was in fact reduced. Tippu Tip left some Zanzibaris in the villages, reportedly to instruct the Africans in agriculture, to supply the large number of personnel he had brought with him. Vangèle was impressed with Tippu Tip, writing that "without being educated, he has general ideas about politics and geography, and seems particularly interested in events in Europe and in affairs concerning the British, the Germans, the French, the Belgians and the Portuguese".[21] Coquilhat patronizingly discusses Tippu Tip's behaviour at dinner:

> Although a bit *gauche*, because of his being unaccustomed to handling a fork, his behaviour was very correct. He drank only water (this was in public), but he encouraged his fellow-Muslims to drink wine.[22]

Tippu Tip was away from Kisangani from January till December 1885, probably in the area between the Rivers Lomami and Lualaba, as he records in a curious postscript to another treaty signed with Wester, this one by himself personally. The treaty itself is a curious document, in that it makes few commitments of substance on either side. In it, Tippu Tip undertakes that he and his people in the islands above the Seventh Cataract of Stanley Falls will not "trouble or interfere with the white men, who stay in Buki just below the same cataract"; that both Arabs and 'Whites' may trade with local Africans in the Stanley Falls district, who should be treated gently and humanely; and that during Tippu Tip's absence there should be "one great Arab, Chief or Niampara" responsible for the Arabs' deeds. In the fourth and final clause, Wester records: "As a sign of the good friendship and understanding between me and Tipo-Tipo, this one has brought me a cow, sheep and goats as present, in return for which he has got two big tusks of ivory from an elephant killed by me with my own gun, and besides many other private things of less value."[23]

This treaty appears to be another attempt to define a border of spheres of influence, but this time Wester has held back from again trying to prevent Arabs from trading downstream. The postscript, written originally in Arabic although only a French translation survives, is a description by Tippu Tip of how he had been absent from Stanley Falls and returned in December 1885; how he had met Wester ("He is an honest man; he has killed several elephants ... and given me some tusks"); how neither the Arabs nor Wester's people will attack the Africans. But, after stating that they will not allow anyone to kill any of the Arabs, this postscript goes on to make clear that Tippu Tip is planning – with Wester's knowledge – a reprisal raid on a village on or near the River Aruwimi. The treaty receives virtually no attention in commentaries on Tippu Tip's life, although Bontinck reprints it from the Tervuren archives.

In the *Maisha*, Tippu Tip makes no mention of either the agreements with Wester or the discussions with Vangèle. He does report meeting Wester and another Swede named Gleerup, and he says that he got on well with them. Gleerup spent several months in Stanley Falls but actually wanted to continue his journey across the continent. Tippu Tip lent him canoes, to go upriver to Kasongo, and supplies to help him reach the coast – in which he was successful.[24]

It may be worth summing up the objectives of Belgians and Arabs in the upper Congo at this time, early 1885. Leopold and his staff were still not sure what the trading opportunities (other than ivory) would turn out to be in the Congo basin generally; the great gains made from rubber would come some years later. They were however determined to establish lines of communication, mainly on the Congo itself but also on some tributaries, and to maintain the stations that Stanley had set up. They were also under pressure to resist the expansion of the slave trade and the violence that was associated with Arab acquisition of ivory, from Manyema on to the Congo below Stanley Falls. For Barghash, the concept of person-to-overlord loyalty (as practised in Arab tribal societies) was more important, and more natural, than actual territorial acquisition. He wished to retain influence over the people – and especially the Arab people – in the interior, wherever they were; and this of course included Manyema and the Lualaba–Lomami river area down to Stanley Falls and beyond. He hoped to be able to maintain this influence with the support of Tippu Tip and other Arab leaders including Rumaliza, who had been entrusted with the restoration of Zanzibari influence north and east of Lake Tanganyika in the anarchy that followed the death of Mirambo in December 1884. Keeping his Arab subjects loyal to him enabled Barghash to levy duty and other taxes on the trade of goods through the still thriving port of Zanzibar. Tippu Tip was content to pay loyalty to Barghash, provided he had freedom of movement in areas where both Arabs and Africans feared and respected him, so that he could make profits from his ivory trading. It is difficult to pin down firm evidence on how he viewed the advantages and disadvantages of using the Congo route for trading. When Ceulemans describes him as "conciliatory", this may have been because he thought at least it was worth keeping his options open. And when in the *Maisha* he stresses his determination to carry out the Sultan's wishes, he would have been anxious that anyone reading it would not have cause to question his loyalty.

His whereabouts through 1885 are uncertain. From the *Maisha* it would seem that he stayed in Kisangani through the year, but he may have taken an expedition to the north or north-east, in the direction of Equatoria, and some evidence suggests that he visited Nyangwe between late January and September. This would have been for a meeting with Rumaliza, who was having difficulty in restoring order in Uvinza, and needed more men and weapons.[25] At any rate, Tippu Tip was still in Kisangani when the British EIC officer Walter Deane arrived to take over from Wester as commander of the Stanley Falls station in January or February 1886. Deane renewed the invitation to visit Belgium, which Tippu Tip declined, on the grounds that he had received an instruction from Barghash to hasten back to Zanzibar. Deane took the opportunity also to tell Tippu Tip that it was not acceptable to capture slaves and send them to the east coast – and received the reply that local slaves would be used only to carry goods to Nyangwe, and would then be allowed to come back to their own land; and that other caravans would be used from Nyangwe to Ujiji and from Ujiji to the coast. Deane seems to have been content with this only moderately satisfactory answer, and went on to ask for an assurance that the violent raids on villages would be stopped. Again Tippu Tip contrived an ambiguous reply – that he wanted good relations with the Europeans.[26]

Carl Peters and the Scramble for East Africa

The command from Barghash was real enough. The Sultan was belatedly coming to realize that European 'interest' in East Africa was developing to the point where his own suzerainty was at risk; the 'Scramble' had spread from Niger and the Congo to the east and southeast. He needed to consult Tippu Tip to consider the implications for Manyema and the interior east of Lake Tanganyika.

How had this come about? Initially, a German private adventurer lay at the root of it, but at a high political level too events were moving fast because of the intensifying competition among European powers for territory – not just influence – in Africa, reinforced by the change of heart on the part of Chancellor Bismarck (page 195). After the conference called by King Leopold in Brussels in 1876, a number of societies had sprung up in Germany with the aim of furthering the policy of developing colonies; but, as we have seen, Bismarck was then opposed to the idea, and the societies made little headway. Nevertheless, one individual named Carl Peters remained determined to move the colonial agenda forward. (See box on page 212–13) He founded a 'Society for German Colonization', and in November 1884 arrived in Zanzibar with two colleagues – all three disguised as 'mechanics' planning to hoist the German flag over territory on the mainland. This they proceeded to do, by means of 'treaties' signed with a number of chiefs, notably on the River Wami, i.e. inland from Bagamoyo. As with the agreements signed by Stanley along the River Congo, these pieces of paper meant little in one sense, and much in another: while giving few rights to the Society, they yet served as proof that the Germans had first claim in these areas. Peters's activities also represented a direct challenge to Sultan Barghash, since the lands in which he had been signing 'treaties' were just those areas through which the caravan routes passed from Bagamoyo and other ports to the interior. Returning to Berlin in February 1885, he founded the German East Africa Company, and ceded to the new company all the rights acquired by the Society. He also managed to extract from the German Emperor a charter giving protection (the *Schutzbrief*) over these territories. Meanwhile, some British businessmen had obtained similar treaties with chiefs farther north, in present-day Kenya, though with the difference that they were acting with the permission of the Sultan of Zanzibar. With these concessions they formed the British East Africa Association.

Events then moved quickly. The Sultan protested to the German Emperor in April 1885, and to Bismarck in May, against the very notion that the chiefs could have authority to cede sovereign rights, and against the declaration of a protectorate in the Carl Peters territories. Kirk, now Sir John, still Consul in Zanzibar, who for years had been working to support the Sultan's influence on the mainland and to maintain British influence with him (and therefore in the area), began to see a weakening of his ability to affect the situation. Barghash sent the former naval officer Lloyd Mathews, now promoted to General in the Sultan's service (see box on page 249), with troops to sign treaties on Zanzibar's behalf with chiefs in areas where they feared the Germans might next intervene. Mathews had some success, but such arrangements lacked durability, and within a very short time German colleagues of Peters arrived and signed up treaties with the very same chiefs.

Carl Peters

Born near Hanover in 1856, Carl (or Karl) Peters studied history and philosophy at three German universities, and was destined for a career as a teacher. However, while staying for a while with a relative in London, he appears to have become interested in ideas of colonization and imperialism, and decided on a change of direction. On his return to Berlin in 1884 he founded the *Society for German Colonization*, with aspirations of annexing areas of East Africa from under the noses of the British. Later the same year he snuck into Zanzibar with a few German companions. Using various (largely unsuccessful) disguises, they kitted out an expedition for the interior and crossed the sea to Saadani.

Moving with speed through areas notionally under Sayyid Barghash's suzerainty, Peters signed treaties with a number of African chiefs, under which they transferred sovereignty and other rights to the Society, in return for 'protection'. As related in the main narrative, he then returned to Germany to found the *German East Africa Company*, which absorbed all the rights of the Society. In February 1885, the Company was granted an Imperial Charter (often referred to as the *Schutzbrief,* protection letter), Bismarck by now having been won over to the idea of German colonization in Africa. This opened the way for further expansion in the area which became German East Africa (roughly present-day mainland Tanzania) under the British–German agreements of 1886 and 1890.

Peters returned to East Africa, now strongly motivated by German nationalist ideology. In 1888, he concluded an agreement with Sayyid Khalifa (Barghash's brother and successor as Sultan of Zanzibar) to lease the

Through the first half of 1885, German efforts to acquire rights to more territories in the interior continued, as did anxious and urgent communications between Zanzibar, London, Paris and Berlin. In August 1885, one German officer, Rochus Schmidt, secured twenty-one treaties in as many days. The German aim seems to have been to impose protectorate status over land in the interior; the fact that the Sultan might retain a coastal strip did not seem to concern them, since their hope was in due course to secure duty-free transit rights to the coast. The Sultan of course saw this as ruinous, his income in large part depending on the customs levies he was able to impose on trade through Bagamoyo and other ports. The British were not able to help him, being unwilling to stand up to German high-pressure tactics in East Africa because of pre-occupations with Egyptian financial crises and the threat posed by the Mahdi revolt in the Sudan.

---

coastal strip on the mainland. The German presence was unpopular, often arrogant and brutal, and led to an uprising which was put down by forces of the Imperial German Government and the British navy. Peters meanwhile decided to try to extend German influence north and east, in an expedition to Uganda and Equatoria, under the pretence of mounting a German attempt to rescue Emin Pasha. He did conclude a treaty with the Kabaka of Buganda, but his hopes of securing Buganda for German rule was thwarted by the division of East Africa into British and German areas under the treaty including Heligoland signed in July 1890.

After a further spell in the homeland, Peters was back in Africa in 1891 as *Reichskommissar*, High Commissioner, for the Kilimanjaro region in the northern part of German East Africa. He was recalled after two years, having earned a reputation for barbarity and immorality, in particular following an incident when he ordered the execution of an African who had broken into the house of his concubines and had sexual intercourse with one of them. (The Germans kept women whom they claimed "had been given to them as presents by local chiefs, and ... were treated as if they were prostitutes by the whites"; Perras 2004: 198.) Peters eventually had his commission removed for abuse of his official position. In disgrace, and to avoid a criminal sentence, in 1896 he moved to London, from where he wrote books and articles, and managed further journeys to East Africa (to explore abandoned gold mines near the River Zambezi). His rehabilitation became a political issue, and in 1905 Kaiser Wilhelm II restored his right to use the title of Imperial Commissioner. He died in September 1918, aged 62. Years later, he was portrayed as a German nationalist and colonialist hero, in various books and articles, and in an epic film produced in 1940.

A showdown came in early August 1885, when a German squadron sailed in to Zanzibar and compelled Barghash to recognize all their protectorate claims. At the same time, the Germans agreed to recognize the independence of his territories – but this was something of a poisoned chalice, since in their view it required prior definition of the limits of his dominions. A further German ship arrived in late August, this one commanded by a Rear Admiral and having on board the Sultan's sister, the former Princess Salme. In a dramatic episode twenty years previously, this daughter of Sultan Sa'id bin Sultan had met and fallen in love with a German trader living in Zanzibar, by whom she became pregnant. To avoid disgrace, and in fear for her life (quite reasonably), she managed to escape with the help of the acting British Consul, and reached Aden on a ship of the Royal Navy. Ruete, her German lover, met up with her there; they were married, and went to live in Germany. Sadly, Ruete died in a road accident only a few years later, and Emily (as she chose to call herself) lived in difficult circumstances, though not in actual poverty, in Hamburg thereafter. It has been suggested that in August 1885 the Germans thought they could threaten to displace Barghash and put Emily/Salme or her son on his throne, but the idea is too far-fetched. The German Rear Admiral may have thought he could embarrass the Sultan to a certain extent, and Emily herself no doubt hoped for some reconciliation with her brother, and perhaps even some financial assistance. But she was not allowed to meet him, and returned to Germany empty-handed and disappointed.[27]

The threat by the German ships was, however, real. The outcome was that Barghash had to acquiesce in the establishment of a tripartite commission composed of British, French and German representatives, tasked with fixing the boundaries of the (remaining) possessions of the Sultan of Zanzibar. Barghash protested even against the terms of reference, claiming that the Delimitation Commission should restrict itself to the region affected by Peters's 'treaties', but his voice was no longer being heard. The Commission's work began in December 1885, but moved slowly, and in time degenerated into a bilateral argument, the British arguing for a more generous, and the Germans for a more restrictive, allocation of territory; but neither would acknowledge the extent of authority that Barghash had come to expect or assume. Partly this was because, as we have seen, the Sultan did not exercise the kind of territorial control which was normal among European sovereigns and governments. His subjects, and especially the local chiefs, owed loyalty to him and accepted that they should pay certain customs dues to him, but what was missing was the sovereign control for which the commissioners were looking. In October 1886, the British and the Germans resolved their differences, to their own satisfaction but hardly to that of the Sultan. They reached agreement to award the Sultan full sovereign rights over Zanzibar, Pemba and Mafia islands, plus a ten-mile coastal strip from the River Miningani in the south to the port of Kipini in the north, plus enclaves round certain ports. Other provisions included the division of territory into British and German spheres of influence, in the north and south, equivalent approximately to present-day Kenya and mainland Tanzania, respectively. Barghash reluctantly bowed to the inevitable, and accepted the terms of the Commission's decision in December 1886 (see map on page 252).[28]

Tippu Tip's return to Zanzibar, 1885–86, and the Arab takeover of Stanley Falls

Tippu Tip made his way back to Zanzibar while all this was in progress. Having left Kisangani in April 1885, he took the normal route via Nyangwe and Ujiji. Arriving in Tabora in August 1886, he was involved in an incident in which a German ivory trader, Giesecke, was shot and wounded by an Arab with whom he was in dispute. In the *Maisha*, Tippu Tip recounts the incident, and the efforts to bring the criminal to justice, in great detail; perhaps it was important because it involved the possible murder of a European, and the Arabs feared reprisals.[29] Despite care from missionaries in Tabora, Giesecke died from his injuries a few weeks later. It was nearly four years later that the culprit was caught and tried; he was hanged at Bagamoyo in June 1890. Present during these events was the Russian-German explorer, Wilhelm Junker, who had been with Emin Pasha in southern Sudan and was making his way down to the coast. He asked for Tippu Tip's protection for the remainder of his journey, which he was given, but at a price – in what he describes as his "critical position" he had to raise his initial offer of MT$750 to MT$1,000 and finally to MT$1,500, of which only about MT$700 would have been the cost of the porters. Tippu Tip's eye for profit was undimmed.[30]

Tippu Tip, travelling with Junker, left the Tabora area in September 1886, and arrived in Bagamoyo in November, where he received a letter from Barghash urging him to make haste to Zanzibar. He crossed the strait early the next morning, and went directly to the Sultan.

Barghash was in the depths of despair. Their conversation would have taken place after Barghash had learnt of the British–German agreement on what should be the outcome of the trilateral Commission, but before he had given his consent to it. He suggested that Tippu Tip should leave again immediately, the local situation being so bad. Tippu Tip said he could not start travelling right away: he needed a rest, and anyway it was the rainy season and routes would be blocked. But if the Sultan commanded him, he would go. Barghash went on:

"Hamed, you must forgive me, but to speak frankly, I don't want anything more to do with the mainland. The Europeans want to take even Zanzibar from me, so how can I keep the mainland? Those who have died without having lived through everything that's happening now, they have been happier. Just now, you are still a stranger here, but you will soon see what the situation is."[31]

Tippu Tip records that when he heard these words of the Sultan's, he realized how grim the outlook was for Zanzibar. Two months later he heard news from the interior which suggested that more trouble lay ahead on the Upper Congo. He appears to have drawn the conclusion – a reasonable one – that Arab interests were threatened on every side.

The news from Kisangani was of a battle between the Arabs there and the Belgian station commanded by the newly arrived Walter Deane. According to Deane's account, given to Herbert Ward in November 1886, he had been wounded by a poisoned spear soon after taking up his appointment as commander, and after a period of recuperation returned to Stanley Falls in January 1886. There, as we have seen above, he met Tippu Tip, who left soon afterwards for Zanzibar, entrusting leadership of the Arabs to his cousin, Bwana Nzige, and Bwana Nzige's son, Rashid bin Mohammed. Deane saw from the outset that things would be difficult: "These fellows did not like me at all, and ... I shouldn't get them to conform to my orders without a row."[32] (It is interesting to note that Deane considered himself in a position of command or authority over the Arabs.) Reckoning that he and his contingent of about seventy men might have to defend themselves against attack, he cleared the area round the camp and improved the fortifications. Relations with the Arabs became worse, partly because Deane tried to protect Africans from being robbed by the Arabs. One day in July 1886, a row broke out over an African woman who took refuge in the camp, claiming that she had been beaten by the Arab to whom she had been given by Tippu

Tip. Seeing no signs of ill-treatment, Deane sent her back; but she reappeared a few days later, this time with severe cuts and bruises. He decided to give her protection, despite demands from Bwana Nzige and Rashid that he should give her back. He was confident that he could withstand an attack, not least because he was expecting a steamer to arrive soon with additional men and ammunition.

The steamer, *Le Stanley*, arrived, but the only fighting man on it was a Belgian lieutenant, and there was no ammunition. Not realizing this and thinking that Deane now had reinforcements, the Arabs sent a message ending hostilities. But a couple of days later they heard the truth about *Le Stanley*'s disappointing cargo, and planned an attack. This started the day after the steamer's departure downriver, on 24 August, and the battle went on for several days, after which numbers of Deane's men deserted, from fear of having their throats cut by the Arabs in the likely event of defeat. Deane decided to destroy the station and leave it. He and a small remnant, including the Belgian officer, set a fire that night and escaped, although the Belgian drowned when they were crossing a tributary. They took refuge in the forest, where they survived on such roots and insects as they could find, and small gifts of food from African villagers who protected them from the Arabs' search parties. Eventually they were picked up by the Belgian officer, Camille Coquilhat, coming upriver from Bangala in the steamer *AIA* (named after the *Association Internationale Africaine*). The Stanley Falls station was thus lost to the Belgians, and not rebuilt for some years.

Interestingly, the Arab side of this event has also come down to us. Bwana Nzige wrote two letters to Tippu Tip in Zanzibar, who showed them to the British Acting Consul, Frederick Holmwood. The originals do not survive, but translations were forwarded as diplomatic reports.[33] Bwana Nzige reported that Deane claimed that all the Africans were under his authority, and that he and his colleagues were faced with a threatening attitude by Deane's armed men when they went to negotiate for the return of the woman. He thought this would lead to an unacceptable situation with regard to all their female slaves (whom the Arabs would have considered legitimate concubines under custom and Islamic law). Deane had said – according to Bwana Nzige – that any slave taking refuge with him would not be restored; and, in addition, he was planning to build in an area where the Arabs did not want construction. In his second letter, Bwana Nzige reported that Deane had been giving refuge to thirteen female slaves, and that when the owner of the original refugee had tried to get her back by a surprise raid, Deane had mounted a reprisal attack, burnt the village, and seized ivory and the woman. Deane had also attacked another village. When the steamer *Le Stanley* had arrived, the Arabs had hoped to negotiate, but received no reply. A few days later, Deane had offered peace, but on unacceptable conditions.

Other accounts contain the hint that Deane actually wanted to buy the 'refugee' woman himself, and that her Arab owner named a price so high that it was clear he did not want to sell her. Whatever the immediate reason for the battle, the underlying reason is likely to have been Deane's excessive assertiveness, in claiming authority on behalf of the AIC or EIC, and Arab concern at seeing their freedom of action (in travelling and trading) curtailed. A Belgian diplomat commented to the Secretary of the British Ambassador in Brussels, probably correctly: "Your countryman Mr Deane is much too much of a soldier and not enough of a diplomatist."[34] The incident was serious for Leopold, who needed to be able to demonstrate security of authority on the Upper as well as the Lower Congo; and it was a forerunner of a greater and more definitive Arab–Belgian battle that would occur later, in 1893.

How did Tippu Tip react, in Zanzibar? At this time, news was coming through about the plight of Emin Pasha, the Egyptian-appointed Governor of Equatoria in Southern Sudan (see next chapter). Emin Pasha was rumoured to have accumulated a huge stock of ivory, and Tippu Tip was considering leading an expedition to bring him out and acquire the tusks. But the new situation created by the fighting at Stanley Falls created an obligation on him to take some kind of action there – either to confront the EIC in order to defend the interests of the Arabs, or to go and make peace. He told the Belgian consul in Zanzibar that he was prepared to go to Belgium and see the King, but that he had no wish to wage war against the Europeans – on the contrary, his interests were aligned with theirs: "I have loved the whites since before I had a beard; now I have a white beard, why should I make war against them? My interests anyway are in having good relations with them".[35]

He may have meant by this that he had in general gained from his contact with European explorers (witness the tidy profit he had just made from Junker), and that a war in the interior would have put at risk his and other Arabs' trading interests.

As he was deliberating on these issues, the decision was made for him by the arrival in Zanzibar, once more, of Henry Morton Stanley, with a proposition to put to Tippu Tip for participation in the most unusual expedition of them all.

CHAPTER 10

Fifth Journey – What a Relief!

TIPPU TIP NOW became closely involved with one of the most extraordinary episodes in the imperial history of Central Africa. Hardly any of the protagonists emerged well from it: reputations were damaged (in one or two cases ruined), money was lost, and repercussions – including for Tippu Tip – lasted for years afterwards. Looking back, it is hard even to see why the enterprise was undertaken at all. Let us see if rational explanations can be found.

The province of Equatoria

The province of Equatoria had no defined boundaries. Rather, it represented an aspiration on the part of mid-19th century rulers of Egypt (notably the Khedive Ismail, r. 1863–79), who had hopes of extending their rule or their influence southwards beyond Sudan through what is now Uganda and Somalia.[1]

Initially, areas alongside the Nile and in its basin to the west became trading areas of agents employed by business people in Cairo and

Khartoum to exploit the ivory resources of the region. This trade was of mutual benefit, since the European and North American craving for ivory (described in Chapters 1 and 3) could be satisfied by exchange for Western manufactured goods, and also for guns. After the Napoleonic Wars, European armies updated their weaponry, and second-hand guns found a ready market in Africa. This ivory trade depended on the reasonably well-developed trading routes north, on the Nile but also beside it, to Khartoum and Cairo. The agents then added trade in slaves to that in ivory, the male slaves being useful as porters (as we have seen in East Africa), and the females as concubines.

Ismail Pasha became *Wali*, Governor, of Egypt in 1862, on behalf of the Ottoman Sultan, though in reality rulers of Egypt at this time were more or less independent; he was later granted the Turkish title of Khedive. He was ambitious and determined, and took forward the policy of pushing Egyptian control south and south-east into Ethiopia and Somalia. He had been educated in Paris, and aimed to bring Egypt into modern times through Western-inspired reforms and industrial investment. Employment of Europeans was consistent with these objectives (although it would eventually be the French and British governments that secured his downfall). In Equatoria, the southernmost province that covered much of present-day South Sudan and northern Uganda including Lake Albert, he appointed Sir Samuel Baker as Governor in 1869.

We have encountered Baker previously, on his 1861–65 Nile expedition when he met Speke and Grant following their discovery of the Nile outflow from Lake Victoria. Now he had a mandate from Khedive Ismail to ensure Egyptian authority in the province, to suppress the slave trade and to establish systems of 'regular commerce'. Ismail seems to have subscribed to the view, common in Britain at the time, that slave trading could be done away with if only there were adequate means for local populations to make money through other, legitimate, commerce. However, in Equatoria as elsewhere, slave-trade abolitionists from Europe encountered the standard objections from those who believed that slavery was sanctioned by Islam, and that in any case it was part of the cultural heritage of their society.

Baker was succeeded in 1873 as Governor of Equatoria by General Charles Gordon, who in 1876 became Governor-General of Sudan, and met his death in Khartoum in 1885. Although both Baker and Gordon felt strongly about the slave-trade abolition item in their instructions, they made little headway against the determination of the traders and the corruption of the Egyptian bureaucracy. They did succeed in setting up a string of military garrisons, mainly on the Nile, and improved communications on the river, for example by means of two steam-driven boats which had been brought there in pieces, assembled and launched.

However, the extent of Egyptian administrative influence was very limited. Communications were extremely poor, both within the province but also to 'headquarters' in Khartoum and Cairo. The Nile itself was unreliable as a means of communication, largely because of the huge marshy region known as the *Sudd* (from the Arabic word for dam or barrier), where the river is clogged up with vast islands of floating vegetation. Sometimes it was possible to get a boat through the winding channels; at others the whole waterway was entirely impassable, as it was for two years between 1878 and 1880.

The garrisons set up by Baker and Gordon could therefore do little more than administer themselves. This they did quite comprehensively, becoming communities complete with women and children, where they grew their own food, and even wove their own cloth. There were about fifty such stations, mostly on the Nile but some in almost forgotten locations in the countryside both east and west of the river.

The province of Equatoria could hardly be said to be administered in any real sense, even under the energetic leadership of Baker and Gordon. They themselves would visit the stations on the river infrequently, and the more distant ones hardly at all. The Egyptian soldiers, and the additional Sudanese recruits, seldom ventured out of the safety of their stations or the immediate vicinity. In addition, as Egyptian finances dwindled in the 1870s – causes included an ill-advised war in Ethiopia and the Khedive's extravagant plans for reform and modernization – the government in Cairo had fewer resources to devote to the intended expansion southwards and thus to maintaining the control (such as it was) over Equatoria.

Emin Pasha, Equatoria and the Mahdist revolt, 1878–86

After Gordon left Equatoria in 1876, the province saw further decline. In 1878, Gordon, now Governor-General of the Sudan, appointed as Governor there a slight, academic-looking, former doctor of German origin, who would become the unwitting and largely unwilling target of a major expedition aimed at bringing him relief.

On the face of it, and certainly if we were to make a judgement on appearances, this was a curious appointment. The person now known as Emin Pasha was a Prussian, originally named Edouard Carl Oscar Theodor Schnitzer until his conversion to Islam, who was born in 1840, the same year as Stanley and a couple of years after Tippu Tip. He left Germany soon after qualifying as a doctor, and set up in practice in Albania, where he demonstrated formidable linguistic skill in adding Turkish, Albanian and Greek to his already existing stock of French, English and Italian – as well as his native German. He travelled extensively in the Ottoman Empire, established a liaison with the widow of the Ottoman Governor of Northern Albania, and then travelled (without her) in 1875 to Cairo, and then on to Khartoum.

As well as possessing an extraordinary gift for languages, Emin was meticulous, precise and well organized. Gordon, when still Governor of Equatoria, had appointed him to be Chief Medical Officer in the province, and then asked him to go on a delicate diplomatic mission to the Kabaka (Chief) of Buganda, a territory lying west of Lake Victoria, to secure the release of an Egyptian force of 160 men being held by him. Emin succeeded in this task, and stayed on at Lado, one of the garrison stations on the Nile. He used this as a base for expeditions over wide areas of Equatoria and neighbouring territories, making plans (never realized) for developing the province with greater independence from Khartoum. He was appointed Governor of Equatoria in 1878, and was there in 1882 when Sudan became engulfed by the revolt of the Mahdi.

The concept of the Mahdi, meaning the 'Guided One', goes back to the early days of Islam, and denotes a leader guided by God who would restore Islam's purity and strength. As a title it was applied to, or adopted by, some of the early Caliphs (*Khalifa*s, successors of the Prophet Muhammad). Among some Muslims, particularly the Shi'a, the term took on a messianic connotation: some believed that a leader would at some point emerge, possibly heralding the Day of Judgement. Through history a number of leaders have claimed the title. Our focus is on Mohammed Ahmad bin Abdullah, born in 1844, who after religious study became a prominent Sufi sheikh and, in 1881, proclaimed himself the Mahdi and initiated a revolt in the Sudan against the oppression of Ottoman Egyptian rule. Within two years he had gained control of most of what is now the Sudan, and destroyed three Egyptian armies sent against him. In January 1885, his forces captured Khartoum, killing the Governor General, Charles Gordon, a victory that enabled him to set up a theocratic Islamic state. His own rule was short-lived, since he died (probably of typhus) six months later, aged forty-one. His three deputies took over; rivalry between them ended with the emergence of Abdallahi bin Mohammed as *Khalifa*, a term deliberately chosen to echo the title adopted by the Prophet Mohammed's successors.

In the early 1880s, Emin Pasha had begun to think that the best possibilities for developing his province lay in the south, especially if the provinces of Equatoria and Bahr al-Ghazal (to the north-west) could be united. He visited Khartoum for consultations in mid-1882, but soon after his return in August he had cause for alarm because of a revolt among the Dinka people on the border with Bahr al-Ghazal. By March 1883, it seemed to him that Khartoum had failed to control the Mahdist revolt, and that his own position in Equatoria was looking increasingly unsafe. No support was forthcoming from Khartoum; steamers with much-needed supplies were becoming scarce. Nevertheless, he retained a degree of optimism, not least because the province's accounts were in surplus, largely due to ivory imports. In May 1883, he felt confident enough to pay a visit to the south-west corner of his province, possibly envisaging some tie-up with the north-east corner of Leopold's Congo. But on his return at the end of the month he was met by news of Mahdist victories through the Sudan, and the start of the siege of Khartoum. He considered that resistance would be futile, and that the best chance for him and his troops was a pre-emptive surrender of the province. He sent a delegation carrying a letter to this effect to the Mahdists in Bahr al-Ghazal. But this had no effect, and the delegation probably simply defected to the Mahdi's forces.

Through 1884, a direct Mahdist attack on Equatoria was expected, but failed to materialize until the end of the year, when the station of Amadi in the north-west came under siege. Karam Allah Kurqusawi, the *amir* (governor) of Bahr al-Ghazal and commander of the Mahdi's army, captured Amadi in February 1885, and threatened to march on Lado, Emin's headquarters, if he did not receive submission. Emin Pasha took the decision to withdraw to the south. It was a reasonable thing to do: Lado could be retained as a garrison, while new headquarters could be established at Dufile, where there were two steamboats, and from where the river was navigable right to Lake Albert. Furthermore, Emin calculated that the Mahdists would not be able to push their conquests into areas where their ideology and language were unfamiliar. His men, however, were not so easily convinced. Their loyalties were to the Khedive in the far north, in Cairo, and they stood less chance of returning to their homes and families if they were to allow themselves deliberately to be cut off in Central Africa, with hostile Mahdists blocking the way home. They also appear not to have realized, or believed, that Khartoum was in the Mahdi's hands, and considered it possible to break out, downriver, to safety.

Despite this resistance from his men, Emin succeeded in effecting at least a partial withdrawal from Lado: he, his officials and the by now large number of refugees from Bahr al-Ghazal would go upriver to Wadelai, while the troops stayed in Lado – where, as it turned out, they remained free from attack, since the Mahdist army had to go back to deal with a mutiny in Bahr al-Ghazal. Wadelai, where Emin arrived in July 1885, was a sound choice of headquarters, having good supplies of food, and means of communication (through Bunyoro and Buganda) with Zanzibar and Egypt.

In the course of the following year, Emin heard (by means of a line of communication through Alexander Mackay, a Scottish missionary in Buganda) firm news of developments in the north: the fall of Khartoum, the death of Gordon, and the Egyptian Government's abandonment of the Sudan. A letter from Nubar Pasha, the Egyptian Prime Minister, suggested he should take any measures he pleased, if necessary to leave the country – a proposal which Emin scorned, ironically claiming that the Egyptian authorities were suggesting that he go to Zanzibar, an overland distance of 1,000 miles or more, as he would eventually discover, "just as they would suggest a walk to Shubra" (a district of Cairo twenty minutes' walk from Tahrir Square)![2] He concluded, rightly, that he could not hope for any support or relief from Egypt, and that his best bet was to stay put. At one point, under encouragement from Mackay, he even believed that there was scope for a British-protected area in Equatoria, and that he might thus hope for relief from British sources.

A *cause célèbre*: proposals to relieve Emin Pasha

Somewhat surprisingly, although not for reasons of imperial acquisition, this was exactly what was about to be attempted.[3] By the summer of 1886, the only news of Emin had come to Europe from the explorer Wilhelm Junker, who had travelled from the upper Nile to Zanzibar in 1885–86. (It will be recalled that he had met up with Tippu Tip in Tabora and travelled with him for the last part of his Fourth Journey.) Junker had been instrumental in bringing about two

German expeditions to relieve Emin, one from East Africa and one via the Congo, both of them unsuccessful. Junker had also influenced Frederick Holmwood, the often over-enthusiastic acting Consul in Zanzibar, who recommended to Cairo and London schemes for a military expedition to bring about régime change in Buganda ("the infamous conduct of whose King [the Kabaka] has for many years been prejudicial to the development of the interior"[4]) and to relieve Emin Pasha. These suggestions were given short shrift by Lord Salisbury in the Foreign Office, and also in the War Office. But Emin's plight began to receive attention in the popular press, and the idea of an expedition began to gain traction.

A turning-point came with the involvement of William Mackinnon, the businessman whom we met as one of the contributors to the *Comité d'Études du Haut Congo* (Chapter 8, page 185), and who had been interested previously in getting a concession from Sultan Barghash for a British chartered company in East Africa. He remained interested in the Congo, and especially in the possibility of building railways – something that Stanley thought essential to by-pass the river's waterfalls and cataracts. By 1886 Mackinnon's interest was turning towards East Africa, where the signature on 1 November of the British–German agreement on the Zanzibar Delimitation Commission encouraged him to believe that security was now better established in East Africa and the way would now be open for him to develop his commercial investments in the region. And that 'region' might include Equatoria. When in November 1886 it became apparent that Emin needed relief, that the British Government declined to act (armed intervention would be too expensive), and that there might be positive commercial outcomes from a private venture, Mackinnon began discussing possibilities with Stanley and other business people. By early December, the framework of a plan for an expedition was in place, with £10,000 coming from Mackinnon and business associates, another £10,000 from the Egyptian Government, and the promise of arms, ammunition, and the support of officials and naval officers from the British Government.

By now, the inner group driving the idea forward (calling itself the Emin Pasha Relief Committee) had agreed that Stanley would lead the expedition. He had left for a lecture tour in the USA pending the final decisions on going ahead with the expedition, and its financing, and had to be summoned back by telegram – cutting short his tour at considerable financial sacrifice. Lecture tours were useful money-spinners. The question then arose which route should be used. The shortest routes to Wadelai were three, all from the east: one was through Buganda, the second a more northerly route through Masai territory, while the third was the known route via the west of Lake Victoria and to Lake Albert. There were various objections to all of these routes: the Kabaka, paramount chief, of Buganda was known to be hostile (the "infamous conduct" reported by Holmwood), the Masai terrain was difficult, and using the Lake Victoria route might incur German suspicion that the expedition was intended for surreptitious imperial annexation. For these and his own reasons, and against the preferences of the Emin Pasha Relief Committee, Stanley preferred to go via the Congo. Looking at the map it was superficially attractive: the route up the River Congo was relatively well known by now, and river transport could be used for long stretches, and from the highest navigable part of the River Aruwimi it was just over 300 miles to Lake Albert, which appeared a feasible distance.

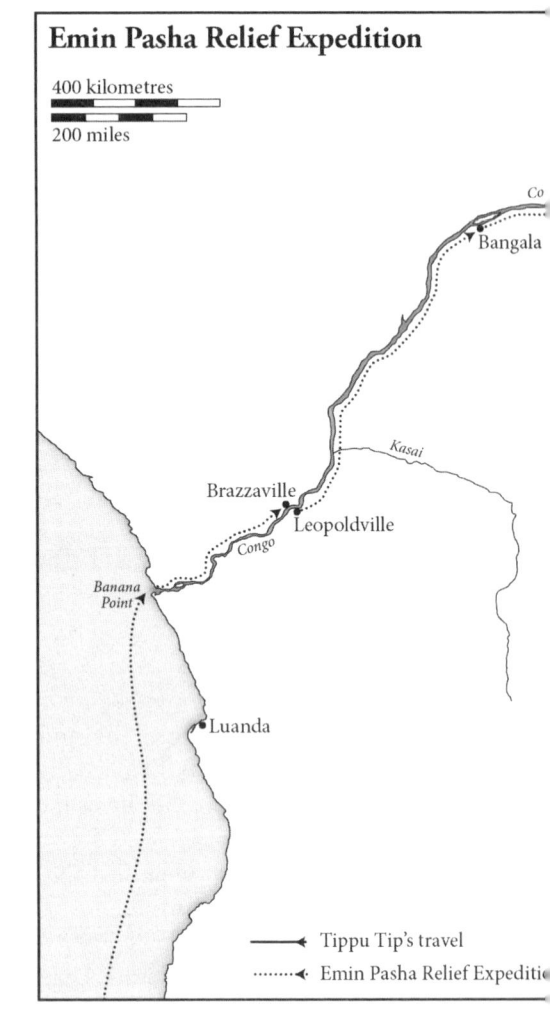

Technically still under contract to Leopold, Stanley needed the King's permission to lead the Relief Expedition. He travelled to Brussels to meet him in December 1886. Both men in fact had a previous interest, going back some years, in the area north-east of the existing Congo Free State territory. Leopold dreamt even of annexing Bahr al-Ghazal to the Congo State, and hoped to extend the State up

Fifth Journey – What a Relief!

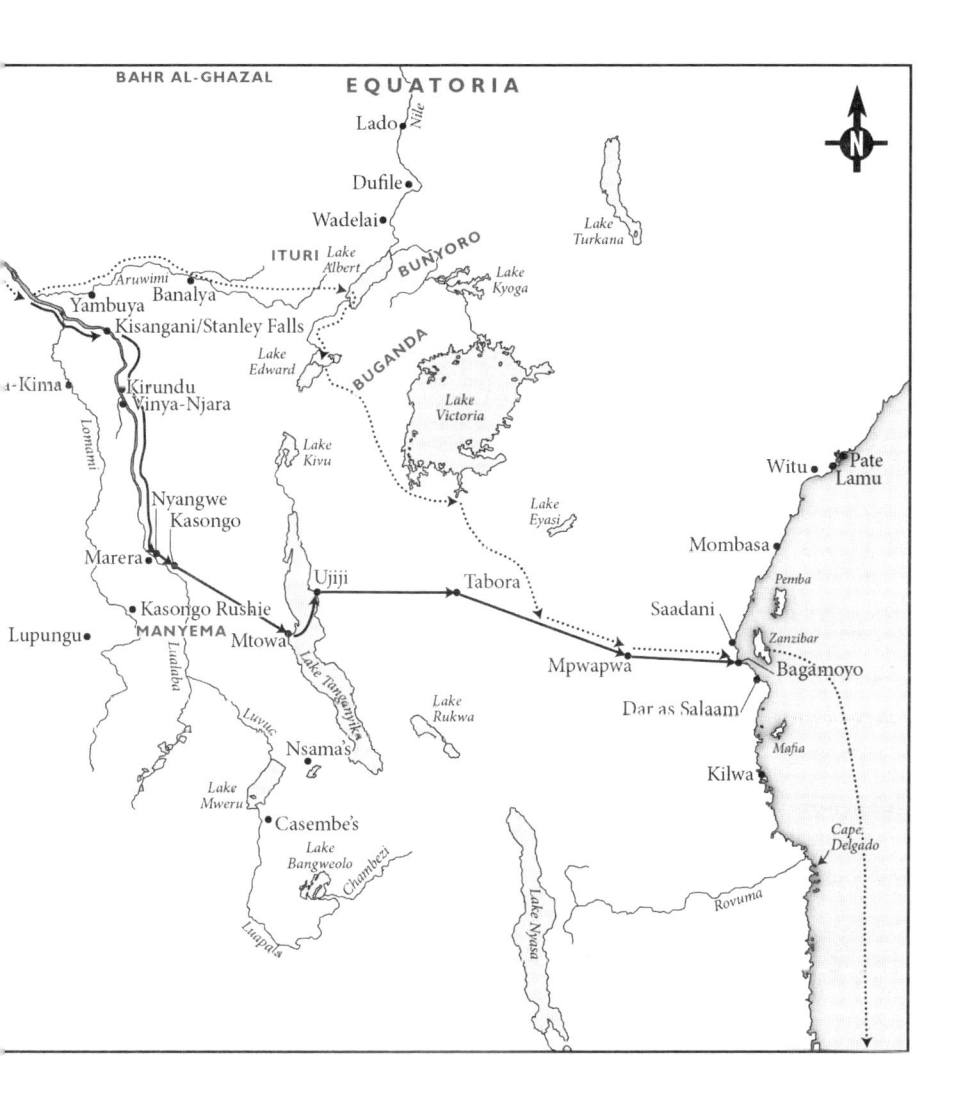

to the west bank of the Nile; Stanley was intrigued by the unexplored region between the River Aruwimi and Lake Albert.

Leopold, however, was reluctant to give Stanley the permission he wanted, reckoning that his services could be useful in recovering the station at Stanley Falls recently lost by Deane to the Arabs. But he then realized that he could resolve the question of the route to be taken, while at the same time opening up the Congo Free State's communications to the north-east, by making the choice of the Congo route a condition of his releasing Stanley. He then made it easier for the Committee to accept his condition, by offering Congo State transport for the river stretches of the route; this would help offset the additional costs of coming to Wadelai from the south-west. In the end, combining the preferences of all concerned, the decision was taken for the Expedition to go out via the Congo and return south-east to Zanzibar.

Tippu Tip, Governor of Stanley Falls

Leopold had one other agenda item for which he needed Stanley's support. It was by now accepted that Stanley would recruit most of the porters and armed personnel for the expedition in Zanzibar; these people were known to him, and risks of desertion could in this way be minimized. Leopold proposed that, while in Zanzibar, Stanley should meet Tippu Tip with a view to neutralizing any Arab opposition which the expedition might face in the region near the River Aruwimi, an area where it was known that Arabs seeking slaves and ivory had been expanding their activity. The base camp to be established on the river would be in territory more or less under Arab control. After the fighting at Stanley Falls, any force linked to the Congo Free State could expect further resistance from Arab traders, and Tippu Tip, with his extensive influence among them, could be brought in, at best to assist the expedition and at the least not to hinder it. He left it to Stanley to decide how best negotiate this with Tippu Tip, who was known to be in Zanzibar.

After choosing the seven officers he needed, Stanley left England on 21 January 1887, and spent a week in Cairo en route to Zanzibar. He had to overcome some Egyptian Government opposition to the use of the Congo route, though Prime Minister Nubar Pasha eventually agreed to the scheme, and expressed the hope that Emin Pasha would be enabled to return to Egypt and bring with him as much as possible of the rumoured stock of ivory he had accumulated. In Cairo Stanley also met the explorer Junker, on his way back to Europe from Zanzibar, who reported that this stock amounted to 65 tons, valued at £60,000 – enough to pay the expenses of the Expedition with a healthy surplus left over.

Stanley arrived in Zanzibar in late February. Frederick Holmwood was acting British Consul-General, Sir John Kirk having departed in mid-1886. Holmwood and Tippu Tip had been discussing events in Central Africa in December and January, both concerned at the front line of hostility opening up between the Congo Free State and the

Arabs on the River Lualaba. In letters to London, Holmwood reported that Tippu Tip seemed willing to instruct his people to withdraw rather than to pursue hostilities with Congo State forces, despite his anger with Congo State representatives and with their attempt to remove Arabs from areas where they had long been established. Holmwood judged that Tippu Tip was likely to be disposed to be helpful to the Relief Expedition; and we know from his conversation with the Belgian Consul of about the same time (see page 218) that he considered his long-term interests to be aligned with those of the Europeans.[5]

Stanley had last seen Tippu Tip when they had separated at Vinya-Njara on the River Lualaba in December 1876. In the ten or eleven years since then, Tippu Tip had extended his trading interests and his personal authority and influence over a large area of Central Africa. (See map on page 252) It would be going too far to describe this as an empire or kingdom, for there was nothing resembling central government or the rudiments of state formation. Renault calls Tippu Tip a 'potentate' in the sub-title of his book, which may also be an exaggeration, as is Iain Smith's description of him as "the chief Arab ruler of a large area of the eastern Congo".[6] But certainly he had acknowledged leadership over the Arabs living and trading in the region, even if at times they could not be said to be under his control the destruction of villages and capture of hostages in order to acquire ivory and slaves does not seem to have been his style. It is probably nearer the mark to think of him as an armed tycoon operating in and opening up non-state territories – an overland expression of the Omani Arab imperial enterprise of previous centuries that had colonized the Swahili Coast. Stanley wrote:

> Tippu-Tib is a much greater man today than he was in the year 1877 when he escorted my caravan, preliminary to our descent down the Congo. He has invested his hard-earned fortune in guns and powder. Adventurous Arabs have flocked to his standard, until he is now an uncrowned king of the region between Stanley Falls and Tanganyika Lake, commanding many thousands of men inured to fighting a wild Equatorial life.[7]

Stanley was therefore right in thinking that his acquiescence at least, and active support if possible, was needed for the Relief Expedition to succeed in its march through the Ituri Forest north and east of the River Aruwimi.

Tippu Tip knew pretty well what Stanley would be aiming at. He had himself been interested in the idea of rescuing Emin Pasha, no doubt because of the reports of the huge quantity of ivory said to be accumulated in Equatoria. The Belgian official Alphonse Vangèle had mentioned it during a conversation in Kisangani in January 1885, actually suggesting that Tippu Tip might lead an expedition to the province. Vangèle was prompted by a letter written to the *Association Internationale du Congo* by an Italian explorer, Gaetano Casati, who had found himself with Emin Pasha and would welcome help in getting home via the Congo. Vangèle reported that Tippu Tip had agreed in principle to establish a channel of communication from the Congo to where Emin Pasha was reportedly isolated.[8] Tippu Tip may indeed have sent an expedition in that direction, which had not returned ten months later; this is what he told Oskar Lenz, an Austrian explorer who was also trying to reach Emin, in February 1886. He had also talked to Junker, while they were travelling together from Tabora to the coast in late 1886, about the possibility of leading an expedition to the area, making it clear that he would expect a share of the ivory there. And, according to a report from Holmwood, he began to organize an expedition to go there in December 1886, but then gave up the project when he heard the news of the Arab capture of Stanley Falls.[9]

While there was a shared advantage in a Belgian–Arab stand-off, or at least avoidance of hostilities, in the Upper Congo, their interests were not really complementary. Leopold wanted the Congo Free State (meaning full territorial control, with administration, justice, right to levy taxes, etc) to extend up to Stanley Falls, whereas Tippu Tip naturally did not wish to recognize such an overt imperial takeover. He wanted the area between the Rivers Lualaba and Lomami (and indeed farther west) to be under his own influence, and himself and his fellow-Arabs to be free to trade without restriction down the Congo at least as far as the confluence with the River Aruwimi. When they met, in the company of Holmwood, Stanley told Tippu Tip that persistence in that attitude could lead to the ruin of the Congo State, and its being consequently handed over to the French (under the 'first refusal' agreement signed just before the Berlin Conference). Stanley could argue that life would be much harder for the Arabs if a major European power took over the Congo basin than if a minor country, Belgium, retained control.

Whether (as Holmwood reported) it was this argument or another that persuaded Tippu Tip, Stanley and he reached agreement on a series of items which effectively tied the Arab into the Expedition, and indeed to the Congo State. Two written agreements were actually signed. For Tippu Tip probably the more important – at least financially – was that concerning the men he was to supply for the expedition, because from this he derived actual profit. Certain clauses in this were to be highly significant later, for example those specifying that Tippu Tip was to supply each man with a gun and 100 bullets, while the powder and percussion caps were to be supplied by Stanley. The second agreement, entered into by Stanley "on behalf of His Majesty the King of the Belgians, and the Sovereign of the Congo State", appointed Tippu Tip *Wali* (Governor) of Stanley Falls, with a salary of £30 per month, and with a commitment that he would hoist the flag of the Congo State at Stanley Falls, and prevent the tribes on the Congo and other rivers, as well as Arabs and others, from engaging in the slave trade. He was to be "at full liberty to carry on his legitimate private trade in any direction, and to send his caravans to and from any places he may desire". Stanley had been given some freedom of movement in his negotiations, but nevertheless telegraphed Leopold to secure his agreement to this outcome.[10]

Tippu Tip hesitated before signing these agreements. He reports them in his customary matter-of-fact style in the *Maisha,* summarizing the requests as:

> Firstly, we wanted you to be Wali of the Belgian area, and your men in those areas to raise the Belgian flag. Secondly we want you to give us men to recover Emin Pasha.[11]

He wanted to consult Sultan Barghash, not least because "we ourselves and our areas were under his authority". Barghash advised him to accept the deal. Tippu Tip complained that the Governor's salary was paltry, but Barghash replied that this should not matter, because he would be able to continue trading on his own account. As for his own interests, Barghash may have thought that Tippu Tip's engagement as Governor could help reinforce the threatened Arab influence in Central Africa. Stanley, looking at the issue through Leopold's glasses, was probably calculating exactly the opposite – namely, that installing Tippu Tip as the Congo Free State representative in Stanley Falls would neutralize Arab influence and go a long way towards reasserting Belgian or Congo Free State authority following the expulsion of Deane.

While the appointment of the new Governor may have suited the protagonists at Zanzibar, the news was not welcomed in Europe. Commentators feared that Tippu Tip would not have the will or the power to stop his fellow-Arabs from bringing the slave trade down the River Congo, and that the licence to continue 'legitimate trade' would be used as a cover for slaving or use of violence in acquiring ivory.

The first agreement, about the provision of porters and armed men, while it contained detail about the conditions under which they were to be employed, did not specify how many there were to be. Presumably neither party was sure at the time of signature. In his report to the Foreign Secretary written soon afterwards, Holmwood stated that the number was to be 600; this was the figure also mentioned by Stanley in his account published after the Expedition, *In Darkest Africa*.[12] In the *Maisha*, Tippu Tip claims that his commitment was only to 500.[13] Unlike the agreement on the Governor appointment, where the salary is in £ sterling, the prices in the first agreement are in Maria Theresa dollars: MT$30 plus food for each man, and MT$1,000 to be paid to Tippu Tip for every 'round journey' from the River Congo to Lake Albert and back. The agreement makes clear that both parties expected to bring back to the Congo a significant quantity of ivory.

The last thing to be sorted out was whether Tippu Tip should accompany the party (answer: partially, but he could delegate a headman to supervise the porters on the journey to Lake Albert), and if so, how he should get there (answer: he should travel with the Expedition on the sea voyage round the Cape). So Tippu Tip with his party of 96 followers, including 35 women, joined the Expedition force on board a steamship of Mackinnon's British India Steam Navigation Company, *Madura*, as she sailed on 25 February 1887. Even without Tippu Tip's party, the total contingent numbered more than 700: 620 Zanzibaris, 61 Sudanese, and 13 Somalis, plus the European officers and their servants.

Carry on up the Congo – and the Aruwimi

Tippu Tip gives us in the *Maisha* some description of the sea voyage, obviously a complete novelty to him. They stopped at Simon's Bay, where "several Europeans, men and women, came on board to see me, as I didn't go on shore", and then overnight at Cape Town. There he and others did go ashore, and walked to the "Queen's Garden" (probably the Botanical Gardens), returning to the ship in carriages.[14] Stanley records a friendly chat with him there, in which Tippu Tip said that, having previously thought the white men fools, he was now – having seen the prosperity of Cape Town – coming to think that "they have something in them, and that they are more enterprising than the Arabs".[15] They reached Banana Point, at the mouth of the Congo, on 18 March.

It is not necessary in this book to retell the story of the Emin Pasha Relief Expedition, which has been well narrated elsewhere.[16] It is difficult even to summarize it, since the various disasters and problems besetting the Expedition gave rise to numerous recriminations afterwards – particularly among the British participants – and therefore to a number of attempts to 'set the record straight' by means of books and memoirs. Several of these are listed in the Bibliography. A by-product of this is a series of glimpses of Tippu Tip, and sometimes long conversations, provided by the British members of the Expedition when they wrote their accounts afterwards. Several of these were delayed in reaching the public, partly because Stanley specified that Expedition members should not publish anything until six months after their return home, but also because, for those members who died, it was left to their relatives to publish.

Tippu Tip travelled with the Expedition as it toiled upriver. Progress was erratic. Due to a breakdown in the telegraph system, advance notice of their arrival had not reached Congo Free State officials, and the promised boats were not available. Stanley had to commandeer boats from missionary stations, and from a Portuguese trading company. Because of the Expedition's size, groups became separated, and even camped apart. Nevertheless, one of the British officers, Mounteney Jephson, kept his good humour and a diary, and records:

> Up came Tippu Tib, in clean white cloths and turban, with his smart gilt sword & light sandals & his servants following him. He nearly embraced me in the effusion of his greeting.[17]

Mounteney Jephson also records that Tippu Tip gave him a "little terrier, 'Spot', a very handsome little dog". (There are several accounts of dogs accompanying 19th-century expeditions in Africa, but they did not survive long.)

For over two months they made their way up the River Congo,

alternating steamboat voyages with marches to by-pass waterfalls and cataracts. Tippu Tip comments in the *Maisha* on the slow progress. But he is impressed by the series of stations built at intervals on the river, and enjoys the way in which "the Europeans accorded me great respect ... Don't underestimate the power of the Belgians!" (or, alternative translation, "The Belgians had a strong presence").[18]

At the end of May, the Expedition arrived at Bangala Station (also written Ba-Ngala), where one steamboat was designated to take another officer, Edmund Barttelot, to accompany Tippu Tip to Stanley Falls. They arrived there on 17 June, and Barttelot left two days later, to rejoin the main part of the Expedition at a base camp which Stanley was setting up at Yambuya, a little way up the River Aruwimi from its confluence with the Congo. (This river is called Usoko in the *Maisha*; farther upstream it was known as the Ituri, and Mature in the *Maisha*.) The purposes of conveying Tippu Tip to Stanley Falls seem to have been various. One was to have the Congo Free State flag, of the gold star on the dark blue background, hoisted again at Stanley Falls – no-one seeming to be bothered by the paradox that this was being done by an Arab Governor, the station having been previously destroyed, as we have seen, during an attack by Arabs. Another was for Tippu Tip to have the opportunity to recruit the men he was due to supply to the Expedition, it being assumed that at Kisangani (or farther up the River Congo/Lualaba, at Kasongo, Tippu Tip's previous headquarters, or at Nyangwe) there would be porters and armed men available. These two factors – the flag and the recruitment – are mentioned in the *Maisha*.[19] We may also assume that Tippu Tip wanted to be on the River Lualaba or Upper Congo, after an interval of seven to eight months, to reassert his authority.

At this point we detect the first signs of the issue that would rupture the friendship (or at any rate the business relationship) between Stanley and Tippu Tip, and be the root cause of the difficulties that beset the Relief Expedition. In the *Maisha*, Tippu Tip records:

> I had asked Stanley for the powder to give the 500 men whom I was supposed to provide to him. But he replied: "I can't give you the powder at present, since I have barely enough for myself, but you will be able to buy some at Stanley Falls."[20]

The reader will recall that, in the agreement signed in Zanzibar, Tippu Tip had contracted to supply men armed with guns and 100 bullets each, while Stanley was to provide powder and percussion caps. As a result of the confusion over supply of boats on the Lower Congo, Stanley had had to leave behind some of the gunpowder, blithely assuming that Tippu Tip would be able to acquire more from Arab sources upriver. But, as we have seen – for example when Tippu Tip had to request additional supplies of powder from Sultan Barghash, in February 1882 – availability of gunpowder could not be taken for granted. Such was the situation on this occasion. In the *Maisha*, Tippu Tip records:

> From the time of our arrival, the Major [Barttelot] and I wanted to buy powder from the Arabs at Stanley Falls, but we could not acquire any. There was none available, nor was there any with the merchants at Nyangwe or Kasongo, because powder had become scarce.[21]

What little powder he did have he gave to the contingent of 500 men whom he had recruited (according to his view of his contract with Stanley). He put them under the command of Ali bin Mohammed al-Hinawi, and they went in canoes down the River Lualaba/Congo, and then upstream on the River Aruwimi. The waters in the rivers were high, and going was difficult. Then, before they reached Stanley's base camp at Yambuya, they were attacked by African tribesmen, their powder ran out, and they were forced to return.

Tippu Tip explained his problems in more detail in a letter (one of very few from him that have survived) written to Holmwood in Zanzibar, in July 1887. Holmwood had it translated and enclosed a translation with a despatch to London.[22] In it Tippu Tip repeats his account of Stanley's expecting him to buy powder from Arabs in one of the river settlements, and explains that either there was none available, or only small amounts at exorbitant prices. Apart from passages making clear the difficulties of getting men through from Stanley Falls to Yambuya, the letter also contains evidence of Tippu Tip having difficulty in maintaining order among the Arabs. For example, he complains that "the followers of Sa'id bin Habib bin Salim al-Afifi have spoiled the river", and "I caused the people who had deserted the villages on the river to return to their places and I keep them in order, and some of the places are not inhabited yet because the people fear". The tone of the letter suggests that, perhaps because of his new position as Governor, and thus on the side of the Europeans rather than the Arabs, the latter treat him with suspicion or even enmity. He asks Holmwood to request Leopold to send him two or three European officers with 40–50 troops to help him keep order.

Stanley had meanwhile decided to push on to Lake Albert with his 'Advance Column', leaving the 'Rear Column' at Yambuya under the command of Edmund Barttelot. He gave Barttelot instructions to wait until the expected supplies arrived from downriver, and until Tippu Tip's 600 porters and armed men came, and then to follow. He would mark their route by burning patches on trees. If Tippu Tip's men were delayed (and Stanley already seems to have had doubts as to whether Tippu Tip would make good on his promise), Barttelot was to wait at Yambuya until Stanley returned from Lake Albert, which he hoped would be within four months, i.e. October or November (1887).[23]

The next few months were probably the worst period for all members of the Expedition. Stanley's advance party suffered terribly in the Ituri forest. The River Aruwimi became impossible for canoes just above Yambuya, so the advance party had to walk through the forest, which was the most dense jungle Stanley had ever come across. It was dark because of the thick canopy, and always wet. Clouds of insects bit them, or made their lives misery. But on top of obstacles of nature, they were subject to human attack. Probably because Arabs had raided villages in their search for ivory and slaves, the local Africans viewed all foreigners with suspicion and hostility. Occasionally Stanley's party would come across a settlement where the villagers had run away, and they could scrounge food from their stores. Very rarely they could barter for food. The more usual pattern was for them to have to clear booby traps or spikes from their paths, or to come under direct attack from Africans armed with spears or bows with poisoned arrows. In their famished and weakened condition, even wounds without poison took a long time to heal, or turned gangrenous. After a slow and agonizing journey of nearly six months, at the end of which fewer than 200 of the 389 were still with him (the others having died or deserted), Stanley arrived at Lake Albert, in December 1887. He was still not sure if he could find Emin Pasha, or even whether (if he found him) he would want to be 'relieved' and escorted out of Equatoria; and his own depleted force had few supplies to offer to Emin.

Things were no better in the Rear Column. Barttelot and his 133 men were soon joined by three other officers plus 125 men, who also brought 600 loads of stores. But they still needed the additional men from Tippu Tip if they were to carry these loads, plus the stores they had already, to follow Stanley's Advance Column. Their diaries and letters recount several journeys to Stanley Falls and Kasongo, aimed at prompting Tippu Tip into action and at finding out when the promised numbers would arrive. Meanwhile, conditions at the Rear Column base camp deteriorated rapidly. From the start, obtaining food had been difficult. Relations with local villagers, never good, reached the point where barter was virtually impossible. They resorted to taking women captive, and releasing them in exchange for provisions. The Zanzibaris relied on eating manioc, which grew quite well there, and was a staple food for local people; but being unfamiliar with the crop they fell into the same trap as Tippu Tip's followers had in Itawa in 1872 – they ate the tuber without giving it the soaking required to leach out the poisonous prussic acid (cyanide), and large numbers of them fell ill and died. They also suffered from dreadful ulcers and other illnesses. Morale sank, and Barttelot's leadership skills were sadly lacking; to maintain discipline he used violence (notably a rawhide whip) which shocked even his fellow-officers.

Tippu Tip's efforts to send men to Yambuya continued, even though he considered that Stanley had still not made good on his undertaking to provide gunpowder. One group arrived in August 1887, and through them the Rear Column officers discovered that it was possible to travel overland to Stanley Falls, possibly more easily than by canoe down the Aruwimi and up the Congo. Two officers, Jameson and Ward, took advantage of this to visit Tippu Tip – the first of three trips there made by Jameson. Tippu Tip explained that supplying the required number of men would be difficult and would take time, since his men were out on expeditions, and after the first unsuccessful attempt to reach Yambuya they were reluctant to take similar risks again.[24]

The problems faced by Tippu Tip were real. As explained above, and as set out in his letter to Holmwood, his position in mid-1887 was very different from that in earlier years, and not only because of his appointment as Governor by a power whom most Arabs were already resenting. As more Arabs had penetrated Manyema and areas west, other powerful figures had emerged, such as Sa'id bin Habib, who may have wished to oust Tippu Tip and resume direct confrontation with the Belgians. Such figures could assert their power through easy purchase of guns and ammunition, and would attract men away from direct allegiance to Tippu Tip. These men would also see little attraction in working as porters for Europeans, for relatively low wages, in poor conditions, and under bullying leadership, as compared with the gains they could make from raiding or trading for ivory. Not only may Tippu Tip have felt that his influence among Arabs was waning; he also believed that he was receiving insufficient support from the King to whom he owed his post – no reinforcements arrived from the Lower Congo, and no steamer visited Stanley Falls until June 1888.

In October came further news from Tippu Tip that he was sending his son Sayf to Kasongo to recruit people from Manyema, to make up for the shortage of his own men. A visit to Stanley Falls by Barttelot himself failed to produce a promise of immediate reinforcement. Weeks passed, and information received from deserters from the Advance Column suggested that Stanley would not return until February (1888). That month, still no Stanley, Barttelot and Jameson went again to Stanley Falls, to find that Tippu Tip was at Kasongo; about 250 men had now been assembled, but were not to proceed to join the Rear Column until Tippu Tip's return. By now there were two Arab camps near Yambuya, relations with whom were also bad; and Barttelot persuaded Bwana Nzige (Tippu Tip's kinsman, and in command at Stanley Falls in his absence) to have one group withdrawn.

Barttelot was in Stanley Falls again in May 1888, and this time did meet up with Tippu Tip. He had just returned from Kasongo, with Jameson, who had been sent to apply further pressure for the despatch of the porters. The meeting was complicated by the presence there also of a Belgian official of the Congo State, Van Kerckhoven, who – like his colleagues – had taken note of the expansion of the Arabs' activities down the Congo and had hopes of distracting them away from the river towards areas farther north, bordering French Equatorial Africa. The Congo Free State's officials' idea was that Arab expansion in that direction would leave the Belgians without competition on and around the River Congo itself, and also save the Belgians the cost and trouble of protecting the ill-defined northern border against incursion by the French. It is not clear whether this idea appealed to Tippu Tip himself, but it does seem that he was doubtful about further or deeper involvement with the Rear Column. Possibly as a way of discharging his obligations, he ensured that Muni Somai, a Manyema headman, signed up with Barttelot to command 400 men to work for the column – at the extraordinary price of £1,000-worth of stores (5 percent of the total estimated costs of the Expedition).

Tippu Tip records some of these travels and meetings in the *Maisha*, but for the dates and for most of the detail we have to rely on the diaries and writings of the Expedition members and the Belgian officials. There are no major inconsistencies, although this section of the *Maisha* reminds us that Tippu Tip had other concerns at this time – for example, what had happened to a large quantity of barter goods which he had sent up-country just as he left Zanzibar at the start of the Expedition. The answer was given to him by Rumaliza (Mohammed bin Khalfan), who reported to him in Kasongo, probably in May 1888, that he had exchanged half the goods for stocks of ivory stored in Uvinza, east of Lake Tanganyika.[25]

Tippu Tip took passage on board the steamer that had brought Van Kerckhoven, to travel to Yambuya. Another steamer, the *Stanley*, arrived on the same day, bringing Lt Alfred Baert, who was to be the long overdue European assistant promised in the agreement signed in Zanzibar sixteen months before. Muni Somai then came, with his 400 Wanyema, and Tippu Tip helped Barttelot merge them and some other recruits into the force that now totalled about 560. The new porters would only carry a lighter weight, so all the loads had to be repacked. In the course of doing this, the Rear Column officers found that some of the ammunition was damaged by damp; but luckily Tippu Tip had enough spare to be able to sell replacements to the Expedition. Some supplies and personal effects which were thought not to be essential were sent downriver to Bangala. Barttelot set out up the River Aruwimi in the hope of finding and assisting Stanley (who, he thought, was probably alive but in difficulty). Tippu Tip returned to Stanley Falls, presumably thinking that he had done with his dealings with the Expedition.[26]

Further disaster befell the Rear Column. Travelling up the River Aruwimi, they ran into obstacles similar to those encountered by Stanley's Advance Column, compounded by desertion and loss of loads. Barttelot marched once more to Stanley Falls to ask Tippu Tip for an additional 60 men to make good the number who had deserted, and for chains to keep them together and prevent escape – all of which he was granted. Two days after his return to the camp, now at Banalya on the River Aruwimi, in an incident fatally typical of his behaviour towards Africans, Barttelot threatened excessive violence to stop some noisy celebration in the camp, and was shot and instantly killed by the husband of the woman he was threatening. William Bonny, a junior member of the Expedition, although he wrote no book afterwards, wrote a report of the incident in a letter to Barttelot's father, which was published in *The Times* newspaper.[27]

In the ensuing chaos, stores were looted and many of the porters deserted. With not enough men to carry the loads, Jameson took command and went yet again to Tippu Tip to request more men and his personal assistance to help salvage the situation. Tippu Tip had already arranged for the arrest, trial and execution of Barttelot's killer, but was unwilling to be further involved in the Rear Column, and agreed with Jameson that his kinsman Rashid, who was at the River Lomami, was the best person to sort out the unruly Wanyema. Rashid was summoned, but declined to help: he was expecting 500 tusks of ivory soon to be delivered to his camp, and needed to protect his interests locally, and no doubt thought that the prospects of success in helping the Expedition were now low – Stanley had left Yambuya over a year previously, and there had been no direct news from him. Jameson, now desperate, sought to persuade Tippu Tip himself to lead the remains of the Rear Column in an expedition to find Stanley, and Emin. The extraordinary conditions negotiated between them reflect Jameson's intense wish to rescue the Expedition if at all possible, and (probably) Tippu Tip's preference to price the deal out of the market. They were that Tippu Tip should receive £20,000 to accompany the Rear Column to Equatoria, the full sum to be paid even if Stanley reappeared or matters were settled sooner than expected; and that the caravan would not go near Buganda or Bunyoro if there were war between those two territories. Tippu Tip probably thought that the Expedition should be ended, and may have been concerned that his reputation with the British was at risk because of his involvement with it. Jameson himself did not think that Tippu Tip was in any way to blame for the disaster, and recorded in his diary that he had done all he could to help it. No doubt conscious that this proposed agreement with Tippu Tip lay way outside any instructions hitherto given to the Rear Column, Jameson undertook to go to Banana Point to telegraph the Expedition Committee, while Tippu Tip agreed to provide support as necessary to the remains of the Rear Column in Banalya. Tippu Tip adds, in the *Maisha,* that "the Belgians" with him (presumably the secretary Baert and the Station Commander Haneuse) said that Jameson would have to request permission (presumably from Brussels) for him to be absent from his post. In the event, no telegram was sent. Jameson fell ill with haematuric fever on the journey downriver, and died at Bangala on 16 August 1888.[28]

On that same day, nearly fourteen months after he had left Yambuya, and having journeyed the 300 miles to Lake Albert and back again, Stanley walked into the camp at Banalya, only to learn of the disastrous collapse of the Rear Column from William Bonny, the one officer surviving there. He quickly reorganized affairs, moved the camp to a new one a few miles upstream on the Aruwimi, and wrote letters to England reporting his meeting with Emin Pasha at Lake Albert and his future plans for the evacuation of the Expedition by the east coast route. He also wrote to Tippu Tip, and sent all the letters via Stanley Falls for forwarding to London. He did not wish to take the time to go to Stanley Falls himself, and in his letter to Tippu Tip simply told him what had happened, expressed the hope that they would meet again before long, and offered to travel slowly, initially, so that Tippu Tip could catch up with him if he wished. Tippu Tip did not so wish, and the Congo Free State authorities were content that he should remain at his post. Salim bin Mohammed, one of his men, was however despatched to meet Stanley, who – while accepting that the Arabs had not deliberately sought to bring disaster on the Rear Column – nevertheless sent Salim back with a message that he would bring an action against Tippu Tip for breach of contract. (This is how Stanley records it in his book; Tippu Tip mentions Salim's conversation with Stanley in the *Maisha*, but says nothing at this stage about the court case.) So, although he never met Stanley again, and had no more dealings with the Expedition, Tippu Tip had not heard the end of it.[29]

The rest of the Emin Pasha Relief Expedition is interesting and exciting, but not part of Tippu Tip's story. Stanley led the remains of the Rear Column to Lake Albert, persuaded Emin Pasha that he should indeed leave Equatoria, and then led a huge caravan past Lake Victoria to Tabora, and then to Bagamoyo. In an absurd postscript to the narrative, and whether from exhaustion, carelessness or having had too much to drink, Emin fell off a balcony at the house in Bagamoyo where a dinner was being given in his honour, and had to stay in hospital there with a cracked skull (from which he recovered), while the rest of the party dispersed and Stanley crossed over to Zanzibar.[30]

Tippu Tip stayed on in Stanley Falls for another year and a half. It seems to have been a very prosperous time for him, and also for the Arabs who brought great quantities of ivory there for transporting down the river – apparently in contravention of the policy on which Barghash had been insisting, namely to export ivory over the eastern route via Ujiji and Tabora to Zanzibar. We hear no record of Tippu Tip's having been in trouble with the Sultan for conniving at the Congo trade. Perhaps what went on in Stanley Falls was simply too far away, and Sayyids Barghash and Khalifa had other more pressing concerns

– the Delimitation Commission and its outcomes. The Congo Free State authorities, not surprisingly, imposed an export tax of about 15 percent, of which Tippu Tip may have been able to keep 6 percent for himself. If his prestige had been declining at the time of the Emin Pasha Expedition, it seems to have recovered during this period at Stanley Falls: the French explorer and journalist Élisée Trivier, who passed through the station in January–February 1889, describes him as "master of Central Africa, sultan, banker, merchant, dealer, catcher of ivory and buyer of men".[31]

Tippu Tip leaves Stanley Falls for Zanzibar

Sultan Barghash died in March 1888. Tippu Tip heard this news, and that of the succession of his brother Sayyid Khalifa, in August; he mentions it in a letter he wrote his half-brother Mohammed bin Masoud the same month.[32] (In the *Maisha* he records receiving the news after Trivier's visit, but this must be an error of memory.) He sent messages of condolence, but does not seem to have considered travelling back to Zanzibar until prompted by other news and events. These were allegations, which he heard about from Leopold, that he was in some way responsible for Barttelot's death and that he was alleged to be in breach of his contract. More seriously, because this would affect his business standing in Zanzibar, his funds with Taria Topan had been blocked, as a result of an injunction brought by Stanley.[33]

Ideally, he would have left quickly for Zanzibar. However, he did not do so, for reasons that are not clear. Even more confusingly, he appears to have left Stanley Falls in January 1890, gone back, and then left definitively between March and May. It is possible that he wanted to wait for the arrival of Lerman, the new commander of Stanley Falls station. He had already nominated his kinsman, Rashid, as his successor. And so he left the Congo, and Central Africa, for the last time.

His colleagues tried to persuade him not to go, arguing that his life (or at the least his liberty) was in danger on the coast, and that he had wealth enough in the interior to live comfortably. They may, as on other occasions previously, actually have wanted to retain the presence of a strong and reliable leader. Tippu Tip's answer was interesting. He said that the Arabs were now confronting a threat completely different to that which they had faced before: previously, African villagers had been relatively easy to combat, partly because of the Arabs' superior strength and weaponry but also because the Africans were divided amongst themselves. The threat posed by the Europeans was of a different order.[34]

News then came that Rumaliza was planning to attack a Capt. Joubert, who had built a stockade camp near Mpala, a little way south of Mtowa on the western shore of Lake Tanganyika, in a position threatening Arab lines of communication; Tippu Tip sent a message to "prevent him from doing anything so stupid".[35] Impromptu attacks on Congo State forces would do no-one any good. He passed through Nyangwe and Kasongo, and at Mtowa met up with Rumaliza, who admitted that fighting Europeans without adequate preparation was not sensible. Luckily he had escaped without harm, because Capt. Joubert's ammunition supply boats had been hit by a storm on Lake Tanganyika and had had to turn back. Not forgetting his instructions from his Belgian masters to "plant the Belgian [i.e. Congo State] flag as far as Lake Tanganyika", Tippu Tip hoisted the gold star at Mtowa before crossing the lake.

Tippu Tip continued his journey eastwards, and reached Ujiji in September 1890. Here he received more letters (he does not say from whom, although he mentions additional letters from Arabs in Tabora) advising him not to return to Zanzibar. He considered these ridiculous, or (according to a different, probably less reliable, reading of the *Maisha*) signs of intrigue, and went on to Tabora. There similar exchanges took place: local Arabs sought to persuade him to stay, on the grounds that the Europeans would not be able to catch him there. Tippu Tip reacted even more violently, saying that they were all mad, that they would not be able to protect him if the Europeans made a serious attempt to find him, and so on. He was determined to finish his journey to the coast.[36]

At Tabora too he received a letter from Emin Pasha, who, having recovered from his post-prandial fall in Bagamoyo, had taken employment with the German East Africa Company, and was on his way back to Equatoria, it was presumed in order to stake further claims for Germany in the interior. Emin's letter was to thank Tippu Tip for the help he had given to the Relief Expedition (for example by the supply of men), and to reassure him that he considered Stanley's charges against him false. Emin's motives were to bring Tippu Tip round to supporting German ambitions in East Africa, and to prepare the ground for establishing good relations with the Arabs at Ujiji.[37]

One last obstacle delayed Tippu Tip's arrival at Bagamoyo. On the day of his planned departure from Tabora, he was struck by a serious illness, probably dysentery, from which he took six months to recover. He was treated by French missionaries, and, after they left their mission station, by British missionaries from Urambo. Feeling better, he set off again in May 1891, but he had not yet recovered his strength, and had to be carried on a litter and then ride on a donkey – one of very few occasions when he is recorded as having travelled other than on foot. In this way he reached Mpwapwa, where again he was looked after by missionaries, these ones from the Church Missionary Society.

The missionaries told him that they had been visited by the brother and widow of James Jameson, the member of the Relief Expedition who had died at Bangala on his way to telegraph for instructions about his proposed deal with Tippu Tip. They wanted information from Tippu Tip in order to salvage the reputation of Jameson, who had been accused of instigating an act of cannibalism when visiting Tippu Tip in Riba-Riba, near Kasongo, in May 1888.[38] The appalling story, which the missionaries said had been told to the family by Stanley, was recorded by Jameson but also appears (with slight variations, as is to be expected) in other contemporary accounts; and it was as follows. Jameson was sitting with Tippu Tip, who commented that the Wakusu, a tribe living farther south between the Rivers Lualaba and Lomami, were terrible cannibals. Jameson said that people in England thought that such stories were "travellers' tales, or in other words lies", and Tippu Tip, having said something to an Arab beside him, asked Jameson to have some cloth brought from his hut, which he did – six handkerchiefs. A Wakusu slave then walked in with a ten-year-old girl, whom he killed by stabbing her twice in the chest. She died without making a sound, and Jameson saw her cut up, and the pieces of her body taken away. In his diary, Jameson describes it as "the most horribly sickening sight I am ever likely to see in my life".[39] The Expedition's Syrian interpreter was also present, and through him modified versions of the story reached other members of the Expedition. On their return, the episode was of course picked up by the British public, and too easily summarized as "Jameson pays six handkerchiefs to have a girl killed and eaten". His family wanted to clear his name; hence the trip to Zanzibar, and the attempt to see Tippu Tip, to have his eye-witness account. Tippu Tip does not mention having met them, the *Maisha* recording that he heard of their presence only from the missionaries; according to another account, Jameson's brother had to turn back because of illness, but his widow met Tippu Tip in Zanzibar, when eventually he arrived there.[40] Would his testimony have been much use? Possibly not, since by his own account he told the missionaries:

> "This is a lie! I was neither there, nor did I hear such a thing before today. That Stanley should say Jameson would do such a thing! Or that I would allow it! Yet I've never seen a European, or for that matter any human being, who is such a liar!"[41]

So Tippu Tip was himself being economical with the truth in the *Maisha*: while it is true that he was not personally present at any act of cannibalism, Jameson's account does confirm that he was present (and probably consenting) at the girl's murder.

He arrived in Bagamoyo in July 1891, but there was still further delay before he crossed to Zanzibar. The Governor of what was now German East Africa, Freiherr Julius von Soden, had written to him en route to request that he should not go to Zanzibar without seeing him first. After ten days, von Soden arrived from a tour of the coast, and they duly met. During the ten-day interval, Tippu Tip had met a Belgian, Capt. Alphonse Jacques, who was leading an expedition into the interior organised by the Anti-Slavery Committee of Belgium. This Committee had been founded as a result of the anti-slavery campaign launched by Cardinal Lavigerie, Archbishop of Algiers, in 1888. (Lavigerie was also the founder – in 1868 – of the 'White Fathers', an order of missionary fathers who established stations first in North Africa, and then in East and Central Africa, where they were sometimes known as the Algerian fathers. It was missionaries of this order who had looked after Tippu Tip when he first fell ill with dysentery.) Jacques was heading for the area west of Lake Tanganyika to try to suppress slave raiding there. Tippu Tip gave him letters of recommendation – one of them addressed to Rumaliza, asking for his support for the expedition. We can only speculate on Tippu Tip's motives for this: perhaps he realized that the practice of slave raiding followed by Arabs in the 1870s and 1880s brought them into a confrontation with the Europeans in which they would inevitably be worsted.

Tippu Tip waited a short time longer on the coast, possibly waiting for assurances that his failure to arrive in good time for his outstanding court hearing would not lead to his arrest. Governor von Soden accompanied him to Dar as-Salaam, where finally he took ship for Zanzibar.

Chapter 11

The British and the Germans:
Protection or Occupation?

IF TIPPU TIP HAD found the Sultan (then Sayyid Barghash) despondent when they met in November 1886, he would have reckoned the situation even more depressing when he returned to Zanzibar in August 1891. He had been away for all of the short sultanate of Barghash's brother Khalifa, who had died unexpectedly, aged only thirty-six, in 1890. The throne was now occupied by Sayyid Ali, also a son of the great Sa'id bin Sultan. The Sultanate had fallen victim to the competition between the British and Germans that characterized this period of the Scramble for Africa, and the Sultan (then Sayyid Khalifa) had become effectively a puppet ruler of a small archipelago – a sad reverse from the mini-empire which his father had controlled.[1] How had this come about?

The Germans face revolt in East Africa, 1888–89

After the conclusion of the Delimitation Commission's work in 1886, the Germans worked hard to consolidate their position in their sphere of influence. During the latter period of Barghash's reign they had been pressuring him to allow them concessions on that part of the coastal strip (left to the Sultan by the Delimitation Commission) opposite the German zone, and they continued this pressure on the young and inexperienced Khalifa. In April 1888, an agreement gave the German East Africa Company the right to administer the coastal territory between the Rivers Umba and Rovuma, under the Sultan's authority and flag. They appointed a Governor of German East Africa, the Freiherr von Soden whom Tippu Tip met in Bagamoyo, and other agents and commanders of military outposts. Things did not always go smoothly for them. Notably, a rebellion broke out in protest at a German agent's high-handed actions, in August 1888 in Pangani, a significant port north of Bagamoyo and only thirty miles from Zanzibar. The leader of the revolt was Bashir bin Salim al-Harthi (known as Bushiri or Abushiri), of mixed Arab and African parentage. It was an expression of resentment against rule from outside, including Omani/Zanzibari rule – but German officials' high-handed actions were undoubtedly the spark that lit the fire.[2] At one point the German agent was trapped with some colleagues, and had to be rescued by troops from the Sultan's army, which was commanded by Lloyd Mathews, the British former naval officer now bearing the rank of General (see box opposite). Sayyid Khalifa had an interest in securing peace on the coast, since under the 1886 Delimitation Commission settlement he still retained sovereignty over the 10-mile coastal strip, and a number of Arab and Swahili traders and others, who considered themselves his subjects, were at risk from the spreading violence.

Mathews found himself unable to mediate between the rebels and the German authorities. Indeed, the rebellion had strong local support, with people in Pangani and other ports unwilling to accept the authority of the Sultan in Zanzibar unless the Germans were removed. The revolt spread over much of the coastal area in the German 'sphere of influence'. After nine months of violence, with a number of German victims, Abushiri first made a truce with a German admiral at Bagamoyo, and then thought to mount one final attack on the port. But by now, May 1889, the authorities in Berlin had taken notice of the peril faced by the fledgling colony. Chancellor Bismarck could not afford to allow his new African colonialist policy to fail at its first hurdle, and persuaded the Reichstag to allocate 2 million marks to equip an armed expedition to sort out the problem. It was to be led by Major Hermann von Wissmann, the explorer whom Tippu Tip had met in Tabora in September 1882.

Lloyd Mathews

It is doubtful that, as a junior officer in the Royal Navy in the Mediterranean in the late 1860s, Lloyd Mathews ever imagined a career ending with a knighthood and a position equivalent to that of Prime Minister in Zanzibar. Born in 1850 in Castle Cary in Somerset, his early naval experience was on the West African coast and then on the anti-slave-trade patrols off East Africa from 1875. His letters home from that time show his revulsion at the trade and the treatment of the slaves being transported, mainly from Zanzibar to the Gulf. In 1877, when John Kirk realized that enforcement of the British–Omani–Zanzibari slave trade agreements required a properly organized local military force, Mathews volunteered for the job of training it. Starting with 300 recruits, the new force – supplied with up-to-date rifles courtesy of the British Government – grew to 1,300 by 1880, and earned plaudits from British Consuls in Zanzibar for its efficiency under Mathews's competent leadership.

In 1881, Mathews left the Navy for permanent employment under the Sultan with the rank of General. He successfully led his little army in various engagements in the 1880s (including the establishment of military posts on the route to Tabora) aimed at enforcing the Sultan's authority on the mainland and pursuing Kirk's policy of maintaining British influence through a strong local ruler. In 1884, alarmed by the news of the signature of Carl Peters's treaties with local chiefs, Sayyid Barghash sent him with some men formally to annex territory near Kilimanjaro.

When the British–German–French Commission was set up in late 1885 to determine the borders of the Sultan's dominions, Mathews was appointed Barghash's agent to represent his views to the commissioners, but the German member ensured that he was sidelined. And, as recorded elsewhere, the Commission's work ended with Barghash's claims virtually ignored. Mathews was brought back into action in 1888, to help quell the 'Bushiri mutiny' in the territories recently acquired by Germany. Law and order was eventually restored by the intervention of German imperial forces, Mathews's troops being used the next year to keep the peace in Zanzibar itself.

By the time the British protectorate over Zanzibar was declared in 1890, Mathews had become a close adviser to the Sultan (now Sayyid Ali bin Sa'id). Now knighted, he was appointed First Minister, in a shake-up of the government system in October 1891, acquiring virtually unrestricted charge of the administration. His management of affairs was not always popular, but he gained immense local prestige. He died in office in October 1901, having served in Zanzibar for twenty-seven years and under five successive sultans.

Abushiri faced not only the expensively equipped Wissmann force, but also a British–German blockade of the coast. This had arisen because Sayyid Khalifa was clearly unable or unwilling to reassert his authority on the coastal strip of the mainland, and Bismarck – intent on restoring hegemony in the German zone – considered a joint blockade to be the only answer, as a means of preventing the supply of arms and ammunition to the rebels all along the coastal strip. He sought British collaboration, and Salisbury was prepared to acquiesce in this because he feared the risk that the Germans, if allowed to act alone, would threaten what was left of Zanzibari autonomy, and possibly even take over the Sultanate altogether. The Germans and the British also needed Sayyid Khalifa's public agreement, because the blockade would be operating in his waters, would be affecting ports that were notionally his, and was intended to restore the Sultan's authority.

However, public presentation of the blockade was quite different. These events were running concurrently with a movement in political circles in Europe favouring the convocation of a conference that would take firm and international measures to end the East and Central African slave trade. While Sultan Barghash had been forced to give in to British pressure in 1873 to close the slave market in Zanzibar and to prevent slaves being carried in Zanzibari ships and dhows, some trading was continuing, including by newly created land routes up the coast to Mombasa. In addition, European public opinion was concerned about the extension of the slave trade, by Arabs, westward from Lake Tanganyika and down the River Congo. So it made sense to present the proposed blockade as a measure to put the lid on slave traders, and also to prevent the import of munitions.

Sayyid Khalifa, not surprisingly, played hard to get, and actually retreated into a palace outside the city of Zanzibar, from where he consented to do business only by telephone. Eventually Charles Euan Smith, the British Consul, secured his agreement to the blockade, and it came into effect early in December 1888. The blockade was not very successful, and crews of both navies thoroughly disliked it. Several hundred slaves were released, but this was not many in comparison with the effort expended; and the operation was even less effective in preventing import of munitions. The blockade was ended in October 1889, just a month before the opening in Brussels of the international conference which had been mooted earlier.

With the combination of the naval blockade and (more effectively) Wissmann's disciplined land force, the rebellion was put down, and

Pangani port reoccupied in July 1889. Trade resumed, as witnessed by the arrival of Tippu Tip's son Sayf with a large cargo of his father's ivory for delivery to Zanzibar. Abushiri escaped, but was eventually captured and executed in December 1889.

German and British interests in East Africa formalized, 1889–90

New arrangements for governing the German 'sphere' were now required. The German East Africa Company, which under Carl Peters had acquired territory and also acquired the right to rule it by means of the *Schutzbrief* (protection charter), had to be replaced by direct imperial government. Carl Peters had in fact been continuing his colony-expanding activities after his initial burst of 'treaty' signatures with chiefs between the coast and Lake Tanganyika. Between June 1889 and January 1890, he took a small but well-armed expedition west from near Lamu, and then north-west, through Masai territory and then to Kavirondo, aiming to reach Buganda and establish a German protectorate there. Most of his route was through land already marked out as 'British sphere of influence'; but neither this, nor the number of African casualties he caused on his violent journey, seem to have bothered him. Writing about this later, Peters claimed that his expedition was aimed at relieving Emin Pasha – the German answer, as it were, from the east, to Stanley's efforts from the west. But the German Consul in Zanzibar, and the German Foreign Office, already sensing that this was unauthorized activity that could lead to trouble, declined to give him any assistance.

Through 1889, while these machinations continued in the Foreign Offices in Berlin and London, and as the threat posed by the Abushiri rebellion receded, it was the abolition of slavery which became the main issue in Zanzibar between the Germans and British on the one hand, and the Sultan on the other. The Europeans were aiming to persuade Sayyid Khalifa to issue an edict making slavery itself, not just the slave trade, illegal from 1 January 1890, but then backed off a little when they considered the social and economic disruption this would bring – and so agreed on a solution whereby all slaves arriving in Zanzibar after 1 November 1889 would be free. Further difficulties arose over a proposal that all children born after 1 January 1890 would be free. And, aware of the direction being taken at the Brussels Conference towards absolute prohibition of slavery, the Arab community of Zanzibar threatened to send all their slaves to the European representatives in

East Africa, 1886

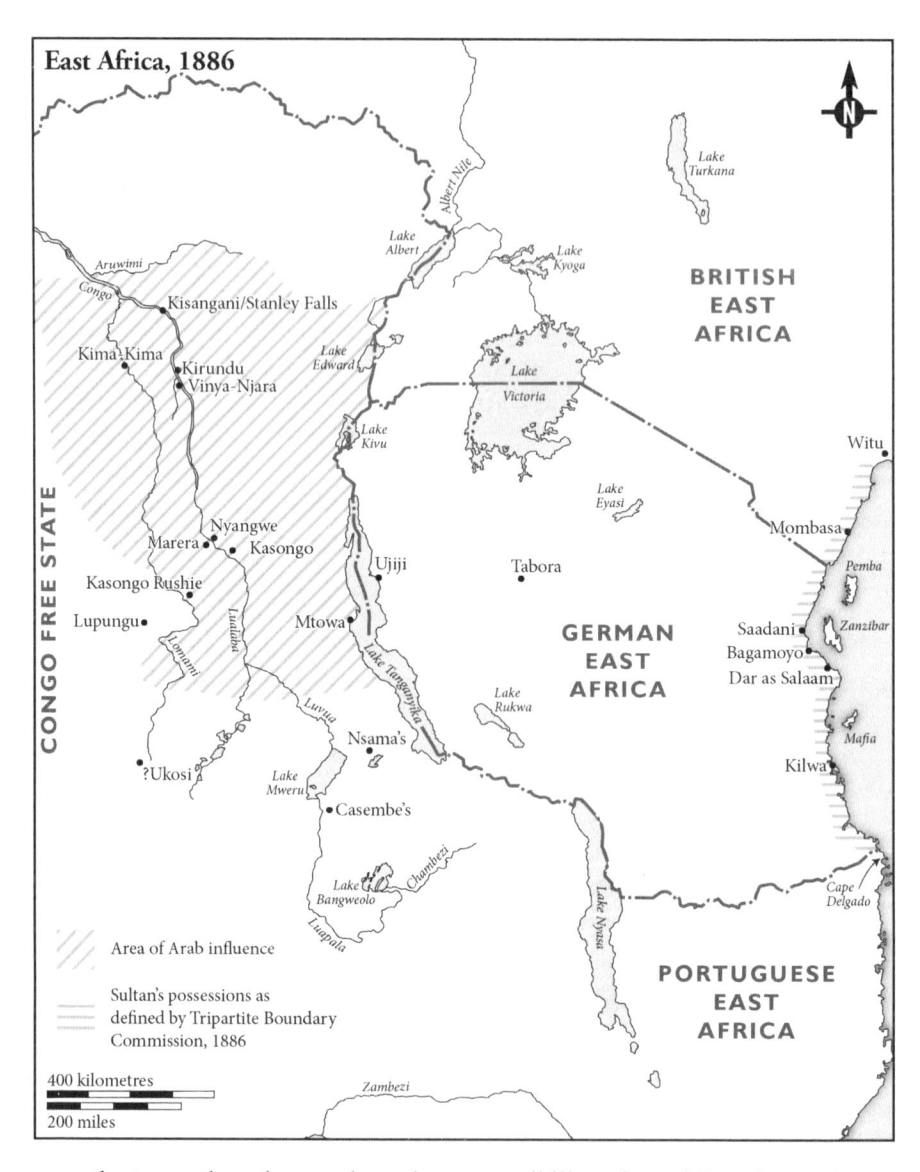

Area of Arab influence

Sultan's possessions as defined by Tripartite Boundary Commission, 1886

the town, throwing on them the responsibility of providing the newly freed slaves with employment and/or financial support. Tippu Tip was still away when this happened, but we may assume that by this time he had acquired estates on Zanzibar island and that he would have been aware of the line being taken by his community.

Meanwhile Lord Salisbury believed that an overall settlement of East Africa could be concluded with Germany, although Bismarck was removed from his post as Chancellor in March 1890: the young and headstrong Kaiser Wilhelm II, whose father had died of cancer after less than three months on the throne, had succeeded in June 1888 and decided to replace the Chancellor of thirty years' standing. Negotiations continued nevertheless, areas of contention being Uganda (north and west of Lake Victoria) and Equatoria, where Mackinnon's Imperial British East Africa Company had interests, and Nyasaland (west of Lake Nyasa), where Scottish missionaries were worried that Germany might take over. Salisbury's position began to look weaker when the German Foreign Office went back on a promise made a year earlier by Bismarck, that Uganda and Equatoria lay outside the area in which Germany had interest.

Salisbury then played an unexpected trump card: Heligoland. How did this North Sea island become connected with South and East Africa? Two years previously, in early 1889, Bismarck had been interested in a British–German defensive alliance against France. In particular, he was concerned that, in the event of hostilities between France and Germany, the French might be allowed to use the island of Heligoland to threaten German naval shipping. Heligoland is a tiny archipelago of two islands, totaling about 400 acres, lying about 40 miles north-west of Cuxhaven at the mouth of the River Elbe; Britain had taken it from Denmark in 1807. For some time – unsurprisingly given its location – Heligoland had been of interest to German people, and as a British colony it became a refuge of German radicals. One of them, Hoffman von Fallersleben, wrote the German nationalist song *Deutschland Deutschland über alles* while at a gathering of such dissidents in Heligoland in 1841. The British managed to stand aside when German–Danish confrontation came within a few miles of the islands in 1848 and 1864, but inevitably covetous German eyes were cast on the tiny colony, and in 1873 the British Ambassador in Berlin reported a speech given by Bismarck in which he "officially declared the possession of Heligoland by a foreign power to be disadvantageous to Germany".[3]

Bismarck was concerned not only to prevent a foreign power (whether Britain or France) having such a commanding position near the German coast, and near the Kiel canal then under construction, but also to develop the main island as a naval base. This did indeed happen in the first half of the 20th century. Today, Heligoland is mainly a holiday resort and bird sanctuary.

Even in 1889, the issues of Heligoland and Africa had been

connected. While Bismarck wanted possession of Heligoland, or at the least denial of it to the French, he also wanted reassurance that the British would not assist the Cape Colony in taking over German South-west Africa (present-day Namibia). Tacit and rather oblique assurances were given at a meeting of the Foreign Secretary and the German Ambassador in London in June 1889. Now, in the negotiations about Africa in May 1890, the cards were laid clearly on the table. Britain would surrender Heligoland to Germany, in exchange for German acquiescence in a substantial list of British requirements in Africa: a British protectorate over Zanzibar, Germany ceding Witu and Lamu, access from Uganda (in the British sphere) to Lake Tanganyika, and much of the land west of Lake Nyasa. This was settled, with small further concessions; and an agreement signed on 1 July 1890 (generally referred to as the Anglo-German Agreement), with the Zanzibar protectorate to come into force on 4 November. It was a deal which met the interests of both parties, and received general popular support in both countries.

The new dispensation marked another step in the ending of the 'informal empire' that Britain had exercised over large areas of coastal Africa. This was how Sir John Kirk, as Consul in Zanzibar, had seen the relationship with the Sultan – a benevolent arrangement, in his eyes. The Sultan ruled, and, for expenditure of little more than the salary of a few officials in the Consulate, the British Government could ensure free (and profitable) trade, protect its subjects (including those of British India), and exert pressure on the Ruler on political matters when it chose (for example over ending slavery). Kirk thought that the best way of ensuring the survival of this system was to assist the Sultan in spreading and consolidating his rule over the interior, particularly the area between the Mrima coast and Lake Tanganyika. This was an area which the Sultan claimed as his, but – as we have seen – his control was weak, the administration virtually non-existent, and the links between him and his Governors subject to vagaries of personal sentiment. Accordingly, in the late 1870s and early 1880s Kirk did what he could to buttress Barghash's power and administration, and to get London's support for this process.

Kirk was summoned back to London in 1886, and retired from service in the summer of 1887, setting up home rather prosaically in Sevenoaks. Though far from his native Scotland, his new home at least enabled him to keep in touch with those in London running African affairs. In the end, he came to accept that his policy was not going to work, and – worse – that if the British did nothing, there was a risk that the Germans would take over Zanzibar itself, as well as the areas of the interior which Carl Peters had acquired. He concluded that, while it went against all that he had worked for over the preceding twenty years, declaration of a British protectorate over Zanzibar was probably in the best interests of the Sultan and his people. And this solution also offered the best chance of ending the practice of slavery in the islands as well as on the mainland.

In all the negotiations in London and Berlin about the new protectorate arrangements being brought in by the Anglo-German Agreement, there was of course no consultation of those actually living in the huge areas of Africa directly affected. Sultan Ali acquiesced, having come to depend on Kirk's successor, Charles Euan Smith, for advice and guidance, and having evidently concluded that accepting a British protectorate was less bad than becoming subjected to German takeover. The Arab community came to a similar assessment. Within a few months, in September 1890, Sultan Ali concluded an agreement with the Germans by which he ceded to them the coastal strip opposite their zone in exchange for £200,000 – an amount he thought barely adequate, considering that he had now lost Bagamoyo and the other ports through which ivory and other goods had come to the Zanzibar market. His income from customs duties, as well as from trading, was noticeably reduced.

Stanley's case against Tippu Tip collapses, Zanzibar 1891–92

Arriving in Zanzibar in August 1891, Tippu Tip thus found himself in a political and administrative system quite different from the one he had left only four years before. Among his first thoughts were concerns over the lawsuit which Stanley had brought against him, with the injunction blocking his accounts with Taria Topan. To his surprise, all was well:

> I stayed there [in Dar as-Salaam] six or seven days, before going on to Zanzibar. There I found nothing amiss. No charges, no questions at all, except a few Europeans asking about Jameson – as a result of Stanley's lies. Mr Nicol [the Zanzibar agent of Mackinnon and of the trading company Smith Mackenzie] came to tell me that there was no case between us, and was anxious that an agreement should be signed. This we did, and Stanley's charges were finished with.[4]

This would have been a considerable relief. Letters about the court case had been reaching him throughout his journey from Stanley Falls. He probably heard first about it in Kasongo, in a letter from Leopold and in the formal notice from the Consular Court that he should present himself there to conduct his defence.

What had happened was this. On arriving back at Zanzibar after the Relief Expedition, Stanley had learnt that an Indian merchant (which must have been Taria Topan) was holding on account for Tippu Tip a large sum of money paid to him by the Congo State for ivory which Jérôme Becker, the Belgian official we have met before, had bought at Stanley Falls. Stanley reckoned that if he could have this money first blocked, then awarded by Court order to the Emin Pasha Relief Committee, then the Committee could be reimbursed the losses it had made as a result – as Stanley saw it – of Tippu Tip's failure to fulfil his part of the contract signed in February 1887. By 19th-century custom, and with the agreement of successive Sultans, the British had the right to hear cases involving British subjects in their own Consular Court. Such courts existed in a number of places world-wide where the British had Consuls; and the Zanzibar Consular Court had been established in 1866, subject to the High Court in Bombay. Stanley therefore had a case lodged at this Court by Nicol, the Smith Mackenzie agent, on behalf of the Relief Committee. Because Tippu Tip was a subject of the Sultan, and not a British subject, Sayyid Khalifa had to give his consent to the case being heard in the Consular Court – which he did. Tippu Tip's son, Sayf, was in Zanzibar, but did not agree to act for his father, and so the judge, named Cracknall (or Cracknell), decided that Tippu Tip should present himself to the Court within six months of receiving notification; and a letter was sent to him in Stanley Falls, though it reached him sooner. Stanley, who could or would not wait for him to return, made a written deposition to the Court, and left for Europe.[5]

As we have seen, Tippu Tip did not make particular haste in returning, even though he had been informed that, if he was not present at the court to defend his case, his property held with Taria Topan would be handed over to Smith Mackenzie – meaning to Nicol, acting on behalf of the Emin Pasha Relief Committee. However, Judge Cracknall would have known that he was on his way. For example, A.J. Swann, a missionary whom Tippu Tip met at Mtowa on Lake Tanganyika in August 1890 on his journey home (but before the delay caused by his dysentery), wrote to the acting Consul, Euan Smith, assuring him that Tippu Tip and his Arab colleagues were leaving soon for the coast. In addition, newspaper reports in *The Times* of London reported on Tippu Tip's illness on his journey back to Zanzibar, and then on the resumption of his journey. Presumably public interest had been aroused by Stanley talking openly of his having sought redress for the losses incurred by the Expedition; he would have wanted the fact of his having started a court case to be interpreted as a sign of his confidence that he was in the right in the matter of the porters and the ammunition.

But the court case was not necessarily in accordance with the wishes of the members of the Emin Pasha Relief Committee. Mackinnon still had important interests in East Africa; better for him to have Tippu Tip as an ally than an enemy. In addition, the grounds presented to the court were not the strongest, and so the chances of success were in doubt. The deposition left by Stanley, supported by one from William Bonny (the person whom Stanley had found alone of the officers of the Rear Column when he returned from Lake Albert in August 1888), dwelt on Tippu Tip's alleged failure to produce the porters contracted for, and accused him of wilfully delaying the supply of the men, harassing and effectively starving the Rear Column, wasting the Expedition's ammunition, etc.[6] It claimed repayment from Tippu Tip of over £11,000. Its intemperate language and exaggerated claims make it easy to see why, on those grounds alone, the Relief Committee may have doubted the chances of success in the court case – especially when Bonny's deposition was undermined by his telling the lawyer representing Tippu Tip that he had written under pressure from Stanley and that on his return to England he intended to make public other facts less favourable to Stanley.

However, even on the detail the Relief Committee's case began to look weak as more information came out after the Expedition members' return from Africa. Stanley's costed claims were for three items: £3,880 for recovery of the cost of food and transport for Tippu Tip and his party of 98 people from Zanzibar to Kisangani/Stanley Falls, £4,200 for arms and ammunition supplied to him by the Expedition, and £3,250 for the salaries and maintenance of the Rear Column (on the grounds that separation of the Advance and Rear Columns would not have been necessary if Tippu Tip had supplied the men he was supposed to). Stanley also claimed an unspecified amount for goods, including weapons, taken from the Expedition by Tippu Tip's men, and damages for the delay caused to the Expedition by Tippu Tip's failure to fulfil his contract and by his "action and conduct". On the "food and transport" item, the Relief Committee considered after more careful calculation that Stanley's original claim for £3,880 was inflated, and reduced it to £2,246 (this amount including the reimbursement of a cash advance given by Major Barttelot when 400 porters had been delivered). In any case, for this item to be accepted by the Court, the plaintiffs would have had to show that Tippu Tip had requested his sea passage – whereas actually he had stated a preference to go to Kisangani by his traditional route, i.e. the caravan route via Tabora and Ujiji; it was Stanley who had wanted to keep his expedition together, and to take Tippu Tip there by sea and river. Even the basic premise, that Tippu Tip had failed to supply the numbers of porters necessary for the Expedition, was difficult to prove given that the contract of February 1887 had not specified numbers; it had only mentioned the sums to be paid per porter, and the distances each was to go.

The month after Stanley left his deposition with the Court, Tippu Tip (who was still in the interior) engaged a lawyer in Zanzibar to protect his position. In London, meanwhile, the Relief Committee members were considering their best course of action. At one point they considered the compromise of bringing Tippu Tip to Europe in order to meet King Leopold, whose employee (as Stanley Falls Governor) he still theoretically remained, with the British Government guaranteeing him appropriate conditions for his journey. A year previously, this might have been a workable plan, although it is hard to say whether it would have mollified Tippu Tip, or how it would have satisfied the unresolved financial disputes. This is because in 1890 Leopold was very keen that Tippu Tip should visit him in Europe, to discuss with him his plans for extending north and east the borders of the Congo Free State, and to look for solutions to the manpower problems faced by the State.[7]

But by early 1891, Leopold had changed his mind. His advisers told him that a visit by Tippu Tip, especially if (as inevitably would happen) it were given high profile and he came with a large entourage, would not go down well with a public opinion that associated senior Arabs with the slave trade. Further, Tippu Tip would be bound to seek contact with arms suppliers, also politically sensitive, given the view current in Europe that many of Africa's troubles were due to the excessive ease in acquiring guns and ammunition. Leopold's advisers also reckoned that the Belgian position vis-à-vis the Arabs was strengthening in the Upper Congo. More importantly, the situation had changed for

Leopold following the British–German negotiations on East African spheres of influence. When Leopold saw which way things were going, but before the negotiations were concluded, he ensured himself freedom of action by reaching a settlement with Mackinnon, acting on behalf of the Imperial British East African Company (IBEAC). By this the IBEAC would recognize a Congo Free State sphere of influence as far as the Nile, in exchange for Leopold's recognition of a strip running north–south along the western side of Lake Tanganyika. This satisfied Leopold's ambition to extend the Congo State north and east of the River Aruwimi, while giving Mackinnon and the IBEAC the possibility of communicating between the British spheres of influence in present-day Kenya and Uganda in the north, and in Nyasaland (now Malawi) in the south. The west-of-Tanganyika strip would by-pass the German territories to the east of the lake, in present-day Tanzania.

Thus, the need for a visit to Belgium by Tippu Tip had fallen away. Although the Congo Free State still had need of recruitment of personnel, and of ensuring supply of ivory to be traded downstream, Leopold could manage these administrative affairs through officials. The Relief Committee had therefore to drop the idea of an honour-filled tour.

And they soon had something else to contend with: Tippu Tip's counter-deposition, answering Stanley's list of claims and accusations with several of his own. These included: that the porters had been engaged to carry ivory back from Lake Albert to the Congo, and that the (changed) plan to go back via the dangerous areas of Bunyoro had caused numbers to desert; that Barttelot's treatment of Africans had made them unwilling to serve; that he had not willfully harassed the Expedition; that certain claims in Stanley's deposition were false, notably about the circumstances of Barttelot's death; etc. Tippu Tip also made counter claims for reimbursements, for the 400 men he had supplied and not been paid for. Once the Relief Committee's claims had (by Tippu Tip's reckoning) been reduced or annulled, and his own set against them, the account balance came out clearly in his favour.

The Relief Committee had no appetite for continuing this wrangling in a court thousands of miles away, especially since Tippu Tip's support might be needed for business purposes later. In October 1891, less than two months after Tippu Tip's return from the interior, a settlement was reached under which neither side would any longer pursue the other, and no more was heard of the case.[8]

During the negotiations on the court case, the proposal to visit

King Leopold in Belgium had been raised, but for Tippu Tip there had not been any direct connection between that and the peaceful resolution of the lawsuit. So he believed he still had the invitation in his pocket. He also wanted to make a pilgrimage to Mecca. He planned to leave Zanzibar in May 1892, on a journey including both the Muslim holy places and several European capitals, and even made arrangements for his son Sayf to send enough ivory to cover his expected expenses. This caused some consternation among Belgian officials, who looked for ways of putting him off. They were all the more determined to do this, since they held him in part responsible for the deterioration of affairs in the eastern Congo, where – as they saw it – he had "not been able or willing to make himself useful to the [Congo Free] State ... [and] had not been able to exert enough authority to prevent the crimes of his Arabs".[9] Fortunately they were spared any embarrassing confrontation, because the deterioration in the interior kept Tippu Tip in Zanzibar.

Chapter 12

Arabs versus the Congo Free State

TIPPU TIP NOW found himself watching from afar as the confrontation between the Arabs and the Belgians in the Congo Free State reached its climax. The battle that resulted in the expulsion of Walter Deane from Stanley Falls in 1886 initiated the overt growth of tension, although the underlying problem had existed for some time before. That is, Arabs had been extending their reach downstream from Kisangani/ Stanley Falls, and – by raids for ivory and slaves – had been incurring the enmity of local villagers living mainly on or near the River Congo and its principal tributaries. While he was at Kisangani up to early 1886, Tippu Tip had realized that compromise with the Europeans was the best way forward for protecting Arab trading interests, and had sought to restrain his fellow-Arabs from excessive or provocative violence. He had not always been successful, but the policy had resulted in a stalemate in which the Belgians had occupied, but not controlled, the river up to Stanley Falls, and the Arabs had traded (and sometimes raided) down as far as Bangala.

The Congo Free State tightens its grip, 1887–92

This continued up to, during and after the Emin Pasha Relief Expedition. By this time, King Leopold had invested considerable financial capital in the Congo, with so far little return, and needed to consolidate the political and economic basis of the fledgling Free State, and at the same time to show Belgian public opinion that he was taking action to reduce the slave trade or at least minimize its spread. This was why it was possible for him to install Tippu Tip as Governor of Stanley Falls – someone who might exert some restraint, and who might allow the reassertion of Congo Free State control over the Upper Congo.[1]

As we have seen, both sides were to be disappointed with the arrangement. Tippu Tip found that his authority in the Arab community was waning, and the Free State authorities, not realizing this, failed to give him adequate support in the form of dispatch of steamers or response to his request for men and weapons. Nevertheless, Leopold still wanted to use Tippu Tip to further his ambition of linking the Upper Congo with the Nile. Jérôme Becker was instructed in 1889 to negotiate with him a deal by which he would establish three posts of the Congo Free State in the Bahr al-Ghazal, an area well inside Equatoria, and a fourth on the Upper Nile, and maintain lines of supply for them. Leopold later described Becker's mission as an attempt to "get the Arabs, in exchange for money, to serve my policy".[2] Tippu Tip agreed to the plan, for which he was to be well paid, but in the end it fizzled out, with Tippu Tip, already overburdened by his efforts to support the Relief Expedition, complaining that he was not being given adequate men and munitions for the task. Trust between the two parties was breaking down, and indeed hostility growing between Arabs and Belgians, fomented by, among other things, the Free State's construction of a post at Basoko, at the confluence of the Rivers Aruwimi and Congo, which Tippu Tip considered in his zone of control. His immediate reaction to Becker's proposed contract was to ask:

> "How can the [Congo Free] State send someone to buy my ivory and demand my services, just when I have proof that they are thinking of making war against me?"[3]

More generally, the Arabs were also inconvenienced by the Free State authorities' imposition of a ban on import of arms and powder, supplies of which from the east coast were under pressure as a result of the British–German blockade.

In place of using Tippu Tip's support, Leopold meanwhile found other ways of trying to push the Congo Free State borders outwards in the north and east, by ordering expeditions led by Vangèle and van Kerckhoven to raid in the area around and north of the Rivers Uele and Bomu, where they clashed heavily with Arab parties, killing a large number and taking a huge quantity of their ivory.

Despite this growing tension, Arabs and Belgians made a success, for a few years, of their commercial transactions. Pursuing the policy of persuading Arabs to trade their ivory westwards instead of back to the east coast, Belgian officials were encouraged (including by a percentage take) to buy ivory and export it via the River Congo. We have seen how Jérôme Becker bought a large quantity from Tippu Tip – the income from this was the sum deposited with Taria Topan and blocked by the Zanzibar court injunction. The Arabs also helped the Congo Free State relieve its labour shortage, by selling slaves whom the Belgians 'freed', but kept to work on the stations and later on the railway being built beside the Lower Congo. This labour force became the notorious *Force publique*, whose violent and abusive behaviour towards Africans caused Leopold to come under fierce criticism in the 1890s. Belgian officials also received commissions for the slaves they 'freed' in this way. Tippu Tip was party to this arrangement. He records in the *Maisha*:

> During my stay in Zanzibar, Mr B [Jérôme Becker] came to see me, wanting men. He had been sent by a Belgian firm who were building a railway. [We] made an agreement that I would provide them with 800 men from Rumami [i.e. the River Lomami area] – Wanakamba – every three months ... Each man for 70 dollars. We made an agreement for 30,000 dollars' worth of men.[4]

The text of the contract, made in Zanzibar in December 1891, has survived, showing that this was indeed a big deal.[5] Tippu Tip was to deliver 2,600 Africans in four contingents of 450 men and 200 women each, in the course of the following year. The total value of the contract can be seen by the high value of the penalty clauses – each party put down a deposit of £3,200, to be forfeit in case of non-delivery on the principal conditions of the contract. £3,200 was equivalent to MT$ 30,000 at the then rate of exchange: the value of silver dropped sharply in the later years of the 19th century, bringing the rate to between MT$9 and MT$11 to the pound sterling, in contrast to about MT$5 or MT$6 a few decades earlier.

But the balance of advantage between the Arabs and the Belgians was shifting. As ivory trade down the River Congo increased and Belgian traders wanted more of the action, Leopold could see the opportunity for monopolizing it. As one historian of the Congo puts it: "Competition over control of ivory pushed Leo to change from collaboration to confrontation."[6] At the same time, Leopold thought he could polish his (by now rather endangered) public image. In 1890, the Brussels anti-slavery conference had given Leopold the opportunity to strengthen his reputation for being a philanthropic developer. From the start of the Congo operation he had presented himself as bringing civilization and trade to this central region of the 'dark continent', and now he was able to claim that he was responding to the anti-slavery campaign conducted by Cardinal Lavigerie and to the Brussels Act signed in July 1890, in asking for more resources to tackle the slavery menace. The Belgian state advanced him a substantial loan (badly needed since expenditure wildly exceeded income in the Congo Free State), and the Brussels Conference gave him the right to levy import duties.

In the Free State itself, this new political situation gave him a reason to start moving towards resolving the growing problem of the Arab presence. By 1892 actual incidents of armed conflict were increasing in frequency, as the Free State raised duties and thereby squeezed Arab profits from the ivory trade. The Arab centres in Manyema and on the Upper Congo were well established, but the leaders in each place retained stubborn independence, and were reluctant to form a united front against an increasingly well-organized antagonist. Tippu Tip's relatives were among these leaders: he had left his kinsman Rashid in charge in Stanley Falls when he left in about January 1890, and his son Sayf in Kasongo, and the Arab leader in Kabambare was his kinsman Bwana Nzige.

The local Africans were ambiguously placed as the confrontation built up. A few years previously they had considered Free State officials their supporters against the raids of the Arabs. In 1886, Bakumu tribal chiefs had told Camille Coquilhat, commander of the Bangala Station, after they had rescued Deane following the battle at Stanley Falls:

> You should give rifles to all the enemies of the Arabs; they'd very quickly be chased out of the country if the whites helped us. Will

you abandon us completely to these bandits? If we weren't your sincere friends, we wouldn't have taken in your white brother.

Coquilhat adds:

The whole village got together in a dance of joy at having helped to rescue the former commander of the Falls, the protector of the oppressed natives.[7]

But with the passage of time, the local people became equally hostile to both parties: the Arabs stole their ivory, their food and their people, while the Belgians forced them into labour and – later in the 1890s – used shocking violence in their demands for rubber from jungle vines.

Progression from minor engagements to what came to be termed a 'massacre' raised the stakes and began to make it likely that a definitive solution – either consolidation of the Arab zone, or their expulsion – would have to come about. The 'massacre' was the killing, in May 1892, of a Belgian trader named Arthur Hodister, together with several European and other members of his substantial trading expedition, at and near Riba-Riba on the River Lualaba downstream from Nyangwe. Although some Africans were involved, they were probably egged on by Arabs, and the Arab-Swahili chief at Nyangwe, Mohara (or Tagamoyo/Mtagamoyo bin Sultan) was judged to be responsible. It was Mohara's men who had been responsible for the infamous massacre at the market in Nyangwe in July 1871, which was witnessed by Livingstone and was the cause of his turning back from Manyema to Ujiji. Hodister was in fact an Arabophile, and Tippu Tip describes him as "a great friend of mine".[8] To begin with, and while his contacts were with Arabs from Tippu Tip's network, his trading expedition went smoothly. But news was coming through to the Arabs of the large-scale killing and pillage wrought by the van Kerckhoven expedition on the River Uele, and Mohara evidently decided that the large European expedition led by Hodister should not be allowed to establish itself. Hodister's party were reportedly killed and eaten by Africans under Mohara's command, and their mutilated heads were sent to Mserera, the Arab chief at Riba-Riba. Mserera was said to be angry at the incident.

The situation was therefore not one of simply defined antagonism between Arabs and Belgians. Among the Arabs, some leaders responded to Tippu Tip's policy of restraint and compromise, while others were prepared to use or order intense violence either to protect territory they considered theirs, or to avenge outrages committed against their colleagues. Among the Europeans, the interests of trading companies were not always aligned with those of the Congo Free State; indeed, some traders directly blamed the Free State and its officials for wrongheaded policies or failure to provide adequate security. Local Africans sometimes looked to the Free State for protection, and sometimes took sides with (or were employed by) Arab leaders.

The Free State goes to war against the Arabs, 1892–93

Despite the appalling nature of the Hodister massacre, and Mohara's overt opposition to the Free State, a kind of uneasy peace persisted for a few months longer. Policy-makers in Brussels even considered dangling a cash incentive in front of Tippu Tip to tempt him back to Stanley Falls, so that they could use him to conciliate Arab leaders while quietly building up military capacity.

But the plan was dropped when, in September 1892, the process leading to full hostilities began.[9] South and west of Nyangwe, one of Tippu Tip's leaders named Ngongo Lutete (also Gongo Lutete) had been raiding west of the River Lomami; Ngongo had been placed as Tippu Tip's representative in Utetera, between the Rivers Lomami and Lualaba, and was subject to his son, Sayf. A Belgian commander, Lt Francis Dhanis, attacked him, successfully, and Ngongo sued for peace and was forced to accept the River Lomami as the limit of Arab influence and trading. Dhanis then put further pressure on Ngongo, resulting in the latter declaring himself (in September 1892) answerable to the Free State. Sayf tried to reassert his father's authority, but Ngongo stayed with his new masters. Sayf gathered a significant army of reportedly 10,000 men, and joined forces with Mohara in open hostilities against the Free State. This was in spite of Tippu Tip's explicit instructions, sent to his kinsman Rashid in Stanley Falls, to stay on friendly terms with the Europeans. Sayf's reaction can be attributed to his considering Ngongo's defection as a personal betrayal, as well as resulting in direct losses – the trading profits in the considerable area west of the River Lomami, and the tribute that he had hitherto received from Ngongo.

But it was a foolhardy decision, and probably not the course of action his more carefully calculating father would have taken.

Although the Free State forces in the field were fewer, they were better disciplined and much better armed, and the Arab leadership was poorly co-ordinated. From early in the campaign the Arab forces were on the defensive, losing about 1,600 guns and several hundred men in an engagement on the River Lomami, in which Sayf was wounded. In this and ensuing engagements the numbers of fighting men on both sides were large, as were the numbers of casualties; and these men were of course recruited Africans, the numbers of actual Arabs and Free State Europeans being low. Dhanis, for example, had a few officers and 350 regular soldiers. The brutality of the fighting was exceptional; and there are reliable reports of cannibalism after the battles. Harry Johnston, the British explorer who became colonial administrator in south-east and south central Africa, commented: "Prisoners seem to have been issued as rations by the native commanders of both the armies."[10]

Dhanis advanced with his Free State forces. After a battle in which Mohara was killed, he pushed the Arabs back to the River Lualaba, and with Ngongo's help succeeded in subverting more local chiefs to come over to give allegiance to the Free State. Under further pressure, the Arabs abandoned Nyangwe, leaving Dhanis able to regroup in order to attack the Arab forces now led by Sayf and encamped in Kasongo. Sayf's forces also included a number who had concentrated on the main remaining Arab stronghold after another Free State campaign, led by Lt Chaltin of the *Force publique*, had scored several successes against other Arab-held villages. Dhanis captured Kasongo in April 1893, taking a vast amount of booty including 25 tons of ivory, many luxury goods, and quantities of stored food, growing crops and cattle. Kasongo was by now a relatively advanced and well-administered Arab town: Sidney Hinde, an English doctor attached to Dhanis's forces, describes the wealth of the settlement, and also its high state of organization and elaborate horticulture and agriculture.[11]

Late in 1893, Rumaliza (Mohammed bin Khalfan), who had been at Ujiji, came to join the fighting, heading for Kasongo. Previously, in mid-1892, he had been operating at the northern end of Lake Tanganyika, both at Ujiji (on the east) and at Mtowa (on the west), where he had come into conflict with a force of the anti-slavery *Mouvements anti-esclavagistes*, led by the Belgian commander Capt. Alphonse Jacques. They had reached a stand-off, although Jacques remained determined to follow his instructions to prevent ivory trading to the east coast ports, or at least to levy taxes – on behalf of the Congo Free State – on any ivory traded by those routes. A complicating factor was that Rumaliza was holding a quantity of goods and ivory belonging to Tippu Tip. He advanced through Manyema, using religious slogans to help raise Muslim or pro-Muslim forces on a kind of *jihad* against the infidel Europeans. Initially he achieved some success, and other Arab leaders came together in a co-ordinated campaign. But the Free State forces brought in reinforcements, and drove the Arabs out of Kabambare (south-east of Kasongo) in a major engagement in which Tippu Tip's son Sayf was killed. The Belgian commander Hubert Lothaire continued the advance, forced Rumaliza to flee into German territory, and asserted Free State authority to the shores of Lake Tanganyika, also linking up with the *Mouvements anti-esclavagistes* forces under Jacques.

After capturing Kasongo in April 1893, Dhanis had too few men to be able to pursue the Arabs in flight, but spent several months reorganizing Nyangwe and Kasongo. This was a complex task, since thousands of former slaves of the Arabs were without direction, until settled on land round the towns and told to cultivate crops which then supplied Free State forces. Further operations to clear the area of Arabs were led by various Belgian officers, including Nicolas Tobback who, as former Belgian Resident at Stanley Falls, had had a good relationship with Tippu Tip. In one of these engagements, Tippu Tip's nephew Habib bin Saʿid was killed, and Rashid (the kinsman who had been left as Acting Governor in Stanley Falls) narrowly escaped capture by Free State forces. He was later interned, his life spared, and he was then deported to the Kasai region and put to service in the Free State. There is some evidence that, after the Free State forces had unambiguously secured their ascendancy, Tippu Tip intervened through the British authorities in Zanzibar to help the Arab survivors. Some were retained to continue the systems of agriculture and river transport that they had developed.

Ngongo, whose men had given Dhanis essential support in his campaign, was allowed to return home, but came to an unfortunate end: for reasons that are not clear, he was brought to trial for treason by a Belgian post commander, and executed. Not surprisingly, his men felt deep resentment at this example of European treachery, and a number of chiefs hitherto loyal to the Free State defected.

As a result of the campaign, a huge additional area was brought under effective control of the Congo Free State – to the River Aruwimi in the north and stretching now to Lake Tanganyika. This became the *Province orientale* of the Free State. In propaganda terms, the campaign was presented as having been prosecuted for the humanitarian purpose of ending the slave trade which the European public believed was entirely in the hands of the Arabs. But we should not forget that the Free State then adopted many of the Arabs' methods, merely calling them by another name. Raiding villages was done in the name of enforcing law and order, appropriating ivory was collecting taxes, and the Africans taken prisoner in the campaign, if they survived, were absorbed into the *Force publique* and used as forced labour.

Tippu Tip and the Belgian–Arab war

Considering that the war between the Arabs and the Congo Free State was so conclusive for his community, Tippu Tip's commentary on it is surprisingly brief, while focusing on Rumaliza's role in the campaign with an emphasis disproportionate to its importance.[12] Probably this is because of his later lawsuit against Rumaliza, and his wish to defend his side of the dispute and denigrate Rumaliza's reputation. Before starting his account of the Hodister massacre and the Arab–Belgian fighting, he mentions Ngongo Lutete (Ngongo Ruweteta in the *Maisha*), but only in the context of a deal he had apparently made with Becker for the supply of men for building the railway: it was Ngongo who was instructed by Tippu Tip to provide them to his son Sayf, presumably for onward 'delivery'.

In Tippu Tip's account, Rumaliza incited Mohara and the Arabs of Manyema and Nyangwe to attack the Europeans, alleging that Tippu Tip's people in Kasongo were in the Europeans' pay. As a result of this, they had killed Hodister, his friend. After the 'massacre', Tobback and Sayf had consulted in Stanley Falls, and Sayf had assured Tobback of mutual support. The next thing Tippu Tip knew was the deal sealing the alliance between Ngongo Lutete and the Free State; he considered it a great mistake on the part of the Belgians not to have taken Sayf and Rashid into their confidence – if they had done so, then Sayf would not have thrown himself into the fray. Tippu Tip was probably correct in this assessment – except that by that stage the Belgians (or at least Dhanis) were not interested in peaceful coexistence and reckoned that it was to their advantage to bring over Ngongo Lutete and set him against his former masters or allies.

Tippu Tip tells how Sayf came to involve himself in the conflict:

> The intelligence of youngsters is small; he didn't question the situation nor send messengers to me. ... He decided to go and deal

with his slave Ngongo Ruweteta on his own but was unaware of his alliance with the Belgians .... If he had realized that Ngongo and the Belgians were in league then he would never have gone to attack him .... He was no fool, and respected his father.[13]

This is all consistent with Tippu Tip's assumption that his own understanding with the Free State authorities was firm, and known to Sayf.

Tippu Tip summed up his analysis in the penultimate paragraph of the *Maisha*: "Now the cause of this intrigue, and the root of the trouble, basically it was Rumaliza."[14] He claimed that Rumaliza had not only been responsible for the war, but had also lost huge quantities of his, Tippu Tip's, goods, both those that he had sent up-country, and ivory that Sayf had sent to him from Manyema for onward transmission to the coast. Finally, he wrote that he had sent warnings, either to Rumaliza or to the Belgians, which had been ignored.

In writing this, Tippu Tip was allowing his prejudice against Rumaliza to run away with him, and corrupt a fair evaluation of the situation. Even by the time that he had left Stanley Falls in 1886, it was clear that fault-lines were opening up in his attempts to hold the line between the Free State and the Arab community. As we have seen, he and his close colleagues (for example his son Sayf, and his kinsman Rashid) were sometimes able to establish a relationship of trust with Belgian interlocutors such as Tobback, but even these relationships were subject to failure, and the Free State was erratic in supplying Tippu Tip with the communications, men and munitions that he needed. Within the Arab community, other leaders were showing increasing independence and enterprise in exploring and exploiting areas which the Belgians considered 'theirs'. Leopold's ambitions to push the Free State boundaries north-east to the Nile and east to Lake Tanganyika would naturally bring conflict closer. Once the Brussels Conference of 1889–90, giving concrete form to feelings in European public opinion, had given Leopold the 'moral authority' to use force against the Arab slave traders, open war became almost inevitable. Tippu Tip could do little or nothing from his absentee position on the sidelines. Captain Dhanis took advantage of his successes against Ngongo Lutete, and in crossing the River Lomami into hitherto uncontested Arab territory, opened the curtain for the final act. He received his reward from Leopold: promotion from District Officer to a Barony.[15]

Tippu Tip's personal losses from the war were significant. By this time he already owned considerable property and cash in Zanzibar, together with property on the mainland. Frank Vincent, an American journalist, visited him in 1892, before either of them knew about the war that had broken out, and describes a household of obvious luxury:

> He is now said to be the richest native in Africa, having property to the value of about $800,000. He is just building a fine, large, three-storey house in Zanzibar. ... Tippo received me at the street door and led me to a long, narrow sitting-room. ... Upon the wall hung many fine swords, daggers and pistols, and upon the centre-table were a set of tea-things and smoking utensils in delicate filigree silver-work. ... Through an interpreter [we] had a long chat about Central Africa, Stanley, Zanzibar and Europe.[16]

In an interview given to a German journalist, Eugène Wolff, in 1891, Tippu Tip said that he had on several occasions been extremely rich, but had also often lost a lot of money. At the time, he owned "only a house in Zanzibar, some houses in Bagamoyo, and several plantations", and he had given large sums of money to many friends. At the same interview he complained that the Belgians had raised the export tax on ivory from 14 to 50 percent, making it impossible to export his ivory to the east coast; and at the time he had 3,000 *frasila* of ivory in the Congo Free State.[17]

The loss of the Arab zone did not affect his assets in Zanzibar and on the coastal region of the mainland, but it did make it impossible for Tippu Tip to extract the quantities of ivory, trade goods and weapons that had not been already repatriated to Zanzibar.

Tippu Tip's influence in Africa dwindles

If his political usefulness to the Belgians was now a wasted asset, Tippu Tip was still considered of some value to the British. In 1893, soon after the expulsion of the Arabs from eastern Congo, the British government were concerned at the insecure and ill-defined borders of south and south-east Sudan, where the Congo Free State and the French respectively were encroaching. Not willing to commit armed forces, they decided to attempt to conclude treaties with local chieftains, and looked for an intermediary to do this on their behalf. Eyes turned to Tippu Tip, who (as some saw it) had been able to source men on the

Equatoria Province borders during the Emin Pasha Relief Expedition.

However, the proposal failed to find favour with Gerald Portal, the Agent and Consul-General in Zanzibar, who reported that Tippu Tip had himself said that he had little influence in that region; and the Foreign Office dropped the idea. Within a year, Leopold had signed his deal with Mackinnon's Imperial British East Africa Company (see Chapter 11, page 259), assuring the King of a border going up to Lake Albert and the Nile, and the Company of its access to the strip of territory along the west shore of Lake Tanganyika. So the treaties with the local chiefs were no longer needed.

CHAPTER 13

Last Judgements

FURTHER EROSION of Tippu Tip's capital was to follow. We saw how he had fallen out with Rumaliza (Mohammed bin Khalfan), formerly a business associate and one to whom he had lent money and goods in the past. Rumaliza had escaped from the Arab–Belgian war, and made his way to Zanzibar. Here he came forward with a document purporting to be a partnership agreement between himself, Tippu Tip and his kinsman Bwana Nzige, according to which all profits earned by any of them were to be shared in the proportions 50 percent to Tippu Tip, and 25 percent each to the other two. Rumaliza thereby laid claim to a quarter of all Tippu Tip's assets.

Tippu Tip sued by Rumaliza and the heirs of Taria Topan

Tippu Tip and Bwana Nzige of course challenged the authenticity of this document, and claimed that their alleged signatures on it were forgeries. But Rumaliza persisted, and took the claim to court. Because he had been born in Lindi, which was now subject to German control, the case was heard in Dar as-Salaam. Judgement was given in favour of Rumaliza. There was then a long dispute about the value of a quarter of Tippu Tip's assets; and the outcome was that he was required to hand over to Rumaliza his property and goods on the mainland, which were listed in an inventory.

We have to rely only on Heinrich Brode for this episode in Tippu Tip's life. In the *Maisha,* after a long paragraph blaming Rumaliza for the Arab loss of the 1892–93 confrontation, Tippu Tip says only: "And in all this, he [Rumaliza] did not suffer. I was compelled to pay up with my property on the Mrima coast. And I can't say anything, because this is how the State chose to compel me."[1] Brode records that some of the mainland assets "did not exist" – meaning that they had been stolen or could not be found; examples were a quantity of ivory that had been buried in Itawa (where Tippu Tip had travelled on his Second Journey), and a claim for a debt of MT$6,000.[2] According to another account, the court decided on the cash value of one-quarter of Tippu Tip's fortune, then confiscated his property in the German zone, and then found that the property was not sufficient in value to cover the amount due.[3] Rumaliza claimed for the recovery of the missing amount in the court in Zanzibar, since Tippu Tip – now having no property in the German zone – could not be sued in Dar as-Salaam. Rumaliza however, who did have property on the mainland, and was therefore recognized as a German subject, was able to claim the right to have a German consular representative in court with him.

This turned out to be important for our knowledge of Tippu Tip's life. The German consular representative was Heinrich Brode, who thus came to meet Tippu Tip and persuaded him to write or dictate the account of his life which we now have in the *Maisha.*

The judgement in the Zanzibar court, given in the end by the Sultan in the Court of Appeal, was that Tippu Tip should pay Rumaliza a further MT$6,000, by then equivalent to about £500, but still a substantial sum of money. It is not surprising that Tippu Tip should give vent in the *Maisha* to such animosity against his court opponent, especially after (as he claimed) he had supported him so much in their business careers in the more peaceable past. Brode comments that Rumaliza did not profit much by the decision since most of it was taken up by the lawyer's fees, and that what was left was subject to claims by creditors, such that he had soon to declare himself bankrupt. Tippu Tip reportedly consoled himself with a Swahili proverb, *Mali ya haramu yanakwenda nyia ya haramu*: "Ill-gotten gains never prosper."

Since we have only Tippu Tip's and Brode's accounts of the dealings between him and Rumaliza, both in their earlier careers and in court in Zanzibar, it is difficult to judge whether factors other than commercial ones were at play. Alison Smith speculates that the underlying cause of their mutual enmity lay actually in their different assessments of the political situation and the best policy for the Arab community to adopt in the light of Congo Free State encroachments on their zone of influence.[4] On this reading Tippu Tip, with his preference for coming to terms with the Europeans, was bound to differ from Rumaliza with his uncompromising insistence on forceful defence of Arab interests, and his hopes that the Europeans might be driven out of Central Africa. Tippu Tip records having made his position clear to Rumaliza when he was in Kisangani during the Emin Pasha Relief Expedition:

"I advised him [Rumaliza] to comply with the Europeans in so far as they wanted. ... He agreed to do this. He had come from Ujiji, especially to see me, and we saw one another for one day."[5]

That Rumaliza was proved wrong in his hopes for Arab supremacy or survival may have added to Tippu Tip's sense of grievance.

Finally, Brode reports another lawsuit, this one involving the heirs of Tippu Tip's former banker and supplier, Taria Topan, who claimed that Tippu Tip had owed him 15,000 rupees at the time of his death. Tippu Tip counter-claimed for money owed to him both by Taria Topan and by his grandson, and the court awarded him Rs 300,000, equivalent to about MT$100,000. But Brode reckoned that, because Taria Topan's grandson had spent his inheritance, there was not much chance of Tippu Tip receiving what he was owed, and that he too, like Rumaliza, had high legal fees to pay.

Retirement on Zanzibar

These court cases occupied Tippu Tip's time and attention in the period after the Arab–Belgian campaign, possibly for some years; final judgement in the Rumaliza case was not given until 1902. In the meantime, he may have been tempted to resume a role on the mainland: rumours began to circulate in 1895 that he might return to Ujiji and be appointed governor there by the German administration, but nothing came of it, and a colonial administrator was installed instead. Tippu Tip stayed quietly in Zanzibar. Records show that he intervened periodically on behalf of his relatives, for example his kinsman Rashid, who had been 'exiled' to the Kasai region and ordered to run an agricultural project. Not surprisingly, given that Rashid's skills and experience were in ivory trading, this was not a great success, and, after lengthy negotiations through the British authorities, Tippu Tip succeeded in having him brought to Zanzibar, but not until 1899. It took another three years to get permission for his family and household to be allowed out of the Free State and across to Zanzibar.

In the absence of records of his activities in his retirement from the mainland, we must assume that Tippu Tip had enough to occupy him with the management of his properties and farms on Zanzibar. He had hoped to visit Europe, and at least make the pilgrimage to Mecca, but neither of these plans were realized. Perhaps he felt, now in his sixties, that his health was not strong enough. Col. Richard Meinertzhagen, the soldier, adventurer and game-hunter, was taken to see him in January 1903, and recorded that "he is not allowed to leave Zanzibar, nor does he want to" – a judgement for which we have no other evidence. Some of his writings have earned Meinertzhagen a dubious reputation, and so we should hesitate before relying on him here. A little anecdote he relates tells us something of both men:

> I tried to get him [Tippu Tip] to talk of slave raiding days, but he clearly did not like it. He gave us coffee from a gorgeous silver pot which I admired, so he had to give it to me. Sinclair [Meinertzhagen's companion] told me afterwards that I must never admire anything in an Arab house, as they are under an obligation to present it to the admirer. I offered to take it back, but Sinclair says that would be an insult, so I shall keep it.[6]

Despite Tippu Tip's losses in the law courts, and the impossibility of bringing back to Zanzibar his assets of ivory, weapons and cash in the Congo Free State, he was still a wealthy man. Brode, writing in the late 1890s while Tippu Tip was still alive, says that he "attends untiringly to his numerous personal affairs", and that "his fortune still amounts to £50,000 in round figures, and is very advantageously invested in stone houses and landed property".[7] The British Consul estimated it more modestly at £13,000–£14,000, though this was still substantial. His plantations were of cloves, a crop brought from Indonesia via Madagascar in the 1820s. Planters in Zanzibar itself and on the neighbouring island of Pemba had found that it flourished, to the extent that in the 1860s and 1870s they were responsible for over half of global production. Tippu Tip was said to be the second largest clove-plantation owner in the islands, but thought he could improve production by inviting the (by now British protectorate) government to take over management of his farms. The Director of Agriculture refused, on the grounds that the public service could not take responsibility for privately owned properties.

The clove plantations relied on slave labour, even after the measures taken to reduce and remove the slave trade on which plantation owners had increasingly depended through the century. When the British assumed the protectorate of Zanzibar in 1890, the administration was subject to increasing pressure from UK public opinion, and in particular the Anti-Slavery Society, to make slavery illegal altogether. As mentioned above, in late 1889 Sultan Khalifa agreed to a proposal from Euan Smith to issue a decree declaring that anyone entering his dominions would be free, and another decree giving freedom to all children born in his dominions after 1 January 1890. But this latter decree was not implemented, and even British officials in Zanzibar advocated a more gradual approach to abolition. They believed that conditions for many slaves, particularly those in domestic service, were tolerable, and they feared the potential disruption to society, possibly detrimental to the slaves' own interests, that might follow mass emancipation. Thus it was only in 1897 that the Zanzibari government abolished the legal status of slavery. It is possible that Tippu Tip, who probably owned several thousand slaves, worked to persuade fellow-owners in the Arab community to accept what he saw as an inevitable process leading to abolition.

Death of Tippu Tip

Tippu Tip's peaceful old age came to an end on 13 June 1905 when, according to most sources, he died from a cerebral haemorrhage following a severe attack of malaria, aged about sixty-eight. His death was reported by the British Consul, who remarked that, whatever one might think of Tippu Tip's previous career, he could only regret the loss of someone whose behaviour, in his personal experience, had been correct and loyal, and whose influence had been used always to the good. *The Times* reported his death as occurring a day later:

Zanzibar, 14 June: Tippoo Tib died today. Hamid Bin Mohammed, *alias* Tippoo Tib, was the famous Arab merchant and slave trader of the Upper Congo, who was associated with Cameron and Stanley in their expeditions across Africa.[8]

His death came a year after that of Stanley, and two years before the Congo Free State, at the end of many years of protest at the atrocities committed there against the African population, was taken out of the hands of King Leopold II into the administration of the Belgian Government. As Tippu Tip passed, so his world passed with him.

A touch of charisma

We are fortunate in having more evidence about the character of Tippu Tip than of almost any Arab or African living in Central and East Africa in that period, partly because of his own *Maisha*, but also because of his dealings with the various Europeans who recorded their impressions of him. We know him as a tall, broad man, with features rather African than Arab. He must have had a very strong constitution, withstanding hazards to health that European travellers kept at bay only with heavy doses of quinine and other medicines. In the thousands of miles he travelled in his lifetime, by far the majority would have been covered on foot; among beasts of burden, only donkeys are mentioned in the accounts of his journeys, and those very rarely. He records himself being carried only once, when he was ill with dysentery during his last journey back to Bagamoyo, in 1891. His energy seemed limitless.

He took great care of his appearance. Frequently observers comment on his impeccable white *thawb*, the long Arab garment worn by most Omani Arabs with a belt and *khanjar*, the curved dagger often decorated with fine silver filigree. (How he managed to have his *thawb*s laundered, when journeying through the swamps of Central Africa, is not recorded; presumably this would have been among the duties of the women camp followers.) His headgear seems to have been more rough-and-ready than that of modern Omanis or other Peninsular Arabs. We have already seen how Cameron described him on meeting him in August 1874:

> He was a good-looking man, and the greatest dandy I had seen amongst the traders. And, notwithstanding his being perfectly black, he was a thorough Arab, for curiously enough the admixture of negro blood had not rendered him less of an Arab in his ideas and manners.[9]

In similar vein, Herbert Ward records:

> Tippu-Tib himself is a very remarkable individual in every way – of commanding presence, and a wonderful degree of natural ease and grace of manner and action. He stands nearly six feet in height, has brilliant, dark, intelligent eyes, and bears himself with an air of ultra-imperial dignity, without a trace of effort or affectation. He was always dressed in Arab costume, of spotless white. His wives carried his food and baggage. They were all well developed in every way; most were fairly good-looking; necessarily very dirty – as they never washed; and very high-smelling. He must have married all these females for love, as none had any money, and they certainly had very little trousseau.[10]

He obviously enjoyed conversation. While this is a characteristic shared by many Arabs and Africans (and others), and would have been useful in order to exchange news, give and receive warnings of dangers ahead on the road, hear about trading opportunities, and so forth, with Tippu Tip we find that many Europeans he met record long talks with him. His interests were wide: conversations would cover not just African topics, but the politics of Europe and America, with Tippu Tip constantly curious to learn and hear more. He spoke Swahili primarily, but also Arabic (which he would have used with the Sultan and on other formal occasions), but is not recorded as having spoken any European language.

It is difficult to tell whether he was humorous in his discourse. Some pictures of him show a twinkle in his eye; but the main impression he gave was one of courtesy and politeness, rather than humour. One writer, A.J. Swann, who came to East Africa in 1882 to take a lifeboat to Lake Tanganyika for the London Missionary Society, records:

> His activity was astonishing. He possessed a frank, manly character, enlivened by humour, and loved immensely to play practical jokes upon his intimate friends.[11]

He was vivacious, and his natural curiosity showed in the ceaseless movement of his eyes. Bonny, of the Emin Pasha Expedition, in describing his eyes, says that they were "restless and turn often. When talking he often shifts about on his seat."[12] He may also have had a twitch in his eyelids, giving rise – possibly – to his nickname. He preferred to attribute his name to the rapid fire of his men's guns.

Slaver as well as ivory trader?

In character Tippu Tip was determined and forceful. He was ruthless in the sense that he would use violence, including the killing of opponents, in order to have his way, and in particular in the course of subduing African chiefs and their villages. In this he was no different from his contemporaries, Arab and African. But he does not seem to have relished killing or to have been gratuitously cruel. The one exception in the record is the incident with Jameson and the African girl during the Emin Pasha Relief Expedition, when he must have known what would happen from the moment he suggested Jameson have some cloth brought from his hut. Although he was guilty of burning villages, there is no record of his having followed the pattern of some of his fellow-Arabs, of attacking a village simply to seize slaves, or of kidnapping women and children so that the menfolk would bring ivory to secure their release. Indeed, his whole narrative – not contradicted by the Europeans he met – is of trading, not raiding, for ivory. He was at pains to explain this in a discussion with van Kerckhoven in Yambuya in 1888:

> We know the advantages of regular trade, and we stop at nothing to create it. You've seen the loads of iron, copper, and cloth which my caravan has brought to Kasongo. Most of this merchandise is destined for paying for ivory.[13]

He was a trader to his finger-tips, not swayed by personal prejudice, but concerned simply to conclude a deal at the best price.

His relationships with the Europeans he met were complex. Almost invariably he made a favourable first impression, no doubt because of his politeness and his natural personal charm. At the individual level, this did not always last long. He fell out with Stanley; the members of the Rear Column of the Emin Pasha Relief Expedition grew exasperated with his non-delivery of the promised men and weapons. Even Tobback, the Resident at Stanley Falls who was a natural ally, lost patience with him. This was because Tobback expected more of him than he was able to deliver – control over fellow-Arabs' raiding into the territory of the Congo Free State. Yet Tippu Tip saw himself as prepared to work with 'the Europeans' in order to smooth the rough edges of the relationship, and to allow for Arab co-existence with the Free State. As we have seen, this was a false hope. And, as time passed, Tippu Tip came round to a kind of passive acceptance of the changes arriving in Central and East Africa in his day – for example, the colonial takeover by the Belgians, British and Germans, and the abolition of slavery as well as the slave trade.

This was not recognized by his contemporaries in Europe. There, because he was an Arab and the Arabs were (with some justification) seen as the brutal and violent exponents of slave raiding down the Congo, he was automatically tarred with the same brush. He is still described primarily as a slave trader in much modern literature. He did of course own slaves, both for transporting ivory and on his clove plantations; but at an early stage he realized that he could earn more profits from ivory trading than from making trade in slaves his primary occupation. This is implicit in his comment in the *Maisha* that his half-brother Mohammed al-Wardi had made paltry profits "in Ngao or Benadir", which his readers would have recognized as well-known slave-trading routes, as contrasted with the surplus he had achieved through the ivory trading on his early trading journeys.[14] Brode makes it explicit, reporting how he had asked Tippu Tip about his brother's trading, and that Tippu Tip

> had to own with a smirk that his brother had undertaken slave-hunts in the south, and sold his booty in more northerly regions. He had not grown rich from it.[15]

Later, when they met in Tabora in September 1881, Tippu Tip gave Jérôme Becker his opinion about slavery and European attitudes to it:

> White people have quite false ideas about our customs and habits. Everything which doesn't exist with them – even if it has ended recently – they insist on abolishing immediately everywhere else! ... When it comes to it, what is the difference between a slave and a domestic servant? A domestic is free and leaves his master when he feels like it. My slaves wouldn't think of leaving me – they're too content with what they have. If I were unfair to them, perhaps they would run away. But what good would it do them? They'd come under the control of others like themselves [i.e. tribal enemies], or be sold again, or mistreated, or perhaps killed, or have to work twice as hard as before.

When Becker asked about human dignity, the immorality of

treating people as chattels, and the cruelty of the slave trade ('human hunting'), Tippu Tip replied:

> There's no lack of human dignity in falling under the protection of an Arab, whose religion enjoins kindness and justice. We have brotherly relations with the blacks, since we bring up our children with theirs, and we're much more fatherly with them than you are with your servants. I'd never dare treat a black person as I've seen some explorers punish their white companions. If we buy men, it's because they're offered to us for sale, and we couldn't get them otherwise [meaning, there are some places where free men are not available for hire]. And it's much better for them that they should be in our hands, than in the hands of their tribal enemies, who massacre and mistreat them.

Tippu Tip goes on to complain about the British pressure on Barghash to end the slave trade, an interdiction that had been impossible to implement "more than 20 leagues from Bagamoyo", because the Africans themselves did not want the trade ended. A few days later, after several visits in both directions, Tippu Tip offered Becker a couple of goats and a young female slave, on the grounds that "your servants don't know how to make good coffee, and you must be eating awfully badly". Becker accepted, remarking, "My team is just about complete"![16]

We may reasonably conclude that Tippu Tip's decision to concentrate on trading in ivory rather than slaves was a conscious commercial calculation; that he owned slaves, and bought and sold them when necessary; but that to describe him, as is sometimes done, as 'the notorious slave trader' is an assessment that needs moderating.

Colonizer as well as businessman?

Tippu Tip is also sometimes described as a kind of king or emperor in Central Africa. This is harder to disentangle. As we have seen, his influence was felt over large areas from his bases at Kasongo and Kisangani, particularly between the Rivers Lomami and Lualaba. Slade considers that he "saved the Manyema from utter anarchy", pointing to the violence and bloodshed between tribes and villages in the area even before the Arabs came on the scene. Ruth Slade judges that Tippu Tip reckoned that he could best achieve his commercial objectives by first establishing a degree of stability through political power, and that he did this through his network of agents and allies. He also built up a well-ordered 'capital' at Kasongo, with its fields of rice and orchards of fruit.[17]

This is true, but only up to a point. The settlements built by the Arabs at their centres such as Tabora, Ujiji, Nyangwe, Kasongo and Kisangani (and perhaps others, unrecorded) were established towns, surrounded by farms and plantations, and with facilities for handling the large and frequent trading caravans that passed through. They were colonies; but not colonies that had aspirations to regional or national administration, or to statehood. Tippu Tip's influence in Manyema was not that of a government. Nor was he a ruler or a potentate. He may have settled disputes, but he did not supervise courts or any system of law and order, and such taxation as he levied was more in the nature of a periodic tribute than a means of protecting or providing facilities for the populace. To attempt a comparison with the British in India, or the French in North Africa, may be tempting but does not aid our understanding.

Perhaps there is one area of similarity. Like some other colonizers, Tippu Tip and his Arab companions never set out initially with the intention of creating these settlements with their agricultural estates. Their objective was simply to trade, and the settlements were a consequence of, and an aid to, that objective. A place like Tabora, at the junction of five major trade routes, was a natural location for a market and for revictualling caravans. Ujiji and Mtowa, almost facing each other on opposing shores of Lake Tanganyika, had similar advantages. These places, and Nyangwe and Kasongo, were at least partially settled by Africans before the Arabs came along with their commerce and then with their organized agriculture.

We may also ask if there are useful comparisons to be drawn with other leaders or (European) pioneers of the period. Figures such as Nsama and the Casembes, paramount chiefs in areas south of Lake Tanganyika, stayed in one place, and did little more than establish hegemony over a number of villages for a few generations, and were either defeated in battle by Tippu Tip or agreed to do business with him (or both). Mirambo, the piratical leader who operated west of Tabora, led his men to a number of victories and captured booty, but his overlordship, exercised over a very limited area, quickly fizzled out. Can we make a comparison between Tippu Tip and European pioneers, grouping together King Leopold, Cecil Rhodes, and Mackinnon, who all combined armed force and money to gain control over large areas of Africa – a category of 'armed businessman' into which Tippo Tip might fall? Asking the question clarifies the distinctness of Tippu Tip: he had no aspirations for statehood in the area he controlled (as Leopold had for the Congo), nor did he have any concept of, or wish to set up, a business empire like Mackinnon's or an entity such as the East India Company; nor did he have imperial ambitions such as those of Rhodes. He probably did, however, have what we would now consider racist views on the ability of Africans to organize their society, believing them prone to inter-communal violence, disorder, irreligion and (in some places) cannibalism – all of which evils could be reduced (he believed) by external intervention.[18]

Emperor, ruler, leader?

It is tempting to ask what might have happened to the Arab settlements in East and Central Africa, and the areas of land between them (i.e. the region west of Lake Tanganyika) if the Arabs had managed to hold off the Belgians and establish a border with the Congo Free State on, say, the River Lomami. Leaving aside, for a moment, a very proper scepticism about the value of counter-factual writing of history, we can see in this confrontation the clear differences between Arab, African and European concepts of the organization of society. Contemporary records by explorers, and by Tippu Tip himself, suggest that African villages in this area were often relatively small, self-contained units, ruled or ordered by a headman or chief, occasionally with several grouping themselves into a kind of federative structure of a few square miles under a paramount chief. Such chiefs are often (confusingly to us) called 'king' or 'sultan' by Brode and other writers, presumably because of the use of *sultani* in Swahili for 'chief'. Both the paramount chiefs and village headmen would have had authority over the people in that village or those villages – in other words an authority over people in a certain quite well-defined area, even if land and animals might have been property held in common. The Europeans brought a similarly domicile-based concept of authority, although they had more sharply defined concepts of ownership of land and moveable and immoveable property. Hence the campaigns by Stanley up the Congo, and Peters in East Africa, signing 'treaties' on a European model, whereby the local chiefs surrendered 'sovereignty' (though they may not have had a clear understanding of what they were surrendering) in exchange for protection and promises of trade.

The Arab model was quite different: it was less territorial, and based more on personal loyalty of family members to family head, and upwards to tribal chief and to paramount chief or sultan. In Oman there was a parallel loyalty to the Imam, as leader of the Muslim faithful, fully and clearly analysed by Wilkinson,[19] but this did not spread to Zanzibar and East Africa, even among Arabs of Omani origin (as most of them were). Repeatedly in the *Maisha*, Tippu Tip reminds us that his loyalty, and that of his fellow-Arabs, is to the Sultan. Yet the Sultan claimed authority only over the people, and only over certain people, the Arabs, in what he described as 'his domains'. This lay at the root of the problem he faced when the Delimitation Commission set to work in 1885: although Sayyid Barghash had no doubt that the Arabs from the coast to Lake Tanganyika were 'his Arabs', he could not demonstrate to the European diplomats (with their notions of sovereignty over land and people, with concomitant administration and government) that he was exercising any of the responsibilities expected of a sovereign ruler. He charged import and export taxes on certain trade routes and in certain ports, but had no courts, no bureaucracy, no administration, and only one or two *Wali*s, governors. The Europeans saw a semi-vacuum, where the Sultan (and also John Kirk) saw a complete network of personal connections and loyalties.

It was this kind of network that Tippu Tip had constructed in order to exercise his influence west of Lake Tanganyika, always in deference to the Sultan in Zanzibar. In Tippu Tip's lifetime, the Sultan never went farther on the mainland than Dar as-Salaam or Bagamoyo, but distance was irrelevant. Tippu Tip, as a 'first among equals' of the Arabs of the region, does not appear to have owned any land himself there, beyond a simple house in each of his centres of operation. Was authority exercised through such a network sustainable? Doubtful: its weakness, in the face of the European 'Scramble', had already been exposed in the eastern sector.

What of Tippu Tip's personal authority and prestige? He clearly had a very high reputation among his fellow-Arabs, gained from his wealth and the organized force with which he acquired it. His travels west of Lake Tanganyika, and northwards down the Lualaba up to the River Aruwimi (notably after his journey there accompanying Stanley in 1876) helped open up areas to the Arabs, from which they gained huge profits. But his influence with his fellow-Arabs declined, at any rate in his later years, since he failed to restrain them from raiding down the Congo, and failed also to persuade them that some kind of accommodation needed to be made with the Congo Free State if they were to survive at all in the area where formerly they held sway.

There are few available assessments of him locally in the oral tradition: they range from judging him, at one end of the scale, as a traitor who sold Muslim interests out to the Belgians for personal gain, to – at the other end – considering him a great chief whose Arab people developed commerce and agriculture in Manyema. He certainly must have had outstanding leadership qualities to take such large numbers of men and women on long journeys in an extremely tough environment, enterprises from which he himself seems to have gained the major part of the profit.

Finally, without doubt, the modern observer must conclude that, even if Tippu Tip was not himself actively involved in the brutal violence of the slave trade, his ivory trading itself had immensely damaging effects on the people, elephants and countryside of Central and East Africa. Even in the 19th century, the elephant herds that used to roam from Somalia down to southern Africa were hugely diminished, and in our own day we can see the damage done by the ongoing demand for elephant tusks. Moral judgement is hard to avoid. These were cruel times and violent places, and Tippu Tip was a man of those times, those places.

APPENDICES

Appendix 1
Tippu Tip's family tree

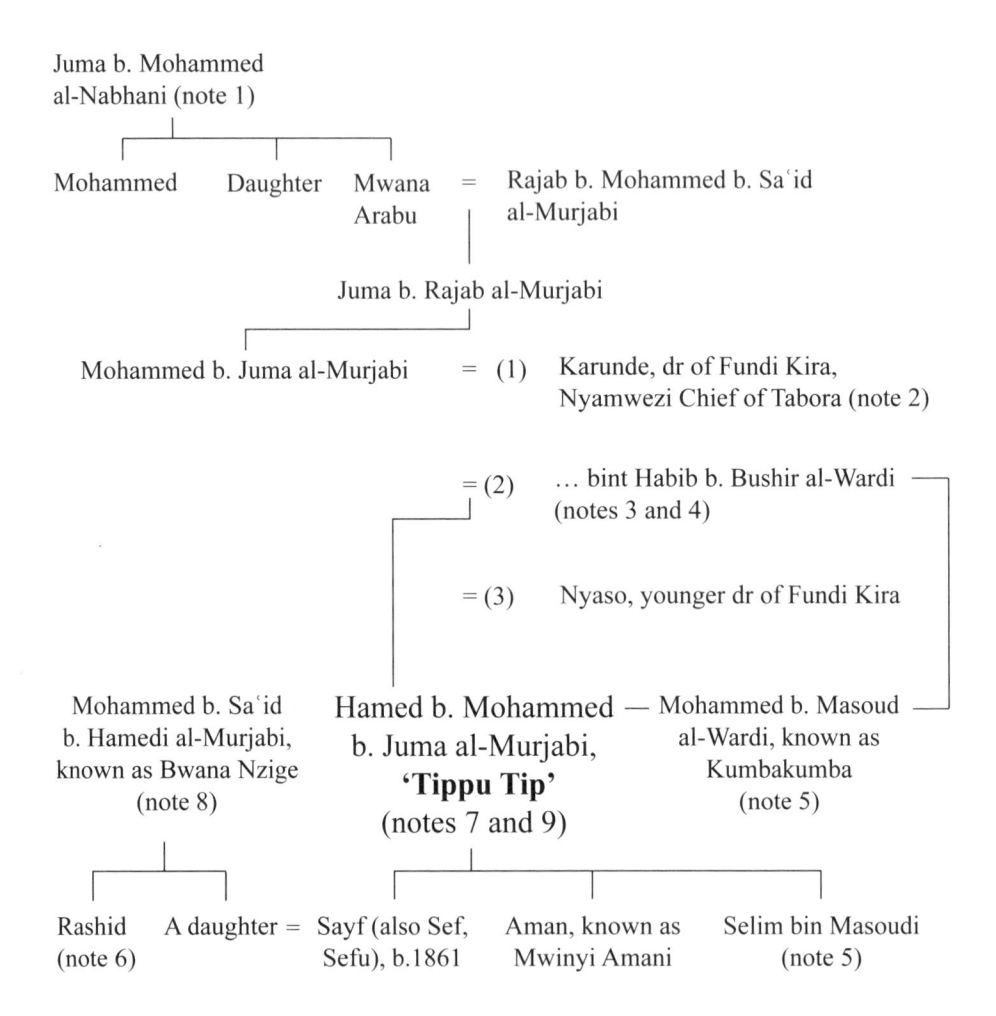

Juma b. Mohammed al-Nabhani (note 1)
├── Mohammed
├── Daughter
└── Mwana Arabu = Rajab b. Mohammed b. Sa'id al-Murjabi
    │
    Juma b. Rajab al-Murjabi
    │
    Mohammed b. Juma al-Murjabi
      = (1) Karunde, dr of Fundi Kira, Nyamwezi Chief of Tabora (note 2)
      = (2) … bint Habib b. Bushir al-Wardi (notes 3 and 4)
      = (3) Nyaso, younger dr of Fundi Kira

Children:

- **Mohammed b. Sa'id b. Hamedi al-Murjabi, known as Bwana Nzige** (note 8)
  - Rashid (note 6)
  - A daughter = Sayf (also Sef, Sefu), b.1861

- **Hamed b. Mohammed b. Juma al-Murjabi, 'Tippu Tip'** (notes 7 and 9)
  - Sayf (also Sef, Sefu), b.1861
  - Aman, known as Mwinyi Amani
  - Selim bin Masoudi (note 5)

- **Mohammed b. Masoud al-Wardi, known as Kumbakumba** (note 5)

Notes

1. Brode asserts that Juma b. Mohammed had an African wife.
2. Fundi Kira, Chief of Tabora, died in 1858 and was succeeded by Msabila (also known as Mnywa Sela or Manwa Sera).
3. Tippu Tip's mother's given name is not found. She is referred to only as 'bint Habib bin Bushir al-Wardi' (daughter of Habib etc). In *Maisha* §100, Tippu Tip refers to his 'uncle Bushir bin Habib', i.e. his mother's brother.
4. Tippu Tips's mother had a husband other than, and before, Mohammed bin Juma. He refers to "my brother Mohammed bin Masoud al-Wardi, older than I but of the same mother" (*Maisha* §1 and 11), and Brode records that she had been married to her relative Masoud al-Wardi but had been divorced by him (Brode 1907: 14).
5. Ceulemans (1960: 49) records 'Selim ben Massudi' as an illegitimate son of Tippu Tip, without explaining why he is called 'son of Massudi'. Roberts (1967a) records that Tippu Tip had a brother known as Kumbakumba, and the British official text on which he is commenting names him as 'Mohammed Masudi'.
6. Ceulemans (1960: 49) also mentions nephews of Tippu Tip: Rashid (also Rachid), Sa'id, Abibu (or Habib) ben Sa'id, and Sa'id ben Ali. It is not clear if these are the sons of his brother(s) or of his sister(s); and the 'Rashid' mentioned may have been the son of his cousin or relative – see note 8.
7. Wilkinson (2015: 186–7) says that Tippu Tip had only one wife, daughter of Salim bin Abdullah al-Barwani (her own given name not recorded), though she was not the mother of his children. Eugène Wolff, after an interview with Tippu Tip in 1891 (quoted in Renault 1987: 333–5), says he had 15 children.
8. Bontinck records (1974: Introduction, p. 22) that Bwana Nzige, Tippu Tip's relative (and, according to Bontinck, half-brother), had a son Rashid bin Mohammed bin Sa'id, named Kamanga; and a daughter who became the wife of Sayf, Tippu Tip's son.
9. Bontinck also comments that in the *Maisha* Tippu Tip mentions two 'brothers': Juma b. Sef b. Juma, named Mpembamoto (*Maisha* §127) and Salum b. Saleh al-Nabhani (*Maisha* § 51).

Appendix 2

British Representatives in Muscat and Zanzibar, 1837–1900

Muscat	Political Agent	Zanzibar	Consul
		1822–36[1]	
		1839	Capt. Robert Cogan[2]
1840	Atkins Hamerton	1841–57	Atkins Hamerton[3]
1843 on	Non-British Agents appointed		
		1858–61	Capt. C.P. Rigby
1861	Agent[4] Lt W.M. Pengelly[5]	1861	Maj. Lewis Pelly
		1863–65	Col. R.L. Playfair
1862	Maj. M. Green	1865–67	G.E. Seward (Acting)
1863–66[6]	Lt-Col. H. Disbrowe		
1867–69	Capt. G.A. Atkinson	1867–70	Henry Churchill[7]
1869–70	Lt-Col. Disbrowe[8]		
1870 – May 1871	Maj. A. Cotton Way*	1870–86	Dr (later Sir) John Kirk[9]
1871–72	Capt. E.C. Ross		[10]
1872–87	Lt –Col. S.B. Miles[11]		
1887–89	Lt-Col. E. Mockler	1887–88	Sir Claude McDonald[12]
1889	Lt W.C. Stratton		
1889–90	Maj. C.E. Yate	1888–91	Sir Charles Euan-Smith
1890–91	Lt-Col. E. Mockler		**British Agent and Consul-General**
1892–96	Maj. J. Hayes Sadler[13]	1891–92	Gerald Portal (Sir Gerald, 1892)[14]
		1893	Rennell Rodd[15]
1896–97	Capt. F.A. Beville	1894–1900	Sir Arthur Hardinge
1897–99	Capt. (later Major) C.J.F. Fagan		

* died in the appointment

Note: the British Embassy in Oman has a fine collection of photographs of British Political Agents, Consuls, Consuls-General and Ambassadors in Muscat, complete except for the period 1932–39. The dates recorded on those photographs do not completely tally with those given in the table, since the 19th-century custom was for officers to take long leave ('furlough') from time to time, during which a deputy would be Acting Resident or Acting Political Agent. Several of these acting appointments are recorded in the footnotes to the table, below.

1. Bennett (1978: 20) says that an Omani subject was appointed British Agent in Zanzibar under the Moresby treaty, 1822, and a successor appointed in 1826.
2. On returning from accompanying Ali bin Nasir, Governor of Mombasa, on an official visit to England, bearing appointment as "Her Majesty's Commissioner and Plenipotentiary at the Court of the Imam of Muscat".
3. In 1840 Hamerton accompanied Sa'id to Zanzibar; Bennett (1978: 46) dates his arrival at 4 May 1841. He died in July 1857, and there was an interval of about a year before his successor arrived.
4. From 1861 until 1949, the appointment in Muscat was styled 'Political Agent and Consul'.
5. After a gap since 1840, with Indian and local agents standing in.
6. The Political Agency was closed in early 1866 when Sayyid Salim seized power after killing his father, and reopened in January 1867, a year after recognition had been granted to Salim, under Atkinson.
7. Churchill was appointed by the Foreign Office, unlike his predecessors, who were appointed by the Indian Government.
8. The British Embassy in Oman has a photograph of Surgeon Lt-Col. Jayakar IMS, recorded as being Agency Surgeon 1870–1900, and as having acted as Political Agent "many times".
9. John Kirk was first appointed to Zanzibar in 1866, as Agency Surgeon and Vice-Consul.
10. Col. Miles acted as Consul in Zanzibar during Kirk's absence on leave, August 1881 to August 1883.
11. P.J.C. Robertson was acting as Political Agent in June 1877, Maj. C.B. Euan-Smith from July 1879 until January 1880, Maj. C. Grant for periods in 1880 and 1881–83, and Maj. E. Mockler for periods in 1883 and 1886.
12. Frederick Holmwood was Acting Consul-General in Zanzibar, after the departure of Sir John Kirk and until the arrival of Sir Claude McDonald.
13. For a period in 1893–94, Sadler stood in as Resident in Bushire; and for a period in 1895, Capt. J.F. Whyte acted as Political Agent in Muscat.
14. Portal stood in during Euan-Smith's temporary absence in Europe in 1889. Appointed as Consul in succession to Euan-Smith, he became British Agent and Consul-General in October 1891, soon after the British Protectorate was promulgated in November 1890.
15. Awarded KCMG in 1899, and in 1933 created Baron Rennell of Rodd.

Appendix 3

Al Bu Saʿidi Sultans of Muscat and Zanzibar, 1800–1910

Ruled	Name
1804–07 (possibly 1806)	Sayyid Badr bin Saif, nephew of Sultan bin Ahmad, murdered at Barka, probably by Saʿid bin Sultan
1807 (or 1806) –1856	Sayyid Saʿid bin Sultan, died on passage to Zanzibar

Ruled in Muscat	Name	Ruled in Zanzibar	Name
1856–66	Thuwaini bin Saʿid (murdered by son Salim, 1866)	1856–70	Majid bin Saʿid
1866–68	Salim bin Thuwaini		
1868–71	ʿAzzan bin Qays, killed in battle at Mattrah by Turki bin Saʿid, 1871, also Imam	1870–88	Barghash bin Saʿid
1871–88	Turki bin Saʿid bin Sultan		
1888–1913	Faysal bin Turki	1888–90
1890–93
1893–96
1896–1902
1902–11	Khalifa bin Saʿid
Ali bin Saʿid
Hamad bin Thuwaini
Hamoud bin Muhammad*
Ali bin Hamoud (abdicated)

* In August 1896, Sayyid Khalid bin Barghash seized the Sultanate, but was accused of poisoning Sultan Hamad, deposed after three days (after the 45-minute British naval bombardment sometimes called the 'shortest war in history'), and exiled.

Appendix 4

Timeline: events in Tippu Tip's life set against events elsewhere

Date	Events in Tippu Tip's life	*Maisha* paragraph
1837	Tippu Tip (TT) born in Zanzibar	
1840		
1841		
1849–50	Early trading in gum-copal	1
1855–?	1858: death of Chief Fundi Kira	2–4
		5
	War over succession to Fundi Kira	6–19
1857–59		
1860–61		11
1860–63		
1864		13–43
1866		
1867	May: TT's battle with Nsama, Chief of Ruemba, in Itawa	
1867	29 July: meets David Livingstone in village 3 days' journey from Lake Mweru	
1869	7 Jan. (22 Ramadan): arrives Dar as-Salaam After the 'Id: sails to Zanzibar, stays 12 months	
1870	Leaves coast for start of Third Journey	44–152
1871	*ca.* 1871: Gets sovereign rights from Kasongo-Rushie	

Appendices

Tippu Tip's journeys	Other events
	March 1840: Emin Pasha born
	January 1841: H.M. Stanley born
Early journeys with his father (1) to Ugangi, (2) to Urua	
	Burton and Speke expedition
	1858 Speke finds Lake Victoria (Victoria Nyanza)
First Journey	
	Speke and Grant expedition
	1862 Speke finds Ripon Falls
Second Journey, 1864–69	March: Baker finds Lake Albert, and Murchison Falls
	1864: plan for debate in Bath; Speke dies
	Livingstone starts last journeys
Third Journey, 1870–82	
	Jan.: Stanley arrives in Zanzibar
	1871–75 Arab war with Mirambo
	Nov.: Stanley meets Livingstone at Ujiji

Tippu Tip

Date	Events in Tippu Tip's life	*Maisha* paragraph
1872	July–Sept.: reaches Itawa Nov: defeats Casembe VIII Mwongo	
1873	In Utetera (from mid-1872 until late 1874)	
1874	Aug.: Cameron meets TT at Nyangwe and they travel together to TT's camp.	
1875	In Nyangwe and Kasongo July: drives out 'Portuguese traders' from Utetera	
1876	Oct.: Stanley arrives near Nyangwe, and TT agrees to help him go downriver Dec.: Stanley and TT separate at Vinya-Njara	
1877	TT in Nyangwe and Kasongo, and between the Lualaba and Lomami	
1878	Remains in Nyangwe and Kasongo	
1879	Recalled to Zanzibar	
1880	Dec.: arrives at Mtowa, on Lake Tanganyika	
1881	Feb.: arrives at Ujiji; then to Ruanda Sept.: meets J. Becker at Tabora	
1882	Aug.–Sept.: meets Wissmann in Tabora Nov.: arrives in Zanzibar; Barghash commissions him to consolidate and extend Upper Congo territories	
1883	Aug.: leaves Zanzibar for Tabora, Ujiji and Manyema Nov./Dec. (or early 1884): meets Mirambo Rescues Juma Merikani	153–169
1884	May: arrives at Kasongo and then Nyangwe Dec.: arrives at Stanley Falls	
1885	TT travelling January–December, and returns to Stanley Falls Dec.: signs treaty with Wester	

Appendices

Tippu Tip's journeys	Other Events
	May: Stanley reaches Bagamoyo
	May: Livingstone dies near Lake Bangweolo
	Nov.: Stanley sets out from Bagamoyo on 2nd expedition
	Nov.: Cameron arrives near Benguela, having made first east–west crossing
	Sept. 1876: Leopold hosts International Geographical Conference. International African Association (AIA) formed.
	Aug.: Stanley arrives at mouth of the Congo
	Comité d'études du Haut-Congo formed.
	Comité becomes Association internationale du Congo. Stanley returns to Congo.
	Mahdi declares revolt in Sudan
Fourth Journey, 1883–86	
	Feb.: Anglo-Portuguese Treaty signed, not ratified (June) Peters signs treaties in the interior Nov: Berlin Conference starts
	Jan.: Gordon killed at Khartoum Nov.: Delimitation Commission on Zanzibar sovereignty starts work

Tippu Tip

Date	Events in Tippu Tip's Life	*Maisha* paragraph
1886	Apr.: leaves Stanley Falls for Zanzibar Sept.: meets Junker in Tabora, then returns with him to Bagamoyo (Nov. 1886) Nov.: meets Sultan Barghash in Zanzibar	
1887	Feb.: Stanley does deal with TT at Zanzibar TT, appointed Governor at Stanley Falls, returns to Congo with Emin Pasha Relief Expedition (EPRE) June: Arrives Stanley Falls, with Barttelot	170–180
1888	In Kisangani, Nyangwe and Kasongo	
1889		
1890	March/Apr.: TT leaves Stanley Falls for Zanzibar, to defend himself against Stanley's accusations and lawsuit Sept.: arrives at Ujiji	
1891	July: TT having been ill in Tabora en route, arrives Zanzibar Oct.: EPRE agents withdraw case against TT	
1892	Arab campaigns: TT's son Sayf ousted	181–182
1893	Nov.: Sayf killed	
1903	Meinertzhagen sees TT in Zanzibar	
1905	June: TT dies in Shangani district of Zanzibar	

Appendices

Tippu Tip's journeys	Other events
	Feb.: Deane takes over at Stanley Falls from Wester
	Aug.: Arabs eject Deane from Stanley Falls
	Nov.: UK–German agreement on Delimitation Commission
	Dec.: Barghash accepts Commission findings
Fifth Journey (EPRE), 1887–91	
	March: Death of Sayyid Barghash; succeeded as Sultan by Sayyid Khalifa
	Nov.: Brussels Conference opens
	Dec.: Stanley arrives back in Zanzibar after Emin Pasha Relief Expedition
	Feb.: Sayyid Khalifa dies
	July: Second Anglo-German Agreement
	Apr.: Belgians capture Kasongo from Arabs

Notes

Introduction

1. Alston and Laing 2014: 101–4.
2. Jones and Ridout 2015; Cooper 1977.

Chapter 1: A Young Arab in East Africa

1. Bontinck 1974: 21.
2. Brode 1907: 13.
3. Stanley 1890: 7 and 11.
4. Wilkinson 2015: 23.
5. Coupland 1938: 67–9.
6. J. Prior in *Voyage along the Eastern Coast of Africa* (p. 32), quoted in Coupland 1938: 70.
7. Wilkinson 2015: 33–5.
8. Villiers 2006: 263.
9. Ibn Ruzayq 1871.
10. Jones and Ridout 2015: 27 ff.
11. For the dating of Ahmad bin Sa'id's election, see Kelly 1968: 9–10 (footnote 5).
12. Jones and Ridout 2015: 36–7.
13. For example: *Maisha* §19: "We saw one old Arab, by name Amer bin Sa'id esh Shaksi. He said, 'Don't go to Samu's place … we went there with Mohammed bin Saleh en Nabhani … and a group of Arabs'." (References to the *Maisha* in this book use the paragraph numbering system introduced in the English translation by Whiteley, and followed also by Bontinck.)
14. Sheriff 1987: 49–50.
15. Burton 1860 i: 324.
16. Waller 1874: 6–7.
17. Stanley 1890: 2 and 4.
18. Abdul Sheriff 1987: 207.
19. Whiteley 1959: *Maisha* §1 and §11.
20. Brode 1907: 14.
21. Burton 1860 i: 392.
22. Ward 1890: 173.
23. Brode 1907: 14.
24. Whiteley 1959: *Maisha* §1.
25. Burton 1860 ii: 403.
26. Brode 1907: 48.

Chapter 2: Nile-seekers, Africa-crossers

1. Kennedy 2007: 1.
2. Waller 1874: iv and v.
3. Jeal 2011: 26.
4. Speke 1864: 1–2.
5. Jeal 2011.
6. Some modern writers refer to this place, at this time, as Kazeh; but Stanley, who records his visit there in June 1871 in *How I Found Livingstone* (1872), was adamant that its name was Tabora.
7. Speke 1864: 319.
8. Notably in Jeal 2011. See also biographies of Burton, e.g. Farwell 1963 and Lovell 1998.
9. Speke 1863: 96.
10. Middleton 1949; Hall 1980; Baker 1866 and 1874.
11. Jeal 1973: 225.
12. Ibid.: 202–73.
13. Notably in Jeal 2007. Other biographies are listed in the Bibliography.
14. Waller 1874. See also Coupland 1945.
15. Cameron 1877 i: 169.

16. Ibid. i: 2.
17. Wissmann 1889: 270 (author's translation).
18. Wissmann 1891: 224.
19. Brown 1892–95 ii: 22 and 24.

Chapter 3: Boy Trader

1. Renault 1987: 13; *Maisha* §2; Brode 1907: 15.
2. Stanley 1872: 416.
3. Ward 1891: 8.
4. Becker 1887: 473; author's translation.
5. Coupland 1945: 52.
6. For these and other details on the porterage business, see Simpson 1975 and Rockel 2006.
7. Stanley 1872: 64.
8. Dodgshun 1969: 69.
9. Pruen 1891: 6.
10. Waller 1874: 268.
11. From a letter, quoted in the biography written by his brother: Thomson 1896: 57.
12. Stanley 1878: 81.
13. Stanley 1872: 33.
14. Dodgshun 1969: introduction ix–xxii.
15. Galbraith 1972: 76-7.
16. For example, Tippu Tip himself: *Maisha* §179.
17. Ward 1891: 6.
18. Simpson 1975: 186.
19. Hopkins 2008: 676.
20. Stanley 1872: 122.
21. Burton 1860 ii, Appendix 1: 383 ff.
22. Ibid.: pp. 383 ff.
23. This and the next few quotations are from Pruen 1891: 4-7.
24. Stanley 1872: 136–40.
25. Farrant 1975: 17.
26. Brode 1907: 15.
27. Jeal 2011: 311.
28. Renault 1987: 14.
29. *Maisha* §3.
30. Abdul Sheriff 1987: 78 ff.
31. Ibid.: 103, citing Loarer 1845–58.
32. Details of the rates are in Abdul Sheriff 1987: 124-5.
33. Speke 1863: 77.
34. Brode 1907: 22.

Chapter 4: Business Start-up

1. Whiteley 1959: Maisha §11.
2. Ward 1890: 174–5.
3. *Maisha §11*.
4. *Maisha §11*.
5. Brode 1907: 25.
6. *Maisha §14*.
7. Waller 1874 i: 218.
8. *Maisha §16*.
9. Stanley 1872:8.
10. *Maisha §16*.
11. *Maisha §35*.
12. *Maisha* §18.
13. Waller 1874 i: 197.
14. Roberts 1967: 244; Bontinck 1974: 192 (note 66).
15. *Maisha* §19.
16. The small war with Nsama is related in *Maisha* §20–§28.
17. Waller 1874 i: 230.
18. Waller 1874 i: 210.
19. *Maisha* §25.
20. *Maisha* §30.
21. *Maisha* §32.
22. Waller 1874 i: 209.
23. *Maisha* §32
24. Letter dated 12 September 1867; Foskett 1946: 137.
25. Roberts 1967.
26. Coupland 1945: 58–70; Waller 1880: i: 282ff; ii 1–6.
27. For a graphic description of Katanga and its mining industry

in modern times, see Butcher 2007.
28. This and the following account of Tippu Tip's journey to Zanzibar is based on *Maisha* §34–§35, and Brode 1907: 42–5.
29. Roberts 1967: 253.
30. Brode 1907: 45.
31. Brode 1907: 46.
32. This and the following account of Tippu Tip's preparations for his third journey is based on *Maisha* §38–§43 and Brode 1907: 48–50.
33. *Maisha* §39.
34. Brode 1907: 48–9.
35. Thomson 1881: 18.
36. Stanley 1872: Introductory xvi–xvii.

Chapter 5: Third Journey: The Far Side of the Lake

1. Kirk to Governor of Bengal, 25 November 1869, cited in Robertson 2010: 82.
2. See also the description of cholera, and in particular how it affected London, vividly given in Dobson 2015: 91–115.
3. Christie 1876: 389–90; also quoted in Robertson 2010: 85.
4. *Maisha* §46.
5. Ibid.
6. Livingstone, *Last Journals*, in Waller 1874 ii: 172.
7. *Maisha* §50.
8. Roberts 1967a: 253.
9. *Maisha* §56.
10. Bennett 1971: 34.
11. *Maisha* §154.
12. *Maisha* §63.
13. Brode 1907: 65.
14. Livingstone, *Last Journals*, in Waller 1874 i: 250–1.
15. *Maisha* §69.
16. *Maisha* §75.

Chapter 6: Between the Two Rivers

1. *Maisha* §84.
2. Wilkinson 2015: 101–15.
3. Wissmann 1891: 183; author's translation.
4. *Maisha* §84.
5. Cameron 1877 ii: 37.
6. Ibid.: 28–9.
7. Ibid.: 29. The 'ants', also commonly known as white ants, are actually termites, ubiquitous in sub-Saharan Africa.
8. *Maisha* §88.
9. *Maisha* §89.
10. *Maisha* §92; Brode 1907: 85–6.
11. Farrant 1975: 61.
12. *Maisha* §89
13. Ward 1890: 183.
14. Cameron 1877 ii: 22.
15. *Maisha* §100–101.
16. Renault 1987: 67.
17. Brode 1907: 91.
18. *Maisha* §107.
19. *Maisha* §103.
20. Livingstone, *Last Journals*, in Waller 1874 ii: 139.
21. Wilkinson 2015: 108.
22. Renault 1987: 70.
23. Coupland 1945: 124–5.
24. Stanley 1879 ii: 119–20.
25. Cameron 1877 ii: 2
26. Cameron writing in Brown 1892–95 ii: 266.
27. Cameron 1877 ii: 1.
28. Ibid.: 12.
29. Cameron writing in Brown 1892–95 ii: 278.
30. Cameron 1877 ii: 25.
31. *Maisha* §104.

32. *Maisha* §105.
33. Bontinck 1974: 22, and 244 note 295.
34. Cameron 1877 i: 373.
35. *Maisha* §107.

Chapter 7: Down the Lualaba: Nile or Congo?

1. For example, Jeal 2007 and 2011.
2. Coupland 1945: 136–7.
3. Stanley 1878: 214–15.
4. Stanley 1879 ii: 92–3.
5. Ibid.: 95–6.
6. Bontinck 1974: 248 note 310.
7. *Maisha* §111–112.
8. Stanley 1879: 129.
9. *Maisha* §113.
10. *Maisha* §115; Stanley 1879 ii: 199 etc.
11. *Maisha* §116.
12. *Maisha* §117; Stanley 1879 ii: *189–92*.
13. Stanley 1879 ii: 193.
14. *Maisha* §118.
15. Brode 1907: 126.
16. Becker 1887 ii: 37; author's translation.
17. Brode 1907: 235–6; also *Maisha* §179.
18. Brode 1907: 235–6.
19. Lenz 1895: 140; Meinertzhagen 1957: entry for 30 Jan 1903.
20. *Maisha* §120.
21. *Maisha* §121.
22. *Maisha* §123.
23. *Maisha* §124.
24. Renault 1987: 86.
25. Hore 1892: 86–7.
26. Wilkinson 2015: 202.
27. *Maisha* §126.
28. Becker 1887 ii: 44.
29. Wissmann 1889: 270.
30. *Maisha* §128.
31. Becker 1887 i: 461 ff.
32. Becker 1887 ii: 47.
33. *Maisha* §148.
34. *Maisha* §134–136.
35. Ward 1890: 187–8.
36. *Maisha* §142.
37. Wissmann 1889: 255, 262.
38. Ibid.: 270; author's translation.
39. *Maisha* §147.

Chapter 8: Tippu Tip and the Scramble

1. *Maisha* §147.
2. *Maisha* §148–149; also Brode 1907: 156–9, although some of his chronology is awry.
3. Emerson 1979; Hochschild 1998.
4. "Il faut à la Belgique une colonie"; famously, he had it inscribed on a paper-weight (Hochschild 1998: 38).
5. Money 1861.
6. Jeal 2007: 220–32.
7. See Stanley 1885: *passim*; Jeal 2007: 239–79; Hochschild 1998: 61–74; Ceulemans 1959: 55–66.
8. See works cited above, plus Miers 1975: 169 ff., and Pakenham 1991: *passim*, but especially 201 ff.
9. Hochschild 1998: 81.
10. That is, St Lucia in present-day KwaZulu Natal, South Africa.
11. Derby to Granville, 28 December 1884, quoted in Pakenham 1991: 217.
12. Quoted in Jeal 2007: 293.

Chapter 9: Tippu Tip's Fourth Journey: Back to the Centre

1. *Maisha* §150.
2. Lyne 1936: *passim*.
3. Renault 1987: 108.
4. *Maisha* §149.

5. *Maisha* §151.
6. Ibid.
7. *Maisha* §152.
8. *Maisha* §153; Brode 1907: 160.
9. *Maisha* §155.
10. Renault 1987: 113.
11. Wissmann 1889: 190–1.
12. *Maisha* §159.
13. Cameron 1877: 69, 98; *Maisha* §160.
14. *Maisha* §163.
15. Bontinck 1974: 159, quoting from Archives Africaines, Bruxelles, A.I. (1377).
16. Coquilhat 1888: 403.
17. *Maisha* §163.
18. Hawker 1909. 215.
19. Coquilhat 1888: 408–9.
20. Ibid.: 407-411
21. Ceulemans 1960: 66–7, quoting *Mouvement Geographique* 1885: 53; author's translation.
22. Coquilhat 1888: 410; author's translation.
23. Bontinck 1974: 161, quoting Brussels *Archives Africaines* (1377) 25IX, B, 1.
24. *Maisha* §162.
25. *Maisha* §164.
26. Coquilhat 1888: 415–16, relating a report written by Deane to an EIC superior.
27. Coupland 1939: 336–8, 437–9; Ruete 2009: *passim*; Jeal 2011: 359–61; Jaffer 2015 *passim*.
28. Coupland 1939: 451–68; Bennett 1978: 129–32.
29. *Maisha* §167.
30. Junker 1892 iii: 559 ff.
31. *Maisha* §168; translation amended from Whiteley's.
32. Ward 1890: 197; Deane's narrative is on pp. 194–214.
33. Ceulemans 1960: 75–6.
34. Ibid.: 78, quoting Gosselin's letter of 25 November 1886, FO 84/1753/40.
35. Belgian Consul de Cazenave's letter to his Foreign Minister, 14 February 1887, quoted in Ceulemans 1960: 79; author's translation.

Chapter 10: Fifth Journey: What a Relief!

1. For this chapter see Smith (1972) and Stanley (1890), but also the personal accounts of members of the Expedition, listed in the Bibliography.
2. Letter, Emin to Schweinfurth, 3 March 1886.
3. For this part of the narrative, see also Galbraith 1972: 111 ff.
4. Holmwood's letter to Baring, 25 September 1886, quoted in Smith 1972: 43.
5. See Chapter 9, p. 218 (penultimate paragraph of chapter): Belgian Consul de Cazenave's letter to his Foreign Minister, 14 February 1887, quoted in Ceulemans 1960: 79.
6. Smith 1972: 84.
7. Stanley 1890: 63.
8. Ceulemans 1960: 68.
9. Junker 1892: 566–9; Holmwood to Salisbury, 8 January 1887, FO 84/1851 (Smith 1972: 107).
10. The agreements are given in Werner 1889: 309–10 and Gray 1944: 26–7, and reprinted in Bontinck 1973: 163–5.
11. *Maisha* §169.
12. Holmwood to Salisbury, 25 February 1887, in FO 84/1851;

Stanley 1890 i: 64.
13. *Maisha* §172.
14. *Maisha* §170.
15. Stanley 1890 i: 74.
16. Mainly in Smith 1972 and Stanley 1890; but see also other books listed in the Bibliography.
17. Middleton 1969: 86.
18. *Maisha* §171.
19. *Maisha* §172–173.
20. *Maisha* §172.
21. *Maisha* §173; author's translation of Bontinck's 1974 French version.
22. The text is in Foreign Office papers, FO 84/1906, 28 March 1888; and reproduced in Renault 1987: 314–17.
23. Stanley 1890: 114–17.
24. Jameson 1890: 128.
25. *Maisha* §174.
26. See Jameson 1890: *passim*; Troup 1890: *passim;* and especially Barttelot 1890: 211 ff.
27. *The Times*, 15 November 1890; see also Bonny's report to Stanley, reproduced in Stanley 1890 1: 490–1.
28. *Maisha* §175; Jameson 1890: 359 ff.
29. *Maisha* §175; Stanley 1890 ii: 18–19.
30. Stanley 1890 ii: 416.
31. Trivier 1891: 36, quoted in Bontinck 1974: 282.
32. Translation sent by Euan Smith in Zanzibar to London, in FO 84/1975, reproduced in Renault 1987: 317–18.
33. *Maisha* §176.
34. *Maisha* §177.
35. Ibid.
36. *Maisha* §178; Brode 1907: 216–17.
37. *Maisha* §179.
38. Bontinck 1974: 288.
39. Jameson 1890: 291.
40. Bontinck 1974: 289.
41. *Maisha* §179.

Chapter 11: The British and the Germans

1. For this period, see Bennet 1978: 124–64; Pakenham 1991: chapters 12, 16–19; Coupland 1939: 448–88.
2. Detailed accounts of the revolt, sometimes called the 'Bushiri revolt' or the 'Bushiri war', are given by Wilkinson (2015: 274–86) and Glassman (1995: 240 ff.) The latter interprets the uprising as being directed as much against Omani rule as against German colonialism.
3. Russell to Granville, 17 May 1873, quoted in Rüger 2017: 71.
4. *Maisha* §180.
5. Gray 1944: 11–26.
6. Stanley's deposition, dated 18 December 1890, is reproduced, in English, in Renault 1987: 338–43.
7. Smith 1972: 295.
8. Renault 1987: 271 ff.
9. Instructions sent from Brussels to the Italian Consul in Zanzibar, acting for the Congo Free State in the absence of the Belgian Consul, quoted in Renault 1987: 290.

Chapter 12: Arabs versus the Congo Free State

1. For this period, see Ceulemans 1960: 269 ff.; Wilkinson 2015: 397 ff.; Hinde 1897: *passim*; Slade 1962: 84 ff.
2. Letter to Van Eetvelde, 6 October 1890, quoted in Ceulemans 1960:

157, where Ceulemans also quotes the operative clauses of the draft contract with Tippu Tip.
3. Tobback writing to his family, 20 March 1889, quoted in Ceulemans 1960: 161. Author's translation.
4. *Maisha* §180.
5. Belgian Ministry of the Congo archives, quoted in Ceulemans 1960: 231.
6. Nzongola-Ntalaja 2002: 21.
7. Both quotations from Coquilhat 1888: 457; author's translation.
8. *Maisha* §181.
9. As well as those mentioned in note 1 above (Ceulemans 1960, Wilkinson 2015, Hinde 1897, and Slade 1962), see also Renault 1987: 283 ff.
10. Johnston 1908 i: 429.
11. Hinde 1897, quoted in Slade 1962: 112.
12. *Maisha* §181, an unusually long paragraph.
13. *Maisha* §181, paragraph 2.
14. *Maisha*, §182, paragraph 1.
15. Slade 1962: 118.
16. Vincent (1895), *Actual Africa*. London.: Heinemann Page 282; quoted by Bontinck 1974: 292.

17. Interview published in *Le Patriote de Bruxelles*, 4 November 1891, quoted in Renault 1987: 333–5.

Chapter 13: Last Judgements

1. *Maisha* §182, paragraph 3.
2. Brode, 1907: 249–51.
3. Renault 1987: 299.
4. Smith in *Maisha*, Introduction: 29.
5. *Maisha* §174.
6. Meinertzhagen 1957: 79.
7. Brode 1907: 253.
8. *The Times*, 15 June 1905, p. 5.
9. Cameron 1877 ii: 12.
10. Ward 1890: 491.
11. Swann 1910: 86.
12. Bonny diary entry for 1 May 1887, quoted in Jeal 2007: 411.
13. Renault 1987: 332.
14. *Maisha* §11.
15. Brode 1907: 25.
16. Becker 1887: 45–8. Author's translation.
17. Slade 1962: 88–9.
18. Conversation with Becker, referred to above; Becker 1887: 45–6.
19. Wilkinson 1987: *passim*.

Bibliography and Notes on Sources

Sources for Tippu Tip's life

We are fortunate in having Tippu Tip's memoirs as a primary source for his life and times. He wrote it (or had it written) in Swahili in Arabic script. Heinrich Brode transcribed it into Roman script, and translated it into German; and he then wrote a biography based closely on it. Brode's biography of Tippu Tip was translated into English by H. Havelock. His German text of Tippu Tip's memoirs was translated by W.H. Whiteley, and published in 1959 in Nairobi with an introduction by Alison Smith. A later French translation was given a detailed commentary by François Bontinck, whose edition contains copious and well-researched notes. These books are:

BONTINCK, F. (tr. and ed.) (1974): *L'autobiographie de Hamed ben Mohammed el-Murjebi, Tippo Tip.* Bruxelles: Koninklijke Academie voor Overzees Wetenschappen

BRODE, H. (1907), *Tippoo Tib: The Story of his Career in Central Africa. Narrated from his own account by Dr Heinrich Brode; and translated by H. Havelock.* London: Arnold. (Modern facsimile edition published by Hardpress, Miami)

WHITELEY, W.H. (ed. and tr.) (1959), *Maisha ya Hamed bin Muhammad el Murjebi yaani Tippu Tip kwaa maneno yako mwenjene.* Introduction by Alison Smith. Nairobi: Supplement to the *East African Swahili Committee Journal* nos. 28/2 of July 1958, and 29/1 of January 1959

Tippu Tip also wrote letters. As with his memoirs, manuscripts of these do not survive, but they are reproduced in translation as annexes to reports from European consular agents in Zanzibar.

Leda Farrant, in the following work, mentions 'Murjebi family papers' as one of her sources. But she does not say where they are stored, I have not been able to find them, and no historian of the period refers to them:

FARRANT, L. (1975), *Tippu Tip and the East African Slave Trade.* London: Hamish Hamilton

Otherwise, to hear Tippu Tip's voice we have to rely on reports from consular agents or explorers and travellers. These are often vivid and detailed, even if skewed by writers' wishes to present their own or Tippu Tip's actions and character in a certain light. Official reports are in the Foreign Office papers at the National Archives in Kew, or (because the Agents in Zanzibar were appointed by the Governor of Bombay or the Governor-General in Calcutta) in the India Office papers in the British Library. Mostly these are to be found in the Foreign Office's 84 Series, and references in the footnotes to FO 84 refer to these papers. Explorers' books published in the 19th century can be found in second-hand bookstores and libraries; the original publishing dates are given below, but increasingly they can be found in new print-on-demand editions, either in facsimile by photography or by optical character reader – the latter being much less satisfactory, since words are often scrambled and the original page numbering is lost.

Much detail on Tippu Tip's life can also be found in François Renault's work:

RENAULT, F. (1987), *Tippo Tip, un potentat Arabe en Afrique Centrale*. Paris: Société française d'histoire d'Outre-Mer

Classic general works on Arabs in East Africa in the 19th century are Coupland's two books of 1938 and 1939.

Notes on other sources

There is a treasury of literature by and about the explorers of East and Central Africa in the 19th century (Chapter 2). Those by Baker, Burton, Cameron, Speke, Stanley and Wissmann are among those listed below. Livingstone's diaries were edited by Waller. Several of the explorers have their biographers; for Stanley, the best modern biography is Jeal (2007) (who also wrote about Livingstone, and about the search for the source of the Nile), but see also Hird (1935) and McLynn (1989).

Stanley himself wrote four important books. After his first, *How I Found Livingstone*, he wrote up his major journey across Africa and down the Congo in *Through the Dark Continent*. His work for King Leopold was described in *The Congo and the Founding of Its Free State*. His account of the Emin Pasha Relief Expedition comes in *In Darkest Africa*. All are listed below; and all are available in reprint editions.

Good descriptions of life in the caravans, and as viewed by Africans, are in Simpson (1975), and an excellent and detailed study of the 'porterage industry', and especially the Wanyamwezi, is in Rockel (2006).

The narrative of Tippu Tip in Itawa, Lunda and Urua in mid- to late 1872 is supported by the account and analysis in Roberts (1967a). Later, while on the Emin Pasha Relief Expedition, Tippu Tip related some of his experiences in Itawa, Urua and Utetera to Herbert Ward, who recorded them in Ward (1890).

For the period October–December 1876, when Tippu Tip and Stanley were travelling together, we rely on both the *Maisha* and Stanley's detailed account in *Through the Dark Continent*.

For Tippu Tip and the Scramble, and the story of King Leopold II's acquisition and exploitation of the Congo, see especially Anstey (1962), Hochschild (1998), and Slade (1962). Stanley's work for Leopold is well covered in Jeal's biography, Jeal (2007). Stanley's own account is in *The Congo and the Founding of Its Free State,* Stanley (1885).

For the pressures on the Sultan of Zanzibar, leading to the settlement of December 1886, see especially Bennett (1978). The story of Princess Salme, later Emily Ruete (possibly Reute), is told by herself in Ruete (2009); and for a fictional account of her and her mother's life, see Jaffer (2015).

A full and clear history of the Emin Pasha Relief Expedition is in Smith (1972). Stanley's account is in *In Darkest Africa.* Several of those with Stanley on the Expedition wrote their own accounts, for example Hoffmann (1938), Jephson (1890), Parke (1891), Troup (1890) and Ward (1891). Other near-contemporary biographies and accounts of those on the expedition include Jameson (1890) and Barttelot (1890).

Joseph Conrad's *Heart of Darkness* gives an unparalleled and vivid description of colonial life on the River Congo in the 1890s, though without any direct reference to historical events. Coppola's film *Apocalypse Now* was based on Conrad's book, with the renegade commander Kurtz bearing the same name as the parallel figure invented by Conrad.

In a surprising departure from novel-writing, Olivia Manning wrote an account of the Expedition, based closely on the sources but with some added conversations, in *The Remarkable Expedition*, published first by Heinemann in 1947, and reissued by Weidenfeld and Nicholson in 1985.

A play by Simon Gray, *The Rear Column*, portrays in dramatic but not entirely historical fashion the trials of Barttelot and his company. The play was staged in February 1978, and the text published by Methuen, London, 1978.

For the European politics surrounding the Berlin and Brussels conferences, see Miers (1975), as well as Coupland (1939). The confrontation between the Arabs and the Belgians in the Congo Free State is written up in detail in Wilkinson (2015) and Ceulemans (1960).

Curiosities

The Emin Pasha Relief Expedition brought Tippu Tip's name to the attention of the British public. His picture is given a full front-page spread in *The Illustrated London* News of 7 December 1889. A search through newspaper archives reveals that a Mr T. Cannon owned a horse named Tippoo Tip, which won the Trial Plate at Newmarket in October 1893. The horse was later owned by Mr H. Hyam, when it won at Sandown Park in April 1894.

The Times also records a volume of short stories among the Christmas books of December 1895, in which one story has a central character named Tippo Tib – a sparrow!

An adventure story about a search for an alleged hoard of Tippu Tip's ivory is in Mundy, T. (1920). The reader should be prepared for a number of hostile references to the German administration of their zone in East Africa.

Bibliography

ABDUL SHERIFF (1987), *Slaves, Spices and Ivory in Zanzibar*. London: Currey

ALDRICK, J. (2015), *The Sultan's Spymaster*. Naivasha (Kenya): Old Africa Books

ALSTON, R., and LAING, S. (2014), *Unshook till the End of Time: A History of Britain and Oman, 1650–1975*. London: Gilgamesh Publishing

ANSTEY, R. (1962), *Britain and the Congo*. Oxford: Clarendon

BAKER, S. (1866), *The Albert N'yanza: Great Basin of the Nile*. London: Macmillan. Reprinted 1962, London: Sidgwick & Jackson

—— (1874), *Ismailiya: A Narrative of the Expedition to Central Africa for the Suppression of the Slave Trade*. London: Macmillan

BARBIER, E.B. (ed.) (2009), *Elephants, Economics and Ivory*. London: Earthscan

BARTTELOT, W.G. (1890), *The Life of Edmund Musgrave Barttelot: Captain and Brevet-Major Royal Fusiliers, Commander of the Rear Column of the Emin Pasha Relief Expedition*. London: Bentley

BECKER, J. (1887), *La vie en Afrique*. Paris: Lebègue

BENNETT, N. (1978), *A History of the Arab State of Zanzibar*. London: Methuen

—— (1988), *Mirambo of Tanzania, 1840?–1884*. New York: Oxford University Press

BROWN, R. (1892–95), *The Story of Africa and Its Explorers*. 4 vols. London: Cassell

BURTON, R. (1860), *The Lake Regions of Central Africa*. 2 vols. London: Longman

—— (1872), *Zanzibar: City, Island and Coast*. London: Tinsley

BUTCHER, T. (2007), *Blood River: A Journey to Africa's Broken Heart*. London: Chatto & Windus

CAMERON, V.L. (1877), *Across Africa*. 2 vols. London: Daldy Isbister

CEULEMANS, P. (1960), "La question arabe et le Congo (1883–1892)". In *Proceedings of the Académie royale des sciences d'Outre-mer*, vol. 22 (1959–60). Brussels

CHRISTIE, J. (1876), *Cholera Epidemics in East Africa*. London: Macmillan

COOPER, F. (1977), *Plantation Slavery on the East Coast of Africa*. New Haven: Yale University Press

COQUILHAT, C. (1888), *Sur le Haut-Congo*. Paris: Lebègue

COUPLAND, R. (1938), *East Africa and Its Invaders*. Oxford: OUP

—— (1939), *The Exploitation of East Africa, 1856–1890*. London: Faber

—— (1945), *Livingstone's Last Journey*. London: Collins

CROWE, S.E. (1942), *The Berlin West Africa Conference, 1884–85*. London: Longmans Green & Co.

Bibliography

DOBSON, M. (2007 and 2013), *Murderous Contagion: A Human History of Disease*. London: Quercus

DODGSHUN, A., ed. Bennett, N.R. (1969), *From Zanzibar to Ujiji*. Boston: African Studies Center

EMERSON, B. (1979), *Leopold II of the Belgians*. London: Weidenfeld

EWANS, M. (2002), *European Atrocity, African Catastrophe: Leopold II, the Congo Free State and its Aftermath*. London: Routledge

FARRANT, L. (1975), *Tippu Tip and the East African Slave Trade*. London: Hamish Hamilton

FARWELL, B. (1963), *Burton: A Biography of Sir Richard Francis Burton*. London: Longmans

FOSKETT, R. (1946), *The Zambesi Doctors: David Livingstone's Letters to John Kirk*. Edinburgh: University Press

GALBRAITH, J.: *Mackinnon and East Africa*, CUP, Cambridge, 1972

GANN, L.H. and DUIGNAN, P. (1979), *The Rulers of Belgian Africa, 1884–1914*. New Jersey: Princeton University Press

GLASSMAN, J. (1995), *Feasts and Riot: Revelry, Rebellion and Popular Consciousness on the Swahili Coast, 1856–1888*. Portsmouth NH: Heinemann

GRAY, J. (1944), Stanley vs Tippoo Tip. In *Tanganyika Notes and Records*, vol. 18, 11–26

—— (1955), Tippu Tip and Uganda. In *Uganda Journal*, xix, No. 1

HALL, R. (1980), *Lovers on the Nile*. London: Collins

HAWKER, G. (1909), *The Life of George Grenfell*. London: Religious Tract Society

HAZELL, A. (2011), *The Last Slave Market*. London: Constable

HINDE, S.L. (1897), *The Fall of the Congo Arabs*. London: Methuen

HIRD, F. (1935), *H.M. Stanley: The Authorized Life*. London: Stanley Paul

HOCHSCHILD, A. (1998), *King Leopold's Ghost*. London: Macmillan

HOFFMANN, W. (1938), *With Stanley in Africa*. London: Cassell

HOPKINS, A.G. (2008), Explorers' Tales: Stanley Presumes – Again. In *Journal of Imperial and Commonwealth History*, Vol. 36, no. 4, pp. 669 ff

HORE, E.C. (1892), *Tanganyika: Eleven Years in Central Africa*. London: Stanford,

IBN RUZAYQ (1871), published as Salil-ibn-Razik, *History of the Imams and Seyyids of Oman*. Tr. G.P. Badger. London: Hakluyt Society

INGHAM, K. (1962), *A History of East Africa*. London: Longmans

JAFFER, J. (2015), *Love in the Time of Zanzibar*. Muscat: Mazoon

JAMESON, James S. (ed. Mrs James S. Jameson) (1890), *The Story of the Rear Column of the Emin Pasha Relief Expedition*. London: R.H. Porter

JEAL, T. (1973), *Livingstone*. London: Heinemann

—— (2007), *Stanley: The Impossible Life of Africa's Greatest Explorer*. London: Faber

—— (2011), *Explorers of the Nile*, London: Faber

JEPHSON, A. J. Mounteney (1890), *Emin Pasha and the Rebellion at the Equator: A Story of Nine Months' Experiences in the Last of the Soudan Provinces*. London: Sampson Low

JOHNSTON, H.H. (1908), *George Grenfell and the Congo*. London: Hutchinson

JONES, J., and RIDOUT, N. (2015), *A History of Modern Oman*. Cambridge: CUP

JUNKER, W. (1892), *Travels in Africa*. London: Chapman and Hall

KELLY, J.B. (1968), *Britain and the Persian Gulf, 1795–1880*. Oxford: Oxford University Press

KENNEDY, D. (2005), *The Highly Civilised Man: Richard Burton and the Victorian World*. London and Cambridge, Mass.: Harvard University Press

—— (2007), British Exploration in the Nineteenth Century: A Historiographical Survey. In *History Compass*, 5/6

LENZ, O. (1895), *Wanderungen in Afrika*. Vienna: Verlag der literarischen Gesellschaft

LOVELL, M.S. (1998), *A Rage to Live: A Biography of Richard and Isobel Burton*. London: Little Brown (Also 1999, London: Abacus)

LYNE, R.N. (1936), *An Apostle of Empire, Being the Life of Sir Lloyd William Mathews*. London: Allen and Unwin

MACLAREN, R. (ed.) (1998), *African Exploits: The Diaries of William Stairs, 1887–1892*. Liverpool: Liverpool University Press

MCLYNN, F. (1989), *Stanley: The Making of an African Explorer*. London: Constable

MAURICE, Albert (ed.) (1955), *H.M. Stanley: Unpublished Letters, 1841–1904*. London: W. & R. Chambers

MEINERTZHAGEN, R. (1957), *Kenya Diary, 1902–1906*. Edinburgh: Oliver

MIDDLETON, D. (1949), *Baker of the Nile*, London: Falcon

—— (ed.) (1969), *The Diary of A. J. Mounteney Jephson: Emin Pasha Relief Expedition, 1887–1889*. Cambridge: CUP

MIERS, S. (1975), *Britain and the Ending of the Slave Trade*. London: Longman

MOLONEY, J.A. (1893), *With Captain Stairs to Katanga*. London: Low, Marston

MONEY, J.W.B. (1861), *Java: or How to Manage a Colony*. London: Hurst and Blackett

MUNDY, T. (1920), *Ivory trail*. London, Constable

NZONGOLA-NTALAJA, G. (2002), *The Congo: From Leopold to Kabila: A People's History*. London: Zed Books

Bibliography

PAKENHAM, T. (1991), *The Scramble for Africa*. London: Weidenfeld

PARKE, T.H. (1891), *My Personal Experiences in Equatorial Africa as Medical Officer of the Emin Pasha Relief Expedition*. London: Sampson Low

PEDERSEN, M.C. (2015), *Ivory*. London: NAG Press

PRIOR, J. (1819), *Voyage along the Eastern Coast of Africa*. London: R. Phillips

PRUEN, T. (1891), *The Arab and the African*. London: Sampson Low

ROBERTS, A. (1967a), The History of Abdullah bin Suliman. In *African Social Research* no. 4, December 1967

—— (1967b), Tippu Tip, Livingstone and the Chronology of Kazembe. In *Azania* II (1967), pp. 115–31

ROBERTSON, E. (2010), *Christie of Zanzibar: Medical Pathfinder*. Glendaruel: Argyll Publishing

ROCKEL, S.J. (2006), *Carriers of Culture*. Portsmouth NJ: Heinemann

RUETE, E. (2009) *Memoirs of an Arabian Princess*. Tr. L. Strachey. New York: Dover

RÜGER, J. (2017), *Heligoland: Britain, Germany and the Struggle for the North Sea*. Oxford: Oxford University Press

SEMPLE, C. (2005), *A Silver Legend: The Story of the Maria Theresa Thaler*. Manchester: Barzan Publishing

SIMPSON, D. (1975), *Dark Companions*. London: Elek

SLADE, R.M. (1962), *King Leopold's Congo: Aspects of the Development of Race Relations in the Congo Independent State*. Oxford: OUP, for Institute of Race Relations, London

SMITH, I.R. (1972), *The Emin Pasha Relief Expedition, 1886–90*. Oxford: OUP

SMITH, R.H. (1890), *Stanley in Tropical Africa*. London: Ward Lock

SPEKE, J.H. (1863), *Journal of the Discovery of the Source of the Nile*. Edinburgh: Blackwood

—— (1864), *What Led to the Discovery of the Source of the Nile*. Edinburgh: Blackwood

STANLEY, H.M. (1872), *How I Found Livingstone*. London: Sampson Low

—— (1878/1879), *Through the Dark Continent*. London: Sampson Low / New York: Harper

—— (1885), *The Congo and the Founding of Its Free State, 1841–1904*. London: Sampson Low

—— (1890), *In Darkest Africa*. London: Sampson Low

—— (1909), *The Autobiography of Sir H.M. Stanley*. Ed. Dorothy Stanley. London: Sampson Low, Marston & Co.

STANLEY, R., and NEAME, A. (eds.) (1961), *The Exploration Diaries of H. Stanley.* London: Kimber

STEVENS, T. (1890), *Scouting for Stanley in East Africa.* London: Cassell

SWANN, A.J. (1910), *Fighting the Slave-hunters in Central Africa: A Record of Twenty-six Years of Travel and Adventure round the Great Lakes and of the Overthrow of Tip-Pu-Tib, Rumaliza and Other Great Slave-traders.* London: Seeley & Co.

THOMSON, J. (1881), *To the Central African Lakes and Back: The Narrative of the Royal Geographical Society's East Central African Expedition, 1878–1880.* London: Sampson Low

THOMSON, J.B. (1896), *Joseph Thomson, African Explorer: A Biography.* London: S. Low, Marston

THE TIMES newspaper, 15 June 1905: notice of Tippu Tip's decease

TRIVIER, E. (1891), *Mon voyage au continent noir: la Gironde en Afrique.* Paris: Firmin-Didot

TROUP, J. Rose (1890), *With Stanley's Rear Column.* London: Chapman & Hall

VILLIERS, A. (2006), *Sons of Sindbad.* London: Arabian Publishing

WALLER, H. (ed.) (1874), *The Last Journals of David Livingstone.* 2 vols. London: Murray

WARD, H. (1890), *Five Years with the Congo Cannibals.* London: Chatto & Windus

—— (1891), *My Life with Stanley's Rear Guard.* London: Chatto & Windus

WERNER, J.R. (1889), *Visit to Stanley's Rear-Guard at Major Barttelot's camp on the Aruhwini. With an Account of River-life on the Congo.* Edinburgh: William Blackwood & Sons

WILKINSON, J.C. (1987), *The Imamate tradition of Oman.* Cambridge: CUP

—— (2015), *The Arabs and the Scramble for Africa.* Sheffield: Equinox

WISSMANN, H. (1889): *Unter deutscher Flagge quer durch Afrika von West nach Ost, von 1880 bis 1883, ausgefuehrt von Paul Pogge und Hermann Wissmann.* Berlin: Walther & Apolant

—— (1891), *My Second Journey through Equatorial Africa, from the Congo to the Zambesi in 1886 and 1887.* Tr. Bergmann. London: Chatto & Windus

YOUNGS, T. (1994), *Travellers in Africa.* Manchester: Manchester University Press

Index

In alphabetizing, al- and bin are ignored

Abbreviations

TT   Tippu Tip
EPRE   Emin Pasha Relief Expedition
aka   also known as
d.   daughter
s.   son

Abdul Sheriff 31, 74
Abdullah bin Nasib/Nasibu 110–11, 114, 117, 178, 199
Abdullah bin Suliman, narrative of 93–7, 114
Abed bin Salim *see* ʿUbayd bin Salim al-Khaduri
Abushiri *see* Bashir bin Salim al-Harthi
Aden 40, 42, 214
Africa
  Central 1–2, 7, 24, 27, 48, 185, 192, 229, 281, 284–6
  exploration of 1–2, 6, 37–60. *See also* Baker; Becker; Burton; Cameron; Grant; Lenz; Livingstone; Peters; Speke; Stanley; Wissmann
  North 191
  South 185
  West 13, 74, 195–7
  See also East Africa
Africans
  and Belgians 263–7
  society in Central 284–5
  villages 71, 73
  on Zanzibar 26–8
  See also Casembe; Fundi Kira; Kasongo; Mirambo; Mkasiwa; Mnywa Sere; Nsama; Nyangwe; slavery; Swahilis
Ahmad bin Saʿid Al Bu Saʿidi, Imam 18
  Al Bu Saʿidi dynasty of Muscat and Zanzibar 8, 18–19, 20, 293
Al Saud 17, 20
Albert, Lake (Luta N'zige) 46, 48, 52–4, 56, 151–2, 220, 223, 226–7, 232, 235, 240–1, 257, 259, 271
Albuquerque, Afonso de 13
Ali bin Hamoud Al Bu Saʿidi, Sayyid, Sultan of Zanzibar (1902–11) 8
Ali bin Isa (kinsman of Rumaliza) 201
Ali bin Mohammed al-Hinawi 235
Ali bin Saʿid Al Bu Saʿidi, Sayyid, Sultan of Zanzibar (1890–93), 247, 249, 255
Aloton, Robert J
America, United States of 2, 13, 67, 149, 172, 193, 197, 225
  and cloth trade 13–14, 69
  consul 100

  and ivory trade 4–5, 13, 15, 74–6, 136–7
  recognizes Leopold II's claim to the Congo 193
Amir bin Sultan al-Harthi 117
Angola 6, 32, 48, 111, 144
Angra Pequena 195
'ants' (*sic*; termites), dried as food 128–9
Arabia 4, 191. *See also* Hijaz; Oman; Yemen
Arabic 8, 20, 27, 33, 39, 48, 94, 279
Arabs 11–24, 72, 177
  as colonizers/imperialists 7, 11, 22, 76, 134, 145, 242–3, 282–5
  concept of sovereignty 285–5
  conflict with Belgians/Congo Free State 5, 58, 77, 172, 192, 205–7, 216–18, 228–32, 237–8, 260–71
  violence against Africans 136–9, 145, 159, 203–4, 208–10, 216–17, 229, 232, 235–6
  and Indian financiers 28
  at Nyangwe and Kasongo 136–40, 142, 145, 189, 265–7
  penetration to the Great Lakes and beyond 21–4, 75–6, 97, 127, 135, 139, 154, 189–91, 203–5
  sphere in East Africa 48
  takeover of Stanley Falls 216–18, 227–8, 230, 234, 261
  traders 2, 7, 11–12, 21–4, 53–4, 57, 59, 76–9, 85, 96–7, 112, 116–17, 167–8, 203–5, 241
  slave traders 3–4, 53–4, 112, 139, 152, 159, 189–92, 202–3, 208, 258, 261, 263, 265
  on Zanzibar 24, 26
  See also Bwana Nzige; Juma Merikani; Oman; Mwinyi Dugumbi; Mwinyi Mtagamoyo; Rumaliza; Saʿid bin Ali bin Mansur al-Hinawi; Saʿid bin Habib al-Afifi; Tabora; Tippu Tip
Arthur, Chester A. 193
Aruwimi (aka Usoko, Ituri, Mature), River 190, 207–9, 226–30, 234–7, 239, 241, 250, 262, 268, 285
Association Internationale Africaine (AIA; aka International African Association) 118, 172, 183, 185–6, 188, 193

Brussels conference (1876) 183, 186, 211
Association Internationale du Congo (AIC) 186, 188–9, 192–4, 206, 218, 230
  transformation into state entity 193–4
Austria, Austro-Hungary 180, 197

Baert, Alfred 239–40
Bagamoyo 3, 5, 8, 32, 45, 54, 56, 70, 75, 77, 82, 101, 104–6, 108, 140–1, 152, 176, 201, 205, 211, 213, 215, 241, 243, 245, 248, 255, 270, 278, 282, 285
Baghdad 190–1
Bahla 32
Bahr al-Ghazal 223–4, 226, 262
Baker, Samuel 38, 46–8, 52, 68, 220–1
  wife former slave 48
Bakumu tribe 264
Baluchis, Baluchistan 113
Bambarré 54
Banalya 239–40
Banana Point 76, 233, 240
Bangala (Ba-Ngala) 217, 234, 239–40, 244, 261, 264
Bangweolo, Lake 52–4, 56, 91–2, 97, 120–1, 123, 138, 141

Bantu languages 27
Banyans on Zanzibar 29, 99–100. See also Hindus; Indians
Barghash bin Sa'id Al Bu Sa'idi, Sayyid, Sultan of Zanzibar (1870–88) 29–30, 32, 72, 78, 102, 111, 161, 163, 170–1, 173, 191, 199–202, 205–7, 209–11, 225, 241–2
  accession (1870) 135, 170
  concept of overlordship 209–10, 214–15, 254, 285
  and Delimitation Commission (1886) 214–16
  and Germany 211–15
  health 171
  and Scramble 171, 200, 204–7, 211, 247, 249
  and slave trade 47, 200, 250, 282
  and Tabora Arabs 78, 113, 117–19, 178–9
  and Tippu Tip 7, 166, 169–73, 178–9, 197, 199–201, 210, 215–16, 231, 235, 241, 247
  visits Europe (1875) 171, 200
  barter 69–70, 85–5, 88, 99–100, 113–14, 236–7, 239
Barttelot, Edmund 234–40, 242, 258–9
Barwani family (of al-Hirth) 35, 100. See also Harthi clan (al-Hirth); Rumaliza
Bashir bin Salim al-Harthi (aka Bushiri, Abushiri) 248–51
Basoko 262
Batoka plateau 49–51
Bechuanaland 195
Becker, Jérôme 6, 58, 62, 179
  and Tippu Tip 58, 162–3, 169, 172–3, 256, 262–3, 269, 281–2

beer 113, 140
Beira 13
Belgians, Belgium 2–3, 9, 58–9, 65, 177, 179–80, 259, 270
  and slavery (inc. Anti-Slavery Committee and Mouvements anti-esclavagistes) 245, 263–5, 267–70
  conflict with Arabs 5, 58, 77, 172, 192, 205–7, 216–18, 228–32, 237–8, 260–71, 284
  imperialism in Africa 7, 118, 172–3, 177–92, 200
  takeover of the Congo 179–98, 205, 278
  court/negotiate with TT 207–10
  initial aims on the Congo 209–10
  lose Stanley Falls to the Arabs 216–18
  slavery and the Force publique 263–4, 267, 269
  See also Congo Free State; Leopold II; rubber; Stanley
Bemba 87, 121
Benadir 81, 281
Bengal 106, 146
Benguela 6, 57, 112, 144, 182
Bennett, James Gordon 55, 103, 149–50
Bennett, Norman 116
Berbera 41–2
Berlin Conference (1884–85) 194, 197, 230
Berlin Act (1885) 197
Bismarck, Otto von 194–5, 211–12, 248, 250, 252–4
Bombay 170
Bomu, River 263
Bonny, William 239, 241, 257, 279
Bontinck, François 9, 11, 34, 145, 154, 209, 309
Boston, Mass. 75
Botswana 48
Boundary Commission see Delimitation Commission
Branconnier 190
Brazza, Pierre de 188–9, 193, 195
Britain, British 16–19, 21, 59, 74, 208, 220
  British East Africa Association 211, 225
  Canning Award (1860) 78
  Delimitation Commission on Zanzibar (1885–86; aka Tripartite Commission) 171, 214–15, 225, 242, 247–9
  Anglo-German Agreement on E. Africa (1890) 171, 213, 254–5
  and Congo 185–6, 194–5
  and EPRE 224–5
  and Germany 8, 171, 195–7, 212–14, 226
  imperialism 7, 180–1, 185, 195, 283
  and ivory trade 73–7
  jurisdiction over Indians in Zanzibar 30–1
  and Maria Theresa thaler 68
  protectorate over Zanzibar (1890) 47, 171, 247–55, 277
  Royal Navy 47, 57, 141, 213–14

Index

and slave trade 30–1, 46–7, 102, 141, 170–1, 185, 191, 197, 200, 220–1, 249–52, 254–5, 277
Anti-Slavery Society 4, 277
and Zanzibar 8, 25–6, 102, 117, 170–1, 212–15, 247–55, 277
See also Christie; Churchill; Euan Smith; Frere; Gray; Hamerton; Kirk; Mathews; Playfair; Portal; Rigby
Brode, Heinrich 8, 11–12, 33, 61, 72, 79, 82, 87, 99–100, 122, 134, 140, 162–3, 165, 274–6, 281, 284, 309
Broyon, Philippe 118
Bruce, James 42
Brussels conference (1876) 183, 186, 211
Brussels Conference (1889–90) and Act 14, 250–1, 264, 270
buffalo 121
Buganda 32, 213, 222–3, 225–6, 240, 251
Buki 208
Bunyoro 22, 151, 223, 240, 259
Burton, Richard Francis 6, 14, 21–2, 24, 33–4, 38–45, 69, 78–9, 84, 88, 110, 128, 171
Hajj/pilgrimage to Mecca (1853) 39–40
bad relations with Speke 41–5, 52
Bushiri uprising *see* Bashir bin Salim al-Harthi
Bwana Nzige (Mohammed bin Sa'id bin Hamedi al-Murjabi, kinsman of TT) 145, 166–7, 169, 174–5, 201, 216–18, 238, 264, 273, 288–9
Bwana Shokka 157

Cairo 42, 45, 190, 219–25, 228
Cambier, Ernest 118, 172–3, 179, 200
Cameron, Verney Lovett 1, 117, 128–9, 152, 191, 204
Across Africa 142, 144
crosses Africa east–west 57, 141–4, 182
and Mwinyi Dugumbi 140
fails to penetrate north of Nyangwe 144, 154, 164
at Kasongo 145
and Kasongo Rushie 133
and Leopold II 182–4
expedition to find Livingstone 140–1
and Stanley 144
and Tippu Tip 6, 57, 132, 140–1, 277–8
Cameroon 195
cannabis (*bhang*) 140
cannibalism, cannibals 133–4, 139, 152, 154, 159, 244–5, 265, 267, 284
Canning Award (1860) 78
cannon 108
canoes 73, 124, 126, 138, 142–4, 150, 157–62, 167, 174, 207, 209, 235–7
Cape Delgado 16–17, 70, 123, 171
Cape of Good Hope, Cape Colony 187, 195, 232, 254
Cape Town 163, 232–3

caravans, trade 63–7, 99–100, 105, 108–9, 114, 116, 119, 121, 157, 165–9, 174–6, 201–2, 204–5, 207, 231, 283
bullock carts 65
donkeys 65, 150, 160
elephants 65
horses 65, 150
mules 65
tsetse fly 65, 150
flags 67
guides and translators 66–7
rate of progress 67, 98, 167
women 67
See also pagazi; porters
Casati, Gaetano 230
Casembe (Kazembe), Chief and village 53–4, 72–3, 91–2, 97, 112, 122–4, 283
cassava (manioc, yucca, tapioca) 121, 237
Ceulemans, P. 137, 191, 208, 210
Chaltin, Louis-Napoléon 267
Chambezi, River 81, 92
China, Chinese 2, 14
and gum-copal 34
and ivory 14–15, 74, 137
Chipili Chipioka *see* Nsama
cholera 26, 39, 106–9
Christie, James 26, 107
Chungu (Urungu chief) 91
Churchill, Henry A. 30–1, 102, 140, 171
Circassians 191
cloth 28, 69, 74, 82, 86, 93, 100, 122, 126, 130, 162, 280
as currency 14, 113, 125, 146
viramba palm-fibre cloth 125, 129, 134–5, 146
See also merikani
cloves 4, 13, 20, 25, 171, 276–7
coinage and barter 67–70
Comité d'Études du Haut Congo 185–6, 188, 206
agreement signed with TT (1884) 206
Congo 3–5, 24, 82, 104, 114, 118, 172, 176, 211, 223
Democratic Republic of the 25, 187
Leopold II and 179–86, 200
Congo Free State (aka EIC; *État Indépendant du Congo*) 2, 58–9, 182, 193–8, 226–8, 258–9, 278
and Africans 263–5, 268–9, 278, 284
conflict with Arabs 77, 172, 206–7, 228–30, 260–9, 271
and Tippu Tip 230–4, 238, 241–3, 256, 258, 266–71, 275–6, 280–1, 286
Province orientale 268
See also État Indépendant du Congo (EIC)
Congo, River 1, 3, 6–7, 25, 55, 57–9, 62, 76, 123, 127–8, 144, 160–1, 163–4, 172–3, 183–4, 186, 193, 197, 232–5, 237–8, 258, 261–3, 286

as alternative trade route out of Central
    Africa 76–7, 137, 172–3, 178, 190, 200,
    204–10, 241, 250, 263, 267
  and R. Lualaba 140, 142–3, 164, 205
  Stanley's operations on (1879–84) 186–92, 209
  and EPRE 226–8
  railway 263, 269
consuls 9, 26, 30, 49, 52, 78, 98, 102, 214, 250,
    290–1. *See also* Christie; Churchill;
    Euan Smith; Gray; Hamerton; Kirk;
    Playfair; Portal; Rigby
  consular courts 256
Conrad, Joseph 311
copper 32, 69, 90, 97–8, 100, 123, 127, 136,
    165, 202–3, 280. *See also* Katanga
Coquilhat, Camille 206–8, 217, 264–5
Coupland, Reginald 16, 62, 139, 150, 310
cowries 13, 130, 162
Crimean War 43, 102
Cunha, Tristão da 13

Damascus 190
Dar as-Salaam 11, 84–5, 98–9, 105, 108, 245,
    255, 273–4, 285
Deane, Walter 210, 216–18, 227, 231, 261,
    264–5
Delimitation Commission on Zanzibar
    (1885–86; aka Tripartite Commission;
    British–German–French Commission)
    171, 214–15, 225, 242, 247–9
Denmark 253
Dhanis, Francis 266–70
Dhofar 17
dhow sailing/trade 12–13, 17–18, 73
Dinka 223
disease 24, 26, 50, 54, 58, 106–8, 141, 152,
    160, 172, 236–7, 240, 243–4. *See also*
    cholera; malaria; smallpox
Disraeli, Benjamin 185
Dodgshun, Arthur 63, 165–6
drums, communication by 159
Dufile 223
Dugumbi *see* Mwinyi Dugumbi
Dunlop tyres 5
Dutch 16, 18, 21, 177, 180, 186
  imperialism 181

East Africa 1–4, 7, 12–24, 106–7, 110, 176–7,
    211–15, 225, 247–55, 281, 284–6
  Indians in 28–31
  Swahili language 27
  tribes of 24–5
  1914–18 war in 66
East India Company, English 15–16, 39–40,
    45, 284
East Indies 181
Egypt, Egyptians 7, 42–3, 185, 190–1, 195, 213,
    219–22, 224–5, 228
elephants 14, 74, 76, 121, 125, 129, 190, 209

  decline of 14, 24, 286
  incident in Ituru 109–10
  valued for meat and hide, not ivory 136, 165
  See also ivory
Emin Pasha 59, 213, 215, 218, 221–4, 243, 251
  British campaign to relieve 225
  Junker's two attempts to relieve 225
  Emin Pasha Relief Committee 225–6, 256–9
  Emin Pasha Relief Expedition (EPRE,
    1887–89) 2, 7–9, 33, 55, 59, 62–3, 65–6,
    82, 94–5, 114, 121, 131, 144, 153, 163,
    174, 185, 191, 205, 225–41, 244, 256–9,
    262, 272, 275, 280
  EPRE Rear Column 121, 236–40, 257,
    279–80
  and TT 243
Equatoria 7, 210, 213, 218–25, 230, 236, 240–1,
    243, 253, 262, 272
Equatorville (Mbandaka) 189
État Indépendant du Congo (EIC; aka Congo
    Free State) 207, 210, 218. *See also*
    Congo Free State
Ethiopia 41, 72, 191, 220–1
Euan Smith, Charles 250, 255–7, 277
Europe, Europeans 105, 108
  concept of sovereignty 284–5
  exploration of Africa 1–2, 6, 37–60, 61–7,
    70–2, 172
  explorers 9–10, 25, 37–60
  imperial expansion 1, 172, 177, 179, 242–3.
    See also Belgium; Britain; France;
    Germany; Leopold II; Scramble for
    Africa
  and ivory trade 3–5, 13, 15, 73–6, 136–7
  trade with East Africa 13, 18–19

Fallersleben, Hoffmann von 253
Farrant, Leda 72, 87, 131, 164, 309
Fashoda 42
firearms 13–14, 66, 87, 89–90, 94, 113, 122–3,
    126, 135, 138, 144–5, 152, 155–7, 159,
    166–7, 172–4, 205, 229, 231, 237,
    249–50, 264
  unfamiliar to Central Africans 129, 131,
    136–7
  arms trade into Africa 94, 147, 197, 220, 258,
    262–3
France, French 9, 18, 21, 58–9, 172, 188–9,
    193–7, 208, 220, 230, 238, 253, 270,
    283
French Equatorial Africa 238
Frere, Bartle 47, 102, 171
Fundi Kira 32, 77–8, 98, 116, 175

Gabon 188
Ganda tribe 111
Germans, Germany 7–8, 58–9, 194–7, 208
  and Britain 8, 66, 74, 195–7, 212–15,
    247–55, 263

Anglo-German Agreement on East Africa
  (1890) 171, 213, 254–5
 in East Africa 176, 211–15, 243, 247–55, 263
 Delimitation Commission on Zanzibar
  (1885–86; aka Tripartite Commission;
  British–German–French Commission)
  171, 214–15, 225, 242, 247–9
 German East Africa Company 211–13, 243,
  248, 251
 German East Africa (Tanganyika) 212–13,
  245, 259
 German South-west Africa (Namibia) 195,
  254
 imperialism 7, 195, 247–55
 Schutzbrief, royal protection charter 211, 251
 Society for German Colonization 211–12
 See also Bismarck; Emin Pasha; Junker;
  Peters; Wilhelm II
Giesecke 215
Gleerup 6, 209
gold 16, 67, 127, 213
Gondokoro 42
Gordon, Charles George (of Khartoum) 7,
  220–2, 224
Grant, James Augustus 22, 45–8, 110, 220
Gray, John 35
Greindl, Jules 184–5
Grenfell, George 207
Gujarat 29
Gulf, the 12–13, 16, 47, 190, 249
gum-copal 13, 28, 34, 76
gunpowder 86, 101–4, 108, 117–18, 167,
  169–72, 229, 231, 234–5, 237, 262–3.
  See also firearms

Hadramawt 12
Hajj (Muslim pilgrimage) 106, 260, 276
Hamburg 34
Hamed bin Mohammed al-Murjabi ('Tippu
  Tip') 1, 11, 77–9, 81–91. *See also* Tippu
  Tip
Hamerton, Atkins 78
Haneuse, L. 240
Harar 41
Harthi clan (al-Hirth, of Sharqiya) 32, 35
 Amir bin Sultan al-Harthi 117
 Barwani family 35, 100
 See also Amir bin Sultan al-Harthi; Bashir
  bin Salim al-Harthi; Mohammed bin
  Khalfan al-Barwani *aka* Rumaliza;
  Mohammed bin Sa'id al-Harthi; Rashid
  bin Mohammed bin Sa'id al-Harthi
Heligoland 213, 253–4
Herodotus 42, 56
Hijaz 190
Hinde, Sydney 267
Hindus 29, 74, 108. *See also* Banyans
Hochschild, Adam 182, 193
Hodister, Arthur 265–6, 269

Holland 197. *See also* Dutch
Holmwood, Frederick 201, 217, 225, 228–30,
  232, 235–7
hongo, transit dues/protection money 70, 77,
  117, 130, 172, 176, 201
Hore, Edward (missionary) 168
Hormuz 16
hunting 121–2, 125

Ibadi sect 13, 19, 27
Ibn Battuta 3
Ibn Ruzayq 18
'Ibri 17, 20
Ilunga Kabare, Chief 124
Imam, as title 19
India, Indians 12, 16, 39–40, 69, 180, 185, 254
 Banyans on Zanzibar 99–100
 as bankers and money-lenders 28, 31,
  99–100. *See also* Jairam Sewji; Ladha
  Damji; Taria Topan
 and gum-copal 34
 and ivory 2, 13, 15, 74, 136
 Muslims 28–30
 rupee 67–8
 and slavery 30–1, 190
 as tax-farmers 29–30, 99
 on Zanzibar 27–31, 99–100
Indian Ocean 4
 sea trade 12–19, 190
Indonesia 4, 20, 181, 276
International African Association *see*
  Association Internationale Africaine
  (AIA)
Irande 126
Iraq *see* Mesopotamia
Islam 13, 19, 27
 Bhoras/Bohoras 29
 Isma'ilis 29
 Khojas 29
 Shafi'i school 27
 Shi'a Muslims 28
 and slavery 28, 282
Ismail Pasha, Khedive of Egypt 7, 219–21, 223
Istanbul 190
Italians, Italy 68
Itawa/Itahua 25, 87, 90, 95–6, 110–11, 120–2,
  126, 146, 274
Ituna 87
Ituri forest (in north-eastern Congo) 190, 229,
  236
Ituri, River *see* Aruwimi
Ituru 72, 101, 109, 111, 169
ivory 1–5, 13, 14–15, 22–4, 28, 54, 63,
  72–3, 82, 85, 88, 90–3, 96, 98, 109–14,
  117–19, 121–6, 128–37, 139–40, 143–7,
  159, 165–9, 173–6, 179, 189–92, 201–2,
  204, 206–9, 215, 220, 223, 228, 232,
  236, 238–42, 255–6, 259–65, 267–71,
  274, 280, 286

billiard balls 15, 73–4, 137
bought in advance 121
carrying tusks 63, 65
combs 74–5
cost and price of 75–6, 85–6
craftsmanship in 14–15, 137
cutlery handles 74, 137
Emin Pasha's 223, 228, 230, 232
exhausted east of Lake Tanganyika 126
exporting from East Africa 73–7
large vs. small tusks 73, 79, 86, 167
Leopold II and monopoly on 264
more profitable than slaves 82–4, 281
not valued by Africans 2, 24, 86, 136, 165
ornaments 137
piano keys 15, 73–4, 137
re-exports from Bombay 74–5
types and grades of 73–4

Jabrin 17
Jacques, Alphonse 245, 267–8
Jairam Sewji 30, 99
Jameson, James S. 95, 144, 237–8, 240, 244–5, 255, 280
Japan 15, 137
Jeal, Tim 43, 49–51, 72
Jephson, Mounteney 233
Jiddah 190
jihad 268
Johnston, Harry 267
Joubert, Ludovic 243
Juma Merikani (Juma bin Salim al-Bakri) 69, 126–9, 202–4
  dealings with explorers 128
  pioneering Arab trader 127
Juma bin Rajab al-Murjabi (grandfather of Tippu Tip) 11–12, 119
Juma bin Salim al-Bakri ('Merikani') *see* Juma Merikani
Juma bin Sayf bin Juma (cousin of TT) 100, 112, 121, 126
Junker, Wilhelm 6, 215, 224–5, 228, 230

Kabambare 264, 268
Kaboga 167–8
Kagera, River 151
Kajumbe Chakuma, Chief 124–6
Kamolondo 125, 128
Kapela, uncle of Mirambo 120
Kapoma, s. of Nsama 91
Karangosi, River 122
Karema 118, 172–3
Karombwe ('Kafumfwe'?) 120
Karunde (d. of Fundi Kira; step-mother of TT) 32, 78, 109, 175
Kasai, River 58, 175, 203, 268, 275
Kasanura 174
Kasili, Lake (now Lukenga) 125–30, 147, 204

Kasongo (settlement near Lualaba river; aka Kwa Kasongo) 1, 7, 25, 28, 59, 95, 128, 134, 136, 143–7, 153–4, 157, 160, 163, 165, 175, 202, 209, 234–5, 237–9, 243–4, 256, 264, 267–8
Kasongo Luhusu 145
  TT takes control of 144–7
  as base of TT 165–6, 269, 282–3
Kasongo Karombo (Urua chief) 202, 204
Kasongo Rushie, Utetera chief/settlement 130–4, 143–5, 166, 202
  alleged kinship with TT 130–3
  eccentricities of chief 133
  Ibari village 132, 166
  TT takes power in 130–5, 146
Kasuku, River 159
Katanga 6, 32, 53, 56–7, 69, 90, 97–8, 112, 123–4, 126–7, 136, 138, 144, 147, 152, 155, 165, 203
Katarambura 174–5
Kavirondo 251
Kawambwa (N. Rhodesia) 95
Kazeh *see* Tabora
Kazembe *see* Casembe; Mwonga
Kenya 71, 215, 259
Kerckhoven, Guillaume Van 238, 263, 265, 280
Khalifa bin Saʿid Al Bu Saʿidi, Sayyid, Sultan of Zanzibar (1888–90) 171, 212, 241–2, 247–8, 250–1, 256, 277
Khartoum 7, 42, 220–4
Kilimane 48–9
Kilimanjaro 213, 249
Kilwa 32, 53, 75, 85, 93, 123
Kima-Kima 164–5
Kipini 215
Kirembwe 130–2, 134
Kirk, John 31, 51–2, 54–5, 92, 102–3, 107, 118–19, 179, 200–1, 212, 228, 254–5, 285
  and Livingstone 102, 140
  and suppression of slavery 47, 102, 171, 249
Kirua 128, 130
Kisanga 205
Kisangani (Kisanga) 2, 5, 25, 76, 127–8, 160, 205, 208, 210, 215–16, 230, 234, 257–8, 261, 275, 282–3. *See also* Stanley Falls
Kitete, chief 133
Kivira, River 22, 45–8
Kizingo 101
Kovende 168
Kutch, Kutchis 29–31, 74
Kwere 105–6, 108

Ladha Damji (Set Ladda) 30, 99–100
Lado 222–4
Lady Alice, Stanley's launch 151, 157–9, 162
Lafu, River 88
Lamu 17, 75, 251, 254

Index

Lavigerie, Cardinal Charles 245, 264
Lenz, Oskar 59
  and Tippu Tip 59, 164, 230
Leopold II, King of the Belgians 1–2, 7, 55, 58, 76, 118, 137, 172–3, 176–7, 200, 211, 223, 278
  character and family 179–80, 182–3
  evolution of imperial aims 181–3, 184–6, 261–72
  turns gaze on the Congo 179–83
  involves Stanley in Congo project 183–94
  and Congo Free State 193–8, 227–8, 230, 258–9, 262–4
  and EPRE 226–8
  and TT 104, 230, 236–7, 242, 256, 258–60, 262, 283–4
  See also *Association Internationale Africaine* (AIA); *Association Internationale du Congo* (AIC); *Comité d'Études du Haut Congo*
Leopoldville (Kinshasa) 187, 190
Lerman, Dragutin 242
Levant 191
Lindi 32, 273
Livingstone, David 1, 4, 6, 9, 22, 37–9, 63, 110–12, 154, 163, 191
  and V.L. Cameron 57, 117, 140–1
  and Casembe 123
  death (1873) and funeral 56–7, 118, 120, 141, 150
  explorations in East Africa 47–55
  first European to cross Africa 48–9
  on ivory 85, 87
  at Kasongo 145
  and Kirk 102–3
  and Mwamba 87
  as medical missionary 48–9
  medicine chest 62
  and massacre at Nyangwe (1871) 138–9, 142, 145
  servants Chuma and Susi 57, 94, 118, 141
  and slave trade 37, 48, 50, 52
  and source of the Nile 52–6, 123–4, 138, 140, 156, 182
  in southern Africa 48
  and Stanley 6, 55–6, 62, 140, 152–3, 185
  and TT 6, 53, 84, 88–9, 91–4, 96–8
  and TT's war with Nsama 88–9, 94, 96–7
  Zambezi expedition 49–52, 102, 181, 185
  on Zanzibar 25
Loarer, Capt. 75
Lomami (aka Lomani, Rumami), River 3, 56, 58, 72, 112, 126–8, 130, 132, 135, 139, 142, 143–4, 175, 202, 204, 207–9, 230, 240, 244, 263, 266–7, 270, 282, 284
  TT's HQ near 132, 135, 143
  TT pioneers to northern Lomami 164–5

London 184. *See also* Royal Geographical Society
Lothaire, Hubert 268
Lualaba, River 3–4, 6, 22, 53–4, 56–7, 59, 65–6, 73, 76, 92, 122–7, 134–6, 138–41, 152, 163, 200, 202, 204–5, 208–9, 229–30, 234–5, 244, 265–7, 282, 285
  established as headwater of R. Congo 140, 142, 150, 152
  Kamolondo/Landji lake at confluence of E and W branches 125, 128
  'Lake Sankoru', alleged confluence with Lomami 142–3
  Stanley's expedition down 153–64, 173, 190
Luanda 32, 48, 58, 111–12, 144, 175
Luapula, River 53
Lukosi/Lukasi 202
Lukuga, River 141–2, 152
Lunda *see* Runda
Lupungu (Rupungu) 202
Luvua, River (eastern branch of Lualaba) 124–5

Mackay, Alexander 224
Mackenzie, Bishop Charles 50
Mackinnon, William 185, 195, 225, 232, 253, 255, 257, 259, 272, 283–4
  Imperial British East Africa Company 253, 259, 272
Madagascar 16, 276
Madina 190
Mafia Island 215
Mahdi, the (Mohammed Ahmad bin Abdullah, of Sudan) 222
  Mahdist Revolt 7, 213, 222–4
Maisha ya Muhammed el Murjebi yaani Tippu Tip (TT's autobiographical memoir)
  citations/mentions 8–9, 11–12, 33–4, 46, 59, 61, 72–3, 77, 82, 85, 87, 91–3, 94–5, 98–9, 103, 105, 111–12, 121, 123, 125, 129–30, 134, 143–4, 155, 157, 160, 162–3, 165, 167, 169, 173, 178, 202, 209–10, 215–16, 231–2, 234–5, 238–45, 255, 263, 265, 269–70, 274–5, 278, 285
  publication history 309–10
Majid bin Sa'Id Al Bu Sa'idi, Sayyid, Sultan of Zanzibar (r. 1856–70) 30, 78, 96–9, 101–3, 105, 107, 111, 114, 133, 170–1
Makoko, Chief 188
Makololo (Botswana) 48–9
malaria 50, 62, 141, 152, 160, 187, 277
Malawi *see* Nyasaland
Malindi 13, 16
manioc *see* cassava
Manyema 25, 54, 76, 86, 95, 97, 117, 119, 124, 152, 173, 175, 178–9, 189–90, 199–202, 205–6, 209, 237–8, 264–5, 268–70, 282–3, 286

323

Marera (Malela) 135, 166, 202
Maria Theresa thaler/dollar 30, 67–9, 155, 162–5, 215, 232, 263–4
Marseille 184
Masai 226, 251
Mascarenes (Mauritius and Réunion) 21, 50
Masoud al-Wardi 33
Matabele 49
Mathews, Lloyd 200, 212, 248–9
Mature, River *see* Aruwimi
Mauritius (Île de France) 4, 21
Mazru'i clan 17, 20
Mecca 106–7, 190, 260, 276
Meinertzhagen, Richard 164, 276
Merere, Urori chief 85, 98
'Merikani' (Juma bin Salim al-Bakri) 69, 126
'*merikani*', cotton cloth 14, 69
Mesopotamia 3, 12
messengers 70
Mgombera, chief 174
Miles, S.B. 179, 200–1
millet 113–14, 116
Miningani, River 215
Mirambo, Nyamwezi chief 70, 77, 110, 116–20, 146, 167, 173–4, 210, 283
  and Europeans 118–20
  and Stanley 117, 151–2
  and Tippu Tip 119, 174–6, 201–2, 283
  war against Arabs (1871–75) 116–20, 140–1, 169
missionaries, missionary endeavour 2, 6, 9, 16, 37–8, 48–52, 58–60, 64, 118–20, 165, 167, 172, 183, 197–8, 207, 224, 233, 244, 256
  Baptist 190
  Church Missionary Society 107, 198, 244
  French 244
  London Missionary Society 58, 63, 167, 198, 279
  Protestant 176
  Roman Catholic 176
  Scottish 253
  Société des missionaires d'Alger 198, 245
  Universities Mission to Central Africa 50
  See also Dodgshun; Hore; Lavigerie
Mitamba forest 157
Mkahuja 130–2, 134
Mkasiwa, chief of Tabora 46, 77–9, 98, 109–10, 175
Mnywa Sere (Unyamwezi chief, Tabora) 45, 70, 77–9, 109, 112, 119
  and Speke 77
Moffat, Robert 141
Mogadishu 3
Mohammed Bogharib 54, 97
Mohammed bin Juma bin Rajab al-Murjabi (father of Tippu Tip) 11, 21–2, 32, 61, 72–3, 77–8, 98, 109–10, 113–14, 119, 146, 169, 175
  wife, d. of Habib bin Bushir al-Wardi and mother of TT 32–3, 131, 169
  wife Karunde, d. of Fundi Kira 32, 78, 109, 175
  wife Nyaso 109–10, 175
Mohammed bin Khalfan al-Barwani *see* Rumaliza
Mohammed bin Masoud al-Mugheri 178
Mohammed bin Masoud al-Wardi (half-brother of TT) 33–4, 79–87, 105–6, 112, 120, 122, 126, 146–7, 201, 242, 281
  slave-trader 81–3, 281
Mohammed bin Rajab al-Nabhani 11
Mohammed bin Sa'id al-Harthi 84
Mohammed bin Sa'id bin Hamedi al-Murjabi (aka Bwana Nzige) 145, 166–7, 169, 174–5, 201, 216–18, 238, 264, 273, 288–9
Mohammed bin Salih al-Nabhani 97
Mohara *see* Mwinyi Mtagamoyo bin Sultan, aka Tagamoyo
Mombasa 8, 13, 16–18, 20, 42, 137, 171, 250
Mountains of the Moon 42
Mozambique 16, 49–50, 112, 123
Mpala 243
Mpwapwa 82, 106, 176, 178, 244
Mpweto, Chief 123
Mrima coast 33, 75, 84, 112, 136–7, 144, 201, 254, 274
Mrongo Kasanga 125
Mrongo Tambwe 73, 125–6, 130
Mserera 265
Mshama/Mushama (nephew of Mkasiwa) 110
Msiri (Mushili), Chief 124–6
Mtowa 32, 77, 135, 167–8, 175, 243, 256, 267, 283
'Plymouth Rock' 167
Mughal Empire 16
Muni Somai 238–9
Munza 156
Murchison, Roderick 52
Musa Mzuri 78–9
Muscat 4, 11, 13, 16–18, 29, 33, 78, 170
  and suppression of slave trade 47, 191
Muttrah 18
Mwamba 87, 95
Mwana Mapunga, Utetera chief 130
Mweru (Moero), Lake 53–4, 64, 89, 91–2, 96–7, 112, 122–5, 135, 202–4
Mwinyi Amani (son of TT) 206
Mwinyi Dugumbi ('Dugumbi') 135, 138–9, 142
  and Livingstone 138
  and massacre at Nyangwe (1871) 138–9
  and Stanley 140
Mwinyi Khayri bin Mwinyi Mkuu al-Ghassani 167
Mwinyi Mohara *see* Mwinyi Mtagamoyo

Index

Mwinyi Nsara, Utetera chief 130
Mwinyi Mtagamoyo bin Sultan ('Tagamoyo', aka Mwinyi Mohara) 135, 139–40, 265–7
  and massacre at Nyangwe (1871) 138
  pioneers north and west of Nyangwe 139, 154
  and Hodister massacre (1892) 265–6, 269
  and TT 142
Mwonga (Casembe/Kazembe VIII Mwonga) 122

Nabhani (Omani clan) 11, 17, 32–3
Najd 17
Namibia 195. *See also* German South-west Africa
Ngaliema, Chief 189
Ngombe, River 111
Ngongo Lutete (Kasongo Rushie chief, aka Gongo Lutete, Ngongo Ruweteta) 202, 205, 266–70
Ngoni 88, 110–11, 120
Niger, River 197, 211
Nile, River 6, 21, 22, 205, 219–22, 224, 259, 262, 270, 272
  according to Herodotus 42
  Blue Nile 42
  attempts to identify source 42–8, 52–6, 59, 62, 91, 151–2, 182
Nizwa 17, 20, 68
Nsama (Chipili Chipioka) 84, 87–93, 98, 110, 114, 121–2, 124, 283
  TT's war with 88–91, 93–7
  village of 88, 96
Nubar Pasha 224, 228
Nur Mohammed bin Herji 99–100
Nyamwezi 32, 63, 77, 109, 116–17. *See also* Unyamwezi
Nyangwe 5, 22, 25, 57–9, 76, 95, 128, 134–40, 142–6, 152–5, 159–61, 163, 165, 175, 178, 189, 191, 202, 205–6, 210, 215, 234–5, 243, 265–9, 283
  Arab colonization of 136
  Livingstone at 54–6, 138
  massacre at (1871) 138–9, 265
  Stanley at 157
Nyasa, Lake (Lake Malawi) 3, 12, 25, 47, 59, 61, 81, 93, 123, 253–4
  Livingstone's explorations of 50–3, 81, 102
Nyasaland 253, 259
Nyaso (niece of Mkasiwa and step-mother of TT) 109–10, 175

Ogowe, River 188
Oman, Omanis 4, 11–13, 17–21, 32–3, 110, 113, 170, 248, 278, 285
  currency 68
  division of empire (after 1856) 78
  expansion inland in E. Africa 21–4, 127, 168, 229
  Ghafiri–Hinawi rivalry 17, 20
  maritime empire 16–21, 229
  and Swahili population 27–8
  Ya'rubi dynasty 17–19
  on Zanzibar 24, 26
Ottoman Empire, Ottomans 7, 16, 220, 222
  and slavery 190–1

pagazi (porters) 28, 61, 63–7, 77, 108, 117, 157, 163, 165, 169, 173
  behaviour of 65–6, 160–1, 168, 172
  and railways 66
  See also porterage
Pangani 70, 107, 248, 251
Pange Bondo, Utetera chief 132
Paris 184, 200, 213, 220
Pate 16–17
Pemba 4, 12, 16, 20, 28, 47, 171, 190, 215, 276
Persia, Persians 4, 16, 26–7, 47, 190
Peters, Carl 211–15, 249, 251, 255, 284
  barbarity and immorality 213, 251
Philippines 106
Playfair, Robert Lambert 103
Pocock, Frank 156, 159, 161, 164
Pogge, Paul 58
Portal, Gerald 272
porterage, porters 1, 7, 28, 63–7, 98, 122, 126, 145, 201–2, 231–2, 234, 236–40, 257–9
  free porters 4–5, 25, 63, 77, 90–1. *See also* Unyamwezi/Wanyamwezi; *waungwana*
  slave porters 4, 221
  of ivory 63, 75, 86–7, 90, 119
  unruly Zaramo 84–5
  See also pagazi
Portugal, Portuguese 13, 16–17, 21, 27, 48–50, 110, 112, 123, 144, 147, 186, 194–5, 208, 233
Pruen, Septimus Tristram 64, 70–1
Ptolemy, Claudius 42
pygmies 139, 154

Qalhat 17
Qawasim 21
Qur'an 27, 33, 107

railway 263
Ramadan 107
Ramaeckers 173
Rashid bin Mohammed bin Sa'id al-Murjabi (kinsman of TT; s. of Bwana Nzige) 210, 212, 264, 266, 268–70, 273–6, 288–9
Rashid Warsi Adwani 99–100, 106
Red Sea 3, 16, 47, 190–1

Renault, François 9, 72, 134, 139, 167, 200, 202, 229, 310
Réunion 4, 21
Rhodes, Cecil 283–4
Riba-Riba 139, 244, 265
Ribwe, relative of Kasongo Rushie 132
rice 136, 142, 145–6, 283
Rigby, Christopher 31, 112
Riuva, Ugalla chief 113–14, 120
Roberts, Andrew 95
Rovuma, River 50, 52, 81, 93, 112, 248
Royal Geographical Society, London 14, 37–8, 45, 48, 52, 57, 62, 64, 103, 140–1, 149, 159, 182
Ruanda, village 168
rubber 5, 192, 265
Rubuga 109
Ruemba 87, 121–2
Ruete, Emily *see* Salme bint Saʻid bin Sultan Al Bu Saʻidi
Ruete, Rudolph 214
Rumaliza (Mohammed bin Khalfan al-Barwani) 8, 167–9, 175, 201, 210, 239, 243, 245, 267–70
  sues TT 273–5
Rumba, Irande chief 128
Runda (aka Lunda) 91, 122–3
Rungu Kabare/Kumambe, Urua chief 130, 204
Rusizi, River 44, 56
Rusuna (Lusuna), Marera chief 135, 166
Russell, Lord John 51
Russia 197

Saadani 32, 58, 70, 176, 212
Safavids 16
Sahara 190–1
Sahel 190
Saʻid bin Ahmad bin Saʻid Al Bu Saʻidi, Imam 18
Saʻid bin Ali bin Mansur al-Hinawi 122, 126–7, 147, 168
Saʻid bin Habib bin Salim al-Afifi 111–12, 135, 168, 235, 237
  crosses Africa in late 1840s 112
Saʻid bin Mohammed al-Mazruʻi 135
Saʻid bin Salim al-Lamki, *Wali* of Tabora 109–11, 113, 118
Saʻid bin Sultan al-Ghaythi 169
Saʻid bin Sultan Al Bu Saʻidi, Sayyid, ruler of Oman and Zanzibar (d. 1856) 2–4, 7, 18–21, 47, 72, 103, 170, 191
Salem, Mass. 34, 75
Salih bin Haramil/Huraymil 21
Salim bin Abdullah al-Marhubi 168, 174
Salim bin Mohammed (companion of TT; informant of Herbert Ward) 174, 241
Salim bin Sayf al-Bahari 78
Salisbury, Lord 225, 250, 252–3
Salme bint Saʻid bin Sultan Al Bu Saʻidi, Sayyida/Princess (Emily Ruete) 214, 311
Samad 32
Sanford, Henry Shelton 184–5, 193
Sangwa, Irande chief 128
Sankoru, alleged lake 142–3
Sayf (Sefu), s. of TT 2, 58–9, 94, 119, 168–9, 175, 201, 238, 251, 256, 260, 264, 266–7, 269–70, 288–9
Sayyid, as title 19
Sefu *see* Sayf
Selim bin Mohammed 82
Scandinavia 197
Schmidt, Rochus 213
Scramble for Africa 1, 6–7, 171–2, 177, 179–98, 211–15, 247–55, 285
  term coined by Lord Derby 195
Seward, G.E. 102
Sharqiya (of Oman) 32
Sheikh bin Nasib 111, 114, 117
Shire (Shiré) River 50–1, 59
silver 67–8, 73, 155, 263–4
Simba 112–14
Slade, Ruth 282–3
slavery, slaves 1, 3–6, 13, 28, 37, 50, 52–3, 63, 77, 82, 86, 116–17, 122–3, 125, 142, 145–6, 165, 167, 179, 185, 202, 229, 236, 261
  Anti-Slavery Society 4, 277
  Belgians and 179, 182–3, 192, 206, 210, 245, 263, 268
  Britain and slave trade 30–1, 46–7, 102, 141, 170–1, 185, 191, 197, 200, 220–1, 249–52, 254–5, 277
  castration/eunuchs 190
  Germany and slave trade 250–2
  history of 3–4, 12, 18–19
  and Islam 3, 28, 220
  in Ottoman Empire 190–1
  sources of 190
  trade in 63, 85, 93, 108, 171, 190, 220, 231–2, 263–4
  trans-Atlantic slave trade 47
  See also pagazi; porterage
smallpox 72, 86, 160, 176
Smith, Alison 275, 309
Smith, Iain R. 229
Smith Mackenzie 255–56
Soden, Julius von 245, 248
Sofala 13
Sohar 13
Somalia, Somalis 14, 38, 40–3, 81, 219–20, 232, 286

Spain 180–1
Speke, John Hanning 6, 21–2, 38, 40–8, 110, 128
  bad relations with Burton 41–5, 52
  first European to L. Victoria 44–5
  identifies L. Victoria as source of Nile 44–8, 151, 220
  proposed debate at Bath and death (1864) 52
  and Mnywa Sere 45–6, 77–9
spices 20–1, 25. *See also* cloves
St Lucia (Natal) 195
Stanley, Henry Morton 1–2, 6, 9, 24, 38, 55–6, 63–4, 75, 86, 137, 167, 206, 244, 277–8, 284, 310–11
  origins 55, 147, 149, 184
  expedition down Lualaba/Congo 140, 142, 150, 152–64, 183, 189
  and source of the Nile 150–2
  and King Leopold II 7, 183–92, 194, 200, 226–8
  life of 55–6
  'finds' Livingstone 6, 13, 39, 55–6, 62–3, 103, 138, 140, 149, 152
  expedition organization 63–7
  and Mirambo 117, 151–2
  operations on Congo (1879–84) 186–92
  leads EPRE 7–8, 33, 62–3, 65–6, 82, 94, 218, 225–36, 240–1, 251
  tendency to exaggerate 150, 161
  and Tippu Tip 6–8, 66, 139, 147, 153–65, 189–90, 192, 205, 218, 228–33, 241, 243, 255–60, 277–8, 280, 285
  treatment of Africans 149–51, 184, 187, 192
  vision for Congo 184–6, 192–3, 225
  on Zanzibar 25–6, 64–5, 171
Stanley Falls (Wagenia Falls) 2, 7, 25, 76, 112, 127, 160, 164, 189–92, 205–10, 234–5, 256–7, 268–70, 280
  Arab takeover of (1886) 216–18, 227–8, 230, 234, 261, 264
  TT as Governor of 7, 25, 231–2, 234–42, 258, 262, 264, 266
  See also Kisangani
Stanley Pool (Malebo Pool) 186–9
steamboats 50–1, 221, 223, 234, 237, 239
  AIA 217
  Le Stanley 187–8, 217–18, 239
  Madura 232
  Ma-Robert, Livingstone's steamboat 49–50
Storms, Émile 172–3, 177–9, 207
Strauch, Maximilien 188
Sudan, Sudanese 7, 14, 68, 190–1, 213, 215, 219–22, 224, 232, 271
Suez Canal 74, 181, 185
Sulaiman bin Ali 101
Sultan, as title 19

Sultan bin Ahmad bin Sa'id Al Bu Sa'idi 18
Sur 17
Swahili 8, 14, 20, 27, 33, 71, 187, 274, 279, 284
Swahilis 94, 142, 167, 201, 248, 265
  animism among 27
  and Arabs/Omanis 27–8, 229
  calendar 27
  Islam among 27
  'Shirazis' 27–8
  on Zanzibar 26–8
Swann, A.J. 256–7, 279

Tabora (Kazeh) 5, 11–12, 21–2, 24–5, 32–3, 43–6, 53, 59, 61, 63, 72, 77, 79, 82, 90, 98, 100–1, 104–5, 109–14, 117, 119–20, 123, 135–6, 140–1, 143, 146–7, 151, 162, 167–9, 172–6, 199–201, 205, 215, 230, 241, 243, 248–9, 258, 281, 283
  Kwihara village 111
  relations with Zanzibar 32, 78, 109–10
  TT refuses governorship of 177–9, 199
  See also Ituru; Unyanyembe
Tagamoyo *see* Mwinyi Mtagamoyo bin Sultan
Taka, Ugalla chief 113, 120
Tanganyika/Tanzania 71, 215, 259
Tanganyika, Lake 1–4, 6–7–8, 11–12, 14, 21–2, 24–5, 32, 39, 47–8, 52–4, 56, 58–9, 72–3, 77, 87–8, 92, 95, 97, 105, 110, 112, 116–20, 123–4, 126–7, 135–6, 141, 143, 167, 169, 172, 192, 198, 200, 210–11, 239, 243, 250–1, 254, 256, 259, 267–8, 270, 272, 279, 283–5
  Burton and Speke at 43–4
  Cameron at 141–2
  Stanley's expedition to 150, 152
  See also Kaboga; Mtowa; Ujiji
Taria Topan 28, 30, 100, 103, 106, 146, 162, 164, 166, 168–72, 176, 178, 199, 202, 242, 255–6, 263, 275
taxation/customs dues/tribute 134, 178, 210, 213, 242, 255, 264, 267, 271, 282, 285. *See also* hongo
tax-farming 29–31
telegraph 233, 240, 244
Thomas Cook 61
Thomson, Joseph 14, 38, 64, 103
Thuwaini bin Sa'id Al Bu Sa'idi, Sayyid, Sultan of Muscat (r. 1856–66) 78, 170
Tinné, Alexine 42

Tippu Tip (Hamed bin Mohammed al-Murjabi)
assessment 1, 5, 278–86
birth (ca. 1837) 11, 23, 32–3, 84
early life 33–5, 61
education 33

character and appearance 72, 85–6, 92, 139–40, 143, 153–4, 176, 233, 277–80
health 161, 278
leadership qualities 85, 286
nicknames 1, 11, 85, 91, 94–5, 279
sets up in business on own account 79–82
as trader 43, 58–9, 65, 165, 204–5, 271, 280.
    See also caravans
as ivory trader 1–2, 46, 63, 72–3, 75–6, 79, 82, 93, 96, 98, 109–14, 117–19, 121–6, 128–35, 146–7, 165–9, 174–6, 201–2, 210, 251, 280–1
and slavery/slaves 1, 4–5, 63, 82–4, 88–90, 93, 96, 122, 146, 169, 210, 230, 245, 252, 263–4, 276–7, 280–2
and Arab and Indian financiers 28–9, 84, 98–9, 106. *See also* Taria Topan
refuses governorship of Tabora 177–9, 199
as 'ruler' or overlord 1, 121, 124–5, 134–5, 146, 200, 229, 282–6
at Stanley Falls/Kisangani 205–10
as Governor of Stanley Falls 7, 25, 231–2, 234–42, 258, 262, 264, 266
and Congo Free State 230–4, 238, 241–3, 256, 258, 266–71, 275–6, 280–1, 286
estates and property 5, 100, 252, 271, 273–7, 281
dwindling influence in Africa 270–1, 285–6
retirement on Zanzibar 275–7
memoirs (*Maisha*) 8–9. *See also* Maisha
death (1905) 2, 277–8

Tippu Tip's journeys 1–2, 24, 46
early travels 34, 61, 70, 72–3, 77–9, 124
First Journey (1860 or 1861) 82
Second Journey (*ca.* 1864–69) 5, 83–99, 121, 274
Third Journey (1870–82) 76, 99–106, 108–15, 119–26, 127–47
Fourth Journey (1883–86) 119, 179, 199–210, 215–16
Fifth Journey (EPRE, 1887–91) 1–2, 219–45

Tippu Tip's relations with other Arabs
Juma Merikani 69, 126–9, 202–4
Rumaliza (Mohammed bin Khalfan al-Barwani) 8, 167–8, 175, 201, 210, 243, 245, 268–70, 273–5
Sa'id bin Habib al-Afifi 112
Sultan Barghash 7, 166, 169–73, 178–9, 197, 199–201, 210, 215–16, 231, 241, 247
Sultan Majid 96–7, 99, 101–3

Tippu Tip's relations with Africans 143, 145, 235
view of Africans 284
and slavery/slaves 1, 4–5, 63, 82–4, 88–90, 93, 96, 122, 146, 169, 210, 230, 245, 252, 263–4, 276–7, 280–2
and cannibalism story 244–5, 280
and Chief Casembe 53
fights the Ngoni 110–11
subdues Casembe 122–4, 283
subdues Kajumbe Chakuma 125
takes control of Kasongo 144–6, 153
takes power in Utetera 130–5, 146
war with Nsama 87–91, 93–7, 99, 283
and Kasongo Rushie 130–5, 144–5, 202
and Mirambo 119, 174–6, 201–2, 283
and Mkasiwa at Tabora 46, 78
and Riuva incident 113–14
and Mwinyi Mtagamoyo bin Sultan ('Tagamoyo')142
See also Kasongo; Nyangwe

Tippu Tip's relations with Europeans 5, 6, 7, 39, 59–60, 164, 197–8, 209–10, 215, 218, 228, 233, 242–3, 266, 275, 280–1
Belgians 2, 104, 172–3, 177, 216–18, 230, 234, 236–9, 242, 258–61, 265–6, 270
conflict with Belgians 206–9, 261–71
Congo Free State 230–4, 238, 241–3, 256, 258, 266–71, 275–6, 280–1, 286
drives Portuguese out of Utetera (1875) 147
Germans 273–5
missionaries 59–60
useful to Britain 170–1
Becker 58, 162–3, 169, 172–3, 256, 262–3, 269, 281–2
Cameron 57, 132, 140–4, 277–8
Emin Pasha/EPRE 7–8, 94, 205, 218–19, 228–41, 243
Hodister 265
Holmwood 228–9, 235–7
Jameson 144, 237–8, 240, 244–5
Kirk 103
Lenz 59, 164, 230
Leopold II 104, 230, 236–7, 242, 256, 258–60, 262, 283–4
Livingstone 6, 53, 84, 88–9, 91–4, 96–8
wins race against Frank Pocock 161
Speke 46
Stanley 6–8, 55, 66, 139, 147, 153–65, 186–90, 192, 205, 218, 228–33, 241, 243, 255–60, 277–8, 280, 285
Stanley's dispute with and lawsuit vs. TT 8–9, 162–4, 241–3, 245, 255–60
Storms 173, 177–8, 207
Wissmann 6, 57–9, 169, 174–6

Tippu Tip's family 11–12, 17, 32–3, 72
family tree 288–9
African antecedents 28, 33, 72, 143
Omani antecedents 11–12, 17, 19–20, 32–3
father (Mohammed bin Juma bin Rajab al-Murjabi) 1, 11, 21–2, 32, 61, 72–3, 77–8, 98, 109–10, 113–14, 119, 146, 169, 175

Index

paternal grandfather Juma bin Rajab al-Murjabi 11, 119
maternal grandfather Habib bin Bushir al-Wardi 28, 33, 130–1
mother (d. of Habib bin Bushir al-Wardi) 32–3, 131, 169
step-mother Karunde (d. of Fundi Kira) 32, 78, 109, 175
step-mother Nyaso (niece of Mkasiwa) 109–10, 175
half-brother Mohammed bin Masoud al-Wardi 33–4, 79–87, 105–6, 112, 120, 122, 126, 146–7, 169, 201, 242, 281
uncle Abdullah bin Habib al-Wardi 34, 87
uncle Bushir bin Habib al-Wardi 34, 87, 89–90, 133, 140
grandmother 17
great-great-grandfather Juma bin Mohammed al-Nabhani 33
son Mwinyi Amani 206
son Sayf (Sefu) 2, 58–9, 94, 119, 168–9, 175, 201, 238, 251, 256, 260, 264, 266–7, 269–70, 288–9
cousin Juma bin Sayf bin Juma 100, 112, 121, 126
nephew Habib bin Sa'id 268
kinsman Mohammed bin Sa'id bin Hamedi al-Murjabi (Bwana Nzige) 145, 166–7, 169, 174–5, 201, 216–18, 238, 264, 273, 288–9
kinsman Rashid bin Mohammed bin Sa'id al-Murjabi (s. of Bwana Nzige) 240, 242, 264, 266, 268–70, 275–6, 288–9
alleged kinship with Kasongo Rushie 130–3
wives and concubines 34–5, 100–1 160, 279
  bint Salum bin Abdullah el-Barwanie 35

Tobback, Nicolas 268–70, 280
Tora 109
trade goods 69–70, 76, 108–9
  bangles 130, 165
  bark-weave products 136. *See also* cloth/*viramba*
  beads 69, 82, 86, 91, 93, 100, 108, 112, 122, 125–6, 165, 167
  bracelets 125
  brandy 79
  brass wire 69, 92, 162, 167
  cattle 113, 117, 167
  chickens 206
  foodstuffs 136
  goats 125, 146, 167, 206
  iron 136, 167, 280
  lake fish 123
  salt 97, 136, 174
  soap 86
  spices 86
  See also barter; cloth/*viramba*; copper; gum-copal; gunpowder; ivory; *merikani*

Trivier, Élisée 241
Tunis 191
Turkey 106, 191
Turki bin Sa'id Al Bu Sa'idi, Sultan of Muscat 47

'Ubayd bin Salim al-Khaduri (aka Abed bin Salim) 136, 191
Uele, River 263, 265
Ugalla 112–14
Uganda 48, 59, 213, 219–20, 253–4, 259
Ugangi 61, 70, 72
Ugogo 24, 45, 82, 106, 108, 112, 176, 201
Uhehe 82
Ujiji 22, 25, 32, 44, 46, 53–6, 58–9, 62, 70, 72, 77–8, 92, 97–8, 117, 119, 128, 135–6, 138, 140–3, 151–2, 167–9, 172–5, 179, 200, 202, 205, 210, 215, 241, 243, 258, 265, 267, 275, 283
Ukonongo 112–14, 120
Ukosi 95, 202–3
Ukusu 139
Ulyankulu 116
Umba, River 247
Unguja 12
Unyamwezi 4, 24–5, 32, 45, 72, 75, 109–10, 119, 140, 199
  porters 25, 63, 84, 98, 168
Unyanyembe 24, 32, 56–7, 72, 86, 111, 116–20, 140–1, 175, 178. *See also* Tabora
Urambo 24, 116, 119–20, 244
Urori 25, 82, 85–6, 98, 105
Urua 25, 73, 77, 109, 122, 124, 127–30, 144, 202, 204
Urungu 25, 82, 90–3, 95–6, 120
Usagara 106
Usoko, River *see* Aruwimi
Utetera 130–5, 144, 146–7, 165, 266
  TT takes power in 130–5, 146
Uvinza 119, 168–9, 210, 239
Uyowa 116, 119

Vangèle, Alphonse 207–9, 230, 263
Vasco da Gama 13
Victoria, Lake (Victoria Nyanza) 3, 8, 12, 14, 22, 24, 32, 42, 47, 119, 222, 226, 241
  as source of Nile 44–8, 52, 150–2, 220
  Stanley's expedition to 150–1, 184
Victoria, Queen 180
Villiers, Alan 18
Vincent, Frank 270
Vinya-Njara village 159–62, 164, 205, 229

Wadelai 224, 226, 228
Wagenia tribe 165
Wahhabis 4, 17, 20
Wakusu 244
Walungu *see* Urungu
Wami, River 211

329

Wangwana *see waungwana*
Wanyamwezi 63, 98, 131, 145, 157, 187. *See also* Unyamwezi
Wanyema 239–40. *See also* Manyema
Ward, Herbert 33, 62, 82, 95, 114, 131, 174, 237, 278–9
Warsi Adwani *see* Rashid Warsi Adwani
Watetera 130–2. *See also* Utetera
waungwana 63, 90–1, 155, 179
Wavinza 168
   TT's war with 173–4
   See also Uvinza
Wester, A.M. 206, 208–10
Whiteley, W.H. 167, 309
Wilberforce, William 47
Wilhelm II, Kaiser 213, 253
Wilkinson, John C. 16–17, 24, 127, 138, 168, 285
Wissmann, Hermann von 1, 57–9, 126, 128, 204, 248–50
   and Tippu Tip 6, 57–9, 169, 175–6
Witu 254
Wolff, Eugène 270

Yambuya 234–40, 280
Yemen 3, 12

Zambezi River 13, 16, 48–52, 56, 59, 112, 123, 213
   Livingstone's Zambezi expedition 49–52, 81, 181, 185
   Victoria Falls 48–9
Zambia (Northern Rhodesia) 52, 95
Zanj rebellion (Mesopotamia) 3, 12
Zanzibar 1–5, 7–9, 11–13, 16–18, 20–1, 32–5, 42–3, 45, 52, 54, 58, 67, 70, 72–9, 92, 96, 99, 101, 140, 146, 150, 163, 166, 176–9, 187, 200–1, 205–6, 208, 210–11, 216, 218, 223–5, 232, 235, 237, 239, 241–2, 244–5, 268, 271, 285
   Banyan community 29, 99–100
   Bayt al-Aja'ib 171
   British Consular Court 256
   British protectorate over (1890) 47, 171, 247–55, 277
   cholera 106–8
   cyclone (1872) 136, 171
   decline in influence in E. Africa 197, 247–55
   Delimitation Commission on (1885–86; aka Tripartite Commission; British–German–French Commission) 171, 214–15, 225, 242, 247–9
   and EPRE 228–32
   Indians on 28–31, 99, 108
   ivory imports and exports 75–6, 117, 137, 176, 202
   life in 25–31
   and missionaries 118
   plantations 20, 28, 30–1, 33, 47, 171
   population 24, 26, 30
   prison 103
   and the Scramble for Africa 177, 179, 204, 211–15, 247–55
   slave market, slavery 47, 63, 190–1, 250–2, 277
   society in 25–31
   succession after 1856 78
   Swahilis on 26–8
   taxes and duties 75, 96, 99, 117
   tax-farming 29–31, 99
   'Zanzibar subsidy' 47. *See also* Canning Award
   See also Ali bin Saʿid Al Bu Saʿidi; Barghash bin Saʿid Al Bu Saʿidi; Khalifa bin Saʿid Al Bu Saʿidi; Majid bin Saʿid Al Bu Saʿidi; Saʿid bin Sultan Al Bu Saʿidi
Zaramo tribe 84–5, 91
Zulus 110